Funding Exploration

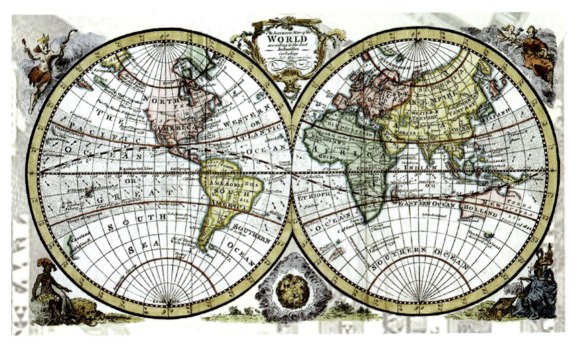

THE CHALLENGE AND OPPORTUNITY FOR FUNDING SCIENCE AND DISCOVERY IN THE 21ST CENTURY

By William F. Vartorella and Donald S. Keel

Edited by Sheldon Gosline and Lester Ness

MPM 9

MARCO POLO MONOGRAPHS
2004

SHANGRI-LA PUBLICATIONS

WARREN CENTER, PENNSYLVANIA

FUNDING EXPLORATION

**The Challenge & Opportunity for Funding
Science and Discovery in the 21st Century**

ISBN 0-9719496-1-1 (CLOTH)
ISBN 0-9719496-2-X (PAPER)

ISSN 1527-2265 (no. 9)
LCCN 2003013474

2004

William F. Vartorella and Donald S. Keel

CLOTH BOUND $44.95 US / PAPERBACK $36.00 US

EDITED BY SHELDON GOSLINE AND LESTER NESS
PUBLISHED IN WARREN CENTER, PA USA
BY SHANGRI-LA PUBLICATIONS
NON-PROFIT UNINCORPORATED ASSOCIATION PA # 2903414
SHANGRILAPUBLICATIONS.ORG
Phone: 570-395-3423 Fax: 570-395-0146 E-mail: shangrila@egypt.net

Library of Congress Cataloging-in-Publication Data

Vartorella, William F.
    Funding exploration : the challenge & opportunity for funding science
    and discovery in the 21st century / William F. Vartorella and Donald S.
    Keel.
        p. cm. -- (Marco Polo monographs ; 9)
    Includes bibliographical references.
     ISBN 0-9719496-1-1 (alk. paper) -- ISBN 0-9719496-2-X (pbk. : alk.
paper)
     1. Research--Finance. 2. Endowment of research. I. Keel, Donald S.
II. Title. III. Series.
Q180.55.F5 V37 2004
507'.9--dc21

                                                                    2003013474

{Gobi}**PLATE 1--**For two years, explorers Denis Belliveau (right) and Francis O'Donnell followed Marco Polo's route through 22 countries (here, in the Gobi Desert) traveling 33,000 miles in jeeps, trains, rickshaws, and on horse and camel. They are the first to approximate Marco Polo's steps entirely by land and sea without resorting to helicopters or airplanes. Photograph and text courtesy of and© by Denis Belliveau (California) and Francis O'Donnell (New Jersey).

{Iwokrama}**PLATE 2--**Iwokrama's Information and Communication Officer, Wycliffe McAllister, offers His Excellency President Bharat Jagdeo of Guyana a bottle of Crab Wood Oil. "Crab Oil" or "Karaba Oil" (as it is called by the indigenous AmerIndians) is extracted from the seeds of the Crab Wood tree (*Carapa guianensis*) and, as bioprospecting has demonstrated with other rainforest plants, has intriguing medicinal and other applications. Through support from The Department for International Development (DFID), a two-year-study on production and market prospects in Guyana has begun. Indigenous and ethnically mixed riverine communities of rural and interior Guyana produce the oil. Photograph courtesy of Iwokrama International Centre for Rain Forest Conservation and Development, Georgetown, Guyana.

{Dinosaur) **PLATE 3**--Peter Makovicky collects the skeleton of a *tyrannosaurid* known as *Gorgosaurus* in Dinosaur Provincial Park, Alberta, Canada. Photograph courtesy of Dr. Philip J. Currie, Royal Tyrrell Museum of Palaeontology, Drumheller, Alberta, Canada.

{Race Car} **PLATE4**--Ohio University's Electric Bobcat Race Vehicle uses an AC motor to convert the power stored in sets of 28 12-Volt batteries to race at speeds in excess of 100 mph in competition with other teams in University Consortium for Electric Vehicle Racing Technology (U.S.). Student team members are responsible for all vehicle design and race preparation activities. Here Adam Covington adjusts the front suspension while Mike Desguin employs a Digital Multimeter to test battery voltages and motor controller connections. Photograph courtesy of Dr. Gregory Kremer and e-Bobcat Racing, Ohio University, Athens, Ohio.

{Jaguar} **PLATE 5**--A scientist inspects the paw of an anesthetized jaguar as part of the long-running endangered species study and partnership between the Wildlife Conservation Society (WCS) and Jaguar Cars in the Cockscomb Basin Reserve in Belize. Photograph courtesy of Wildlife Conservation Society, Bronx, New York and Alan Rabinowitz.

AMUNDSEN IN WINTER COSTUME.

{Amundsen}**PLATE 6**--Plagued by financial difficulties, Norwegian explorer Roald Amundsen nonetheless persevered and, on December 14, 1911, stood victorious at the South Pole. Source: Amundsen's The South Pole, Volume I (1912), p. 390. Photograph courtesy of the Archives of The Explorers Club, New York City, New York.

{Mt. Everest}**PLATE 7**--Kenneth M. Kamler, M.D., examines a Sherpa at Base Camp (17,500 feet) on Mount Everest as part of a telemedicine study that tested the hypothesis of a physiologic cipher -- non-invasively identifying a climber's real-time physiologic status by monitoring vital signs, biochemical, and other parameters using sensors worn by the individual. Photograph courtesy of Kenneth M. Kamler, M.D., New York.

{Mars} **PLATE 8**--Mars instrument developers Peter Smith, seated holding an engineering model of the Beagle 2 microscope, and Roger Tanner, examining a section of a robotic arm with a camera attached, prepare operational tests for their camera systems at the Lunar and Planetary Lab, University of Arizona (U.S.). On the table in front of them is a model of the Pathfinder panoramic camera (IMP) that is also being readied for test. The actual IMP flight model is seen in the photograph on the wall behind them. Photograph courtesy of Dr. Peter Smith, Lunar and Planetary Lab, University of Arizona, Tucson, Arizona.

{Galapagos}**PLATE 9**--Dr. Alex Antoniou, Field Director of the Shark Research Institute, examines a whale shark in the Galapagos Islands. Photograph courtesy of Shark Research Institute (SRI), Princeton, New Jersey.

{Hunley}**PLATE 10**View of bow of *H.L. Hunley* resting in its lifting cradle on transport barge during five-and-one-half hour voyage from retrieval site to Warren Lasch Conservation Center at former Charleston Navy Base on August 8, 2000. On that day, the Confederate submarine rose from murky waters off Charleston, South Carolina's harbor, secure in custom steel truss and slings, 136 years after its fateful encounter with Union warship, *U.S.S. Housatonic*. On 17 February 1864, the Confederate submarine rammed its spar torpedo into that ship's hull sinking it and, soon thereafter, the *Hunley* itself slipped from view, the first submarine ever to sink an enemy vessel. In foreground is Christopher F. Amer, South Carolina State Underwater Archaeologist, South Carolina Institute of Archaeology and Anthropology, Columbia, South Carolina. Photograph courtesy of Tristan F. Amer, Archaeology Assistant, *Hunley* Recovery Project, South Carolina.

Funding Exploration

CONTENTS

BOOKS IN THE SERIES
MARCO POLO MONOGRAPHS

MPM1: Written in the Stars – Lester Ness

MPM2: God's Scribes – Charles D. Isbell

MPM3: Archaeogender – Sheldon Gosline

MPM4: The Coins of Pontius Pilate – Jean-Philippe
Fontanille & Sheldon Gosline

MPM5: Male & Female Circumcision – Sami Aldeeb
Abu-Sahlieh

MPM6: Roman Hospitality – John DeFelice

MPM7: Philistines – Neal Bierling

MPM 8: Manetho – Gary Greenberg

MPM 9: Funding Exploration – William F. Vartorella &
Donald S. Keel

MPM 10: Goddess and God – Valerie Abrahamsen

Shangri-La Publications, 3 Coburn Hill Rd, Warren Ctr., PA 18851 USA   866-966-6288

SHANGRILAPUBLICATIONS.ORG

Series Foreword
By Sheldon Lee Gosline, series editor

"*While other civilised nations have encountered great expence to enlarge the boundaries of knowledge, by undertaking voyages of discovery, and for other literary purposes, in various parts and directions, our nation seems to owe to the same object, as well as to its own interests, to explore this, the only line of easy communication across the continent…*" Thomas Jefferson, 18 Jan. 1803

During this the bicentennial year of Meriwether Lewis and William Clark's expedition, many people are expected to retrace their journey even though it was not significant in terms of discovery, and was mostly ignored for years. It failed to find a navigable cross-continental river, because such a link does not exist. It did not reshape the known world, as did Humboldt, Cook, or Darwin. For much of their journey, the Corps of Discovery, led by native guides, followed pre-existing trails and maps. They were not even the first Caucasians to traverse North America: Alexander MacKenzie completed the trek for Britain's North West Company in 1793. What now fires U.S. imagination is that this particular expedition became America's archetypal odyssey, recounting a mythology of America's vastness. Like Homer's *Odyssey*, the Corp of Discovery is America's first and greatest epic of this genre. So, unlike the 500th anniversary of Columbus' voyage, over-shadowed by Native American objections, this bicentennial reflects a huge popular appeal in the United States.

The year 2004 also marks the centennial founding of the esteemed Explorers Club, which emulates a broader and more inclusive vision. As I turn to editing this, the ninth volume in the *Marco Polo Monographs* series, named for that legendary explorer and diplomat, I note that this work diverges from our typical subject matter, involving cross-cultural academic research, to that of the "how-to" genre. However, *Funding Exploration: The*

Challenge & Opportunity for Funding Science and Discovery in the 21ˢᵗ Century is far more than a "how-to" book. The authors provide a vivid roadmap into the perils and possibilities of obtaining those all too illusive pearls of donor support for fields of study that this series highlights. Our general goal of the series is to challenge specialists to tackle broader issues by combining in-depth scholarship with broadly based theories and methodologies. As we consider the history of exploration, it is only fitting to gaze toward the future, and imagine how we might fund exploration in the 21ˢᵗ century, and beyond. Without such vision, we can set no goals and dream no dreams. Jefferson asked Congress to fund Lewis and Clark with just $2,500, "for the purpose of extending the external commerce of the United States," but in reality Thomas Jefferson entrusted them to produce a scientific record. Individual vision fueled the Lewis and Clark expedition, as it continues to fuel exploration and discovery in the 21ˢᵗ century. This volume is a vital tool for the continuation of such vision.

Between 20 and 15 years ago, I could have made great use of this book. I was the field director of a small but promising archaeological expedition in a remote Egyptian oasis, named Bahariya. The project had all the romantic 1920's amenities; the ubiquitous aged Land Rover, old army tents, kerosene lanterns, buried ruins of a lost city, sand dunes, hot mineral springs, palm groves . . . in short an exotic locale right out of a movie about the French Foreign Legions. But alas, I knew little then about how to market the possibilities of this project, and by the time donor and institutional support began to trickle in, the first Gulf War was in full swing and the project died. I had wasted too much time applying for nearly impossible to obtain organizational and governmental grants, and I learned too late what the authors of this work know so well. Private, individual,

personally motivated funding is the best way to finance any field project.
The only funding that I ever received for the Bahariya Oasis Project was
from such private sources from individuals who shared my vision.

It is therefore with great pleasure that I introduce William F.
Vartorella and Donald S. Keel's collaborative contribution. They have
rekindled my belief and desire to seek out funds for worthwhile science and
exploration. I am convinced this guide shall prove to be a vital resource for
any and all non-profits as they seek financial support for developing science
and discovery in the 21st Century. The future is bright for those who dream.

Prof. Sheldon Lee Gosline, *Marco Polo Monographs* series editor
Publisher and Director of the Hieratic Font Project, May of 2004

Volume Foreword

By Kathryn A. Monk, Ph.D.

Funding Exploration: The Challenge & Opportunity
For Funding Science and Discovery in the 21st Century

The world was a very different place for a scientist twenty-odd years
ago. My postgraduate research was fully funded based on a proposal only
half a page long. Society regarded universities as institutions in which to
stretch the mind and as reflections of their cultural aspirations. Scientists
were financed well by governments and civic societies, even though these
benefactors were frequently unsure as to what it was that the scientists were
actually doing, and few questioned if it was done effectively or efficiently.

Throughout history, in times of peace and plenty, science has enjoyed
political patronage as a show of cultural sophistication. The cynical might
say that the desire for a commercial profit might have been hidden; the
search for the philosopher's stone, the religious or political high ground, or

even tax relief, can be said to provide the true reason for such philanthropy. A more obviously commercial basis for funding science and discovery has also played its part many times before. In the fifteenth and sixteenth centuries, European exploration of the world was basically funded to discover the source of rare commodities, albeit mixed at times with religious fervor. The desire for profits, for gold or for souls, provided explorers with the key to attract their financial backers.

Funding for science and discovery is now once again in serious decline, and proposal writing is an art form that can leave scientists with little time to implement their successfully funded projects. In my own field of biodiversity conservation and utilization, taxonomists reformat studies to provide indicators of biodiversity change that can be linked to climate change, and hydrological studies must be linked to potential water wars. Without reference to the demands of the wider political and corporate world, these studies would now probably not be funded. It is fashionable to say that 11 September 2001 has caused this change. The perception of American society is perhaps permanently refocused, but actually changes in science and discovery have been emerging for some time. Noted international NGOs had already started to engage the corporate world. They recognized that scientists and their development colleagues could not meet many of the scientific challenges, particularly in biodiversity conservation and sustainable development, in isolation. Conversely, businesses were responding to increasing consumer demand and saw, for example, implementation of environmental policy statements as being a necessity rather than a luxury. The need for linkages with the scientists was clear.

The authors of this timely book guide scientists to an understanding of how the corporate mind works and how to attract it more directly toward scientific activities. Amidst increasing donor fatigue and global crises, the message is clear. Scientists must discover new important skills, of building relationships with the business world and of managing and being managed with efficiency and effectiveness. Scientists have long been accountable to too few within and outside their organizations on the basis of their effectiveness. As these programs look at increasingly comprehensive approaches, management systems push the skills of scientists to limits in running and participating in such large programs. These are no longer just technical issues but are also fully involved in social, political, and business development. Old style management approaches do not work. Management cannot be rigid but evolutive and collaborative. Scientists are no longer in their ivory tower, but must share work with colleagues, as any corporate team must. Territories cannot exist. Once again, scientists have to adapt to the demands of the economy and present their wares and visions in such a way as the people with the purse strings will understand and want to share those visions. The historical cycle of scientific world has come full circle once more and scientists must join the real world.

The authors have compiled a wealth of practical advice for the lost scientist. They provide insights into the thinking of, and discuss strategies to use, the corporate world. Practical advice on targeting corporate donors, developing appropriate proposals, and identifying selling points abound. Their detailed discussions on budget construction are essential reading. They must be commended for providing this information in such a synoptic manner as to be accessible to all. Indeed, this may be their downfall. This advice may prove to be so useful, that those discovering this book may wish to keep it secret from their competitors.

They offer some comments on even the most difficult of problems. What threatens to cause an implosion within the system is the need felt by all donors, be they governments or corporations, to launch new initiatives, to fund "sexy", new projects. Even established, successful projects are now threatened by insufficient continuity of commitment or lack of operational costs. Everyone expresses admiration and praise but no one picks up the utility bills. This is a challenge that should encourage scientific institutions to move further into the business world by developing income-generating activities themselves.

Throughout my career as a scientist, I have been fascinated by the synergies to be found at borders and crossroads, be it at the fundamental level of seeing how plant-insect relationships might be enhanced by the inclusion of understanding how birds and mammals feed on the same plants, in the vital debate of whether biodiversity conservation means preservation or utilization, or in the realization that developmental projects are akin to medium-sized enterprises, demanding managerial and political skills beyond the technical. Borders and crossroads are, however, often areas of conflict, be they verbal or physical. For scientists, protection of the ivory tower and unquestioning patronage because of intellectual prowess or even clear logic has gone. If science and discovery are to continue in this new century, if new worlds are to be explored, scientists must understand where the money is, who controls it, and how to get it. They need to develop understanding of, and skills for dealing with, corporate agencies. The authors of this book have provided us with a timely and essential guide to that new world.

Dr. Kathryn A. Monk, Georgetown, Guyana.   November of 2002

Dedication

To George R. Vartorella, Dr. Norman H. Dohn, and Robert DuBose Burbank, A.I.A.--three men who fundamentally shaped my view of the modern world.

William F. Vartorella
Camden, South Carolina
December, 2002

To Don and Kay Keel, my parents, who gave me the gift of life, and to Wilson and Stephanie Keel, my son and daughter, who give it to me over and over again.

Donald S. Keel
Providence, Rhode Island
December, 2002

Acknowledgments

Funding Exploration has been a six-year odyssey from a 17,000-foot peak in the Andes to the bowels of the Great Pyramid at Giza, malaria-stricken scientists in the rainforest, remote petroglyphic sites in Europe, an erupting volcano in Central America, fishery tagging programs in South America and off isolated "islands" in Lake Nasser, Egypt, rough landings in cargo planes, medical Institutes in Eastern Europe, a 7.1 R-scale earthquake, lecture halls at Cambridge University and at The Smithsonian Institution, geothermal energy generation in Iceland, several embassies and consulates, NGOs in a host of climes, and back to the Map Room/Archives at The Explorers Club in New York City, from whence it all began in a random conversation with my now old friend, explorer Peter Hess, Esq. In between, I have had meetings with Prime Ministers and Presidents, tea with Bedouin, worked in exotic labs in the heart of darkness, participated in a project involving ancient Egyptian mummies, and the occasional disquieting *coup d'état*; all in the name of Science (?).

The major players in this narrative deserve our thanks. Vartorella's business partner, Joanna B. Craig, heads the list for her relentless encouragement. Terry McKendree, President of a small NGO (Conservation Outdoors), provided tremendous infrastructure in South America, Iceland, North Africa, and the Middle East. The Prime Minister of Guyana, the Hon. Samuel A. Hinds, M.P., arranged an introduction to Dr. Kathryn A. Monk, Director-General of Iwokrama International Centre for Rain Forest Conservation & Development, who provided access to scientists and a one million-acre rainforest--and then generously wrote the "Foreword" to this volume. Co-author Donald S. Keel helped prepare two fundraising workshops for field scientists and explorers and contributed to an initial *Proceedings*, which gave us the impetus to write this hefty volume. EgyptAir, KLM, Cara Hotels, South Sinai Travel, Historic Camden/Blue House Dig, Wilderness Explorers, the (then) Egyptian Antiquities Organization (EAO), and African Angler have provided essential help.

Indispensable insights and/or assistance have come from Michael Adams (Environics), Chris Amer (SCIAA), Denis Belliveau (Marco Polo 700th Anniversary Expedition), Brion Battin Black (consultant), Dr. Philip Currie (Royal Tyrrell Museum of Paleontology), James Dinsmore, D.V.M. (Sinai Wildlife Projects), Clare Flemming (The Explorers Club), Peter Fritz (editor, *F1 Sport*, Central European Edition), Nisia Hanson (consultant), Peter Hess, Esq. (attorney), the late Dr. Michael Allen Hoffman (predynastic Egypt), William Jamieson (ancient Egyptian mummies project), Kenneth Kamler, M.D. (E[3]), the late Pamela Kolar (UNDP), Dr. Gregory Kremer (e-Bobcat Racing), Tamara Krizek (The Wildlife Conservation Society), Marie Levine (Shark Research Institute), Paolo Mangiafico (Duke Papyrus Archive), Dr. Robert Maybury (IOCD), Dr. Alfred McLaren (polar/underseas explorer), Shea McLean (*H.L. Hunley* Project Archaeologist), Dr. Robert Neyland (*H.L. Hunley* Project Director), Francis O'Donnell (Marco Polo 700th Anniversary Expedition), Dr. Bruce Rippeteau (SCIAA), Sally Shelton (The Smithsonian Institution), Dr. Mila Simões de Abreu (Congresso Internacional de Arte Rupestre), Dr. Steven Sidebotham (Berenike Expedition), Dr. Peter H. Smith (Lunar and Planetary Laboratory, The University of Arizona), Richard Wagner (science writer), and Dr. Graham Watkins (Senior Wildlife Biologist, Iwokrama International Centre for Rain Forest Conservation & Development).

Editors Ephimia Morphew (*Journal of Human Performance in Extreme Environments*), Ron Fellows (*The Glyph*, AIA/San Diego), Dr. P.J. Capelotti (*Into the Field: Strategies for Funding Exploration--Proceedings*, etc.), Jill Muehrcke (*Nonprofit World*), Jill Johnson (*Fund Raising Institute*), and Steve White (*Action Asia*) offered opportunities to flesh out our views on strategies for exotic funding, sections of which served as the touchstone for specific Chapters. Our book Series Editor, Prof. Sheldon Lee Gosline, distinguished himself as both scholar and diplomat, which we much appreciated. Like freed gladiators, they have all earned their wooden swords.

Finally, the authors have made every effort to cite properly ®,™,© logotypes, registrations, trademarks, and slogans within the context of our examples. Any omission is either inadvertent or consistent with the original advertisement, etc. The opinions expressed in this book are those of the authors, unless otherwise attributed.

For the authors,

William F. Vartorella
Camden, South Carolina USA
December, 2003

***

Chapter 1: "Challenge and Opportunity for Funding Science and Discovery in the 21st Century"

By William F. Vartorella

> *"To give away money is an easy matter and in any man's power. But to decide to whom to give it, and how large and when, and for what purpose and how, is neither in every man's power nor an easy matter." Aristotle*

I. Harnessing Chaos--A Survival Manual for the "Lost Scientist":

The challenge to serious science and exploration in the 21st century is not political unrest in some far-flung, exotic land or the ravages of Nature. It is, pure and simple--"funding." Competition for money is keen in a global village driven by the Internet and the desires of "have-not" nations for access to technology, transnational dollars, and just, sustainable futures.

Simultaneously, the nonprofit or "Third Sector" is beset with its own dramatic growing pains, complete with thorny governance issues, territorial desires, and an insatiable need for cash.

Large nongovernmental organizations (NGOs) are vying with nation states to receive diminishing governmental and other supplemental funding. Yet, small scientific Institutes and expeditions, pressing hard at the Frontiers of Knowledge, teeter on the brink of disaster when it comes to money. Their Boards are seemingly at war, often with themselves. "Donor fatigue" has taken its toll as the loyal are asked, repeatedly, to bail out an expedition or Institute that has no apparent plan for self-sustainability. No relief seems in sight. Foundation assets are down and grant applications are up.

Real-politik is the new philanthropic mantra. And you, the scientist, are in the *middle* of it all, a stranger in a strange land, forced to chase money—any money—to keep your research alive. Some 6,000 expeditions worldwide are poised to go into the field this year. Few truly have the money they need and some are dramatically, some might argue "dangerously," under-funded.

Funding Exploration is not for the faint-of-heart.

It is a **modern survival manual** for the most extreme of environments: the arcane, highly competitive, shadowy world of donor egos, Byzantine corporate culture, and foundation labyrinths that comprise modern philanthropy. Best estimates of annual *non-governmental* funding available for science and exploration worldwide fall easily in the U.S. $50-100 *billion* range. The money is out there. ***Funding Exploration*** will show you how and where to get it using specific strategies and tactics as part of your survival training. The donor pool is global and so is the focus of this book. We make assumptions based upon experience worldwide, trends, and serious scholarship. One assumption is that governmental funding for science is at risk. Hence, governmental funding is not a focus of this book. What is the focus is the private sector: individuals, corporations, and the foundations both underwrite.

There are reasons our book quotes Niccolò Machiavelli (*The Prince)*, Sun Tzu (*Art of War*), and François de Callières (*De la manière de négocier avec les Souverains*). And they aren't about literature. Yours is a zero-sum game played for high stakes. You either get funded or you don't. In the words of a government functionary we once knew, "What price success unless your friends fail?" This book is about success, rugged individualism, and entrepreneurship. It is about developing and implementing a *plan* of reasonable, cost-effective action. It is intended as a catalyst for change.

Your authors have 50 years of combined experience worldwide raising money for nonprofits and/or foundations and, in some cases, giving it away. We know the "strategic landscape" and how to avoid the minefields.

Every survival manual needs a map. ***Funding Exploration*** works on two levels: as a tool for planning and as an instrument for action. For example, the book maps out Board recruitment, retention, and actualization and then applies lessons learned to Capital Campaigns and endowment, etc. We show you how to get out of trouble, raise money now, and—with perseverance and this book--become a self-sustaining Institute or expedition.

Our survival manual for the "lost scientist" is part *Zen and the Art of Motorcycle Maintenance* and *A Year of Living Dangerously*. On the one hand, it extols the romantic view of the scientist as scholar/adventurer, sallying forth to engage Knowledge wherever she lurks. On the other, it is boardroom intrigue and high stakes parlor games--the underlying classical view of how the world works. There is a saying that all of us who have ever spent serious time on Expedition heed: "It isn't what you see that kills you." The same is true here, both literally and figuratively. What you don't see or read are our anecdotes about a year of living dangerously (parts of six, actually) with scientists from all over creation.

Then there is the stuff you will see: proven best practices and lessons learned that lead to cold, hard cash:

Donor Dynamics

Corporate and Expedition "co-branding"
Sponsorships
Free Gear
Foundations from "inside-the-box."
Asian Funding
Direct Mail/Direct
Marketing…

In short, this book has a full-blown, easy-to-use Capital Campaign model.

This book is short on theory and polemics and long on proven practical advice. The devil is in the details and you are well advised to plunge into the footnotes, especially those that explore studies of wealth, corporate giving, or finance/budgets.

In addition, *Funding Exploration* "names-names" when it comes to unusual donor sources, both within the context of Chapters and in the "Donor Bibliography" at journey's end. There are hundreds of millions of U.S. $, £, ¥, €, etc. lurking in these pages. Take a peek.

If you are involved in archaeology, paleontology, biomedical research, astrophysics, biodiversity/endangered species, expedition logistics, remote sensing, mountaineering, developing the next generation of Super Car, establishing or expanding your Institute or expedition, or an oceanographer, environmentalist, gifted graduate student, botanist, university development officer, or a scientist tied to a lab coat, etc., this book is for you.

Trust us, you ain't seen nothin' like this.

Stow your field kits (and preconceptions) in the cargo webbing, grab your copy of *The Prince*, and tighten your seat belt. It's going to be an eventful, bumpy ride certain to shake your conventional wisdom.

II. *Market Forces, Expeditions, and Cautionary Tales:*

Napoleon once remarked that an acquaintance could take everything Napoleon had, but not his "time." Time is money. Let's begin there.

Ironically, if we look at nonprofit funding worldwide for virtually every imaginable kind of charity, some U.S. $10,000 *per second* is donated as either in-kind contributions (equipment, supplies, etc.) or cash. In the U.S. alone, corporations donate about U.S. $50,000 per hour in equipment and supplies. And by its own reporting, the U.S. National Science Foundation (NSF) historically has funded some *one in three proposals for research, training, and educational projects.*[1]

Scientific field seasons and related laboratory analyses can no longer be carried out on "shoestring budgets," as affiliated universities clamor for ever-escalating indirect cost support--70% or more in some cases--at least in the U.S.[2] That "override" on the budget--legitimate or not--raises serious questions with governments, foundations, corporations, and individual donors who strive to allocate limited financial resources to core science only.

Historically, science, exploration, and Patrons were inextricably intertwined. The Fifth Earl of Carnarvon spent some £50,000 over 18 field seasons in his quest for an unplundered tomb of an ancient Egyptian pharaoh before that glorious day of discovery in 1922 of Tutankhamun. Carnarvon's realm was one of caprice and culture, both of which he could easily afford to indulge. Science as indulgence has rapidly moved into the gun sights of science as business--and business costs money.

For example, U.S. $65,000 is roughly the cost to:

- put one high-altitude physiologist on Mt. Everest to measure and monitor vital signs of a summit team;[3]

- underwrite the per kilogram cost of a 10 kg. payload heading for a low-earth-orbit (LEO) on board the Space Shuttle;

- send an archaeological expedition into the field in most of the developing world for four to six weeks, depending upon airfares and remoteness of site.

Yet, historical perspective can be misleading, especially during

---

[1] But even the NSF recognizes that, while environmental issues cross national borders, public support in the U.S. for international cooperation is mixed--at best. In the late 1990s, The President's Council of Advisors on Science and Technology released its recommendations in the areas of ecosystems and biological diversity entitled, *Teaming with Life: Investing in Science to Understand and Use America's Living Capital.* It functionally advocated increased support for *only* studies on U.S. biota. This is symptomatic of a point made continually throughout our book, namely that Governments cannot be depended upon as a financial safety net for science--especially consortial, global science. The paradox is that the money, globally, for projects is available, but seemingly just out of reach. The purpose of *Funding Exploration* is to *extend* one's reach, to enable Tantalus to stoop down and drink deep of the funding that is flowing by.

[2] U.S., Congress, House, Committee on Energy and Commerce, *Financial Responsibility at Universities, Hearings,* before the Subcommittee on Oversight and Investigations of the Committee on Energy and Commerce, House of Representatives, on Indirect Cost Recovery Practices at U.S. Universities for Federal Research Grants and Contracts, 102d Cong., 1st sess., March 13 and May 9, 1991, p. 2.

[3] Lest anyone is confused about the cost of serious research on Mt. Everest, the royalty charged by Nepal for a recent seven-member team on the sacred slopes was U.S. $ 50,000.

periods of turbulent stock markets, as foundations and corporations peg donations to performance.

Furthermore, philanthropy is becoming much more entrepreneurial. Gone are the days of a formula for donations. Corporations, for example, are moving more and more to a sponsorship model, in which niche constituencies (read: specific target consumers and their geo-demography) are central focus. IEG, which tracks sponsorship data worldwide, estimated global sponsorship for the year 2000 at roughly U.S. $22 billion.[4] Only some 40% of this was in North America (mostly for sporting events)--which means the rest of the planet is fertile ground for ambitious scientists capable of matching their missions to those of multinational companies seeking new, high-profile, cost-effective opportunities for distinct niches without a lot of competitive clutter.

Foundations--more than 62,000 in the U.S. alone--are receiving record numbers of proposals and applications, estimated well above **1 million** annually. That translates to about 2,740 daily, with some 192 funded. In other words, for the uninitiated randomly tossing proposals "over the transom," chances are roughly 7%.

Plus, other forces are at work, which cloud the picture:

1) Post-"September 11th" U.S. giving surged for projects and programs related to the tragedy (nearly U.S. $2 billion), but has flagged as a general result of the U.S. recession. "Giving USA," an annual survey on philanthropy, has widely reported U.S. corporate giving as decreasing 14.5%, in 2001.[5] The broader picture is murky,[6] with donors hardly ebullient over all the global "saber-rattling," the war in Iraq, and cascading oil prices. Overall giving for environmental and international efforts saw increases of 1.1% and 9.9% respectively [7] --but has to be seen perhaps as a response to changing U.S. governmental policies toward global warming and the rash of earthquakes and terrorism worldwide. Regardless, in 2004 foundation grant support seems to be stabilizing, in spite of plunging assets (25% in some cases), with selected sectors even experiencing modest growth.

---

[4] IEG, Inc., "Spanning The Globe," *IEG Sponsorship Report*, December 20, 1999, pp. 4-5.

[5] Nicole Lewis, "Charitable Giving Slides," *The Chronicle of Philanthropy*, June 27, 2002, p. 27.

[6] Independent Sector, "A Survey of Charitable Giving After September 11th, 2001," on-line at <http://www.IndependentSector.org>.

[7] Nicole Lewis, "Social-Service and International Groups Were Winners in 2001, Report Says," *The Chronicle of Philanthropy*, June 27, 2002, p. 28.

2) Some **110,000 new nonprofits** have been created in the U.S. alone during the past three years and are competing for the less restrictive funding traditionally awarded by corporations.

3) Science monies are under attack, as the U.S. Federal Government moves away from funding pure research to encouraging private enterprise to fill the gap. In developing nations, clean water and food security challenges continue to plague society, exacerbating the constant "brain drain" of scientists who seek safe havens in laboratories in the West. The early Johns Hopkins Comparative Nonprofit Sector Project, which profiled nonprofit economic activity in 12 nations, pointed out that 43% of nonprofit income in the average of seven of the countries studied was governmental.

4) Roughly **6,000+** Expeditions will take to the field this year - in almost direct competition for dollars, with **6,500 natural history museums and collections** around the world, which are mainly in desperate straits for funding to conserve their collections and to detail biodiversity.

5) "Accountability" is now the watchword, as expeditions long on adventure and short on science must face corporate managers, who demand to know how such projects help their companies meet the bottom line through exposure to new markets or patents.

6) **Corporate Volunteerism** is now the lead component in a successful funding equation that includes first - corporate employee support, second-- in-kind contributions of equipment and supplies, and--finally--cash.

7) Foundations, globally, are demanding **consortial efforts**, and thereby discouraging the single applicant.

8) Developing Nations are clamoring for access to technology--especially the Internet--and are increasingly protective of their natural resources and biota collections, which they fear will be digitized and available on-line, thereby making visits to their countries unnecessary and choking much-needed foreign exchange in hard currency.

9) Finally, states and provinces worldwide are now competing with scientists for funding from central governments. The era of scientific dependence upon Big Government for funding is virtually over. To borrow a title from Aldous Huxley, scientists are facing a "Brave New World" in which arcane, academic projects must stand up not only to the rigor of peer

review, but the brutal competition of an ever-changing global marketplace.

In short, the day of funding science and exploration for their own sakes and "pure knowledge" is over--if it ever truly existed.

Also highly at-risk are those ambitious projects that attempt to retrace the steps and exploits of past explorers, such as Marco Polo, yet maintain a reasonable scientific context. The two-year, 33,000-mile-trek through Afghanistan and nearly 20 other countries by explorers Francis O'Donnell and Denis Belliveau ("The Return to Venice: 700th Anniversary Expedition"),[8] in spite of some incredible ethnography, would now probably be beyond the capability or daring of most funders in a post-September 11th world.

Belliveau and O'Donnell cobbled together funding from top-drawer multinational corporations, such as **Kodak** (which supplied film and developed some 50,000 slides; Belliveau had won the prestigious Kodak Gallery Award in 1992), **DHL** (the international shipping company), **Canon** (video equipment), **Hoffman-LaRoche** (medicines donated for a host of potential health crises),[9] **Peninsular and Oriental (P&O) Steam Navigation Company** ("a passage to India"), and **United Technologies** (whose offices in remote locales provided access to international telephone lines and faxes). Others, such as **Merrell Boots**, gave boots and jackets to the intrepid explorers. The lead financial backing came from a former president of Sikorsky Helicopters.[10]

To put this in perspective for the early 1990s (when O'Donnell and Belliveau embarked on the Marco Polo re-tracing) provides insight into just how precarious the funding environment was (and can be). Before 1996, less than one percent (1%) of Eastman Kodak Company's annual gifts supported projects overseas. (By 1999, that figure rose to 12% of its U.S. $12 million gifts budget.[11]) Clearly, both Belliveau and O'Donnell fundamentally understood Kodak's evolving world-view and developed a

---

[8] Francis O'Donnell and Denis Belliveau, "Marco Polo's Guide to Afghanistan," *Smithsonian*, Volume 32, Number 10 (January 2002), pp. 44-47, 49-51.

[9] Lillian Africano, "Eight War Zones, 20 Visas, 17 Countries, and 33,000 Miles: Two Friends Retrace Marco Polo's Treacherous Route," *Biography*, February 1999, p. 83.

[10] Vartorella is indebted to Belliveau and O'Donnell for sharing additional information regarding their funding sources, both in a face-to-face meeting at The Explorers Club in New York City in November, 1999 and in subsequent telephone calls with O'Donnell on 5 and 15 November 2002.

[11] Debra E. Blum, "Companies' Charitable Gifts Follow Their Revenue and Go Overseas," *The Chronicle of Philanthropy*, July 15, 1999, p. 12.

cutting-edge project at the frontier of a shared, global vision.

In short, by serendipity or design, Belliveau and O'Donnell followed a model we advocate throughout this book, namely entrepreneurship, an urgent and compelling (and interesting) Case for Support (700th Anniversary, etc.), and high-profile donors capable of providing gear, in-kind services, and cash.

Funders demand results and expect that risk will be manageable. Mt. Everest has been climbed and continues to take its human toll. Tales of "there we were, there we were in *darkest Africa*" now too often evoke the response of "been there, done that" or conjure up visions of neo-colonialism.

Yet, amidst what should be obvious to most scientists are what might be termed the seven deadly sins of science and discovery fundraising.

The Seven Deadly Sins of Science and Discovery Fundraising [12]

1) Focus upon the end results of the Project, rather than a potential Donors Needs and Mission ("unenlightened self-interest"): This sin is the most deadly and easiest to avoid. A successful request for funding is centered upon how a project helps a corporation, foundation, governmental entity, or individual donor meet core aspects of *its* Mission (Vision Statement), marketing goals, "dead donor wishes," or individual aspirations.

2) Creation of a concept for which no funding source is in sight ("the mirage"): People give money to people, not ideas. An identified constituency of potential donors is critical at the point of concept. (See #1, above.)

3) Development of project done better, elsewhere, for less money ("re-inventing the wheel"): If one looks at *all nonprofit projects*, regardless of description, published U.S. figures indicate that some **33%** fall within this sin. The same is probably true for most expeditions that seek to re-trace someone else's steps. Funders would rather have the shock of the new, rather than a travelogue. Plus, there seems to be a conventional wisdom among funders that risk of the new is actually less risky than supporting a "re-creation," which usually has most of the risks of the original adventure.

4) Lack of appreciation for the marketing concepts of "new, improved,

---

[12] William F. Vartorella, "Seven Deadly Sins of Expedition Fundraising," *Expedition News*, Volume Four, Number Two (February, 1997), 3-4. This article, with a slightly different focus than the revised text herein, emphasizes strong strategic and financial planning, which shall be detailed later in this book.

or free" ("Corporate Culture 101"): Access to new markets, improved infrastructure or scientific advances, and a free, public component are important aspects of a successful grant application to a corporation, foundation or pitch to an individual donor. The more market-driven in terms of concept, without sacrificing underlying science, the better the project is.

5) Misjudging the financial requirements ("exploring the Amazon on a dollar a day"): Many expedition leaders (and scientists, generally) are so accustomed to razor-thin budgets, that they either a) grossly downsize the request to near-danger levels or b) inflate the budget with the expectation that a funder will give less and, thereby, still meet the project's needs. Both approaches flirt with disaster. Rising floodwaters, political intrigue, theft of provisions, etc. are nuisance enough, without the added stress of limited financial resources. **Strategy:** determine clearly the expedition's goals and the amount of money and in-kind donations (including corporate volunteerism and governmental infrastructure) necessary for safe passage. Funders realize that field science costs money. Entrepreneurs (key potential underwriters) are acutely aware of the dangers of under-capitalization as most have suffered through this themselves. A bare-bones budget can lead to bare bones. No funder wants to contact next-of-kin or explain lawsuits to shareholders.

6) A project too good to be passed up by funders ("insidious narcissism"): Ideas that seem too good to be true, often are. Such expeditions also tend to be poorly articulated and usually have an adventure focus. Laboratory science that implies an imminent cure to a dread disease also raises "red flags" with donors.

7) A Board comprised of experts, rather than donors ("The Trojan Horse"): If you have a Board, it needs to be comprised of members exhibiting the three C's—connectedness to Mission, clout with donors, and capacity to give money. The old model--the 4Ws: the wealthy, the wise, the workers, and the worriers--suffers from passivity and inertia. The *only reason* anyone should sit on a scientific nonprofit board is for his/her ability to give or get money. If you need advice, buy it. Your Board should have 100% participation in terms of giving/getting money for your project. Taking "ownership" of the concept pays dividends when the laboratory or field project seeks corporate--and especially Asian--support.

But the above is just the tip of the proverbial iceberg.

Central to the challenge is an inherent corporate culture *within* science that can make long-term sustainability of a laboratory project, Institute, or expedition at-risk with funders. As this Chapter's author is partially trained in archaeology, perhaps the best analogue is one from experience. Consider these traits within the context of your own scientific discipline.

The Quest for a Sustainable Archaeology [13]

1) The Archaeologist as Divine King:

All too common--especially in Egypt, Mesopotamia, and Central America--are the charismatic, brilliant archaeologists who build careers and mystique on exotic sites. Donor monies flourish and are attached *specifically* to the persona of the Archaeologist. When s/he *dies* the natural transfer of power, responsibility, and--most importantly--donor cash flow is impossible, as the Archaeologist (rather than the site and its relative scientific goals) *was* the total focus.

2) The Impenetrability of Archaeology as Divine Mysteries: The
implication of archaeology as fundable science and romantic adventure is a two-edged sword. Generally speaking, the more rarefied the jargon employed to explain a project, the more difficult to convince a donor to participate. If *Europe* could be invaded successfully in W.W.II on the basis of a clear one-page summary, it stands to reason that an archaeological project could be detailed simply in a similar document. The balancing act is keeping archaeology intellectually accessible to donors, the general public, and other constituencies.

3) The Myth of Corporate (Donor) Interference (and Tainted Money):
Archaeologists traditionally seem suspicious of corporate culture and the requirements of budgets, public exposure, and the utilization of site imagery as part of marketing campaigns. Fine corporate partners such as **IBM** and **American Express** have long since dispelled this myth, but the "true-believers" (e.g., those archaeologists without funding) perpetuate it to the detriment of the profession. Isolated problems may exist, but they seem more a function of a lack of communication than blatant interference.

Corporate types understand trench warfare, but not trenching.

---

[13] William F. Vartorella, "Digging for Dollars: the Quest for a Sustainable Archaeology," *The Glyph*, Volume 1, Number 11 (December, 1997), 13-15.

4) The Misreading of the Text, *"Publish before you Perish"* as *"Publish or Perish"*: Donors expect to see results within reasonable time frames. *Posthumous* publishing is not reasonable. The goal is to provide cogent reports and discussions to *each* of the major constituencies (professional, donor, public(s)) within definable time limits. In the words of one donor, "An archaeologist who does not publish is nothing more than a highly-trained *looter.*" Archaeologists who disseminate knowledge widely *and frequently* have the best chance for attracting serious funding.

5) The Belief that People Give Money to Ideas: They do not. "People give money to People." It is the reason that the Archaeologist as Divine King has been successful in the *short term*. The challenge is to translate the interpersonal to the intellectual as planned giving, endowments, multiple annual gifts, etc.

6) Trojan Horse Boards: The creation of a nonprofit with an active Board is *the* vital first step toward sustainability in the 21st century. Remember the three C's (connectedness to Mission, clout with donors, and capacity to give money).

   *Note: the only reason any person should be recruited for an expedition-related Board is her/his ability to **give or get funding (wealth)**.* **Period.**

   The most powerful phrase to secure funding from an individual donor is "Won't you join *me* in giving XYZ $$$ to this project?"

   Boards comprised of advisors (other archaeologists and university types) serve little purpose. A nonprofit can *buy* this kind of expertise, but it cannot *buy* donors. A better strategy is a Board of Donors, plus a second-tier **committee** of ex-officio advisers (scientists) who are experts in their fields and can help explain needs cogently to the larger Board.

7) The Lack of a Compelling and Urgent Case for Support: What distinguishes one archaeological excavation and team from another competing for funding? Is it the science or the *language* of the science? In short, can the team provide a simple, evocative Mission explained in Management by Objective (MBO) terms that any corporate, individual, or foundation donor can understand? Is it interesting? Urgent? Intellectually compelling? Does it have educational components for the *entire* family?

   Finally, and most importantly, can the needs of the team be translated into terminology/projects that *meet the donor Mission* without sacrificing strong scientific goals?

Clearly, what we are outlining in **Funding Exploration** is a fundamentally different way for scientists to see the world, particularly as it relates to opportunities for funding.

> *The real voyage of discovery consists not in seeking*
> *new landscapes, but in having new eyes.*
> *Marcel Proust*

III. "The Trend is your Friend," or "When in Doubt, Follow the Money":

A quick look at trends in 21st century funding should help round out our global view that funding sources for science and exploration are limited more by one's imagination than any perceived budgetary ceiling.[14]

"Think globally. Act locally."

It may sound trite, but future fundraising comprises seamless international borders with cash, volunteerism, and information essentially manifested as the same commodity.

We are already seeing this trend, as corporations increasingly move away from the simple, unrestricted cash gift to a market-driven composite of employee volunteerism, in-kind donations of product, and (finally) cash.

"Accountability" is the watchword. Simply--companies, foundations, and individual donors expect a bigger bang for their donated buck. Donations--and strategies that drive them--are products of dynamic market forces.

It has been estimated that more than 90% of the technology we shall use by the Year 2008 has not been invented. Worse, some predict that existing technology by that date will become obsolete every 30 days-- virtually as fast as it can be developed.

The evolving marketplace will be highly decentralized, with strategic niche markets consisting of pods of consumers in cyberspace, rather than pushpins on a sales map. Offices, including those your college, Institute, or expedition's development staff occupy now, may only be "touch points" for workers to interact occasionally face-to-face. What this means for the people business of development is, at best, uncertain.

---

[14] William F. Vartorella, "A Catalyst for Change: The New Philanthropy in the Global Village, " *NonProfit Strategist*, Volume 7, Issue 1 (February, 2001), 4-5. The current context is an expansion of this article.

What follows is consistent with our experience working with scientists, nonprofits, foundations, and non-governmental organizations (NGOs) worldwide.

Firstly, know what is on the brink of extinction:

1) grant requests lacking a consortial partner and matching funds: Foundations are beginning to understand "synergy"—the move to required consortia for **all proposals** is inevitable.

2) institutional overhead: Foundations see value in more funding available, if less institutional overhead is granted. Institutional Overhead and the General Operating Grant will be put to rest.

3) state funding for various nonprofit efforts: states are competing with traditional nonprofits for remaining federal dollars.

4) large, unwieldy university development offices: faculty and hard-pressed departments are tired of begging for help. Trend is toward academic "petty fiefdoms" that raise their own dollars. As these gain momentum and power, universities will be at a loss as to how to respond--competition for donor allegiance will intensify. Decentralization of development offices will be the rule.

5) gross duplication of nonprofits will result in shake-out and a healthier non-profit, "Third Sector": Foundations are getting smarter that projects they fund have often been done elsewhere, better, for less cash. And the "replication" of successful grant models (e.g., projects) is more myth than reality.

6) the Board that gives and gets money: like it or not, Boards are shifting their fundraising responsibility to extremely overworked Staff; Board "dysfunction" is growing.

7) a clear line of demarcation between nonprofit and for-profit operations: not-for-profit and for-profit activities will blur, as nonprofits and NGOs (non-governmental organizations) become more competitive, more entrepreneurial--with the result: confused donors.

Secondly, be on the cutting edge:

1) move to "virtual nonprofits" on-line: creation of instant global consortia

in response to defined needs in real-time; ever-changing, easy to match with articulated, precise donor Missions;

2) creation of "virtual foundations" on-line: foundations will combine seamlessly to conserve resources and to be more responsive via on-line applications and peer review of ever-evolving projects that are people and performance-focused;

3) birth of "virtual donor pools"--as donors become more sophisticated (and as "baby boomers" prepare for the U.S. multi-*trillion* dollar infusion of inheritance from parents), expect the use of the Internet to identify suitable nonprofits for support--regardless of borders; estimates for the next decade see 40-50% of all donations occurring "on-line";

4) the emergence of "Seamless Missions" for ever-evolving nonprofits: Missions will become Vision Statements, with annual review; stronger internal accountability;

5) increased synergism between global NGOs and local nonprofits to form strategic alliances aimed at encouraging "shared solutions" to global / local problems, with substantial participation by foundations across traditional borders;[15]

6) global volunteerism as a "just cause" in and of itself.

7) finally, global funding trends will focus on "access" issues—
   - *Access* to New Technologies, including the Internet
   - *Access* to Information and Distance Education
   - *Access* to Better Health Care Delivery Systems and information leading to the *prevention* of communicable diseases
   - *Access* to Social Justice
   - *Access* to safe, Affordable Housing (40-60% of world's population live in adobe-style structures)
   - *Access* to a Global Economy, through the ability to create partnerships, which encourage global / local investment

---

[15] The World Bank has called upon European and U.S. foundations active in developing nations and the former Soviet Bloc to explore greater collaboration, including the potential for consortial projects with the World Bank itself. See Vince Stehle, "European Philanthropy Experts Disagree on Rules for Giving in Era of Euro," *The Chronicle of Philanthropy*, May 21, 1998, p. 37.

- *Access* to Opinion Leaders.

In short, the 21st century will test our notion of what "sustainable futures" mean.

In the words of one sage, "The future ain't what it used to be."

For researchers looking at fundable projects, developing a platform that includes combining "access" issues and easily measured outcomes with hard science is a proven strategy for success.

The trend *is* your friend.

IV. *Everyone Has a Theory--Here is Ours:*

As a scientist you are trained to think "outside-the-box."

Yet, unfortunately, you are not taught about such mysterious corporate techniques as "War Rooms" pasted over with ideas scrawled by bold, felt-tipped markers or the value of "brainstorming" software.[16]

That being the case, indulge us with some of our own counter-intuitive thinking.

While this book will rarely tread in the realm of theory, developing a model way of thinking how to explore a funding universe is more than an exercise in mental gymnastics. It is a way of applying the principles laid out thus far to the most important scientific investigation on your immediate horizon, namely the unique project you hope to have funded.

For the sake of illustration, we have chosen a project in an extreme environment.

---

[16] Corporate leaders such as **Sandoz, Ltd.**--the global pharmaceutical company based in Basel, Switzerland--are known to turn to newly-developed "brainstorming" software in an effort to gain a strategic competitive advantage for new product launches and a host of other applications. Institutes, NGOs, and expeditions may well gain from their example, both in terms of generating new, fundable ideas or approaches and in getting a sense of the corporate mind. "Brainstorming" software and card-kits abound, including IdeaFisher, Idea Generator Plus, and Mindlink Problem Solver. Ask your corporate partners what they use, take a look, and open a dialogue.

A Simple Application of Convergent/Divergent Funding Theory to (Micro-) Extreme Environments [17]

How extreme is "extreme"?

While the question sounds rhetorical, it isn't.

Extreme environments often take on the characteristics of micro-extremes: unexpected changes in temperature, visibility, and mental disorientation (polar "white-outs," etc.).

At this point, an Extreme Mission takes on its own characteristics and eccentricities. That is the stuff of science and the essence of discovery.

It also is probably the most overlooked "window of opportunity" for funding. For the sake of definition, let's call this "convergence vs. divergence funding theory."

In "convergence funding theory," an expedition seeking a grant or sponsor tries to simplify the funding request to reflect one shared, core concept or value ("Big Idea") that will resonate with a donor: "Find bacterial life on Mars." Result: typically, a rather short list of donor prospects as the Mission--no matter how complicated--is narrowly defined in terms of potential underwriting interest. Very focused, yet very little room to negotiate/change direction with funder $$$.

In "divergent funding theory," an expedition would look at the problem differently. "What kind of analogues exist on Earth that can be explored to help us understand the process of finding and identifying life on Mars, if life exists? The analogues may be polar, under-seas, desert, high-altitude environments, etc. Result: a much larger list of donor prospects, as the research possibilities diverge from a core concept to reflect differing extreme environments, their own peculiarities, donor interest, etc.

Still focused, but the underlying funding is spread among a larger number of donors who understand their piece in the broader puzzle. Risk, too, is shared.

Simply, fundable projects in extreme environments need to keep the "Big Idea" in focus, yet investigators should understand that smaller, fundable "victories" build reputations, donor confidence, and may lead to ever-upward spiraling donor investments. In short, a "divergent" strategy for fundraising keeps donors in balance (e.g., no one may represent more than 20% or so of the funding) and, thereby, keeps projects on track and less susceptible to

---

[17] William F. Vartorella, "Simple Application of Convergent/Divergent Funding Theory to (Micro-) Extreme Environments," *Human Performance in Extreme Environments*, Volume 5, Number 2 (June, 2001), 128-130.

donor dysfunction (untimely withdrawal of financial support).

Missions, funders, and extreme environments all have goals and objectives, whether controlled by man-made or natural laws. A scientific Mission has its strategies and tactics, a funder has its Vision Statement and application guidelines, and an extreme environment has a combination of known and unknown characteristics (seemingly) consistent with our understanding of Nature.

In an extreme environment all of these converge, either at a single point or as a group of micro-points. Tactics (and equipment and underlying funding) are put to the test when theoretical science and best-laid plans are pitted against Nature's fury. Sometimes this is predictable (the overall single point convergence, based upon expected micro-outcomes) or as a burst of unexpected micro-outcomes, often roughly analogous to what might have been expected in other extreme environments (but not in the present Mission).

In the "predictable" convergence theory instance, a Mission team

1) identifies and approaches a funder
2) matches its Mission with the goals and objectives of the funding source
3) offers a methodology for testing an hypothesis in an extreme environment
4) (ideally) gets funding
5) sallies forth into an extreme situation with manageable risks.

In a less predictable scenario, the Mission followed steps 1-5, yet is met with new challenges of unexpected micro-extreme environments. These are either dealt with "seat-of-the-pants" or the Mission is aborted or some other outcome occurs. Then, it is back-to-the-drawing-board.

At this juncture, many scientists working in the extreme attempt to re-group to assess what went wrong, re-format the project/methodology, and seek additional funding from either the same or similar sources. Functionally, they are trying to re-direct a convergent strategy (back to the "Big Idea") to a donor for whom the "Big Idea" just did not materialize as a successful Mission. In lay terms, what the scientist tries to do is create some "boiler-plate" language that seemingly will attract an underwriter--"any" underwriter. Yet, this may be absolutely the wrong approach from a funding perspective.

The question is this: does the extreme situation experienced in the Mission (e.g., a high altitude biomedical test) "mimic" something analogous, say, at great depths underwater? If the answer is "yes," suddenly the Mission has multiple points of convergence between funder goals and Mission objectives, albeit in multiple extreme environments.

Translation: instead of a very, very narrow universe of funders for the original Mission concept, now there exist multiple funding targets. The trick is to address these new Donor Missions within the context of a multifaceted project that crosses--diverges--several extreme environmental borders. A real example might be the approach a Mars habitat ("biosphere") experiment takes in a polar setting on earth.

Multiple funding platforms emerge, to wit:

- pure science/space exploration (a very shallow funding pool)
- polar exploration (cold weather adaptations, degradation of the ozone layer, cosmic radiation, etc.--still relatively few donors)
- habitat (new, stronger, cheaper lightweight materials with long-term commercial and humanitarian uses/access to cheap, affordable housing; donor DIVERGENCE begins - more funding opportunities)
- group dynamics and team-building (again, commercial/corporate applications for streamlined decision-making)
- equipment tests (newer, cheaper, highly-adaptable synthetics which conserve heat and human energy with broad applications, e.g., mitten-friendly clothing fasteners also useful for the aged, physically handicapped, etc.)
- food and nutrition (high-energy, minimal/small/low impact packaging, easily portable; commercial and humanitarian applications in exploration and relief efforts)
- ground transportation innovation (often overlooked, highly-fundable, especially if it has urban congestion applications)
- efficacy of pharmaceuticals on humans in extreme cold, etc. (significant opportunity, considering the distribution of humans in northern latitudes and/or at high altitude)
- weather prediction in extreme environments, artificial environments / closed systems--including those ravaged by fire, chemicals, etc. (host of funders, ranging from commercial aviation to producers of heating/ventilation/air conditioning/HVAC), etc., etc.)

Functionally, we have broken the Mission down into fundable sub-Missions in a host of micro-environments (both Natural and Built).

Now, instead of just a handful of funding sources, we have the potential for "donor divergence"--a host of donors tied to multiple Mission objectives, analogous to the hub of a wheel with numerous spokes radiating outward. Each spoke (donor) is important in holding the cohesive Mission (hub and wheel itself) together.

The key, as always, is addressing the outcomes sought by the donors. They may, in fact, be far from mutually exclusive.

A few words regarding "outcomes" are in order:

1) an equipment manufacturer wants to see his gear tested at the "bleeding edge" of its intended use and the "cutting edge" for new applications;

2) a materials company is interested in heat transfer, portability, erection in high winds, stability, ease-of-maintenance, and low-cost repair (habitats);

3) a foundation is intent upon its Mission being met in innovative, cost-effective ways.

Once the scientist recognizes and identifies the extreme micro-environments, the next step is to create a funding checklist for each potential donor type: foundation, corporation, federal, and individual. Then, as if plotting coordinates on a map, the investigator lists the primary and sub-Missions of the project, analyzes the goals and objectives of these multiple Missions (again, staying close to the central focus), and matches them to those Vision Statements of the funders and logs them on the checklist.

What emerges is a chart that looks like this:

Funding Checklist for Project X (foundations, corporations, federal, individuals)

	Primary Mission	Sub-M #1	Sub-M #2	Sub-M #3
Shared Goals:				
1)	Donor A	Donor B	Donor C	Donor D
2)	Donor F	Donor A	Donor A	Donor A
3), etc.	Donor A	Donor E	Donor G	Donor A
Objectives:				
1)	Donor H	Donor A	Donor E	Donor C
2)	Donor D	Donor D	Donor D	Donor D
3), etc.	Donor B	Donor A	Donor C	Donor I

Several things should be apparent from this example.

1) The #1 Mission GOAL has potential support from four funders, thereby expanding the initial funding universe through the addition of micro-Missions.
2) Goals #2-3 see the introduction of three new donor possibilities (Donors E-G), offering still more underwriting potential.
3) Objective #2 surprisingly offers broad support across all Missions from new Donor D.
4) As Objectives are detailed, additional donors H and I surface.
5) Primary Mission now has five strong donor targets (read down the chart!).
6) Donor A becomes a main funding target for the overall Mission and Sub-M #1, thereby increasing the Case for Support with Donor A.
7) Finally, a scatter analysis of funders for this specific set (say, foundations) indicates A=7 points of funding interest, D=5, C & E=3, B=2, F-G-H-I=1 ea.

Total = 9 foundations and 24 target points meeting aspects of funder Vision Statements.

In short, the best way to converge on funding is through a divergent analysis of donors based upon understanding the dynamics and opportunities presented by microenvironments in extreme situations. By separating a project into intertwined components, a scientist may discover
1) unusual mimicry or mirroring of environments (a Mars habitat experiment in earth's polar region) which may establish multiple Cases for Support with donors,
2) b) the existence of donors capable of supporting unusual aspects of sub-Missions, and c) the ability of the project to sustain donor growth within the context of the overall extreme Mission.

V. From Theory to Practice:

The problem is many scientists, while highly-creative in their labs or field research, are "hell-bent-to-leather" to get funded and seem inclined to believe that the shortest point between them and money is a straight line.
It isn't. The answer is non-Euclidean: it's an arc. "Straight-line" solutions may work if you are an investigator trying to decipher an ancient, unknown language, but with funding in a global economy, the money may

be just over the horizon. The "straight-line" solution usually emphasizes aiming at the same, highly competitive funding source that scientists worldwide have used since time immemorial - government.

A non-Euclidean approach understands that funding sources actually have "curvature." The pathways are more complex: donor Missions may be at the center of a sphere, but the Boards, Executive Directors, and program staff are set at different points on the sphere. They may be nearby and seen or just over the horizon.

As noted above, the goal of our discussion in the ensuing chapters is Proust's insight about having "new eyes"--to see beyond the horizon at unexplored funding opportunities.

Too often, scientists tend to imagine their projects as static, rather than in motion as a living entity.

For example, the world's 6,500 natural history museums are faced with the Herculean task of housing, conserving, and managing an estimated 12 to 15 *billion* specimens by the middle of this century. Static? Hardly--particularly with the pressures to record biodiversity and efforts within developing nations to *resist* digitizing their collections and, thereby, reducing much-needed foreign currency from visitors.

Furthermore, many of these same collections are missing a highly fundable point: more than 25,000 plant species are used in medicine. These collections may play an increasingly important role in the delivery of high-quality, cost-effective health care worldwide. *Access* to them and the knowledge stored therein is crucial, as some 80% of the top prescription drugs are either natural products, synthetic compounds modeled on them, or semi-synthetic derivatives, according to the recent United Nations report, *Global Biodiversity Assessment*.[18] Natural History collections are faced with a multi-billion dollar (USD equivalent) burden. Rather than focusing upon what we call "dusty antiquarianism"--storage in hermetically-sealed exhibit cases for ages of casual viewing--the better approach for funding is the active one of access, strategic use, and an entrepreneurial attitude.

---

[18] Kenan Pollack, "Outlook: Species--It's a Tough World Out There," *U.S. News and World Report*, November 17, 1995, p. 23. See also, T. Adler, "Providing the data to protect biodiversity," *Science News*, Volume 148 (November 18, 1995), 326. Adler's summary of the 1,140-page tome points out that since the 1600s, scientists have documented some 654 plant and 484 animal species extinctions. Especially troubling: more than 26,000 plant and 5,000 animal species stand at the near-brink of extinction--because of "human activities." If ever there were an urgent and compelling Case for Support and funding platform for global consortial projects involving shared solutions to the human and Nature interfaces in habits, this is it. As the report points out, the issue is really one of protecting *genetic diversity within species*, rather than a pure focus on individual species.

It is the premise of this book that competing for the increasingly finite financial resources of governments worldwide takes scientists on the slippery slope to a "predator trap." To avoid ending up in the LaBrea Tar Pit morass of the un-funded, scientists need to position themselves to occupy unique funding niches (evolutionary spaces, if you will) which are aggressive, high profile, and capable of attracting the attention of significant funders while remaining consistent with the evolving Mission of their institutions. Inherent in this opportunism is the ability to meet

1) donor needs,
2) constituency needs (Boards, college administrations, Institute dynamics, etc.), and
3) institutional needs (rising costs of doing science, administrative overhead, long-range goals and objectives, etc.) - in *that order*.

Too often the order is reversed--with science seen as some kind of abstract absolute, for its own sake.

Vertebrate paleontology, which the uninitiated might deem as being about "extinction," is probably one of the most robust examples of how great marketing can lead to useful funding in true "win-win" scenarios.

Case Study #1--Dinosaurs Pay Dividends:

In the 1930s, the old **Sinclair Oil Company** staged a major dinosaur exhibit at the World's Fair in Chicago, complete with professional assistance from a paleontologist at the American Museum of Natural History. During the same period, Sinclair sponsored a free dinosaur book for use by school-teachers and librarians. Sinclair continued the tradition of sponsorship well into the 1960s--*30 years*--with a host of exhibits, mechanical dinosaurs, stamp albums, etc. with a combined educational and advertising focus.[19]

The interest in dinosaurs has been unabated ever since.[20] If anyone has any doubt about this, revisit the public outcry and financial stakes over the discovery of the *Tyrannosaurus rex* nicknamed "Sue," whose life ended some 65 million years ago, but generated paper offers of up to U.S. $60

---

[19] Jay Stevenson, Ph.D. and George R. McGhee, Ph.D., *The Complete Idiot's Guide to Dinosaurs* (New York, N.Y.: alpha books, A Division of Macmillan General Reference, 1998), p. 27.

[20] Alvin H. Reiss, "Groups Are Using Strong Visuals to Woo Donors and Audiences," *NonProfit Strategist*, Volume 7, Issue 2 (April, 2001), 1, 6. Discusses fundraising for The Field Museum's exhibit of "Sue," the most complete *Tyrannosaurus rex* fossil found to date, and other unrelated projects.

million, before resolution.[21]

Perhaps the best recent example is the surge in funding for dinosaur research and collections following the release of *Jurassic Park*, to wit [22]:

- Estimated annual funding prior to *Jurassic Park*: U.S. $ 1 million
- Increase in scientific funding immediately following the movie's release: 25%
- Grants from revenue of "The Dinosaurs of *Jurassic Park* traveling exhibit: U.S. $500,000.

Even the most cursory look at advertising in the mass media turns up numerous opportunities for scientific underwriting.

A few examples:

- **Campbell's® Condensed Soup**: "Dinosaur Shaped Pasta with Chicken in Chicken Broth." (The soup can's label includes Tyrannosaurus,[23] Triceratops, and Pteranodon, with other shapes -- Stegosaurus, Brachiosaurus, Parasaurolophus, and Dromaeosaurus -- on the back and inside of the label. Tremendous opportunity for investigators interested in these species and an obvious tie-in to core Campbell's values, interest in education, children, etc.

---

[21] Richard Monastersky, "For the Sake of Sue--What will happen to the world's best *T. Rex*?," *Science News*, Volume 148 (November 11, 1995), 316.

[22] Anonymous, "Outlook: Database--Jurassic Juggernaut," *U.S. News and World Report*, September 25, 1995, p. 16. *USN&WR*--Basic data: *Advertising Age*; American Film Institute; Dinosaur Society; Paleontological Research Institution.

[23] Like it or not, both the public and advertising agencies are focused upon the Theropods, particularly *T. rex*, in terms of "borrowed interest" to elicit notice and readership of their corporate clients' ads. One approach that museums with reasonably representative collections of Theropods might consider is mounting a "retrospective" exhibit, complete with the usual public lectures and, perhaps, a narrowly-drawn scientific symposium of specialists, with a raft of professional papers, panels, and the usual "poster" sessions. The exhibit/focus might hinge on the historically "controversial," for example the confusion over *Troodon*, which was lifted by P.J. Currie (Royal Tyrrell Museum of Palaeontology, Drumheller, Alberta, Canada), or the resurgence of the debate over *T. rex* as predator vs. scavenger . One funding strategy would be to look at the companies using Theropod imagery, create an overlay of corporate subsidiaries active in the museum's membership main zip code (and that of specific, related excavations), and approach companies with a specific plan to a) underwrite the basic costs of the exhibit and b) provide research and travel support for paleontologists participating in the related scientific symposium. A third opportunity for sponsorship might include underwriting "*Proceedings*," which could include separate public lectures for employees of the corporate supporter(s). We explore similar strategies in greater detail in Chapter 5.

- **GDS Systems**: "It appears layer based systems have finally found their place in time." (An "update" of traditional GIS software, this ad not only features a host of dinosaur species, but also offers a *free poster* of the ad from its home office.)

- **GE Information Services:** "If you think you can take your time going to market, think again." (Advertisement with an exposed, *in situ*, dinosaur skeleton.)

- **Mita Copiers**: "Mita copiers can help any office get out of the stone age." ("Still working with prehistoric office equipment?" A humorous appeal with cartoon dinosaurs operating a new line of personal and high-speed photocopy machines. Part of a series of company ads, another of which indicates that companies using the machines become "productive," while "those without become fossils.")

- **Real Enterprise Systems Products**: "We're Back! (And We're Stronger Than Ever)." (An ad for computer servers, with two raptors wreaking havoc in an outmoded office.)

- **TIAA-CREF**: "Paleontologist Paul Sereno has encountered some of the weirdest creatures that ever walked the earth. Yet some of the scariest things he's discovered aren't likely to become extinct anytime soon." (An advertisement aimed at fund management fees.)

- **Wachovia Securities**: "What can a Tyrannosaurus Rex teach us about a Retirement Plan? What's big one day may disappear the next." (An ad for expanded banking services.) [24]

- **Rockport Shoes**: "I'm comfortable chasing monsters." (Dr. Bob Bakker was an unofficial consultant for the film *Jurassic*

---

[24] For an excellent overview of the status of scholarship regarding *T. rex*, see John R. Horner and Don Lessem, *The Complete T. rex* (New York: Simon and Schuster, 1993)--especially p. 217, that might leave some advertisers cringing, to wit: "T. rex as a scavenger isn't a new idea. And it isn't a popular one. For much of this century [20th century], scientists thought *T. rex* was a scavenger. But that's when we viewed all dinosaurs as stupid, sluggish, and swamp-bound." Marketing campaigns, like dinosaurs, have life-spans and undergo change as brands mature and die. *T. rex* as metaphor seems to be long-lived.

Park and is perhaps best known for his theories that dinosaurs were warm-blooded creatures. See, *The Dinosaur Heresies*. His novel, *Raptor Red*, is the story of a year in the life of a female raptor dinosaur some 120 million years ago.)

Bakker, the inveterate scientist-as-entrepreneur/promoter, is an example of financial evolution in an era in which large-scale research fieldwork is prohibitively expensive. For example, an unrelated expedition in New Mexico unearthed a *Seismosaurus* whose entire skeleton could cost some U.S. $1 million to excavate.

Even individual donors can be brought into central focus, as the recent debate over donor naming of new species has historical precedent in the guise of the late steel tycoon-turned-expedition-underwriter, Andrew Carnegie. A paleontologist at the Carnegie Museum in Pittsburgh shrewdly named a new species of the sauropod *Diplodocus* after him (*Diplodocus carnegiei*). Carnegie, responding to the donor recognition, provided additional funds to have the 300 or so bones cast in plaster and replicated, with the resulting skeletons donated to Natural History museums in Mexico City, Paris, Vienna, London, etc.[25]

The point is simple: corporate and individual donor alliances with
Natural History collections have worked for more than a century and are expected to work in the future, whether the project is paleontology, bio-diversity, pharmacology, or ancient flora and fauna. If your project involves a museum[26] as a consortial partner, a key first step is to canvas the collection for both its strengths and its most unusual specimens. Think outside the museum box. Imagine how the collection and your research should evolve in terms of both its competitive components and those that are most opportunistic (ancient birds, for example).[27]

---

[25] Stevenson and McGhee, *The Complete Idiot's Guide to Dinosaurs*, p.199.

[26] In 2003, for example, the Eden Hall Foundation provided U.S. $5 million to the Carnegie Museum of Natural History to expand its Dinosaur Hall.

[27] For an excellent summary of the historic and ongoing debate over the relationship of birds to dinosaurs, see David E. Fastovsky and David B. Weishampel, *The Evolution and Extinction of the Dinosaurs* (Cambridge, England: Cambridge University Press, 1996), pp. 304-321. Essentially, early Darwinian T.H. Huxley outlined 35 characteristics between the two of which 17 are still considered valid. Renewed interest in the dinosaur-bird connection is credited to J.H. Ostrom of Yale University, who documented the relationship between *Archaeopteryx* and coelurosaurian theropods.

As you will learn in our Chapter on corporate funding strategies, such advertisements and corporate news releases often are replete with fundable scenarios--if you know how to proceed quickly.

A missed opportunity (?) for Mycenaean specialists may have involved **Boeing**'s announcement several years ago that its war-horse, the 747, had celebrated its 20th anniversary, logging some 27.5 million hours. That equates to one airplane having taken off when the Mycenaean civilization ended and landing 3,139 years later. An archaeologist capable of a flight of fancy may have been able to translate Boeing's analogy into funding for, say, the Mycenaean civilization's technological prowess, trade, or some other transportation-related project.

It all comes down to another reoccurring theme of *Funding Exploration*: creating a "solicited" idea.

FACT: Many proposals submitted today worldwide began and ended with an "unsolicited idea"--namely, an idea for which the scientist had no precise notion of why or how it would be funded.

A "solicited idea" begins with

- a known donor's Mission or Vision Statement which can be met with your idea and scientific Mission.

Furthermore, the successful grant proposal or sponsorship in the early 21st century will be

1) Consortial (a sharing of Vision and expertise)

2) Matching (e.g., the consortium puts up "non-cash" in-kind contributions of time and resources; *never* match with hard-earned dollars--more on this later)

3) Inclusive, rather than exclusive in terms of the constituencies participating in the project (with sensitivity to gender, cultural and personal differences, etc.)

4) Submitted by women and minorities often under-represented in the

grant review and award processes

5) New, improved or free and have a strong public educational component

6) Easy to evaluate

7) Capable of becoming self-sustaining at end of a grant award period.

VI. *Recommendations for Keeping Adventure to a Minimum, Funding to a Maximum:*

With more than *6,000* scientific expeditions of all descriptions (archaeology, marine sciences, geology, biodiversity, etc.) going into the field worldwide this year--plus countless laboratory investigations--the *perceived* competition for funding is *keen.*

The reality is much different, *if* scientists plan for a **sustainable future** that is a combination of individual, corporate, and foundation funding in which 30% is earmarked for endowment.

In the early 21st century, philanthropy, too, is at an historic crossroads. The old model of the benign patriarch donor is rapidly disappearing. It is being replaced with an aggressive global corporate culture focused upon niche-specific giving. The Corporate Philanthropy of the New World Order is dictated by emerging markets and a compressed marketing cycle in which the spiral from product introduction to maturity to death (or reintroduction) may be months in duration, rather than years.

The implications for funding science and discovery may seem removed, at best.

Time for a "reality check."

Those investigators who survive and thrive will develop innovative partnerships with donors that move away from the starving-scientist-business-as-usual model to an entrepreneurial focus, which is agile, aggressive, donor-focused, and responsive to real-time global Missions of corporations and foundations alike.

The scientist-entrepreneur embraces market forces, thrives on change and New Technologies, and seizes opportunities to explain her scientific Mission and discoveries within the context of funding-rich environments.

So much for the challenge... What, then, is the opportunity?

In general, the **most fundable projects** are those that are

   1) consortial

   2) have well-articulated Mission Statements with an urgent,
      compelling, and *understandable* Case for Support

   3) include a strong free public component

   4) provide insight or solution to a contemporary problem (herbal
      medicines in the Rainforest, etc.)

   5) are **not** controversial

   6) incorporate traditional values

   7) encourage participation by scientists from developing nations

   8) can be easily evaluated

   9) have strong financial oversight

   10) offer the funder an opportunity for volunteerism, in-kind
       contributions, and cash, and

   11) provide readily for donor recognition through the traditional
       press and/or the Internet.

The overall goal is to be unique, without being "trendy." For the field
scientist, perhaps the best way to accomplish this is by joining forces with
one or more institutions in developing nations. The advantages of such an
approach are several:

   First, instead of competing for financial support, the combination
offers added value to any funder through economy of scale within a
consortial framework.
   Second, the scientist or expedition gains prestige and name
recognition and infrastructure within a host country.
   Third, grant applications to foundations are improved dramatically,
as selected funders have regional or national interests in developing nations,
protection of their biodiversity, etc.

Fourth, corporations with subsidiaries in a developing nation often consider the entire country a "community of interest." More importantly, they tend to favor projects in which the fiscal oversight is modeled after Western business practices, with a Western presence part of the process of accountability.

Fifth, occasionally there exist governmental set-asides or special programs for which scientists are only eligible with a training/participation component by non-U.S./Western colleagues.

Sixth, family foundations (some 20,000 in the U.S. alone) sometimes have special offshore interests for which scientists may only be eligible via application by the consortial partner.

A final recommendation is in order: the more specific the focus of the scientific inquiry, the better. Funders like projects they can understand, in broad terms. Scientific plans that are laden with techno-babble and a laundry list of incomprehensive goals ranging from the archaeology to the zoology of a remote region are doomed on the funding front. They are viewed as too diffuse and, especially, difficult to define in specific marketing and public relations terms. Furthermore, donors want assurances that they, the scientists, and their Boards are on strong legal footing and that issues of liability and risk are manageable.

In short, science funders look for simple, easy-to-execute plans with manageable risk, streamlined infrastructure, **proven leadership**, strong science, a reasonable timetable, viable economics, and opportunity for success and return on investment (books, television, new medicines, etc.).

The New Explorer in the New World Order must be as comfortable in the corporate jungle as s/he is in the Rainforest. The law of both jungles can be strikingly similar--and just as deadly.

Someone once said, "Adventure is the result of poor planning."

The message of *Funding Exploration* is to keep the adventure to a minimum, funding to a maximum.

Bibliography for Chapter One

"Challenge and Opportunity for Funding Science and Discovery in the 21ˢᵗ Century"

Adler. T. "Providing the data to protect biodiversity." *Science News*, Volume 148, November 18, 1995, 326.

Africano, Lillian. "Eight War Zones, 20 Visas, 17 Countries, and 33,000 Miles: Two Friends Retrace Marco Polo's Treacherous Route." *Biography*, February, 1999, pp. 78-88, 108.

Anonymous. "Outlook: Database--Jurassic Juggernaut." *U.S. News and World Report*, September 25, 1995, p. 16.

Blum, Debra E. "Companies' Charitable Gifts Follow Their Revenue and Go Overseas." *The Chronicle of Philanthropy*, July 15, 1999, p. 12.

Fastovsky, David E., and Weishampel, David B. *The Evolution and Extinction of the Dinosaurs*. Cambridge, England: Cambridge University Press, 1996.

Horner, John R., and Lessem, Don. *The Complete T. rex*. New York: Simon and Schuster, 1993.

IEG, Inc. "Spanning The Globe." *IEG Sponsorship Report*, December 20, 1999, 4-5.

Independent Sector. "A Survey of Charitable Giving After September 11th, 2001." On-line at <http://www.IndependentSector.org>.

Lewis, Nicole. "Charitable Giving Slides." *The Chronicle of Philanthropy*, June 27, 2002, pp. 27, 30, 33.

_____. "Social-Service and International Groups Were Winners in 2001, Report Says." *The Chronicle of Philanthropy*, June 27, 2002, p. 28.

Monastersky, Richard. "For the Sake of Sue--What will happen to the world's best *T. Rex*? " *Science News*, Volume 148 (November 11, 1995), 316-317.

O'Donnell, Francis, and Belliveau, Denis. "Marco Polo's Guide to Afghanistan." *Smithsonian*, Volume 32, Number 10 (January, 2002), pp. 44-47, 49-51.

Pollack, Kenan. "Outlook: Species--It's a Tough World Out There." *U.S. News and World Report*, November 17, 1995, p. 23.

Reiss, Alvin H. "Groups Are Using Strong Visuals to Woo Donors and Audiences." *Non-profit Strategist*, Volume 7, Issue 2 (April, 2001), 1, 6.

Stehle, Vince. "European Philanthropy Experts Disagree on Rules for Giving in Era of Euro." *The Chronicle of Philanthropy*, May 21, 1998, p. 37.

Stevenson, Jay, and McGhee, George R. *The Complete Idiot's Guide to Dinosaurs.* New York, N.Y.: alpha books, A Division of Macmillan General Reference, 1998.

U.S. Congress. House. Committee on Energy and Commerce. *Financial Responsibility at Universities. Hearings* before the Subcommittee on Oversight and Investigations of the Committee on Energy and Commerce, House of Representatives, on Indirect Cost Recovery Practices at U.S. Universities for Federal Research Grants and Contracts, 102d Cong., lst sess., March 13 and May 9, 1991.

Vartorella, William F. "A Catalyst for Change: The New Philanthropy in the Global Village." *Non-profit Strategist*, Volume 7, Issue 1 (February, 2001), 4-5.

_____. "A Simple Guide to a Fundable Field Season." *The Glyph*, Volume 1, Number 12 (March, 1998), 13-14.

_____. "Creating Sustainable Funding for Natural History Collections in the New World Order--Foundations and Corporations: Old Allies, New Opportunities." *Museum Management and Curatorship* (England), Volume 15, No. 3 (September, 1996), 328-333.

_____. "'Digging for Dollars' or the Quest for a Sustainable Archaeology." *The Glyph* (AIA, San Diego), Volume 1, Number 11 (December, 1997), 13-15.

_____. "Evolution, Predator Traps, and Money Pits: Re-thinking Collection Extinction." *SPNHC Newsletter*, Volume 13, Number 2 (August, 1999), 1, 9, 13.

_____. "Seven Deadly Sins of Expedition Fundraising." *Expedition News*, Volume Four, Number Two (February, 1997), 3-4.

_____. "Simple Application of Convergent/Divergent Funding Theory to (Micro-) Extreme Environments." *Human Performance in Extreme Environments*, Volume 5, Number 2 (June, 2001), 128-130.

***

Chapter 2: "Pushing the Extreme, Managing Risks"

By William F. Vartorella

> *"Only those who attempt the absurd will achieve the impossible."*
> *Albert Einstein*

I. Introduction:

In 2004, an estimated 6,000 Expeditions worldwide will test limits of planning and human performance in the field - often under highly charged, stressful, and potentially life-threatening scenarios in exotic locales. Field research, whether in the cosmos, undersea, in the upper atmosphere, or in the rainforests of the Amazon, carries the burden of "risk management."[1] The same is true in laboratories, particularly those handling toxins, exotic compounds, human DNA, or the latest plague - each of which may have its own controversial media "spin."

It is this "risk management" and a scientist's ability to explain risk to potential funders in terms of a donor's Mission that often proves the razor-sharp difference between success and failure of an ambitious scientific investigation in an extreme laboratory or field environment.

We began our Book with a simple assumption: the greatest threat to science and discovery has little to do with creative researchers working under extreme conditions in exotic environments. The threat is attracting significant funding to conduct investigations with manageable risk.

Too often, it seems, scientists are strapped with "bare-bones budgets" and the most minimalist of infrastructure. Worse, they have secured funding from donor individuals, foundations, or corporations lacking the resources or the will to manage the risk properly. From the beginning, such scientists have labored under the fatal assumption that *their agendas* are fundable and that they can hammer donor needs and aspirations to meet research goals and objectives.

The result: casualties, whether in terms of Mission or human performance.

Question is, how does a scientist about to venture into extreme

---

[1] William F. Vartorella, "Funding in the Extreme: Pushing the Envelope, Managing the Risk," *Human Performance in Extreme Environments,* Volume 2, Number 1 (June, 1997), 27.

environments - whether a polar icecap or a lab with deadly biological or chemical agents - identify funding sources which have a) the greatest potential for grant dollars or in-kind contributions (equipment, free travel, supplies, etc.) and b) the strongest *cash impact*, with the least disruption (best risk management) for both the donor and the hard science?

The first answer is deceptively simple. *Choose foundations, corporations, and individual donors whose Mission/Vision Statements are most easily met by the research agenda. It is the needs and aspirations of donors that come first, with the hypothesis to be addressed - second, and the expedition and lab infrastructure - third (more on this later).*

The second part of the question, much less its answer, is usually a mystery or often leads to dangerous assumptions regarding the viability of an expedition or lab research and its cash requirements (and, thereby, impact on the science involved and the reputation of the donor institution).

Like it or not, most donor institutions - including "operating foundations," with their own research agendas - have to allocate their resources (time, cash, or in-kind contributions) carefully - regardless of whether a project is paid out of their own hard cash or through a grant strategy.

If this is not challenge enough, scientists face growing competition from the 6,500 natural science collections/museums worldwide also in the hunt for cash - as well as zoos, *States* (in the U.S.), and a host of private contractors organized as legal nonprofits (with projects ranging from undersea mining to Mars exploration).

Clearly, competition is keen.

There exist a number of strategies to reduce this competition, the best of which is known as the "consortial project," in which scientific teams and institutions synergistically combine forces to apply for grant funding. Again, regardless of strategy, the bottom line is creating a project with manageable risk capable of meeting the *specific Mission* of a funding source.

We believe this risk can be measured and quantified and that a strong, resourceful budget is central to success.

II. The Fundability Matrix for Investigations in Extreme Environments:

The first step is to evaluate potential projects in terms of both their *capability* of being funded (re: donor Mission) and their *positive financial impact* on the institutions involved, including the funder *and* consortial partners (re: time, indirect costs, "intangibles" such as good will, name recognition, and the potential for securing other underwriting, etc.).

Functionally, the analysis is conducted using four *subjective variables* we categorize as the *4P's - Policy, Programs, Procedures, and Performance.* Each variable quantifies as time, equipment, and money.

The "Fundability Matrix" needed for the decision-making process looks like this, regardless of which of the *4P's* is being evaluated:

Most (+) Financial Impact

〰〰〰〰〰〰:

(3)   xxx :

Least (-)   (4)   Most (+) Fundable

Fundable

4P Study---------------------------------------*4P* Study

(1)   (2)

Least (-) Financial Impact

The procedure is simple. Using standard scientific evaluation criteria for a scientist's particular field of investigation (sample collection and analysis, data crunching, etc.), create overlays, re: *Policy, Programs, Procedures, and Performance.*

The language/standards used should be consistent with an identified funding source and capable of being compared with that donor's Mission.

The goal is to discover whether, for example, on a *Policy Level*, the amount of time and anticipated outcomes *justify* expenditure by a donor and, whether, a consortial institution reaps some positive financial benefits.

Ditto for *Program* costs as measured, again within specialty, against the standard or average costs affiliated with other projects under similar time constraints and conditions.

Procedures analysis begins with traditional procedures with known cost ranges and progresses to new, innovative procedures whose costs may be less static.

Finally, *Performance* is evaluated in terms of potential positive outcomes and some indication of commercial applications for discoveries.

What emerges is a series of x's within various quadrants (depicted as 1, 2, 3, 4 above), plotted on transparent overlays. These quadrants can be characterized as the following:

(1) Least Fundable, with Least Financial Impact;
(2) Most Fundable, Least Financial Impact;
(3) Least Fundable, Most Financial Impact;
(4) Most Fundable, Most Financial Impact.

This matrix is not "rocket science," nor is it intended to provide hard and fast answers. Often the transparencies will disclose a scatter pattern in which one dynamic - say, *Procedures,* does not appear to be particularly fundable. As a scientist is trying to plot *trends* rather than absolutes here in terms of strategy and tactics for securing funding, this exercise serves as a tool for approaching funders, after addressing problem areas; nothing more, nothing less.

Clearly, the goal is to create a proposal that offers the greatest financial impact for the project and consortial partners, while specifically meeting the needs, aspirations, and *Mission* of a donor. Constructed properly, a proposal that falls within Quadrant #4 should receive funding (see x's above).

Some nagging underlying factors to consider in such a matrix include, for example:

- Scientific team time (how much is donated as a potential in-kind matching component vs. actual grant salaries, e.g., "direct costs"
- Indirect cost strategies (does the researcher's institution or consortial partner have a federally-approved institutional overhead rate?; can such a rate be "donated" as part of an actual cash equivalent match?)
- Infrastructure (can the accounting system currently in place handle the segregated accounting/reporting procedures for the grant, especially any offshore/consortial components?)
- Long-term impact (after three years - an ideal grant support period with built-in launch, evaluation, "fine-tuning, final evaluation, etc.
- Can this program become self-sustaining? If not, what is the financial exposure and public relations impact of either continuing the project or abandoning it?)
- Outcomes: commercial applications, patents, emerging technologies.

Once this exercise is completed and a most-fundable project and donor are identified, the second step is to *abstract* the project using *language that is risk-manageable.*

III. The Fine Art of Abstracting "Derring-do" and Hard Science in Risk-Managed Language:

Now that the matrix is complete, the challenge is to word the *grant proposal abstract* in language that

a) imbues confidence and professionalism
b) explains the science in human terms - without excessive jargon
c) details the project in marketing terms of "new, improved, free"
d) underscores a *conservative* return on investment (ROI) for the funder in donor Mission language, and
e) e) manages the risk with *a safe, realistic budget.*

Note the entrepreneurial approach. Core, professional science that meets the Donor Mission, underscores an understanding of corporate culture (e.g., an accountable business environment), is conservative, and manages risk financially.

While item "c)" will be discussed in our corporate chapter, suffice it to say that successful projects are those that embody innovation with some free, public component (usually "education," access via Internet, etc.).

Risk management is the issue here.

Simply stated, successful abstracts for grant proposals for science should share the following positive terminology *written in simple language:*

- A team of professional scientists (rather than *adventurers*)
- Proven Technologies (begin with known and then discuss new)
- Innovative, rather than arcane ("there we were, there we were in *darkest Africa*" is fine for the movies, but not for funders)
- Inclusive, rather than exclusive: consortial and sensitivity to gender and background is important; fewer professional investigators listed on grant applications tend to be women, which means that those that are stand out in the minds of potential funders

- A "Building Blocks" approach: tying your research to the

successes of earlier efforts through the scientific advances of breakthroughs is extremely helpful as it links the project to the scientific community, rather than as a "stand-alone" project

- The choice of high-profile consortial partners, especially "Institutes," rather than mere colleges or universities; "Institute" implies a greater sense of accomplishment and has a very specific meaning to European funders;

- If controversy is inherent in the nature of the project, discuss areas of agreement and position the rest as hypotheses, etc.

- Throughout, a consistent, thoughtful attention to *safety* within a *realistic budget* able to withstand the scrutiny of Certified Public Accountants (CPA's)

- Thoughtful opportunities for the funder - especially corporations – to participate in the project (volunteerism, in-house data crunching, etc.) plus positive imagery suitable for public relations campaigns or corporate marketing.

IV. The Budget Crunch:

Traditionally, proposal budgets are often left to later chapters in books on fundraising or show up as fine-print examples in "appendices."

We choose to discuss them here, as they are central to the issue of "risk management."

Budgets, pure and simple, are often left to **last** when a scientist, Institute, or university creates a grant proposal. The reasons may be complicated - or convoluted logic - depending upon your perspective, but often involve institutions making certain that the math includes the indirect costs (administrative overhead - heat, electric bill, etc.), liberal cost-of-living and inflation models, and a host of other arcane issues which have little to do with the science-at-hand.

The U.S. Federal Government, in its classic report, *Financial Responsibility at Universities*, has listed a number of these mysterious, "unallowable or inappropriate indirect costs" including,

- travel expenses for trustees who donated their travel and did not receive reimbursement
- legal expenses related to lawsuits
- depreciation of equipment no longer in use

- president's house . . . receptions, flowers, travel to sporting events and gifts, e.g., crystal decanters, etc. [2]

This is a formula for disaster, as sooner or later an independent audit is going to find irregularities that some "policy wonk" has embedded in your proposal.

Be that as it may, foundation, corporate, and governmental reviewers tend to critique proposals very quickly, often in this order:

- the abstract
- the budget
- qualifications of the Principal Investigator (PI)
- past and current funding history
- the proposal narrative (attachments, etc.).

In reality, the risk assessment is one of determining the risk associated with a donor giving money to your project vs. another project.

First, we shall start with some "do's-and-don'ts" that could well get you past the "first cut" in a proposal competition.

Then, we'll look at two different budget scenarios: **a field Expedition** and a **laboratory setting**, using the field study as a streamlined budget for time-pressed corporate or individual donors and the lab research as an example of limiting risk via matching funding, in-kind contributions, etc.

Remember this: an expert peer or lay reviewer can dissect a budget in a matter of a few minutes. One of our authors spent *one day* **with a colleague doing a "first-cut" analysis of 65 grant proposals for a U.S. Federal Government agency. That translates into just more than** *eight proposals considered per hour - some seven minutes each.* **Most of that time was a quick, telling analysis of the budget.**

---

[2] U.S. Congress, House, Committee on Energy and Commerce, *Financial Responsibility at Universities, Hearings,* before the Subcommittee on Oversight and Investigations of the Committee on Energy and Commerce, House of Representatives, on Indirect Cost Recovery Practices at U.S. Universities for Federal Research Grants and Contracts, 102d Cong., lst sess., March 13 and May 9, 1991, p. 320.

Avoiding Budget Traps: [3]

10 Simple and Inviolable Rules for Competitive Budgets:

Rule #1: **Be certain that the proposal's abstract, narrative, and funder's guidelines align perfectly with the budget.** Do *not* construct the budget in isolation from the abstract. If you do, you risk the budget veering away from the point of the abstract and proposal. Use the abstract as the major check-and-balance of the budget. Remember: the Mission Statement of the funder is critical and budget narrative (if required) should emphasize Mission language.

Rule #2: **Do not intentionally "pad" the budget.** "Padding" the budget is dangerous because foundations know what science costs and tend not to get involved in paring down a budget request. Rule-of-thumb is never ask for more money than the *average grant amount* provided by the funder during the past three years - the "ease-of-fit" rule. If your project needs more than this average grant size, you may need to target another foundation/corporation based upon its fund's assets, average grant size, and your ability to meet its Mission.

Rule #3: **Keep salaries of personnel below 70% of the budget.** Donors prefer to fund programs, not personnel. The best way to keep salaries below this threshold is to make the project a *matching grant* in which your Institute pays the benefits and part of the salaries and develops an "in-kind" component of volunteer time (see *Rule #7*, below). This increases the project total (but *not* the amount requested from donor) and *reduces the overall percentage of requested salary support* within the total budget. **Result: a much more competitive proposal, as the grant request becomes a matching one rather than an outright award *and*, on a percentage basis, the donor's share is reduced.**

Rule #4: **Avoid hidden consultant fees.** 1) If you need an outside colleague to perform radiocarbon dating, include her cost as part of the radiocarbon suites. 2) Independent evaluation of your project's progress should be conducted at the beginning, middle, and end of a

---

[3] William F. Vartorella, "Avoiding Budget Traps: Ten Simple (and inviolable) Rules for Constructing a Competitive Budget, " *FRI Monthly Portfolio,* January, 1994, 1-2.

funded program. This is a legitimate line item and is a strong, positive argument for funding a project, as it introduces expertise, impartiality, and accountability into the equation. 3) Regardless of fees charged, consultants are usually viewed as expensive or, if not, as suspect in terms of competence. 4) Finally, trying to embed consultant services as "miscellaneous expenses" or within some other dubious category is not only transparent to most budget reviewers, but carries ethical and perhaps legal ramifications.

Rule #5: *Minimize travel expenses.* The best way to do this is to get an airline as a donor/sponsor at either reduced rates or free tickets during the off-seasons or "shoulder" periods of decreased paying customers. Ditto for hotels, especially those that tout their environmental records with nearby coral reefs, endangered flora and fauna, nesting sites, etc. Use these as part of your matching strategy, which, again, reduces the percentage required by a cash donor and brings corporate names/underwriters to your research.

Rule #6: *Never request equipment by brand name.* Generally, most equipment (other than daily laboratory supplies) should be sought separately from manufacturers as loans (the strongest strategy, which we shall discuss later) consistent with corporate Mission (niche markets, geo-demography, new sales territories, etc.). By doing so, your project may be able to leverage these loans as an in-kind/matching contribution that enhances your proposal and reduces cash outlays. Clearly, science can require exotic gear for measuring atmospheric gases in ancient ice cores or "stitching software" and cameras for panoramic documentation of at-risk antiquities sites in Asia. Even if only one manufacturer meets your requirements, list the equipment *generically*, but price it appropriately. The goal is to meet the test of reasonableness and to avoid the appearance of trying to outfit your lab with the latest technology at one donor's expense. Some foundations may require the return (or disposal) of equipment after a project, which makes the brand name issue moot. Yet, at worst, specified brands raise what is known as a "budget flag" that does not need to be waved in front of reviewers who are looking to reduce the number of first-cut proposals.

Rule #7: *Use conservative estimates for donated services, facilities, and*

equipment consistent with regional cost averages. Again, donors know what things cost in specific markets. Discretion here is the better part of valor.

Rule #8: *If a "general reserve" is allowed by the funding body, keep it at roughly five percent (5%) of the budget, no more.* Functionally, this is for unforeseen circumstances, particularly in dicey situations of fieldwork. It is not a "slush fund" for miscellaneous travel or hidden consultant fees. Keep it lean, mean, and seen.

Rule #9: *If you must claim administrative overhead, keep it below the 40% (forty percent) plateau - if possible.* A gutsy strategy is to request *no* administrative/institutional overhead from the donor and to proffer it as an in-kind match. Very persuasive, although a bit edgy if the project is large and the university, museum, or Institute, etc. would have to sacrifice serious cash as a result.

Rule #10: *Keep the proposal's budget in line with your annual budget and management capabilities of your Institute.* A grant proposal whose budget approaches even 20% (twenty percent) of your Institute's annual budget may make funders apprehensive. Staffing and financial capability and accountability become an issue, as does Board oversight and the question whether you can muster that much commitment to donor Mission and carry out the project in the time allotted.

Finally, keep in mind that the budget is intended to put flesh and bones on a proposal - to make it personal, rather than some lofty, theoretical concept. Budgets that are accountable reduce donor anxiety, manage risk, and enhance survival in the review process.

V. Risk Management as a Budgetary Function:

First, we shall use a budget of U.S. $100,000 for one reasonable field season. [4] For illustration purposes in this scenario, let's look strictly at the

---

[4] William F. Vartorella, "A Simple Guide to a Fundable Field Season," *The Glyph*, Volume 1, Number 12 (March, 1998), 13-14.

revenue stream, rather than the expenses. Our second, unrelated example will explore a full budget, including a third being a matching component.

Clearly several assumptions are operating in the first example, the major one of which is each Expedition Member is responsible for his/her own airfare and minimal maintenance, for which we shall assign a value of U.S. $2,500. This amount provides all-important *cash flow* prior to the expedition's launch, primarily in the form of the prepaid airfares, ground transportation, insurance, and meals. In addition, we are assuming that the expedition has an urgent and compelling Case for Support and a strong public educational component. Finally, we anticipate the results will be published in a timely fashion. In short, it does not violate our "deadly sins" of science fundraising and is inherently capable of securing support.

With this said, for a four- to six-week field season with a **U.S. $100,000 budget,** here is how we believe it can be successfully structured:

PRIOR TO DEPARTURE:

Member Contributions:	50%	$50,000
Corporate Participation		
(In-Kind and Cash):	25%	$25,000
Individual Patrons:	15%	$15,000
Foundations:	5%	$5,000

POST-EXPEDITION:

Lectures:	2%	$2,000
Miscellaneous:	3%	$3,000
	100%	$100,000

Or, looked at another way:

20 Expedition members @ $2,500 =	$50,000
5 corporate sponsors @ $5,000 =	$25,000
3 individual patrons @ $5,000 =	$15,000
1 foundation @ $5,000 =	$5,000
20 lectures @ $100 honorarium =	$2,000
Miscellaneous small gifts:	$3,000
Total:	**$100,000**

Discussion

The reason we have chosen corporate and foundation gift increments of U.S. $5,000 (actually - U.S. $4,999) is because below the U.S. $5,000 threshold, corporations and foundations **usually** do not require full Board discussion of the potential awards. These are made at the Executive Director/staff level and are relatively easy to get. In addition, if chosen carefully, the corporations may be helpful in three important ways: 1) with volunteer expertise (GIS training, for example), 2) with free/lent gear and/or supplies, and 3) cash. Supplies and equipment **is** a form of cash. The proper donor approach combines all three of these elements for long-term, sustainable support.

Foundation support will most likely be from one of the small family-related foundations with assets of less than U.S. $1 million (which is the average foundation size in the U.S.) interested in archaeology. This means an average grant in roughly the U.S. $5,000 range, which is reasonable.

The three individual patrons could easily become participating members of the expedition, if only as overnight visitors, and thereby take increasing "ownership" (here meaning intense interest) in the expedition and potentially becoming long-term supporters.

Functionally, the expedition is looking for **nine small donors** in addition to the actual field team support. Looked at from another perspective, one corporation @ U.S. $25,000 plus one foundation (or one patron) @ U.S. $20,000 will provide the same cash equivalent toward the U.S. $100,000 goal.

Clearly, what we are outlining here is a broad base of support capable of providing additional future funding if the expedition is successful and does an excellent job in terms of a public component (free lectures, etc.) and donor recognition (mention in newsletters, public and school talks, etc.).

Broken down in this manner, with a systematic, thoughtful, and easy-to-understand line-item budget of expenses (including specific equipment needs), this expedition *should* be able to raise the U.S. $100,000 needed to go into the field. Again, the key is its ability to meet the Mission Statement of the potential funder with an urgent, compelling, and interesting Case-for-Support.

Now let us look at Case Study #2 [5] for an *actual funded budget* for a

---

[5] William F. Vartorella, "Simple Tools for Navigating a Budgetary `Lunar Landscape,'" *Human Performance in Extreme Environments*, Volume 4, Number 1 (April, 1999), 27-29.

laboratory setting. Assume that you are engaged in an experiment looking at the effect of sleep deprivation on brain and motor function in a high-stress, extreme lunar environment. While the methodology and variables may be intricate, the strategy for creating a relatively easy-to-understand experiment using human subjects is not. What does appear to be "rocket science" to many researchers is the creation of a fundable budget.

What follows is an analysis and discussion of an actual, FUNDED budget. For reasons of confidentiality, the above fictitious project is being substituted for that developed by an experimental psychologist. The point is to follow her logic and tactics of structuring the budget request, rather than the actual cost of lunar module/simulation software.

This budget's strategy of utilizing matching, federal government (FG), and in-kind contributions can easily be adapted to a host of elegantly simple laboratory experiments with an extreme environment focus and relatively modest financial needs.

Case Study #2 - Sleep Deprivation in a Lunar Lander Simulation:

While hypotheses and methodologies are not important here, the underlying themes are sleep deprivation and stress in flying a lunar lander over a software-simulated landscape on the dark side of the moon. The risk we are trying to manage is that of creating an elegantly simple budget that is responsive to donor Mission, maximizes available resources, uses a non-cash matching strategy, and spreads the risk and opportunity among three foundations and one U.S. governmental donor.

First, an overview of underlying strategic financial assumptions:

1) We must be able to create a budget that demonstrates our own institutional commitment, as well as our ability to attract other supporters.

2) Yet, we must minimize our actual CASH contribution in order to maximize our ability to create a proposal that meets the donor's Mission with a convincing, cost-effective approach to our problem/hypothesis while controlling our own expenses.

3) Furthermore, we must appease our in-house administrators who need the

institutional overhead (indirect cost reimbursement) for purposes of "justifying" the project and overall daily cash-flow needs.

4) Because the actual amount needed from each individual foundation is relatively small (see below), we believe this project can be "fast-tracked" with reasonable expectations that it can be funded within six months. We shall facilitate this by not asking for more from any one source than the average amount it gave to a similar project category during the past three years.

5) To ensure a rapid decision-making process, we must make it clear to potential funders that none is carrying an inordinate burden, re: wages and benefits and institutional overhead. (This is particularly important as many foundations are moving away from providing ANY indirect costs, as they see these as the host institution's responsibility.)

6) In particular, we shall be cognizant of the following reviewer questions, re: finances, to wit:

- Who else is participating financially in the project?
- Does the project really need our help or is the entire budget available elsewhere, much more easily?
- Are we convinced that good fiscal responsibility is a hallmark of this Institute?
- Is the budget and the staging of expenditures feasible?
- How much cash/expertise is the potential grantee bringing to the table?
- Is there an annual financial audit in place?
- Is the amount requested consistent with our usual policy (e.g., within our average range of support)? If not, what are compelling reasons for us investing more $$$ in this proposal as opposed to others under review?
- (If the foundation is "corporate" . . .) Which other corporations in the community are being solicited? How much are they giving? Are any of our competitors involved?

With these assumptions in mind, several strategies for securing funding present themselves:

1) Create a consortium of funders: three donor foundations (the 1/3rd

Matching component), the Federal Government (FG), and Non-cash participation (In-Kind) by the Principal Investigator's (PI's) institution. The long-term strategy here is simple: develop three new friends capable of assisting you with future projects.

2) Keep salaries (meaning Salaries and Benefits) at/below a threshold of 70% of the total budget. Little-known to most grant-seekers is the fact that above 70% generates what is known as a "budget flag," e.g., skepticism on the part of the potential donor that the actual project costs (non-salary) can carry the project's implementation.

3) Maintain all other budget line categories below 10% of the total budget. This is an effort to keep the overall project streamlined, easy-to-understand, and consistent.

4) Keep total FG participation well below 50%. Minimizing Federal participation now will pay dividends later, as you build a coalition of private sector and foundation funding sources.

This, then, is how she configured the actual budget:

Line Items Costs for Lunar Project

Budget Categories	Budget	1/3 Match	FG Funding	In-kind	Total
Principal Investigator	$6,000	$0	$6,000	$0	$6,000
Asst. PI (4 weeks @ $17.50/hr.)	$2,800	$0	$2,800	$0	$2,800
3 Crew @ $8.50 per hr. x 480 hrs.	$4,080	$1,360	$0.00	$0	$4,080
15 Vols. @ $5.50 x 20 hrs. x 4 wks.	$0	$0	$0	$6,600	$6,600
Mission Control. @$12/hr. x 420 hrs.	$5,040	$1,680	$0	$0	$5,040
Mission Asst. @$9/hr. x 420 hrs.	$3,780	$1,260	$0	$0	$3,780
Per Diem @$166.50/wk. x 2 x 4 wks.	$1,332	$444	$0	$0	$1,332
Lunar Module Software	$1,300	$433	$0	$0	$1,300
Simulation Software	$1,860	$620	$0	$0	$1,860
Misc. Supplies	$800	$212.50	$162.50	$250	$1,050
Lab Preparation	$0	$0	$0	$250	$250
Equipment	$250	$83.33	$0	$0	$250
Loan Equip. from Extreme Institute x 4 wks	$0	$0	$0	$1,000	$1,000
Printing (100 reports @ $15 ea.)	$1,500	$500.00	$0	$0	$1,500
Sub-Total	$28,742	$6,593.16 x 3	$8,962.50	$8,100	$36,842
Administrative Overhead @ 12.5%	$3,592.75	$1,197.58	$0	$0	$3,592.75
Total Budget:	$32,334.75	$7,790.75 x 3	$8,962.50	$8,100	$40,434.75

A close analysis of her budget discloses the % of total budget by categories and the relationship of the three donor constituencies (Federal Government, P.I.'s institution, and Foundations) in terms of their shared financial commitment. See chart below.

CATEGORY (% of Total Budget)	FG	In-Kind	$$$ REQUESTED FROM FNDNs
Salaries: 69.98%	31.09%	23.32%	45.58%
Software: 7.81%	0%	0%	100%
Per Diem: 3.29%	0%	0%	100%
Misc. Supplies: 2.59%	15.47%	23.80%	60.71%
Lab Preparation: < 1%	0%	100%	0%
Equipment: < 1 %	0%	0%	100%
Extreme Institute: 2.47%	0%	100%	0%
Printing of Reports: 3.70%	0%	0%	100%
Administrative Overhead: 8.88%	0%	0%	100%

Her budget succeeds for a number of reasons:
1) It is by definition **consortial**, with a strong public-private funding base.

2) It provides an in-kind match by the P.I.'s institution, WITHOUT committing CASH. It offers some support in standard supplies, breaks out its Institute support to include lab prep, and calculates the economic value of volunteer subjects (e.g., undergraduate students, who receive bonus points in experimental psychology courses, etc.). (Another variation would have had the Institute as one of the 1/3rd Matching partners - an improvement in terms of strategy, but one that would have cost $6,600 in cash.)

3) At 31.09% FG and 45.5% 1/3rd matching, re: salary support, none of the consortial partners is strapped for carrying an undue burden of wage and benefits.

4) Administrative Overhead (12.5%) is charged ONLY against the outside funding foundations, with an equitable cost share. In addition to being well below the usual university threshold of 40%+ in indirect costs (AO), the budget becomes even more competitive, re: FG $$$, as no AO is requested. Furthermore, the researcher's Institute realizes the full AO, which should please the internal constituency (e.g., Institute administration). The budget could have been strengthened by the Institute reporting the difference between the requested AO and its federally approved AO rate in the "In-Kind" column, thereby increasing its % of $$$ participation overall.

An evaluation component should also have been added, probably as a *pro bono* by a friend of the Institute. This would have strengthened an already strong budget in terms of "In-Kind" contributions.

5) With the non-Salary categories so small as a % of the total budget, the project received little resistance from potential funders, even for Report Printing and minimal Equipment/Software requests, which generally are "flags" to reviewers and often require more detailed explanation.

6) Something that is not apparent in the budget is that the Per Diem rate quoted meets Federal guidelines for the City (here, undisclosed) in which the project takes place.

7) Salaries are also regionally consistent for the Southeastern U.S. (project location), including payment of graduate students as Crew, etc.

· The crowning achievement of this budget is that it clearly moves the Foundation and Federal decision process from an "outright gift" by a funder to a "shared solution." Functionally, this places the proposal in the funding pool with the least competition, e.g., a matching rather than outright gift pool). It also allows non-cash participation by the PI's institution, thereby maximizing the Institute's limited resources.

Finally, it encourages four funding entities, rather than the traditional "one" which most projects requiring less than U.S. $50,000 would have sought. Each of the four was, in fact, approached for slightly different aspects of the research - a strong strategy. More important, it set the tone for **future** support from **four** funders, rather than **one**.

VI. *Risk Management, Daily Operating Expenses, and the Quest for Unrestricted Cash:*

"We just need **money**. Not for specific projects, but just to 'keep the doors open.'"

Sound familiar?

This litany echoes worldwide, especially with cash-strapped Institutes and NGOs focused on serious science, but whose Boards see themselves as advisors rather than advocates (read: donors).

We have worked with scientists worldwide in extreme environments with poisonous plants and animals, temperatures and altitudes that rob the senses of simple logic, and the dictum - "It isn't what you see that kills you."

In all these cases, at some point life may hang in the balance based upon simple, quick decisions.

Yet in many of these instances, these same seasoned scientists have no earthly idea of how many square feet their labs occupy, what they spend on essentials such as petrol or toilet tissue annually on a per project basis, or where money is literally walking out the door in minute, relentless waste.

It isn't what you see that kills an Institute, NGO, or multi-season expedition. It's what you don't see or fail to recognize as important.

Let us begin with a simple assumption:

> *Your Institute, NGO, or long-term expedition is entitled to reasonable operating costs as part of funded science.*[6]

While we believe operating costs and the long-term sustainability of a nonprofit to be the **responsibility of the Board**, there are things you can do to bolster that all-encompassing passion for "unrestricted cash." We shall assume here that you are working in a global setting which is not resplendent with formal institutional overhead charges established by governmental programs or artificially imposed by university honchos.

A. Expenses:

1) Measure you lab space, offices, meeting areas, etc. and come up with square footage for each and the sum of the whole. **You need to know what your science costs based upon the formal space it occupies.**

2) If you have the luxury of support staff (secretarial), total the salaries and benefit packages, etc. and divide that number over all formal projects based upon a percentage of time that staff spends on each. **Now you have some idea what a project might really cost.**

3) Inventory your labs, offices, etc. Establish depreciation schedules and develop a *realistic* assessment of equipment dedication to specific projects, either exclusively or as part of the broader science. **Now you know what your gear costs.**

---

[6] Totally unrestricted grants do exist, but they are exceedingly *rare*. During the past 25 years, the **Bristol-Myers Squibb** Unrestricted Biomedical Research Grants Program has awarded U.S. $100 million in "no-strings-attached funding" to major research institutions worldwide for investigations involving cardiovascular and infectious diseases, cancer, metabolics, neurosciences, and nutrition.

4) Create an estimate of the cost to preserve samples, collections, etc. **Now you probably have some really scary numbers.**

B. Revenue:

1) If you have a Natural Science Collection, what are the revenue streams you have established for it? "Collegiality" is fine and we all help visiting scientists, *but* there are minimum costs (at least) affiliated with accessing samples or turning on the high-tech equipment for a demonstration of evolving lab techniques. Set a simple schedule of fee-for-use, announce it, and follow it. No exceptions.

2) Develop and implement a written, iron-clad policy for visiting scientists and scholars regarding costs affiliated with using your facility. Distribute it. Post it in your lab or field station. Keep the costs reasonable. The issue here is **cash flow**.

3) Establish a formal, written policy for *professional fees* based upon job description, scientific experience, etc. Call these fees "honoraria." These fees should be paid directly to the NGO, Institute, expedition. "Moonlighting" (e.g., professional fees that are garnered off-the-books, but often are the result of a scientist's affiliation with an NGO, etc.) should be forbidden as part of the employee "Handbook."

Now that you are truly horrified or perplexed, consider this. In our entrepreneurial paradigm, a scientist lives in an edgy world. You cannot afford to live in an Ivory Tower where *pro bono* rules. Nor do you wish to live in a castle ruled by Niccolò Machiavelli.

But to quote Machiavelli,

In examining the characteristics of this kind of regime, there is another consideration to be taken into account: which is whether a prince has a state of such resources as will enable him to stand on his own feet in case of need or whether he must always have the assistance of others.[7]

---

[7] Niccolò Machiavelli, *The Prince*, trans. and ed. by T.G. Bergin (New York: Appleton-Century-Crofts, 1947), p. 29.

Self-sustainability is the goal. Success means sacrifice. The barbarians are *always* at the gates. Either you get funded or you don't.

The assessment we advocate above helps you add fair-market-value to grant proposals and to re-capture some of your operating expenses through a fair-minded, though aggressive, program of cost-accounting focused upon generating strong cash flow for projects.

Develop a *cash-flow model* as part of your broader Business Plan. You already know what your science is *worth* in the pursuit of knowledge and a better Society. Now you have a better idea what it *costs*.

After that it is back to Machíavellí, who is alive and well and living under an alias: "Unrelated Business Income."

While the Draconian aspects of space-age accounting are best left to Certified Public Accountants (CPAs) and competent tax attorneys (of which we are neither, nor pretend to be), much has been written in the U.S. and elsewhere on the tax benefits of proper structuring of "unrelated business activity" and write-offs of *operating expenses* against it.[8]

The tax advantages for large Institutes such as the Howard Hughes Medical Institute, which conducts biomedical research and education, and the California Institute of Technology, under a contract "to operate the [U.S.]federal government's Jet Propulsion Laboratory,"[9] are stellar examples of U.S. *billion*-dollar tax savings.

Areas of "unrelated business income" that *may* prove tax-exempt for U.S.-based, nonprofit scientific Institutes or NGOs *might* include,

- Income from contracts to do government research;
- Income from research by a nonprofit . . . whose primary mission is to "conduct fundamental research that has no direct, immediate commercial application"; [10] or,
- Royalty income related to the more than 1,000 credit

---

[8] First and foremost, seek out competent legal/tax advice on issues involving your NGO, Institute, or expedition. For an informal discussion of some of the broad issues in the U.S., see Harvy Lipman and Elizabeth Schwinn, "The Business of Charity: Nonprofit groups reap billions in tax-free income annually," *The Chronicle of Philanthropy*, October 18, 2001, pp. 25-26 ff. For an interesting insight into legal issues of entrepreneurship and commercialization of the nonprofit sector within a global context, see Theodore J. Hopkins, Jr., "Commercializing the Third Sector: Public Benefit and Private Competition," A Paper Delivered at the Fifth International Conference of the International Society for Third Sector Research, July 8, 2002, University of Cape Town, South Africa. Attorney Hopkins argues the Third Sector is "faced with balancing public benefit and private competition and ensuring that benefits to some do not result in unfair advantage of competition with respect to others."("Abstract").

[9] Lipman and Schwinn, "The Business of Charity," p. 26.

[10] *Ibid.* See Table, "What's Exempt From the Federal Tax on Charities' Unrelated Business Income."

cards ("affinity" cards) offered by one or more
commercial banks.

Again, do not under any circumstances take our word for this
"section." Competent professional and legal advice is necessary and the
primary reason why we venture into this arena with trepidation and brevity.

There is also the potential for a dark downside:

*Your Board sees you as picking up the slack (financial short-fall)
through entrepreneurship and spend even less time raising money.*

Solution: rotate the "dead wood" off your Board.

A final word from Machíavellí:

There are indeed three kinds of minds: one understands things by
itself, the second can understand what is explained to it by others,
and the third cannot understand either directly or by the demonstration
of others. The first kind is most excellent, the second is good, and
the third is useless.[11]

These, in fact, are the states of mind of Boards.

The most incomprehensible thing to most of them is "daily operating
expenses" and the Board responsibility inherent therein.

Again, embed "operating expenses" in each project as part of your
fundraising. Know the value of your research and the costs associated with
its success.

VII. *Risk Assessment and Management as Fundable Images:*

The stark reality is many Expeditions into remote regions are
dangerously under funded, often a mixture of poor planning, bravado, and
misplaced urgency. Laboratory research is under similar pressures, as
scientific dollars are linked to market forces. In the words of Bertrand
Russell,

*A life without adventure is likely to be unsatisfying, but a life in which
adventure is allowed to take whatever form it will is sure to be short.*

Yet, this whole issue of risk assessment and management within a science
and exploration context fuels advertisements for companies worldwide.

---

[11] Machíavellí, *The Prince*, p. 68.

Here are a few examples for selected scientific disciplines:

Archaeology:

- **D&B Software**: "Is your mainframe on *your* side?" (A computer mainframe depicted as a "Trojan Horse.")
- Easter Island elicits images of the mysterious stone figures, which tower as much as 65 feet above the landscape and can weigh some 400 tons. Risk assessment with Easter Island as the analogue can be found in numerous corporate advertising campaigns, including:

    Mutual of Omaha Companies: "Has Your Insurance Company Forgotten That Groups Are Made Up of Individuals?" (Plays upon the view that "archaeological data suggests [sic] that the statues represent important individuals who were deified after their deaths.")

    The American Express Card: "You know where you stand." (Message: "No more interest charge `surprises.'")

    interBiz: "Unlocking the mysteries of eBusiness." (Play on words--"Let's face it" and "monumental undertaking. Plan is to "take the mystery out of eBusiness.")

Biodiversity:

- **New York Life**: "Many creatures on this earth have such short life expectancies, they don't really need to worry about RETIREMENT." (Several examples from the air-land-water realms: Butterfly: 2 weeks, Beetle: 21 days, Dragonfly: 48 days, Flicker: 6-7 years, and Tinfoil barb: 7 years.)

"Exploration":

- **Progress Software**: "Between 1519 and 1522, Ferdinand Magellan made his bid to circumnavigate the globe, fighting oppressive conditions, mutiny, and despair." (An evocative advertisement with an adversity focus, with a subtext of "Remind you of deploying applications across your organization?")

Mountaineering:

- **GTE Directories**: "It's amazing what you can conquer with the right information partner." (Series of annotated visual metaphors, such as "Visual Metaphor #5: The Mountain. Represents the daunting task of tackling new marketing opportunities with emerging information technologies."

Partnership focus.)

- **Hoechst Celanese**: "You May Not Know Us, But We Help The North Face Satisfy Their Off-the-Wall Customers." (Dramatic visual risk image of a mountain guide asleep in an expedition bag hanging from pitons at 5,100 feet on the near-vertical face of Mt. Wilson.)

Physical Anthropology:

- **Sonics**: "You Can't Rely on a Bunch of Numskulls to Keep Your Museum Open." (A dramatic advertisement featuring human evolution as a display of skulls such as *Homo sapiens neandertalensis* with a message that "Audiences get bored out of their gourds pretty easily these days." Company produces sound technologies for museums.)

Space Exploration:

- **Blessing White**: "Rocket launcher." (Close-up of a cleaning brush and the story of a NASA employee who, when asked in 1968 what he did, replied, "I'm helping to put a man on the." Pitch: "Business Strategies Made Humanly Possible.")
- **Cray Research**: "The future isn't what it used to be." (Focus is company's "advanced compiler technologies," specifically, "Because no workstation is an island." Image of earth in space.)
- **Deutsche Aerospace**: "The first steps are always the hardest." (Photograph taken in 1891 of Otto Lillenthal and his Mark 3 flying machine, poised for take-off, perhaps for his initial 25-meter flight. Basic progress-begins-with-risk approach.)

What these fine corporations have discovered is that "borrowed interest" (an advertising execution in which a visual or literary image has high inherent interest but no direct connection to the goods or services advertised) with a science, discovery, or exploration focus gets attention and may lead to sales.

A constant theme of our book is that these advertising platforms are themselves *Cases for Support* for approaching corporations for underwriting projects that are central to both the thematic depiction and the Mission and Vision Statements of the companies.

In some cases, the corporations actually encourage the linkage.

Phillips Petroleum Company is an excellent example.

Consider this advertising copy: "To understand our concern for the environment, sometimes you have to look beneath the surface." The full-page, full-color advertisement discusses an artificial reef, "created from a former Phillips Petroleum production platform" and the hundreds of species of fish it attracts. Yet, important within the context of our book is a small message at the bottom of the page: "To find out more about environmental innovations from Phillips, write to: Rigs to Reefs, Phillips Petroleum Company, 16 D-2 Phillips Building, Bartlesville, OK 74004."

The point is that advertising campaigns are potentially fertile ground for the entrepreneurial scientist capable of matching corporate culture - Corporate Mission - to that of her or his research. It's a matter of positioning opportunity to outcomes. Creating innovative, cost-effective, "win-win" situations for both donor and scientists is the message.

VIII.　*Some parting thoughts:*

Clearly, a "Fundability Matrix" serves as a built-in system of checks and balances. It helps to streamline projects in extreme environments to meet the specific Mission Statements of the best potential funding sources, while keeping a keen eye on the grantee's bottom line.

The key, again, is to define projects that remain in the quadrant of the matrix that has both the highest potential for funding and the most favorable financial impact for donor and consortial partners alike. No one "makes money" on grants.

With a keen understanding of the funder's Mission and the matrix in place, fine-tuning can occur in project planning. Choice of positive, risk-managed language is critical in the creation of the abstract. While the laboratory or the fieldwork may be on the cutting-edge of Extreme Exploration, the language must be tradition-bound, interesting - yet non-threatening, non-controversial. Here are several tips to minimize "rejection-risk":

- Abstracts serve as excellent talking points with potential donors and easily expand to three-page Letters of Intent (mini-proposals).
- People give money to people, not to ideas. This is the reason that once the risk-managed abstract is created (following matrix analysis), the time is ripe for a telephone call to an identified funder to explain, in lay English, the concept, duration, and costs.
- When speaking with donors, remember to include Mission language *and* to ask these important questions: 1) How many proposals were received last year?, 2) How many were funded?, and 3) What is the *average grant size/amount*? If the ratio is *worse* than one in five, generally do *not* apply. Take note of average grant size. Grant awards that deviate significantly above average are "trustee-

discretionary grants" for which you are generally unable to apply.
- Finally, if a foundation/corporation has four review cycles, the worst time to apply is generally for the *first* cycle; the best time, the *fourth* cycle, where the competition is usually the least.

Again, analyze a donor's Mission, measure feasibility via matrix, avoid risky "danger language," and use the abstract as the first step to a successful grant proposal.

Budget traps are often self-created, almost a form of "self-fulfilling prophecy" in which a scientist gets mired down, becomes desperate, and generates numbers that bear little semblance to reality. The outcome is never truly in doubt - the project will not get funded.

We offered two budget examples. Both emphasized shared solutions to fundable outcomes. Each was elegantly simple, yet, in the words of Einstein in a note to himself, "Everything should be made as simple as possible, but not simpler."

Point is this: many budgets for corporate and private foundations can be developed in *one page*. Experience tells us that these one-pagers should take between *one and three days* to create. Avoid the budget traps detailed earlier and, by all means, request and read corporate annual reports. They offer their own risk assessments of their business climate, plus internal evidence of corporate philanthropy.

Finally, an underlying theme of all of our discussion of risk management is the nagging concern on the part of donors that scientists generally are focused on their own projects, rather than the need to devote resources, time, and energy to creating sustainable futures ("capacity-building") for their institutions. "Self-sustainability" is the often-asked and rarely answered question posed by corporate and foundation boards when considering dynamic grant proposals.

McKinsey and Company, a management-consulting firm, issued a report in 2001 that detailed, for example, how The Nature Conservancy (Arlington, Virginia U.S.) revised and realigned its Mission Statement and strategies for a decade of growth from 1990 to 2000. During that period, The Nature Conservancy tripled its revenue, doubled its membership, and galvanized its operating units behind clear overall objectives.[12]

"Survival of the fittest" may be Darwinian, but survival of the focused is the Draconian reality of financial competition in the world's funding pools.

---

[12] Anonymous, "Charities Urged to Focus on Management Strategies," *The Chronicle of Philanthropy*, September 6, 2001, p. 42.

***

Bibliography for Chapter Two
"Pushing the Extreme, Managing the Risks"

Anonymous. "Charities Urged to Focus on Management Strategies." *The Chronicle of Philanthropy*, September 6, 2001, p. 42.

Hopkins, Theodore J., Jr. "Commercializing the Third Sector: Public Benefit and Private Competition," A Paper Delivered at the Fifth International Conference of the International Society for Third Sector Research, July 8, 2002, University of Cape Town, South Africa.

Lipman, Harvy, and Schwinn, Elizabeth. "The Business of Charity: Nonprofit groups reap billions in tax-free income annually." *The Chronicle of Philanthropy*, October 18, 2001, pp. 25-26 ff.

Machíavellí, Níccolò. *The Prince*. Translated and edited by T.G. Bergin. New York: Appleton-Century-Crofts, 1947.

U.S. Congress. House. Committee on Energy and Commerce. *Financial Responsibility at Universities. Hearings* before the Subcommittee on Oversight and Investigations of the Committee on Energy and Commerce, House of Representatives, on Indirect Cost Recovery Practices at U.S. Universities for Federal Research Grants and Contracts, 102d Cong., lst sess., March 13 and May 9, 1991.

Vartorella, William F. "Funding in the Extreme: Pushing the Envelope, Managing the Risk." *Human Performance in Extreme Environments,* Volume 2, Number 1 (June, 1997), 27-29.

_____. "Simple Tools for Navigating a Budgetary 'Lunar Landscape.'" *Human Performance in Extreme Environments*, Volume 4, Number 1 (April, 1999), 27-29.

_____. "A Simple Guide to a Fundable Field Season." *The Glyph*, Volume 1, Number 12 (March, 1998), 13-14.

_____. "Avoiding Budget Traps: Ten Simple (and inviolable) Rules for Constructing a Competitive Budget." *Monthly Portfolio,* January, 1994, 1-2.

***

Chapter 3: "Board Dynamics--Trojan Horses vs. Patrons of Exploration"

By Donald S. Keel

> "It is also very useful and fitting . . . to have such a general knowledge of science as may tend to the development of [the Diplomat's] understanding, but he must be master of his scientific knowledge and not be consumed by it. He must give science the place, which it deserves, and must not merely consider it as a reason for pride or for contempt of those who do not possess it.
> . . . [F]or he who enters the public service . . . must consider that he is destined for action and not for academic study in his closet."[1]
>
> François de Callières, De la manière de négocier avec les Souverains, 1716

I. "Boards"-- What are they?

There is an old joke about a Chief Executive Officer (CEO) who is interviewing accountants for the position of Chief Financial Officer (CFO) of his company. The first candidate comes in and the CEO asks: "What is two plus two?" The accountant answers: "Four." "I'm sorry, you won't do," says the CEO. The second candidate comes in, and the CEO asks: "What is two plus two?" "Four," responds the second candidate. "I'm sorry, you won't do," says the CEO. The third candidate comes in, and the CEO asks again: "What is two plus two?" "Whatever you want it to be," answers the candidate. "You're hired," says the CEO.

A "Board" can be whatever its creators and/or members want it to be. There are Boards of Directors, Boards of Trustees, Boards of Managers, Boards of Visitors, Boards of Advisors, Development Boards, Conference Boards, and the list goes on. Some organizations have a Board of Trustees *and* a Board of Directors. Others, such as universities, have a multiplicity of boards of different kinds, all with different purposes and Missions within the fabric of the overall institution.

---

[1] Monsieur de Callières, *On the Manner of Negotiating with Princes; on the Uses of Diplomacy; the Choice of Ministers and Envoys; and the Personal Qualities necessary for Success in Missions abroad*, trans. by A. F. Whyte (Notre Dame, Indiana: University of Notre Dame Press, 1963), p. 50.

Some boards have clearly defined, written purposes and expectations of their members. Some other boards have evolved circumstantially into their present states, with ill-defined purposes and ambiguous expectations of their members.

A. Governing Boards:

One of the most concise yet comprehensive books on boards available today is by Cyril O. Houle, *Governing Boards*. In it, Houle's premise is that organizations function in a "Tripartite System" in which:

1) There is work to be done by someone.
2) The work must be administered by someone; and
3) The policies for administering and doing the work must be created and monitored by someone.[2]

In its purest form, the "Governing Board" sets policy for the conduct of business by the Institute or expedition it governs, and monitors that policy (or policies) to insure that the Chief Executive Officer (CEO), Chief Financial Officer (CFO), and others administer those policies, ensuring in turn that the people doing the work of the organization will carry out that work in accordance with the policies set by the Board.

In the for-profit sector, Boards of Directors of a corporation oversee management strategies and serve as the fiduciary custodians of the stockholders equity in the corporation. Their job is to ensure that the stockholders make as much money as possible -- legally and ascribing to current accounting practices and standards -- and that the corporation is managed in the best way possible toward that end. Corporate Boards of Directors are drawn from the highest levels of corporate executive leadership and are compensated well for their roles.

The Enron scandal shook this structure at its foundations.

In the not-for-profit sector -- the "Third Sector" -- large grant-making foundations have Boards of Directors or Boards of Trustees who are compensated monetarily for their governance work overseeing the policies of the foundations. But elsewhere in the Third Sector, among eleemosynary organizations, governing Board members are prohibited explicitly from personally profiting financially from their work on the Board. Their role on not-for-profit boards is purely charitable and civic.

---

[2] Cyril O. Houle, *Governing Boards* (San Francisco: Jossey-Bass Publishers, 1989), p. 2.

Houle defines a Governing Board of a not-for-profit organization as "an organized group of people with the authority collectively to control and foster an institution that is usually administered by a qualified executive and staff." [3] In Houle's definition, what is contained in the word "foster" is the word of primary focus for us in these pages. "Fostering" an institution encompasses all the actions necessary to enable your expedition or Institute to "advance:" advocacy in local, state, and federal government venues; making major personal financial gifts to the organization; personal contact with major prospective donors, and the making of key decisions regarding the growth and development of the institution. [4]

B. Special Purpose Boards:

While Houle's volume focuses entirely on "Governing Boards," Third Sector organizations also create boards of unpaid volunteers for special purposes. "Boards of Advisors" are created to lend expertise and credibility to organizations, programs, and projects. Other boards are created specifically to raise funds and develop fundraising policy and strategy. For example, in a state university system where there is one Governing Board for the entire University system of multiple universities and individual universities do not have Governing Boards, Special Boards have been created with names like "Development Board" to oversee and help implement institutional advancement strategies at individual universities within the system. They are not, however, "Governing Boards" in that they do not determine and monitor institutional governance policy, hire and fire chief executives, or are vested with the responsibility for stewardship of the assets of their institution.

II. *Boards in the Real World:*

In the "real world," delineation of responsibility is not as "squeaky-clean" as in the Houle model. Boards do not adhere only to policy and governance issues. They get involved with the inner workings of their institutions at various levels and in many ways. In fact, the art of engaging volunteer board members, and keeping them engaged, requires that they get involved with the institutions beyond the oversight of policy and governance issues. The interactions of Board and staff can be like the currents of a

[3] *Ibid.,* p. 6.
[4] *Ibid.,* p. 7.

waterway. In practice, these interactions are not as cleanly defined as they are in the textbooks.[5] Board members get involved with operational issues. Staff members get involved with policy issues. These interactions constitute a living dynamic requiring adroit human relations and communication skills.

A. A Major Potential Asset:

The focus of our Book is fundraising, and fundraising is a major focus (if not the primacy focus) of many boards of not-for-profit institutions, including Governing Boards. A recurring theme throughout this text is that fundraising - and the umbrella concept into which fundraising fits, *"institutional advancement" as it is called in the broader context of fundraising, advocacy, and constituency relations* - is a highly personal enterprise. It is not a science. It is a craft. It is perhaps an art. It is a "People Business" in which people invest in the work of other people because they have identified a shared purpose with the people in whom they are investing, and they believe that the people in whom they are investing will advance that shared purpose.

In that context, a Board of Volunteers - strategically recruited and adroitly managed - can be a major asset to an Institute, NGO, or expedition providing critical elements that would not otherwise be available. A Board can raise the sights and expand the horizons of a program, providing the vehicle for ongoing support and a way out of the cycle of *ad hoc* fundraising.

On a personal note, most boards we have worked with have had more impact in their roles in fundraising, constituency relations, and advocacy (in that order) than they have had in their roles in the "governance" of the institutions. They have generated funding, through their own investments in the organizations and/or in their efforts to raise funds from others, which would have been otherwise out of reach of the staff of the organizations without board involvement. They have provided access to and gained the attention of federal, state, and local officials who would have been out of the reach of the CEO's and staff of the organizations. And, in the broader sense, their identification with the organizations has provided those organizations with a credibility and perception of professionalism that they would not have had without the involvement of those board members.

---

[5] William F. Vartorella, "Board & Staff Consensus: A Powerful Fundraising Tool," *Nonprofit World*, Volume 15, Number 1 (January/February, 1997), 14.

Thus, a Board can be a lifeline for your scientific efforts, opening doors in the public and private sectors not otherwise accessible to the professional staff of your organization, and bringing a cachet and credibility you would not otherwise have had.

B. A Major Potential Liability:

However, there is a "flip side." A Board can become a "Trojan Horse," from which emerge a host of issues and problems that can subvert rather than enhance the Mission for which the Board and nonprofit were created. How can that happen?

1) Kidnapping the Case for Support

Elsewhere in this volume the Case for Support is discussed in detail. It must be perceived as Valid and Urgent by the organization's existing and potential constituencies. A major potential danger for an organization is the well-connected, charismatic board member who "kidnaps" the Case to advance his/her own personal agenda or philosophy.

Here are two Mini-Case Studies:

a. Example: The Chairman of the Board of a university with more than 10,000 students makes a U.S. $1 million-dollar gift to the university. However, the gift is a Trojan Horse. The Case for Support of the university is that it is an institution that puts the interests of the students first. The faculty is well known for nurturing students and for the development of a curriculum that serves students well in the "real world of work" after their graduation.

The Chairman not only restricts his gift, but also specifies *exactly* how his gift dollars are to be used: the creation of an Institute to teach his own political philosophy. He dictates which books will be used as texts, he dictates which courses will be taught at the Institute, and he even dictates who will be the faculty member hired by the university to teach the courses. The proposed faculty member is a well-known advocate for the Chairman's political views, and he has few qualifications to be a university professor. If the president of the university acquiesces to these "specifications" in the Chairman's gift, the faculty of the university will revolt at the circumventing of university hiring policy and the gauntlet of academic peer review for the creation of new courses or new curricula.

b. Example: A conservation organization owns a large tract of land in northern California where thousands of acres of two-hundred-year-old trees majestically cover the landscape. The White House has given the organization cause for concern by making comments to the effect that the timber industry should be allowed to harvest these trees in the name of creating economic activity.

A Board Chair has been recruited who is thought to be a conservationist. The Board Chair was also a major contributor to the President's campaign and a prominent member of the President's political party. The thinking behind his recruitment as Board Chair was that he would use his access to dissuade the White House from pursuing the possibility of timbering in the preserve.

The strategy has backfired. The new Board Chair - immediately and unilaterally - fills enough Board vacancies with his own handpicked people to control a majority of votes on the Board. He then uses his access to the White House, but not to dissuade it from pursuing an economic agenda in the conservation district. To the contrary, his discussions with the White House are on the subject of how most effectively to introduce the timber industry into the conservation district in a way that will cause the minimum of public furor.

2) Micromanaging

Surely the most common liability in board dynamics is *micro-managing*. In the ideal scenario of Houle's Tripartite System, the staff does the work, the directors do the directing, and the Governing Board does the policy making.

In the "Real World," however, the art of board dynamics is to engage your board members in the work of your Institute, so that they can speak passionately about the work that is being done as they engage in their fundraising, advocacy, and constituency relations on behalf of the organization. At the same time, however, allowing board members to become too immersed in the detail of the work being done results in micromanagement of the staff, a totally counterproductive activity for a board member that drains staff time. Artful diplomacy is necessary to deflect such micromanaging without offending the Board member(s). The goal is for the Board member to understand his role(s), much in the same way as that of the Diplomat in the quotation that introduced this Chapter.

Mini-Case Studies:

a. Example: A board member of the above research Institute, a CEO of a major corporation, has agreed to make a presentation to another large corporation with whose CEO and Board of Directors he is well acquainted. He has arranged for a presentation to the corporate board at its annual meeting, at which he is going to ask for a seven-figure commitment from the corporation to underwrite the largest research expedition the Institute has ever mobilized. It has been decided that a computerized presentation will be developed, and it will include video clips from previous expeditions, graphics of the proposed research objectives, travel routes, funding priorities, and other key aspects of the expedition. In the course of reviewing drafts of the presentation he is to give to the corporate board, the Institute board member begins to make suggestions as to alternative approaches to the research priorities, funding priorities, and even travel routes, drawing on his corporate experience. He lapses into his CEO mentality of giving instructions and delegating responsibilities and expecting his "subordinates" to follow through on them. Soon the preparation of a presentation for unprecedented funding for the largest expedition the Institute has ever undertaken has become an exercise in salvaging the original objectives of the expedition, as the director of the Institute is caught in the horns of the dilemma of trying to accommodate the board member who is providing the opportunity for the funding, and at the same time not permitting unfeasible or otherwise inappropriate, erroneous, or irrelevant aspects to creep into the project and subvert its Mission.

b. Example: A university has an Institute for research in herbal medicine. It has gained international acclaim for its discoveries, particularly in the area of medicinal herbs of the Amazon area, where it has conducted numerous expeditions and has developed a history of relationships with the regional government officials and local people. The new Chairman of the Board is a distinguished medical researcher, recruited for his stature in the medical research and for his contacts among major foundations that are targets for the Institute. However, his recent research at his hospital has led to a conclusion that a cure for malaria may be found in a particular plant species indigenous to sub-Saharan Africa. He introduces this to the director of the Institute and to the Board. He becomes convinced that this African possibility should be of higher priority than the South American research in which the Institute already has distinguished itself worldwide. He exhorts the Board to divert funding from the Amazon expeditions to a focus on sub-Saharan Africa, and he hounds the director of the Institute and her fundraising director to identify and pursue sources of funding for the African research.

These are examples of how board members can become "Trojan Horses," actually undermining the very Missions of the organizations they have been recruited to govern. Even well intentioned board members can become more of a liability than an asset, subverting or misdirecting the staff away from the Missions that the board members themselves believe they are supporting by their membership on the Board.

When this happens, the resulting dysfunctions consume more time and effort for organization directors and development officers than the primary work of the organization. Often, such a dysfunctional direction by a board member or group of board members takes the director and/or development officer by surprise, adding confusion and doubt to the dysfunctional scenario.

Prevention of such scenarios is by far preferable and feasible than rectifying them once they have occurred. The old saw that "An ounce of prevention is worth a pound of cure" could not be truer. Prevention of such scenarios, however, begins with the creation of the Board, the ongoing evaluation of board strengths and weaknesses, and careful attention to maintaining a desirable balance on the Board.

The starting point for an organization's CEO is to articulate precisely what he or she wants the Board to be and to do.

III. Building and Assessing Your Board--Know Your Objective:

"When you get to a fork in the road, take it."
Yogi Berra, American baseball legend

In some three and a half decades of working with not-for-profit organizations and institutions as a development officer and consultant, we have been amazed at the board selection processes of even some of the most prestigious institutions:

There is no written "job description" for a board member. There is no analysis of the composition of the current Board in terms of skill sets of the members against a well-reasoned profile of which skills, resources, attributes, and expertise should be represented on the Board.

There is no assessment of specifically which skills or other attributes are needed on the Board to compensate for current weakness or complement current strengths. And often there are no term limits.

Thus, the Board evolves, on its own, through *ad hoc* decisions, by a handful of members at different intervals in time.

In so many situations, the scenario is something like this: A few people (perhaps on a nominating committee, perhaps just an *ad hoc* group) sit around a table (perhaps with a list of names, perhaps not) to identify prospective board members for their organization. Someone surfaces a name: "Sam would be a good addition to the Board. Sam is a good guy. Sam is a doer. He knows a lot of people. He would be good." Heads nod, and Sam is nominated to the Board and is unanimously elected. This scenario replicates at sophisticated and unsophisticated organizations alike.

Another common scenario, though one which is not admitted, is the scenario in which the CEO or Board Chair of an organization nominates board members who s/he knows will go along with what the CEO or Board Chair wants to do. In other words, the new board member will not be a challenge to the CEO or Board Chair of the organization. The new board member will be a vote that can be counted on. He or she will not oppose or challenge the CEO or Board Chair and will serve to strengthen the political position, and therefore security of tenure, of the CEO or Board Chair.

A variation on this theme is the selection of new board members by existing board members, where the existing board members have longevity on the Board and have perhaps been with the expedition from its inception. When it is time for the organization to cross the threshold of its next level of development, a common problem arises. For the organization to cross the threshold, fundraising will have to be conducted at higher levels. These are a form of what this Book has termed *access issues*.

Thus, there will have to be increased *access* to major prospective donors, *access* to local, state, and federal elected officials, and increased public visibility, *ergo* increased *access* to the media.

However, the existing Board does not have the necessary access to funding sources and elected officials and media, nor does it have the capacity to contribute at a level that is necessary to cross that threshold. It is clear that "heavier" board members must be recruited.

If the existing board members find ways to recruit persons of higher corporate rank and philanthropic capacity needed to advance the organization, they risk being "upstaged" by the new members who will in turn bring in other new people at their level of access and capacity to contribute. In the process, the incumbent board members will fade into relative obscurity, not being of the same prestige and means as the newer members, who are now in the process of "upgrading" the Board.

Faced with this possibility, some board members tacitly choose to preserve their status on the board by not recruiting the kinds of people needed to raise the organization to its next level, and, thereby, they *stunt* the growth and advancement of the organization by preventing such people from being recruited.

Yogi Berra's road map does not have a destination. Neither do the board recruitment scenarios described above. The key to successful board development is to know what you want your Board to do, and what kind of people you need on your Board to do those things.

A. Twelve Characteristics of the 21st Century Global Board Member

The co-author of this book has developed a set of characteristics to aim for in the development of a global Board in the 21st century. Boards of organizations focused on exploration must, *ipso facto*, have an orientation that is globally focused in a special way. The larger picture must always be in sight.

In this context, Vartorella has articulated twelve desirable traits emerging as characteristics of board members for science-oriented organizations in the 21st century.[6] A board member:

1) "Acts as an entrepreneurial advocate for the nonprofit institution, accepts ownership of the Strategic Long-Range Plan, and seeks linkages with like-minded organizations worldwide."

This characteristic has a number of implications. For a board member to act as an advocate for the organization whose Board he or she serves on, the board member must have the nonprofit in the forefront of his/her mind. S/he must be thinking about the organization and its work. This is not as obvious a statement as it might appear. Too often, board members are recruited for their "name," in the mistaken notion that their name on the Institute's letterhead alone will attract funding and attention.

---

[6] William F. Vartorella, "Test Your Board's Global IQ: Give your board members this quiz to see if they're prepared for the 21st century," *Nonprofit World*, Volume 17, Number 3 (May/June, 1999), 16-17.

The problem with this notion is that it is too tired after many decades of use. The board members and donors of the 21st century are too sophisticated and discriminating not to recognize token membership on a board (such token membership is not to be confused with "Honorary" or "Emeritus" board positions given in recognition of achievement or long terms of service).

Second, board members are most motivated and, therefore, effective when they see their role as part of a larger whole. Thus, if board members are recruited in presentations that define their role and relate them to the backdrop of a sound Strategic Plan, they derive comfort, confidence, and motivation in the knowledge that their efforts have been well thought out in the context of the long-term direction of the nonprofit. In that mentality, they will take calculated entrepreneurial risks with confidence in the backup of their Business Plan.

Finally, board members will continue to have comfort, confidence, and motivation in their role as part of a larger picture if the ongoing communications vehicles with the Board continue to reinforce that confidence with periodic information about, and communication with, like-minded organizations throughout the world.

2) *"Adopts a universal vision of the nonprofit's Mission, rather than concentrating merely on program content (or internal politics and personalities)."*

While traveling in the car one day scanning the radio channels for some music, we happened upon one of Paul Harvey's broadcasts as he was uttering a famous one-liner: "The Main Thing is to keep The Main Thing The Main Thing." This is especially true of the focus of board members.

Without a continuing flow of information on the institutional Mission in the global context (including progress reporting on critical fronts), substantive involvement in areas where they can see the results of their efforts (e.g. fundraising), board members' focus inevitably deteriorates to narrower vision, micromanagement, and organizational politics.

Seasoned not-for-profit executives pay close attention to the pro-active ongoing communications with each of their board members, and to their involvement in substantive ways with different aspects of their institutions. They know the risks of not maintaining and monitoring closely their Board-Institute relationship, and the value of maintaining such relationships on a pro-active basis.

3) "Understands and promotes the institution's global/local strategy, especially to the mass media and opinion leaders."

There is a sign on a pub in Providence, Rhode Island that says: "Think globally. Drink locally." In the ongoing management of Board-Institute relationships, board members must periodically be given hands-on assignments with immediate action required. This is to keep their focus simultaneously on the global significance of the institution and the necessity for local action to maintain that significance. A Board that comes together only to reflect on global issues is a board of inaction and, ultimately, non-involvement.

One of the ways that board members' stakes in the Institute or expedition can be periodically cemented is through media contact and contact with opinion leaders to advocate for the institution. This is an activity that board members generally enjoy, as it gives them an opportunity to exercise their access and credibility. In preparing for such contacts, board members become re-educated in the key issues addressed by the institution (its Case for Support), they are reminded of the importance of the institution in addressing these issues, and, thus, their appreciation of the nonprofit is re-energized and their stakeholder role is strengthened.

4) "Adapts readily to new people, cultures, and circumstances, recognizing that the nonprofit Mission must take advantage of global opportunities that, while unusual, are central to the historic Mission."

Seasoned not-for-profit executives know that board members must receive an intermittent stream of communications that are current, vital, and varied. If the Board's composition becomes too homogeneous in terms of demographics or political persuasions, or if the communications stream becomes routine, the Board will get "stale." By the same token, successful not-for-profits recognize that perpetuating their historic Missions requires them to be able to make entrepreneurial decisions expeditiously in order not to miss opportunities that may not have been possible in years past.

Continuity with past values considered timeless and valid has in recent years become a more significant component of a Case for Support, as the perception of threats to the civilized world has become more pervasive, especially since 9/11. A concomitant phenomenon has been that, unlike the 60's, for example, meeting the challenges of the future does not mean "changing" in the sense of departing from the values of the past. For a not-for-profit institution, advancing confidently into the future means changing technologies and perhaps *modus operandi* in order to perpetuate the values on which the institutions were founded. The message is that circumstances change, but the values remain constant.

5) "Embraces the 'gold standard' of global best practices and supports the creation of a Center of Excellence to promulgate consistent goals and objectives."

Board members will be more confident and comfortable in their roles in the knowledge that the institution adheres to global best practices acknowledged by similar institutions in the field. Funding sources also will be more inclined to invest in expeditions that adhere to globally agreed-upon standards and practices.

6) "Appreciates new technologies and their advantages for reaching new constituencies, old friends, and consortial partners across cultures."

Given the increasingly global reach of many institutions, the multinational composition of Boards, and the increasingly multinational fabric of partnerships and consortial relationships in the Third Sector globally, technology has become an indispensable resource for intra-board communications and for inter-agency communications.

E-mail is fast replacing conventional mail as the communication of choice. On-line fundraising is emerging among international Third Sector institutions as a method for giving. E-conferences and teleconferences are becoming more common, accelerated with the increased travel concerns of the post-9/11 world.

7) "Enjoys the 'art of the deal' and is not afraid to extol the virtues of the institution and to explain the 'nature of the opportunity to participate' through voluntarism, in-kind contributions, and/or cash."

In another Chapter, "Investment Philanthropy" has been explained as the philanthropic mindset of the 21st century. It is an outlook in which the donor has specific expectations not only with regard to the specific ways in which his/her donation will achieve goals of betterment of the world, but also with regard to the optimum impact of the gift on the donor's tax situation and, in the case of a corporate gift, positive impact on the corporation's public relations and marketing position.

Later in this Chapter, we shall look at an instrument to evaluate a Board's potential to develop philanthropic gifts.

The reality is that much fundraising is accomplished through the network of enlightened self-interest among corporations' leadership. Peer perception is a *bona fide* motivator. One-ups-man-ship, personal, and corporate competition is found in the solicitation meeting as much as it is found on the golf course.

8) "Builds local/global funding networks and partnerships in close collaboration with public and private sector management and staff."

Increasingly, partnerships are being forged between the public sector and the private sector to achieve shared goals and progress in science, social equality, and economic improvement. Public sector institutions are creating private eleemosynary foundations to tap the resources of private philanthropy. And private sector institutions are ever more diligent in the identification and pursuit of funds in the public sector.

Board members in the 21st century must be attuned to the potentials of such partnerships and recognize where they might exercise their access to create and promote them.

9) "Encourages life-long learning about exciting new programs and ideas."

A 21st century Board member must be stimulated to learn and must be excited and have a sense of fulfillment from that learning. A Board member who is not learning in his or her experience on the Board is a Board member who is serving out of obligation. And a Board member who is serving out of obligation is an unmotivated Board member.

So, again, the seasoned not-for-profit executive knows that there must be a varied continuing information flow and substantive involvement of a board member in order to keep the learning process moving forward and preventing a lapse into the mentality of serving out of obligation.

10) "Flourishes on the challenges of relentless change."

It is one thing to resist changing the basic values on which an institution is founded, and it is quite another thing to resist changes in *modus operandi*, communications techniques, and technology. If "change" in an institution's *modus operandi*, communications techniques, and technologies is seen by board members as ways to perpetuate the founding values of their institutions, they will espouse those changes and thrive in them. They will see such changes as opportunities.

If Board members resist change for the sake of resisting change, they doom their institution to obsolescence.

11) "Supports intellectual honesty and the free, open marketplace of ideas within the Board and the not-for-profit institution."

Likewise, the Board of a not-for-profit institution confident enough to entertain new ideas for the pursuit of its Mission is a Board that can contribute to the vitality of its institution, not subtract from it. A Board, however, that has its "wagons circled" and is fearful of new approaches is a Board that will enervate its institution and sap it of its vitality, placing its CEO and others in the unenviable position of having to drag the NGO further into the 21st century instead of ushering it in.

As they advance, institutions develop their own corporate cultures. Some institutions develop corporate cultures whose main agenda becomes self-perpetuation. In those corporate cultures, there is tacit resistance to different perspectives on issues or new approaches to implementation of their Missions. Such resistance to openness is never acknowledged or discussed. People who do not "know better" and introduce such new approaches and perspectives find themselves "out of the loop" of information. When self-perpetuation becomes the main (unspoken) agenda, the institution becomes slow to respond to opportunities and becomes lumbering in its slow progress.

12) "Agrees that his/her primary responsibility is the growth and sustainability of the institution through getting and giving money, time, expertise, and access to those who can help the nonprofit most--donors."

Institutes and expeditions remain viable if they have developed a critical mass of sustaining financial infrastructure and a supportive constituency that is not aware of its resistance to its organizational and cultural environment.

B. Assessing and Building Your Board: The Leadership Assessment Matrix

A Board member who exhibited all of the 12 characteristics listed above would quick-change into his Superman cape and fly off with Lois Lane. In the real world, however, we have Board members who exhibit some characteristics and not others, or they are strong in some characteristics and weaker in others.

For the purpose of assessing and building fundraising strength on our Boards, there are three primary characteristics on which to focus. These three characteristics are only for the purpose of assessing and building fundraising strength on the Board. If a board member has multiple Ph.D.'s in Plasma Physics and Quantum Mechanics and has won two Nobel Prizes, that board member's obvious attributes will not show up on this matrix. It is only for the purpose of assessing strength in fundraising.

Each of these characteristics must be observed and evaluated dispassionately. They are good predictors of Board performance and utility in fundraising, but they must be honestly analyzed without the proverbial "rose colored glasses."

To facilitate an assessment of each board member and the Board as a whole in fundraising strength, Nisia Hanson and I have found a simple matrix to be useful to assist in this process of focusing and evaluating each board member's strength or weakness in each of these characteristics. This matrix can be applied not only to board members, but also to volunteer leadership of any kind, such as volunteer Capital Campaign Leadership.

1) Connectedness

"Connectedness" connotes the board member's degree of connectedness to the institution. It is a subjective judgment, but one which is usually predictable with a considerable degree of certainty because it is predicated on the knowledge of the board member and his/her history of involvement with the institution.

On a scale of one to ten, a board member who had served multiple terms on the Board, had served as Board Chair for two terms, and had a history of 20 years of involvement with the institution would rank at or towards the higher end of the "10" scale. A board member who had been recruited the previous year out of loyalty to another board member and was in the process of being educated and cultivated would rank toward the lower, "1" end of the scale.

The degree of enthusiasm of the board member is the wild card in this category. A board member who has had a dramatic personal experience with the institution or the values it espouses and is passionately articulate in support of the institution, and who is a major donor to it, might rank toward the "10" end of the scale even though he/she had only been associated with the institution for a short period of time.

Often Connectedness is used as the primary determinant of a board member's value to the institution in fundraising. A board member's enthusiasm and passion for an expedition or scientific NGO provides a high comfort level to the CEO and other board members, especially if the Board is not well developed with major donors and/or high level corporate leadership. Without the presence of the other two characteristics, however, Connectedness alone can only render a board member an effective advocate for the NGO accompanied by someone else on the Board (or elsewhere in the institutional leadership structure) who ranks highly in one or more of the other two characteristics.

2) Clout

"Clout" is a term used to connote a combination of access to philanthropic sources and/or corporate leadership, and influence with those sources to which the board member has access. A criterion for evaluating an individual's "clout" which is a good predictor of future fundraising performance is access to major corporations' executive leadership.

We have found the following ranking criteria to be consistently accurate predictors of fundraising performance:

a) Category 5 = Access/Influence with CEO's
The reality is that a board member in this category changes the rules of how you play the game of corporate fundraising.

Decisions are made by the CEO of a corporation and handed down the chain of command. While there are corporate guidelines for corporate giving, rules for grant applications, and a host of other corporate and bureaucratic do's and don'ts, the reality is that the corporate CEO is the corporation's Commander in Chief. When the corporate CEO decides that something will be done, it will be done. Of course there are exceptions to this observation as there are exceptions to almost anything else. But the reality is that if a board member is a major corporate CEO, and/or has access to major corporate CEO's it eliminates layer upon layer of decision-making by various individuals on corporate giving committees, etc. by going straight to the top for decisions.

b) Category 4 = Access/Influence with Executives *near* the Top
Access to the second tier of leadership in a corporation provides indirect access to the CEO. While not as strong as direct access to the CEO, access to the second tier still constitutes an advantageous position to be in, as it

permits a funding request to be decided in the informal conversations of the inner *sancta* of corporate leadership and then validated in the formal process, instead of having to go through the formal process of layers of evaluation in the hope of getting attention at a higher level.

c) Category 3 = Access/Influence with "Gatekeepers"
All of us in the Third Sector are familiar with the corporate positions with titles such as "Director of Community Relations." They are the official recipients of proposals from not-for-profit institutions. They provide guidance to not-for-profit institutions on how to apply for corporate support. They receive and screen proposals. They reject those proposals that do not follow proposal guidelines of format or date of submission. They prepare proposals for review by Corporate Giving Committees by summarizing and categorizing them. And they notify the not-for-profit institutions submitting proposals regarding whether they will receive support from the company.

The people in these positions are generally referred to as "Gatekeepers." Access and influence with this group of individuals may increase the probability that a funding request will find its way to the pile of proposals being reviewed by the Committee (as opposed to the pile of rejects), but such access/influence can rarely achieve more than that.

d) Category 2 = Access/Influence with Someone at the Corporations
Smaller not-for-profits may have individuals on their Boards who are executives at some level of middle management in major corporations and who may have access to their peers in others through their professional associations and acquaintances.

Such access/influence will usually mean that the contact person will know the Gatekeeper at his/her corporation and serve as a proposal conduit to that Gatekeeper for inclusion in the review process. Such access / influence is better than not knowing anyone at all in a corporation, as it is better to have a proposal be given to the Gatekeepers by someone in the corporation as opposed to "being tossed over the transom" with all the myriad other proposals Gatekeepers receive and screen by the hundreds.

e) Category 1 = Access/Influence with No One
The bottom ranking is having access and influence with no one in the community of major corporations. Such board members, if their Connectedness level is high and they are persuasive and perhaps distinguished in some other right, may be effective accompanying another

board member with a Clout level of four or five, but they cannot be effective without any access or influence whatsoever.

In the context of the descriptions above, the Leadership Assessment Matrix attaches values to these Clout Categories as follows:

i)   Category 5 = 10 points
ii) Category 4 = 8 points
iii) Category 3 = 3 points
iv) Category 2 = 1 point
v)   Category 1 = 0 points

3) Capacity

The final characteristic is Capacity to Give. This characteristic is self-explanatory. A Board member who has made a high level gift has an *ipso facto* credibility with others regardless of his/her other access or influence with prospective major donors. Remember this rule:

There is no more effective solicitor than one who has him/herself made a commitment equal to or greater than what that solicitor is asking of any prospective donor.

Ranking Capacity on the Leadership Assessment Matrix depends on the level of fundraising of the Institute or expedition. You choose what values you assign to the point system. It is a 1 - 10 point system, and the intervals between the numbers should correspond with the prospective giving levels anticipated from the board members. The 1 - 10 rankings could represent U.S. $1,000 to U.S. $10,000 and above in U.S. $1,000 increments. Or they could represent U.S. $100,000 to U.S. $1 million and above in U.S. $100,000 increments. Whatever the dollar amounts assigned to the numeric rankings, a picture of relative strength and weakness will emerge from this matrix when completed.

Let's look at an example of Board leadership represented on the matrix and what it tells us:

Figure 1
Leadership Assessment Matrix

Board Member	Connectedness	Clout	Capacity	Total Individual Strength
John	10	0	1	11
Mary	3	10	9	22
George	10	0	1	11
Fred	10	0	2	12
Total Factor Strength	33	10	13	56

Obviously, a matrix for a full Board would contain many more names than this. But for the purpose of illustration, this matrix depicts a Board that is long on Connectedness and short on Clout and Capacity. Look at the total factor strength in Connectedness compared to the two other factors. What this matrix tells us is one or both of two things:

a) If this Board is to embark on any serious fundraising program, it needs to cultivate and recruit new board members with greater philanthropic Capacity and Clout. Those board members who are highly connected to the institution can apply their enthusiasm for the institution to the recruitment of the new board members who will be more effective providing access to potential major donors.

b) However, this matrix also suggests that it might be the case that the majority of the Board, highly connected members without much Capacity or Clout, have resisted the recruitment of new board members with more Capacity and Clout than they have. They do not want to be upstaged by people with higher corporate rank, prestige, and wealth, and they have chosen to preserve their turf rather than facilitate the institution's advancement.

In Figure 2, we see a very different picture:

Figure 2
Leadership Assessment Matrix

Board Member	Connectedness	Clout	Capacity	Total Individual Strength
John	1	8	10	19
Mary	2	10	9	21
George	1	8	9	18
Fred	1	10	10	21
Total Factor Strength	5	36	38	79

In Figure 2, we see a Board that is wealthy and influential, but not connected to the institution. It is apparent that this Board was recruited for prestige and wealth, but, given the low degree of connectivity, it is doubtful that the board members of this Board are making substantial gifts to the institution proportionate to their wealth and prestige. A serious cultivation effort is needed to build a connection with these board members that have so much untapped potential.

In Figure 3, we find a Board with a balance between Connectedness, Clout, and Capacity of its members. Members with high Connectedness but low Clout and Capacity are offset by members with higher levels of Clout and Capacity. Notice, however, that there are no bottom level numbers in the Connectedness column. This suggests that the organization has done its job of cultivating prospective Board members so that by the time they are recruited, they are connected to the organization and capable of advocating knowledgeably about its work.

Figure 3
Leadership Assessment Matrix

Board Member	Connectedness	Clout	Capacity	Total Individual Strength
John	10	5	3	18
Mary	7	10	9	26
George	5	8	8	21
Fred	4	10	10	24
Total Factor Strength	26	33	30	89

C. Care and Feeding of Board Members

1) Recruitment Strategies

i. Sequential Recruitment

In other Chapters in this Book, we discuss the similarity of the psychology of fundraising with the Psychology of an Invitation. One receives an invitation to a party, notes who is giving it and the date, and two questions immediately come to mind:

"Who else is going?" and "What are they going to wear?"

In fundraising, people want to know who else is involved and what is the extent of their participation, i.e., support. This is discussed in the Chapter on Campaigns as a primary strategy for recruiting volunteer leadership and developing the lead gifts in a sequential manner in order to stimulate higher giving by subsequent donors.

The same psychology applies to the recruitment of board members. *Sequential recruitment* is a useful strategy that improves the chances of recruiting a higher caliber of board member. Sequential recruitment simply means that, on the front end of your recruitment process, you review your list of prospective board members and identify those who are leaders among their peers whom others are likely to follow. If you are successful in recruiting two or three of these leaders, what you have developed is a critical mass of leadership that will attract other prospective board members.

ii. Custom-Tailored "Job Descriptions"

It is surprising how many institutions, even prestigious institutions, recruit board members without written "job descriptions" detailing what they will be expected to do as board members. Board members recruited in this manner do not have a clear idea of what will be expected of them, and they may have very different assumptions than the NGO's executive about how much they will be asked to give, or whether they will be expected to give at all, and they may have very different beliefs about what they will be expected to do on the Board.

A clear idea of the specific tasks a board member is being asked to take responsibility for should be articulated succinctly in the recruitment presentation. It should be tailored to the known interests of the prospective board member and to his/her position and life circumstances.

Illustrating this point is a recent experience with a client institution that had recruited to the Board one of the most affluent and visible CEO's in the region. This individual had an enormously busy schedule involving global travel to the various subsidiary companies owned by the parent company he headed. A letter was drafted and sent to him containing a litany of responsibilities he was being asked to take on, some of which were broad in scope and would have required a huge amount of time. The board member became inaccessible to the institution.

Clearly, the job description presented to the CEO was not developed with the realities of his position and life circumstances in mind. It was wholly inappropriate for him. He was presented with an alternative job description that fit his schedule and circumstances. It asked him to perform a small number of *strategically important tasks*, such as making key contacts with major prospective donors and elected officials. He accepted these responsibilities with gusto, became involved with the institution, and subsequently made a seven-figure gift to it.

2) Communication Strategies

There is a saying in higher education institutions that the first thing you do after you recruit your freshmen is start recruiting your sophomores. In other words, the task of recruitment is not finished when the freshman is recruited; you have to keep the freshman's interest up during the freshman year so that he/she returns as a sophomore.

The same principle is true for board members. After a board member is recruited, he or she cannot be taken for granted, and a variety of communications modes are necessary to relate to that board member, both as a member of a group and as an individual.

i. Personal Contact: There is no Substitute

Often not-for-profit executives believe that communicating with "the Board" is a matter of sending out timely newsletters and memos on a regular basis. While regular communication with "the Board" is a necessity, the mentality of thinking about "the Board" instead of "the board members" de-personalizes the communications process and engenders an institutional approach to communicating with an organizational entity instead of communicating with a group of successful and dynamic individuals.

Consequently, communicating with each individual board member, in person, one-on-one, on a regular basis, is absolutely critical to maintaining board interest and enthusiasm. *Such individual communications must include not only board business, but also conversation related to the board member's personal interests and circumstances.*

The term "Moves Management" is current parlance in the Institutional Advancement field to denote the process of developing and structuring a plan for fostering a relationship with a board member or other major prospective donor, sometimes over a period of two years. Such a plan posits specific types of contacts by different people along the path to the solicitation of a major gift.

The seasoned NGO executive knows that each of his/her board members requires a thoughtful plan of sequential contacts in order to continue to involve and motivate the board member toward the objective of that board member doing the most for the institution that the board member can do.

ii. Recognition

In print communications with the Board, there should always be something featured which recognizes and expresses appreciation for the contributions and/or work of a board member.

Another way to personalize board membership is to have group photos of the Board taken each year. These photos are hung in sequence on the Board Room wall, becoming a part of history in future years. Such photos are best taken not in a Board Room setting, but at some appropriate site in the field. For exploration, this could be at a field station conducting a census of avian populations in the rainforest, on board a research vessel charting the health of coral reefs, or dressed in mukluks and analyzing ice cores in the High Arctic. It also adds an additional sense of history if the board members hold a banner with the year (and expedition name) emblazoned on it. All these touches add up to personalize the experience of a board Member in service to your institution.

3) Exit Strategies

i. Term Limits

One of the most difficult issues in board relations is the delicate business of divesting the Board of members who ceased to be productive.[7] It is particularly difficult when those members have served for many years and perhaps been a part of the founding of the scientific group.

The least difficult way to handle such situations is by the use of term limits. If a Board has a policy that no board member may serve more than two consecutive terms, it is the *policy*, not the executive or Board Chair, that dictates that a board member must not be reappointed to the Board. The downside of term limits is that you periodically lose a year of service from your board members whose continued presence would be an asset. But they can always be reappointed after a year off the Board.

ii. The Honorary Society

Especially for board members who have been on the Board for a long time and feel a part of the institution, departure from the Board can constitute a disenfranchisement from both the Board and the institution.

The question becomes how to provide an alternative to the all-to-nothing transition when a board member leaves the Board. An effective strategy is the Honorary Society.

---

[7] Anonymous, "Remove 'problem' members from your board--diplomatically," *Nonprofit Board Report*, March, 1994, pp. 1-2. An interview with a panel of practitioners, this article lists job descriptions, probationary periods, a clear rotation policy, and an assessment mechanism as preventive approaches to dysfunctional Boards.

An Honorary Society, perhaps bearing the name of the Founder of the Institution or some other revered person, can be created to solve the disenfranchisement issue. The Society is created for people who have served one full term on the institution's Board. At the end of his or her first full term of service, an individual is inducted into the Society with as much circumstance as appropriate for the institution. In so doing, the inductee joins all other living people who have served one full term on the Board. Some of the Society's members will be serving currently on the Board, and some will not, either because they are in their obligatory term off the Board or because they have not been invited back on the Board. There will be many such individuals who, for one reason or another, have not been invited back on the Board. The members of the Honorary Society receive social invitations to Board social functions, and they receive newsletters and other Board communications, with the *exception* of meeting minutes and official proceedings. They retain status within the institutional family but do not participate in the business proceedings. Thus, they are not disenfranchised, and institutional executives can continue to maintain and enhance the institutional relationship with them.

Induction ceremonies can be impressive occasions, as, by definition, all living current and former members of the Board are present. It has been particularly dramatic to have a medallion struck for the Society. At the induction ceremonies, usually black tie banquets, all the members assemble on stage (or in front of the banquet hall) wearing their medallions, and the new members are called up individually to have their medallion placed around their necks. A leather-framed, hand-calligraphic five-by-eight scroll provides an additional touch of distinction.

D. Obstacles

Board dynamics involve the complexities of multiple personalities joined together in shared purpose. Within these dynamics, some of which have been described previously in this Chapter and illustrated in the Mini-Case Studies and other examples, there are common threads and patterns that show up in boards across the spectrum of not-for-profit institutions and organizations. Over the years, Nisia Hanson and I have tried to identify the common obstacles that arise to impede the not-for-profit executive's ability to make progress.[8] Sometimes they render a not-for-profit board relationship dysfunctional.

---

[8] What follows is based upon the copyrighted Obstacle-Based Thinking (OBT) Seminar developed

Our experience has been over the last three decades (this is based on personal experience and not a statistical sample) that most substantive obstacles in board dynamics fall into one or more of three categories: Political, Communications, and Organizational.

1) The Political Obstacle

A political obstacle is recognized by the fact that someone's behavior is creating the circumstance that impedes progress. Examples of a political obstacle include

   a. The Board Chair who refuses to introduce term limits because he fears it will end his longevity as Board Chair.

   b. The organization founder who is reluctant to enable the recruitment of high-powered corporate leadership for fear of being upstaged and relegated to obscurity.

   c. The well connected Development Committee Chair who chokes at the thought of asking his/her peers for gifts and focuses on the development of brochures and videos and other materials not to enhance the fundraising process but to procrastinate it.

   The common variables at work in the Political Obstacle are

               i.   Power
               ii.   Territory, and
               iii. Control.

This obstacle is the most common, the most difficult to deal with, and the most serious of the three obstacles, because it usually must be dealt with indirectly, sometimes not even surfacing the real issue for face-saving reasons with the person whose behavior must be changed in order for the institution to advance. It requires the involvement of other people and adroit focus on issues in ways that create a scenario in which the person whose behavior needs to be changed does so out of positive motivations.

---

by Donald S. Keel and Nisia Hanson. This discussion encompasses new materials created for an international conference in Canada by Keel and Hanson and is used by permission of the seminar team.

2) The Communications Obstacle

A communications obstacle is recognized by the fact that a flaw in the institution's message is creating the circumstance that impedes progress.

Examples of a Communications Obstacle include,

a. A fundraising video that is ineffective because it was written and edited to include volumes of information rather than human emotional appeal.

b. A general fundraising appeal to major corporations who have never contributed before, consisting of a letter signed by the Board Chair asking for U.S. $1,000. The letter raises nothing and the Chair, who created the strategy, deduces that the institution has no Case for Support with the corporate community.

c. An appeal for contributions to scholarship endowment at an expensive college is sent to parents of current students who are paying the entire tuition for their children.

The variables at work in the Communications Obstacle are:

i. Content: In the first example above, the content was the problem because the focus was on volume of information, when, in fact, people respond to video presentations more from emotional resonance than from intellectual acceptance of a great quantity of information.

ii. Vehicle: In the second example, a general letter was sent out in a "shotgun" approach to major corporations with sophisticated community relations and grant-making infrastructure. Such a general letter never made it past the Gatekeepers at the lowest level of contact. Therefore, it was not the Case for Support that was the problem; it was the vehicle that transmitted it.

iii. Target Audience: Sending a solicitation for scholarship support for students to parents who are currently paying the entire tuition for their own children couldn't be more misdirected. Why would parents who are struggling to pay the high tuition make additional sacrifice to subsidize someone else's child's tuition?

Communications Obstacles can more often be dealt with directly, in that they are require direct "wordsmithing." Problems arise, however, when the person advocating the faulty strategy or wording is in a position of power and the element of face-saving gets involved.

3) The Organizational Obstacle

An Organizational Obstacle is recognized by the fact that a flaw in the institution's structure is creating the circumstance that impedes progress.

Examples include,

a. Lack of term limits has resulted in a stagnant Board.

b. Lack of Gift Acceptance Policies has enabled a donor to expect major recognition for a six-figure gift, which turns out to be a gift of a life insurance policy taken out on his infant grandson.

c. The Board has no committee vested with responsibility for meeting fundraising objectives. The Development Committee sees itself as approving fundraising policies and nothing more. The Finance Committee sees itself as approving budgets and nothing more. And the Investment Committee sees itself as choosing and monitoring investment strategy for the institution's endowment, nothing more.

The variables operative in the Organizational Obstacle are:

i. Roles: In the first example, the lack of term limits has enabled a Board to perpetuate itself without addressing its roles in the survival of the institution.

ii. Responsibility: In the second example above, the lack of Board-approved gift acceptance policies has enabled a donor to expect major recognition for a "gift" which is so extreme as to be considered bogus.

iii. Accountability: In the third example, no committee of the Board considers itself vested with the accountability for fundraising objectives being met.

Organizational Obstacles can generally be met with a direct approach addressing the relevant issues with the appropriate committees, unless someone on the Board has a vested interest in the status quo, in which case it becomes a Political Obstacle to be dealt with accordingly.

IV. Summary:

In this Chapter, we have

- discussed what Boards are in their various incarnations in the diverse mix of not-for-profit institutions and their varied roles in this institutional mix;
- demonstrated how board members can be a tremendous asset for a not-for-profit institution and examined ways they can be a Trojan Horse and a liability to that institution, going against the grain of its Mission;
- explored the Leadership Assessment Matrix as a tool to evaluate the relative strong points and weak points of a Board with regard to fundraising potential;
- detailed 12 characteristics of 21st century board members;
- revealed strategies for recruiting and retaining board members, and provided a way to avoid disenfranchising former board members.

Finally, we have looked at the most common obstacles that impede progress in fundraising and board development, and we have identified the variables to be aware of within those obstacles.

Boards are groups of individuals. Like any other group of individuals, they have interpersonal dynamics, personal agendas behind the scenes, and the whole host of interacting factors at work whenever a group comes together to support a shared purpose. Boards require continuing adroit attention, as a group and as individuals in order to keep the institutional Mission, in the earlier quoted words of Paul Harvey, "The Main Thing."

Bibliography for Chapter 3

"Board Dynamics--Trojan Horses vs. Patrons of Exploration"

Anonymous. "Remove `problem' members from your board--diplomatically."
    Nonprofit Board Report, March, 1994, pp. 1-2.

de Callières, Monsieur. *On the Manner of Negotiating with Princes; on the
    Uses of Diplomacy; the Choice of Ministers and Envoys; and the Personal
    Qualities necessary for Success in Missions abroad.* Translated by A. F.
    Whyte. Notre Dame, Indiana: University of Notre Dame Press, 1963.

Houle, Cyril O. *Governing Boards.* San Francisco, California: Jossey-Bass Publishers,
    1989.

Vartorella, William F. "Board & Staff Consensus: A Powerful Fundraising Tool."
    Nonprofit World, Volume 15, Number 1 (January/February, 1997), 14-15.

_____. "Test Your Board's Global IQ: Give your board members this
    quiz to see if they're prepared for the 21st century." *Nonprofit World*, Volume 17,
    Number 3 (May/June, 1999), 16-17.

***

Chapter 4:   "Donors as Individuals - Investment Philanthropy and the Psychology of the Invitation"

By Donald S. Keel

"Our deepest fear is not that we are inadequate.   Our deepest fear is that we are powerful beyond measure.   It our light, not our darkness, that frightens us."

Nelson Mandela

I.   It's not about "US," It's about "THEM":

A resonance approach does not begin by asking,   'What do I want to say?'   We seek to strike a responsive chord in people, not get a message across.[1]

In the 1940's and 1950's, before portable tape recorders existed, being hailed as a media guru amused Tony Schwartz.   He became famous for rigging up a makeshift "mobile" tape recorder and going outside to record actual children's voices instead of using women's voices recorded in a sound studio as children on the radio commercials of the day.   He had made a revolutionary step in communications, bringing recording to real-life situations instead of replicating real-life situations in a sound studio.

Tony Schwartz had developed a concept of communication focused not on the sender, but on the receiver:

A listener or viewer brings far more information to the communication event than a communicator can put into his program, commercial, or message.   The communicator's problem, then, is not to get stimuli across, or even to package his stimuli so they can be understood and absorbed. Rather, he must deeply understand the kinds of information and experiences stored in his audience, the patterning of this information, and the interactive resonance process whereby stimuli evoke this stored information.[2]

---

[1] Tony Schwartz, *The Responsive Chord* (New York: Anchor Press/Doubleday, 1973), p. 27.

[2] *Ibid.*, p. 25.

Much of what is practiced and written about in fundraising relates to "*US*," the people raising the funds.   We focus on our institutional needs.   We focus on our message to communicate our needs to our prospective donors.

But the raising of funds is not about "*US*."   It's about "*THEM*," the individuals who, for reasons of   "information and experiences stored" in them, resonate with the work that we are doing and the Missions that we are holding dear and carrying forth, and choose to support our work with their philanthropic gifts.

In this Chapter, then, we are going to focus on our donors as individuals--from the **donor's perspective**.   So we are going to focus on ways to "strike the responsive chord" in our donors and evoke their support.

Specifically, we are going to

- Look at the orientation of donors' different connections with the different types of institutions they support.
- Explore the motivations of donors, dispel some popular misconceptions, and delve deeper into the roots of their motivations beneath the superficial conclusions of surveys.
- Discuss "Investment Philanthropy" and the "Psychology of the Invitation"[3] as cornerstone concepts for the development of our cultivation and solicitation strategies to strike the responsive chords with our prospective donors.
- Propose the "Donor Focus Matrix," as a tool for developing approaches to individual donors based on their connections with our institutions and with each other.
- Examine basic strategies for the cultivation, solicitation, and recognition of our donors.   And, finally--
- Gaze into the future of our donors' motivations and expectations based on recent research into cultural shifts.

---

[3] For an earlier treatment of these issues, see Donald S. Keel, *"Chapter Three*:   Investment Philanthropy & the Psychology of the Invitation," in *Into the Field: Strategies for Funding Exploration— Proceedings of the Conference held at Nesbitt Hall, College of Design Arts, Drexel University, Philadelphia, PA on 20-21 April 1996*, edited by P.J. Capelotti, Ph.D.   (Philadelphia: The Philadelphia Chapter of The Explorers Club, March, 1997), pp. 41-55.

II. Donors as Individuals:

A. The Role of Individuals in Charitable Giving in the U.S.

The language of fundraising is misleading. We talk and read about "501(c) institutions" and "funds" and "programs" and "grants" and "corporations" and "foundations" and "prospect tracking" and "moves management" and "gift acknowledgement," and "strategy" and "donor recognition," and it all sounds so organizational and impersonal.   As we have observed elsewhere in this volume, the fact is that if we strip away all the jargon, what is really going on is that people are investing in the work of other people they believe in.

The "donor" is not a "foundation" or a "corporation."   The donor is an individual who directs the gifts and grants of the family foundation, or the group of individuals that, collectively as a committee, direct the gifts and grants of the large professionally staffed foundation.   The "Corporate Donor" is the CEO, or the group of individuals in the corporate philanthropy committee that direct the gifts and grants of the corporation.

In fact, most money given to not-for-profit organizations and institutions each year in the United States is given directly by *individuals as individuals*, not through foundations or corporations.   *Giving USA*, a publication of the AAFRC Trust for Philanthropy, annually reports charitable giving in the United States.   For the latest year of record at the time of this writing, 2000, individuals had contributed 75 percent of the U.S. $203.45 *billion* contributed in the U.S. that year. Corporations contributed 5.3 percent, and foundations contributed 12 percent. Bequests accounted for 7.8 percent.[4]

So often, people planning to raise funds first think about corporations and foundations as their primary prospects, even though together corporations and foundations contribute less than 18 percent of the money donated in a given year—a figure that has held relatively constant since the American Association of Fund-Raising Counsel began tracking U.S. giving in 1959.

Dr. Kathleen S. Kelly has put this in global perspective:

Total gift dollars . . . equal half the combined profits of all *Fortune* 500 corporations and exceed the budgets of most countries in the world.[5]

---

[4] The Center on Philanthropy at Indiana University, *Giving USA* (Indianapolis, Indiana: AAFRC Trust for Philanthropy, 2001), p. 20.
[5] Kathleen S. Kelly, "Commentary: The Top Five Myths Regarding Nonprofits," <www.prsa.org/Publications/magazines/Tactics/0800comm1.html>.

It is individuals as individuals that are the engine that propel philanthropy in the United States.   And, as co-author Vartorella has noted elsewhere, the U.S. philanthropic model has been investigated, adopted, or adapted by NGOs from Asia to the Amazon.   But, in fairness, a more dynamic global model—as advocated by our book—is required, considering the multiplicity of laws, mores, and opportunities that present themselves internationally.

Hence, in our global context, it is important that scientists worldwide understand this paradigm and explore it within their own cultural, legal, and philanthropic milieu.[6]

III. Donors' Relationship To The Institutions They Support:

The nature of the relationship a donor has with an institution is defined, in part, by the type of institution itself.   Understanding this relationship helps us to identify the nuances of a donors' motivation to contribute and helps guide our thinking on how to develop strategies that will strike a responsive chord with them and their perspective.

Donor-institution relationships can be condensed to four categories:

Donor Relationship Categories:

1) Organizational relationship = The donor is a Member.   The nature of the connection is Belonging. Examples include: Alumni of schools, colleges, and universities and members of churches, synagogues, or mosques.

A prior existing relationship between a donor and an institution engenders a bond that transcends the rational reasons for supporting that institution, especially when that relationship reaches into the past and evokes major life development experiences.   Such a sense of belonging is a powerful tie that provides the foundation for the cultivation and solicitation strategies of schools, colleges, universities, and religious groups.   Such institutions are not starting from a blank page with their prospective donors.   The middle-aged college alum is harkened to his past and recalls his aspirations and dreams nurtured at his/her *alma mater*.   This process in turn inspires a desire to enable a young person of today to have a similar fulfilling experience.   The

---

[6] But this is also a "cautionary tale," as pointed out in an undated, published letter by Thomas Harris (The Virtual Consulting Firm, Paris, France) to *The Chronicle of Philanthropy* recently.   Harris indicates "most countries" make a clear distinction between a donation (which may not carry with it "conditions") and a sponsorship (where a donor demands recognition).   This is a thorny donor issue, best resolved with appropriate legal and tax counsel in the prevailing jurisdiction.

church member recalls the baptism of his/her children, and the elements of ritual echo far into the past in the development of his/her ethics and life principles.   Organizational relationships often engender solicitation strategies that evoke memories of the past and link them with circumstances in the present and a perpetuation into the future.   **A prevalent theme in Cases for Support in recent years has been the concept of perpetuating the values of the past to create a strong future.**

2) User relationship = The donor currently avails himself/herself of services of the recipient organization. Examples include members of YMCA's who exercise regularly to improve their physical health and fitness, and whose children may be in the day care of the "Y" while they, their parents, pursue their careers in the world of work.   Other examples include cultural organizations such as symphony associations, museums, [7] and arts groups, in which donors experience directly the personal uplift of the art forms they are supporting.   A sub-group of this donor category, one that applies to funding for exploration, is the "Would-Be User" group.   These are the donors who have such affiliations as social memberships in riding clubs, adventure-related associations, and other groups in which they identify with the participants but do not actively participate in the activity themselves.   Such "would-be users" "would be there" if they could, climbing the mountains, tagging the sharks, or conducting a census of the exotic animals in the rainforest.   They derive a vicarious pleasure from knowing that they support the perpetuation of the activity they would pursue if they could.

3) Issues Relationship = The donor supports the issue(s) that the organization addresses. The point of connection and relationship with the organization is the issue itself. Examples include environmental groups [8]; right-to-life organizations and pro-choice organizations; anti-discrimination organizations; and the National Rifle Association. Donors to these types of groups are passionate in their support of the issue first, the organization second.   A donor to the Sierra Club is normally not connected to the Club because of fond memories of a long-standing membership in the beloved Sierra Club, but rather a passionate desire to curb development in a tract of "unspoiled" land.

---

[7] Prince & Associates, "Profile: Wealthy Donors to Museums," *The Chronicle of Philanthropy*, September 20, 1994, p. 12.   Of the subset of donors known as "investors," some 87% indicated "supporting the organization is an investment in the community" and 95.7% of this group noted that it provides a venue for "meeting prospective and current clients."   Zoos and aquariums are rather similar, with wealthy donors perceiving them as "important community assets."   See, Prince & Associates, "Profile: Wealthy Donors to Zoos and Aquariums," *The Chronicle of Philanthropy*, May 31, 1994, p. 10.

[8] Prince & Associates, "Profile: Wealthy Donors to Environmental Organizations," *The Chronicle of Philanthropy*, April 5, 1994, p. 14.   While the data are aging, slightly more than half of the donors

4) Former Patient relationship = The donor was cured or helped by a medical organization such as a hospital.[9]   The nature of the relationship is often gratitude: "XYZ Hospital saved your life, now you can give to save someone else's life."   This donor category also applies to the loved ones of former patients.   With this donor category, cultivation and solicitation is often done entirely by staff.   At some medical institutions, advancement staff officers visit patients and family members in their rooms before they are discharged from the facility to make an initial connection and begin the process of relationship building.

When one considers the nature of the donor relationship to the institution from the standpoint of these four categories, it is immediately evident that the nature of the appeals and the presentation of the Case for Support will differ significantly from one category to another, based on the nature of the connection between the donor and the institution, and the values and emotions which those connections can evoke in the donor.

The donors who stick with an institution and sustain it through the progressive stages of its development are donors with whom the institution has plumbed the nature of one of the categories described above to develop a personal relationship for the donor with the institution, its people, and its Mission. Such relationships are not built instantaneously.   They are built over time.   They are cultivated.   Such relationships are built by first understanding the priorities and interests and motivations and experiences of the prospective donors, and by communicating the Case for Support in ways that resonate with the prospective donors' priorities, interests, and motivations.

Major institutions with sophisticated advancement staffs have cadres of major gift officers whose mission it is to chart a "cultivation/solicitation plan" for each of 200 or more major prospects, develop a relationship between each donor and the institution involving the participation of senior staff, the President, board members, and others, and culminate with a "major ask" (e.g., a request for financial support).   In smaller Institutes and expeditions, in the absence of the cadre of professional relationship-builders, such relationships

---

surveyed said they contributed to environmental causes because they considered "environmental protection to be one of the highest priorities among all kinds of philanthropic causes."

[9] Co-author Vartorella also points out that a donor relationship might be cultivated to the underlying biomedical research involved with, say, a drug related to vampire bat saliva used as a treatment of stroke. His view is such a strategy broadens the Case for Support, while keeping it personalized to the donor. In this real example, rainforest scientists involved with vampire bats, their habitat, indigenous cultures, and bio-prospecting might join forces for support of special initiatives of interest to the donor.

are developed directly with the leaders of the organizations and the people advancing the organizations' Missions. Large NGOs also have sophisticated prospect research staffs and the infrastructure of hardware and software to develop comprehensive profiles on their major prospects.

This Chapter, however, is directed at a readership of smaller-shop advancement offices without such sophisticated infrastructure, small shops where the principal officers of the organization (or even the Chief Scientist) have a hands-on central role in the identification, cultivation, and solicitation of prospective donors.

IV. Motivations of Donors:

Writing in *Harvard Business Review,* Chris Argyris discusses single-loop and double loop learning.[10] In single loop learning, we ask one-dimensional questions to get one-dimensional answers. When Yogi Berra was asked why the Yankees did not beat the Dodgers on one occasion, he answered: "We didn't score enough runs." That would be a "single-loop" answer. Double loop learning goes back to ask "Why?" a second time, to look for the reasons behind the one-dimensional answers.

Interviewed in the *New York Times*, Professor of Economics James Andreoni, an economist at the University of Wisconsin "who has studied charitable giving throughout his career," said:

> The main things that predict how much a person gives are how much income they have and whether they can take advantage of the tax deduction for charitable giving. We also consistently find that people with higher educations give more, and that as people age, they give more, too. But we probably see older and more educated people giving more because they also tend to have more savings and better stock portfolios, not because they really care more about charity.[11]

There is a surfeit of survey data that provide information like this in a little more depth. Such surveys ask donors to rank their reasons for giving from the donor's perspective, and they rank motivations such as Belief in the Mission of the Institution, Tax Benefits, Respect for the President, Civic

---

[10] Chris Argyris, "Good Communication That Blocks Learning," *Harvard Business Review*, July/August, 1994, p. 78.
[11] Interview, *New York Times*, November 18, 2002, p. 23.

Duty, A Sense of "Giving Back," etc.   Not surprisingly, the survey results consistently rank the categories such as Belief in the Mission, Civic Duty, and A Sense of "Giving Back" highly, and they rank all categories that appear to be self-serving, such as Tax Benefits, low on the scale.[12]   This is a single loop process.

The purpose in this Chapter is not to replicate such information provided by economists and surveys.   Rather, the purpose here is to take a double loop approach, go beneath such surveys and the economists' conclusions, ask a second "Why?" and to motivators that decades of subjective experience with donors have identified through that compel donors to *invest* in an organization. Our purpose in doing so is to identify bottom-line, lowest common denominator, simple premises - cornerstones, if you will - on which to build donor cultivation, solicitation, and recognition plans.

A. Popular Misconceptions

There are a few popular misconceptions that appear frequently as erroneous assumptions as not-for-profits contemplate accelerated fundraising plans.

1. Donors Give To "Needs"

In *Mega Gifts: Who Gives Them, Who Gets Them*, Jerold Panas--a U.S. fundraiser who wrote several books on fundraisers and donors--reflects on interviews with donors of gifts of seven figures or more.   He observes:

> People do not give because there is a need.   Countless thousands of organizations and institutions have great needs.   Overwhelming financial problems. . . . But donors run away from 'needs.' . . . Large donors give to exciting, heroic programs rather than to needy institutions.[13]

Large donors do not give to programs only because they believe they are "exciting" and "heroic."   They view their "gifts" as "investments" to generate measurable returns on their resources, not in terms of monetary

---

[12] See, for example, the Hudson Institute's study, "The National Survey on Philanthropy & Civic Renewal: 1997-1998," which reports, among other things, how the views of the wealthy (annual incomes of U.S. $200,000 + or net assets of at least U.S. $3 million) on philanthropy compare with those of all Americans. The worthiness of a nonprofit's goal resonated with 87% of the rich donors surveyed.   Another important finding was the similarity of responses across different racial and ethnic groups.

[13] Jerold Panas, *Mega Gifts: Who Gives Them, Who Gets Them* (Chicago, Illinois: Pluribus Press, 1984), p. 41.

returns to donors, but as returns to society at large or targeted segments of society through Missions of the programs they are supporting with their gifts.

Major donors want to see themselves that the gift - the *investment* - they have made will accomplish the purpose for which it was given. It is no longer enough for major donors to have confidence in the leadership of their institution and know that their gift is "going to a good cause," a familiar refrain from the past.

> *Donors have been increasingly asking over the past decades for more focused restrictions on their giving, and they have been interested in defining their gifts in ways that make sure that their funds will be spent on generating specific results in specific areas.*[14]

This is the mentality of *"Investment Philanthropy*," a phrase we coined 10 or 15 years ago to describe this shift in giving posture toward more specific restrictions and increased accountability for specific results.

2. Donors Give To Avoid Taxes

Panas says: "I am convinced that people do not give for tax reasons, although if there is an advantage, that is helpful. I am convinced they do not give logically. Passion, rather than reason, rules." [15]

Even Professor Andreoni, who listed income and tax deductibility as the primary factors in giving, observes:

> There is clearly a lot to charitable giving that goes beyond the usual cold and rational economic analysis.   There is a lot of emotion and empathy and impulse that goes on. . . . The economic data that we collect through surveys or from tax returns really can't get at these other motives very well. Plus, they're really hard to quantify, even for psychologists or sociologists who make it their business to understand such things.[16]

---

[14] Two *free* reports may be of interest: "What's a Donor to Do?   The State of Donor Resources in America Today" and "Doing Well By Doing Good: Improving Client Service, Increasing Philanthropic Capital: The Legal and Financial Advisor's Role" at The Philanthropic Initiative's website at www.tpi.org. Also, see the Mellman Group's study, "On-Line Giving and Activism: What Donors Want," which reported in 1999 that a nonprofit's website can make a charity more accountable to donors (63% of those surveyed).   In 2001, the Better Business Bureau's Wise Giving Alliance released poll results that indicated 79% of respondents would seek, in some fashion, "financial information about how the group spends its money" from a charity's website.   Accountability and results are converging issues, particularly with global NGOs seeking "e-gifts," which by definition are planned gifts in which the cultivation and education process are 50% on-line/interactive or via e-mail solicitations.

[15] Panas, *Mega Gifts: Who Gives Them, Who Gets Them*, p. 50.

[16] Interview, *New York Times*, November 18, 2002,   p. 23.

Tax incentives may affect how a donor gives, but they rarely determine whether a donor will give. Tax incentives will, for example, encourage a donor to contribute appreciated stock rather than cash. But the decision to make a gift, and to whom to make it, has already been made. Tax incentives alone rarely motivate the gift itself. And tax incentives alone will not motivate a gift to your Institute, expedition, or NGO instead of another one. To be sure, there are often instances where at year's end it will be in a donor's advantage to make a few unplanned charitable donations, but these instances are merely peripheral extras and not central features of a development plan.

These observations are based on United States circumstances, where there are substantial tax incentives to encourage charitable giving. Evidence of the secondary nature of these tax incentives to motivate giving is found in Europe, where little or no such tax incentives exist, and where philanthropic giving is evidenced by a proliferation of international conferences on philanthropy and fundraising, and on the increasing influx of American fundraising firms opening European offices and international divisions.

3. Donors Give to Get Their Names On Buildings

While it is true that corporate donors contribute company funds for the value of visibility of the corporate logotype or entrenched brand or image, a name on a building is generally not the primary motivation of a major contribution from an individual. **Such a "naming opportunity" may influence the size of a gift, or even its timing, but a gift of such magnitude comes as a result of a *relationship* with the people of the institution, and a belief in its Mission and the purpose of the building.**

Donors' names on buildings (expedition field houses, research centers) confer prestige on the buildings as well as the donors.[17] They raise the sights of subsequent donors, motivating larger gifts from the other donors in the short run, and in the long run, they elevate the continuing visibility of the role of private philanthropy in the support of those institutions.

---

[17] HNW Digital addressed this issue indirectly in a 2001 survey. It concluded while half of all Americans prefer to give anonymously to nonprofits, two-thirds of wealthy donors prefer to give "with their name attached."

B. The Role of Emotion: Investment Philanthropy's First Requirement

The mentality of Investment Philanthropy requires a focus on measurable returns on investment for the Mission of the institution and the program being supported by the gift, but the donor must be engaged first *emotionally*.

Referring to the donors of very large gifts, Jerold Panas observes:

> Clearly, the mega givers are not motivated by dire need, but rather are captivated by the opportunity, the challenge, the magic of being able to do something special, something others may not be in the position to do.[18]

I believe the same is true of the not-so-mega givers. I started my career in New York City doing corporate fundraising for what is now the United Way. I worked those corporations all the way from the top to the bottom - raising the corporate gifts from the CEO's, and organizing and directing the employee campaigns reaching every single person who worked for the corporation down to the very bottom of the organizational chart.   One of the things I learned from that experience was that the employees who gave the highest percentage of their incomes were the lowest paid employees at the corporations doing the most menial and unskilled work there was to do.[19]   Many of them had had first-hand contact with one or more of the agencies supported by the United Way, and they believed in the people they had encountered in those experiences.

Donors who are willing to give to their capacity (whatever the level of that capacity is) over a sustained period of time, are motivated by passion before reason.

The authors believe this is particularly true for donors who support "non-traditional" scientific causes such as the private enterprise exploration of the cosmos.   Since 1961, only 420 people have traveled in space.[20] Yet, a recent poll of Americans with net worths exceeding U.S. $1 million disclosed,

- 19% would pay U.S. $100,000 for a 15-minute ride 50 miles into space that included a weightless experience;

---

[18] Panas, *Mega Gifts: Who Gives Them, Who Gets Them*, p. 50.
[19] See our Summary Chapter for a detailed discussion of conflicting research regarding the giving patterns and percentages of "rich vs. poor" donors.
[20] "ABC World News Tonight with Peter Jennings," Thursday, August 29, 2002.

- 16% would invest U.S. $5 million for a two-week visit to an orbiting space station;
- 7% would splurge U.S. $20 million for the same two-week jaunt aboard a space station.[21]

A 1998 NASA study, which endorsed the notion of *space tourism*, concluded it could conceivably become a U.S. $10-*billion* industry within decades.[22]

However, after the emotion - the passion - has been engaged and the decision is made to support the program under discussion, then reason kicks in. In the mentality of "Investment Philanthropy," donors want to see the hopes triggered by their passion realized, and in the structuring of their gift, they demonstrate an expectation that they will see a "return on their investment."   In terms of the thorny issue of "risk assessment," which Vartorella detailed early in our book, the satellite launch industry's failure rate of 1% [23] would likely dissuade all but the most ardent of space advocate/donor-tourists.

Fact is, only the satellite communications business has proven viable economically, despite NASA's ongoing efforts to attract "zero-gravity" businesses (biotechnology, electronics, and pharmaceutical companies) capable of affording cutting-edge research in low earth orbit (LEO).

As quoted by Mark Alpert, "To go to space to *stay*, we have to make space *pay*."[24]   The same may well apply to underseas colonization plans, whose donor profiles may mirror those of space ventures in terms of advocacy and wealth.

What, then, employing Argyris' double-loop inquiry, is the "lowest common denominator," the thread between donor and institution, the emotional motivator that engages the passion and results in a major gift?

The authors' experience suggests it has to do with **transcending obligation**.

All of us, rich and poor, have obligations.   We pay taxes.   We work, or, those who are wealthy enough not to have to work for a living at least have to monitor their finances.   Philanthropy affords us the opportunity to feel

---

[21] Futron/Zogby Poll, widely reported in January, 2003.   For the truly intrepid & well-heeled explorer, in 2002 Space Adventures offered a trip to the International Space Station via a Russian rocket for U.S. $2.5 million per day, with two weeks for training in Moscow.

[22] Mark Alpert, "Making Money in Space: Exploring the solar system turns out to be the easy part.   The next great challenge will be creating profitable space enterprises," *Scientific American Presents The Future of Space Exploration Quarterly*, Volume 10, Number 1 (Spring, 1999), 94.

[23] *Ibid.*

[24] *Ibid.*, p. 93.

good about doing something we are not obligated to do.   It is something
we do for someone else.   We derive satisfaction ourselves from doing
something for someone else.   We are not obligated to pay a percentage of
our income in philanthropic gifts like we are obligated to pay taxes.   And
we are not obligated to support one organization over another.   If we feel
"obligated" to "give back" to the community, it is a self-imposed obligation
(or one the more religious may believe is imposed by God), not one that is
imposed from outside ourselves. Even the donors in the "User" category
demonstrate this: the donor to the YMCA is not giving because the donor
will benefit; s/he is giving so that someone else can benefit.

The choice to make a philanthropic gift is a unique kind of choice.
And the choice of who will be the recipient of the philanthropic gift is also a
unique kind of choice.

So, then, our task raising funds - and, equally important,
strengthening our relationships with our donors after they have become
donors - is to perpetuate, fortify, and re-create for our donors that sense of
satisfaction and fulfillment that comes from doing something they were not
"obligated" by someone else to do.   Our task is to find out how to strike
the "responsive chord" between our institutions and our donors that will
evoke the values shared by our donors and our institutions.[25]

C. Levels of Giving

It is useful in focusing on donors to group them into levels of their
giving. Experience has shown that they generally share the characteristics
described with each level.   The descriptions of the donors at each level
refer to the donors for whom that respective level of giving is his/her
maximum level.   It does not refer to the donors capable of higher levels
who are contributing lesser amounts:

1) Donors By Level of Giving:

   a. Seminal Donors: Eight-figure gifts

   i.   They are looking to make the biggest gift of their life.
   ii.   They want to make a truly significant statement.

---

[25] Note: Exempt from this discussion on motivations for giving is the network reciprocal giving that goes
on between CEO's of corporations. Motivations here refer to motivations of individuals to give as
individuals.

iii.   They want to validate a perceived need, e.g., the need for a new breast cancer treatment center. Their investment and its visibility and impressiveness demonstrate the perceived validity of the need for the program, and elevate visibility of the issue.

iv.   They want to create something: A new school, an Institute, a program. They want to set a new precedent, perhaps a new paradigm.

v.   They want to leave a Legacy, by having their creation, i.e., their School or Institute, leave a lasting impact that will benefit generations of people.

vi.   They want to be appreciated. It is not fame they seek. They either have achieved fame through their other activities or they have avoided it.

vii.   They want to set an example for others to follow: they want to set something in motion that other donors will join.

b. Leadership Donors: Seven-figure gifts

    i.   They usually have long-term relationships with the recipient institutions, e.g. their *alma mater*. [Note: There are exceptions. We recall the Chancellor of a public university having lunch with the development officer of one of the colleges and a prospective major donor with whom he had cultivated a relationship. The prospect surprised them by saying that he was so impressed with the institution that he had decided to give them U.S. $1 million dollars immediately. When he asked what they would use his gift for, the Chancellor and the development officer did not have an answer.]

    ii. They can be motivated by personal circumstances such as a high profile CEO wanting to demonstrate his sense of civic / community / charitable involvement by making a high profile seven-figure gift.

       iii. They, too, want to leave a legacy, want to be appreciated, and want to set an example for others to follow.

c. Major Donors: Six-figure gifts

i. Exhibit the same characteristics when giving to smaller organizations as the donors of larger amounts to larger institutions above.

    ii. Tend to contribute in line with their capacity proportionally to the
        Leadership and Seminal donors when solicited in the context of a
        Capital Campaign.
    iii. They want to see their support as part of a larger picture.

d. **Threshold Donors: Five-figure gifts**

    i.   The first U.S. $10,000 gift lifts a small NGO to the next level
       of its fundraising potential, giving it a new level of credibility as a
       good investment.
    ii. Threshold Donors can be very generous, as it is often more of a
       "stretch" for a U.S. $10,000 donor to make that level of gift than it
       is for a U.S. $100,000 donor to make a six-figure gift because of
       the difference in their wealth levels.
    iii. Threshold Donors also appreciate personal expressions of
       appreciation from key people associated with the institutions.
    iv. Threshold Donors will contribute to *existing* programs. This level at
       many institutions is the entry level for establishing named funds.
       Where that is the case, the donor recognition can be more of a
       factor than at other levels which do not represent crossing such a
       threshold.

e. **Sustaining Donors: Four-figure gifts**

    i.   Sustaining Donors constitute the pool of future Threshold and
       Major Donors. U.S. $1,000 is often the level of annual support at
       which social recognition begins in the form of invitation to an
       annual donor banquet of U.S. $1,000+ donors.
    ii. They are often staff members or people of lesser means who make a
       large stretch to meet what they perceive to be their responsibility.
       Often such donors give proportionally more than others with far
       greater means and far lesser sense of connectedness or responsibility
       to the institution and its Mission.

f. **Base-level Donors: Three-figure gifts**

    i. Base-level Donors, usually solicited by mail or phone, provide a base-
      level of support for the organization and constitute the donor's first
      entry onto your Institute, expedition, or NGO's "radar screen" for asks

at higher levels.

ii. They appreciate a timely communication of thanks and look for their names on Honor Rolls of donors.

iii. In Capital Campaigns, they respond to forms of tangible recognition such as their names on bricks in donor recognition walkways and garden walls.

2) Inherited Wealth vs. Made Wealth

Conventional wisdom holds that donor prospects with inherited wealth are motivated by protection of that wealth and therefore make major gifts which are less than the donor prospects who have made their money and are more inclined toward confidence in larger entrepreneurial philanthropic investments.[26]

This conventional wisdom implies that the prospective donors with "Old Money" protect their inheritances out of a behavioral trait. However, the reality is that prospective donors who have inherited "Old Money" are usually much more constrained by the terms of the irrevocable trusts from whose income they benefit, than the prospective donor of new wealth, who may have realized this wealth in the heady days of "Dot-Coms" [27] and the "bull market."

So the statement: "So-and-so is worth U.S. $100 million," may mean something very different in terms of philanthropic potential if "So-and-so" inherited the money from generations past than if "So-and-so" made it in a series of transactions over a period of a few years (or even overnight) such as in the 1990's through dot.com growth or the sale of a business.

Inherited funds are usually in the forms of trusts, where the beneficiary has access to only the income of the trust and not the principal. So our prospective donor who is "worth" U.S. $100 million that s/he inherited may probably be able to spend only the interest from that U.S. $100 million principal. On the other hand, our prospective donor who is "worth" U.S. $100 million that was realized from short-term business deals

---

[26] Again, see the detailed discussion in the footnotes of our Summary Chapter. What is measured and how are central issues in the debate.

[27] See Elizabeth Schwinn, "New Study Details Giving Habits, Preferences of High-Tech Millionaires," *The Chronicle of Philanthropy*, May 17, 2001, p. 29. Main findings: High-tech donors are interested in nonprofits that approach an issue comprehensively, with new approaches that are knowledge-based and which offer opportunities for expansion of successful programs. For an Executive Summary, "Agent-Animated Wealth and Philanthropy: The Dynamics of Accumulation and Allocation Among High-Tech Donors," visit the Association of Fundraising Professionals' website at <www.nsfre.org>.

can spend as much of that money as s/he cares to, and it may very well be to the donor's tax advantage to do so.

I recently had a revealing conversation with a manager of portfolios with U.S. multi-million-dollar minimums. He said that he had been examining the terms of "Old Money" trusts for his clients and learned in the course of doing so that in parts of New England, returning Civil War Union soldiers were given, by their State, deeds to large homestead tracts of land in the Midwest. Not wishing to migrate to the Midwest to take up farming, they got together, created large land trusts, and leased them to farmers. These land trusts grew in value and were sold for substantial sums, from which were created irrevocable trusts for the heirs of the original owner families.

Today's heirs, almost a century later, can only access the income from these trusts. Yet these heirs are "worth" many millions of dollars because the trusts are now theirs.[28]

V. Strategies for Donors--Investment Philanthropy and the Psychology of the Invitation:

The mentality of Investment Philanthropy and the Psychology of the Invitation provide cornerstones on which to construct the strategy for a solicitation of a donor, or the strategy for the creation and execution of a Capital Campaign.

Investment Philanthropy provides the framework for development of a sound Case for Support and well thought out proposals, presentations, and programmatic infrastructure that will stand the test of questions and accountability. We know that the point of entry for the donor is the passion that is evoked by the portrayal of the work and Mission to be supported by the donor's gift. If that passion has been backed up by the donor's reason inspiring confidence that his/her gift is a good investment in actualizing the Mission that has evoked the passion, the presentation of Case for Support has done its job.

Awareness of the Psychology of the Invitation provides the sensitivity to the sequencing of donors' solicitation in the overall development plan, and the identification and involvement of other individuals to add another dimension of motivation for the donor.

A. Usefulness of the Psychology of the Invitation

---

[28] For a list of 300 ZIP codes with the highest per capita incomes in the U.S based on *Worth* magazine estimates, see <www.usc.edu/dept/source/zipcode/index.htm> .

1. What is the Psychology of the Invitation?   And how does it relate to the solicitation of donors?

When you receive an invitation in the mail to a party and you read where it is and when, two questions usually immediately come to mind: "Who else is going?" and "What are they going to wear?"

This is analogous to fundraising strategy in that prospective donors consider carefully

- Who else is involved with the program s/he is being asked to support?
- What is the extent of their involvement?

In years past, awareness of this dynamic was carried right through to the pledge card, which read: "In consideration of the gifts of others . . ." in the pledge line.

When reflecting on a list of prospective donors, it is useful to try to differentiate (if they are sufficiently known to you or your evaluation committee) between those donors who are more likely to be motivated to set the pace or follow the pace, or, in the words of Charles Fazio, cited in our later Chapter on Capital Campaigns, whether they are more likely to be motivated to make a winner, or back a winner.

It is also useful to make (or obtain) some reasonably accurate determination of to what extent a donor is motivated or influenced by another person or other people, through *admiration, aspiration, obligation, or competition.* Examples:

- Admiration: A prospective donor holds in esteem a mentor who is a former professor, colleague, icon in the prospective donor's field, or other charismatic figure whom the prospect admires.
- Aspiration: A prospective donor aspires to be "in the same league" as another individual.   This aspiration can be in terms of wealth acquisition, corporate rank, or professional prestige and recognition.
- Obligation: A prospective donor who is a corporate CEO is attentive to and influenced by someone who is usually also a CEO and whose corporation has a financial relationship with the prospect, such as being the prospect's corporation's biggest customer.[29]

---

[29] I learned about the dynamic of corporate leverage unambiguously early in my career. The CEO of a company had volunteered to take the assignment to call on another CEO, who was the CEO of a *Fortune* 500 company. I was the young development staff person on the call. I did my homework, prepared my

- Competition: A prospective donor is socially and/or professionally competitive with another individual and is attentive to "keeping up with the Joneses."

Determinations on these issues can provide valuable guidance on what sequential order you want the solicitation of your prospects to take place. **It is fundamentally critical to get a maximum commitment from a prospective donor whose level of commitment will influence the level of commitment of another donor for one of the above reasons.**

2. The "Invitation" as Solicitation

Treating a solicitation as an invitation is more than a matter of semantics. It is an era when it is very difficult for any but the most philanthropically developed institutions to recruit and retain high quality volunteers because of the overabundance of campaigns which are present in every metropolitan area throughout the U.S. Volunteer fundraising committee members who choke at the words "I would like you to consider giving the XYZ institution U.S. $10,000," have no problem saying "I would like *you* to join *me* in the President's Club," where the "President's Club" is the donor group of U.S. $10,000+ donors, and the volunteer has handed the prospect a brochure opened to the page showing the donor club levels and their names. Couching the solicitation in terms of an invitation makes it easier on the volunteer and the staff member.

The whole concept of a campaign (annual or capital), or other fundraising program treated as something to which someone is "invited," has a subtle impact on the responses of prospective donors and volunteer solicitors alike. To treat a fundraising program as something to which people are "invited" connotes a movement, a celebration, something positive that is happening that the prospect should want to be a part of, something that other people are involved with in whose company the

---

written presentation, and rehearsed my lines. On the appointed day, I accompanied my volunteer to the *Fortune* 500 company's Madison Avenue executive offices in New York City. We entered the CEO's sumptuous offices, my volunteer strode past the CEO's secretary, entered his office without knocking, and, as the startled CEO (who we'll call "Joe") got up from his desk to cross the room to greet him, he shook his hand peremptorily and said: "Hi, Joe. This is Don Keel," then, to me, "Don, tell him what you want him to do." There was a moment of "dead air" in which I looked at the CEO and he at me. My volunteer sat down on the couch and picked up a magazine. I told the CEO what I wanted him to do and he agreed to all of it without question. The meeting lasted less than ten minutes. I learned the lesson. I subsequently called on the largest banks in New York and, through fortuitous contacts and a little homework, was able to make the calls with each bank's largest depositors. I didn't get a single turndown or response below the ask amount.

prospect would like to be included. Proposals and pledge cards can take the format of **invitations** rather than **solicitations**, and the message becomes "We want you to join us and become a part of this wonderful thing that we are all doing together (bio-prospecting with indigenous tribes in the rainforest; conducting CT scans of pterodactyl skulls; deep-diving Russian MIR submersibles; mapping the ruins of Huanna Picchu, etc.)" instead of "We want You to give Us some of Your Money to do what We want to do." It's about *THEM*, not *US*.   ***Strike the responsive chord.***

B. The Donor Focus Matrix

A useful tool for segmenting prospective donors and focusing on the pertinent issues in their solicitation is the "Donor Focus Matrix."   It is similar to the Leadership Assessment Matrix in Chapter 3 on Board Development. The Donor Focus Matrix, however, is oriented to the evaluation and sequencing of donor solicitation, and to the involvement of the appropriate people who might be influential in the process.

It is a *confidential tool* for your own private use or for use with a small evaluation or strategy committee.

> **It provides a way to rate your top prospects with criteria**
> **that determine the level of their target ask, the sequencing**
> **of their solicitation, and the identification of other**
> **individuals whose role could be influential in their gift**
> **decision.**

The column headings of the matrix are as follows:

- Capacity: The ranking of the prospects estimated capacity to give. The ranges chosen for the numerical rankings would depend on the size and fundraising experience of the institution or organization.   1-10 could be U.S. $1,000 to U.S. $10,000, or could be U.S. $100,000 to U.S.$1,000,000, or anywhere in between.   The ranges are a function of the level of development of the organization.
- Readiness: The degree to which the prospect is connected with your institution and "ready" to make a commitment to it.
- C/B: Denotes whether the prospect is considered to be one who is in the cadre of prospects who are entrepreneurial and motivated by

creating a winner, or whether the prospect is in the cadre of prospects who are more conservative and motivated by backing a winner.

- I/Q: Denotes the "Influence Quotient," i.e., the estimated degree to which the prospect can be influenced by the direct or indirect input from another person or group of persons.

- I/P: Denotes the "Influence Person," i.e., the person considered to be the person by whom the prospect would be most influenced.

- I/T: Denotes the Influence Type that the IP would be most likely to have: Admiration, Aspiration, Obligation, or Competition.

Prospect	Capacity	Readiness	C/B	I/Q	I/P	I/T
Prospect #1	9	10	C	1	A	n/A
Prospect #2	10	8	C	9	Prospect #1	Admiration
Prospect #3	5	5	B	8	Prospect #7	Aspiration
Prospect #4	4	8	B	7	Prospect #6	Obligation
Prospect #5	3	7	B	9	Prospect #8	Admiration
Prospect #6	5	2	B	7	Prospect #5	Competition
Prospect #7	8	3	C	8	Prospect #2	Obligation
Prospect #8	7	1	C	9	Prospect #1	Obligation

For the sake of this example, the matrix above shows donors who are influenced by other Prospects on the same list.   Obviously, this will not work out so conveniently in the real world.   But, in our example, what does this matrix indicate about these prospects?

Prospect #1 has high capacity to give and is ready to do so according to his/her Readiness Rating.   S/he is not influenced by anyone else and is ready to make a commitment.   S/he is the kind of person who is inclined to create, rather than back a winner.   S/he is not influenced by anyone in particular.

Prospect #2 has very high capacity to give.   S/he is not cultivated yet as the low Readiness Rating shows.   This prospect is also a person who is inclined to take the initiative rather than follow someone else's example.   But the Influence Quotient, Influence Person, and Influence Type columns show that Prospect #2 is highly influenced by prospect #1, whom s/he admires.

Prospect #3 is in the middle range of capacity and readiness to give.   This prospect is a person who prefers to back an already known winner and is highly influenced by Prospect #7, whom s/he aspires to emulate.

Prospect #4 is of moderate capacity to give, is not ready to do so, is a person who follows rather than leads, and is rather highly influenced by Prospect #5 with whom s/he is in a competitive position socially or professionally.

Prospect #5 is of relatively low capacity to give, but of relatively high readiness to do so.   S/he is a person who prefers to follow rather than lead, and is heavily influenced by Prospect #8, whom s/he admires.

Prospect #6 is of median capacity to give and little inclination to do so at present.   S/he is a person who prefers to back a winner rather than create a winner who is quite influenced by Prospect #5 with whom s/he is in a competitive posture.

Prospect #7 has high capacity and little readiness to give.   S/he is a leader who is highly influenced by Prospect #2, to whom s/he is in a position of obligation.

Prospect #8 has relatively high capacity and relatively no inclination to give at present.   This prospect is not heavily influenced by anyone but is in a position of obligation to Prospect #1.

What does all this tell us about what sequence we should go about soliciting these prospects?

Prospect #1 is clearly the starting point.   This prospect has both high capacity and high readiness ratings, so s/he is in a position to get the ball rolling with a pace setting commitment.   Being a person determined to be a leader and not a follower, s/he is likely to do so.

Prospect #2 also has high capacity and readiness to give, and is also a leader rather than a follower.   In addition to these attributes, s/he is highly influenced by Prospect #1, whom s/he admires.

So, it is clear that we want to secure Prospect #1's commitment first and then Prospect #2's.   Now we can proceed to the third donor and be able to say that Prospects #'s 1 and 2 have already "come on board."

Who's next? Prospect #7 has high capacity but a low readiness rating. However, s/he is heavily influenced by Prospect #2, to whom s/he is obligated.   And Prospect #2 is already on the roster of donors.   Because of the low readiness threshold, we know that more cultivation will be necessary for this prospect than for the others. Because of our assessment of their I/Q, I/P, and I/T situations, that involvement of Prospect #2 (now a donor) would be productive. Reflecting on our discussion of the Psychology of the Invitation in fundraising, it is evident that, given this scenario, a powerful ask would be for Prospect #2 to say to Prospect #7 (after sufficient cultivation): "I want to invite you to join me as a donor to this program."

After Prospect #7 is on board as a donor, Prospect #3 is our next best bet. S/he is a middle range prospect in both capacity and readiness, but is heavily influenced by Prospect #7, whom s/he admires.   And this prospect is rated already as more ready to give than Prospect #7 was.   The involvement of Prospect #7 in the cultivation and/or solicitation of Prospect #3 will both bolster confidence of Prospect #7 in his/her investment, and encourage Prospect #3 to "join" #7, whom s/he aspires to emulate.

Now, we have a significant donor roster in Prospects #'s 1, 2, 3, and 7. This gives our program credibility of existing support.   But we have our work cut out for us.

Our next key is Prospect #8.   This prospect is the key to Prospects #4, 5, and 6. S/he has relatively high capacity, is a leader, and is heavily influenced by Prospect #1 to whom he is obliged.   But he is not ready to give.   Cultivation of this prospect involving Prospect (Donor) #1 will be critical to our progress in maximizing the gifts of Prospects # 's 4, 5, and 6.

If we are successful in our invitation to Prospect # 8 to join us, however, we are then in a better position to win support from Prospect #5, who has relatively low capacity to give but relatively high readiness.

Then we can approach Prospect #6, who is highly influenced by Prospect #5 and who is a leader.   We will have to take care not to take his/her support for granted, however, as the low readiness rating means that we shall have to think through and execute a good cultivation/solicitation plan.

Finally, with Prospect #6 on the donor roster, we will be in a good position to solicit Prospect #4, an initiative taker who is relatively highly influenced by Prospect #6, to whom s/he is in a position of obligation.

Of course, things are not so neat and tidy in the real world as they are in this example. Prospect lists are larger and everyone does not relate to everyone else. However, you will find that within your prospect list you will have several scenarios such as the example. You will find several such subgroups of people who relate to each other in the ways indicated by the example. Identifying and following such a sequential solicitation will maximize your success and generate higher results than if you simply solicited everyone without regard to their relationships with other prospects and without use of the roster of donors already on board.

When you consider the "Rule of Thirds" discussed in Chapter 8 (a widely practiced tenet that, in Capital Campaigns, you must get the first third of the financial goal from the top 10 gifts, the second third from the second 100 gifts, and the final third from everyone else), effective use of this matrix at the top level of your prospect list can mean a difference of thousands or even millions of U.S. dollars.

Unfortunately, the flip side is also true. If the prospects in a position of influence over your subsequent levels of prospects *decline* or enter your donor roster at low levels, the sights of your subsequent levels of donors whom your initial donors influence will be proportionately lower for the same reasons that they would be higher if your prior donors came in at higher levels. Again, considering the Rule of Thirds, low-level response from just a few of your top group of prospects can spell disaster for your chances of successfully reaching your goal.

The obvious conclusion is that the Donor Focused Matrix is best used in the development of carefully considered cultivation/solicitation plans for each of your best prospects, because the results you generate from them - positive or negative - will reverberate down the line as you solicit your subsequent prospects.

C. Communication Strategies

1. Remember: It's About *"THEM,"* Not About *"US"*

Just as institutional directors often miss the boat by communicating with their constituencies of prospects and donors in terms of their (the institutions') needs instead of the opportunities and bold initiatives that excite their constituents, they often forget that their communications are for their constituents and not for themselves. For example, institutional publications staffs often unwittingly write many college and university alumni magazines for themselves and for the people they report to, not for their alumni.   Most alumni receive their alumni magazines, skim through them, and look at the pictures, captions, and graphics as they proceed immediately to the "Class Notes" section to see what their classmates are doing. But most alumni magazines are heavy on verbiage and short on photos.   Usually, the only people that read the alumni magazines cover to cover are the alumni director, the staff that produced the magazine, the college president, and a few board members.

It is both fundamental and important in prospect/donor communications to keep reminding oneself that these communications must be in the terms of the interests of the prospects/donors, not in terms of the institutional directors' interests.   It is our job as communicators of institutional priorities and needs to remind ourselves constantly of this fundamental point.   We must strive to communicate our institutional priorities and needs in the terms of our prospects and donors' interests, priorities, and values.

2. Conduct or Replicate the In-Person Conversation

It is a common trap to think of communications in terms of brochures, mailings, and other mass-produced print media.   The most effective form of communication is the in-person conversation.   Keeping this reality at the forefront of your communications strategy leads to two premises:

a) An institutional director or development officer will communicate with as many major prospects and donors as possible on a continuing basis with in-person conversations.   The cultivation/solicitation plans and on-going communications plans will include as the first priority the periodic personal conversations with top prospects, donors, board members, elected officials, and, for communications directors, personal conversations with as many media representatives (i.e., editors and reporters) as possible.   NOTE: Too often, communications directors retreat to the safety of their offices and focus entirely on writing and producing print media and ignore "media relations," i.e., the necessary in-person relationship development with the people who are doing the reporting and commenting.

b) All other communications will replicate as closely as possible the in-person communication.   Hand-written notes are always opened and read.   Personal letters are next in the pecking order of reading material.   Letters that are individually addressed, with passages underlined (e.g. the *Kiplinger Letter* format) usually receive a relatively complete read unless they are transparently mass-produced.   And mass-produced newsletters are skimmed or ignored and discarded unless there is something of special interest to the reader that catches his/her attention in the first few seconds of observation.

3. Personalize Impersonal Media

Always personalize the Case for Support. Give it life.
Portray it in the lives of the people who benefit from it or
experience it.

Recognizing the reality of the Relationship Dynamic between the prospect/donor and the institution/Mission - a dynamic which is heightened by the ever-increasing sophistication of the already sophisticated institutions, making it ever more difficult for the less sophisticated and/or newer organizations and institutions to make inroads into developing relationships with prospective donors - communications of all kinds must replicate as closely as possible the personal interaction between a person at the institution and the prospect/donor.   Mailboxes have been stuffed so tightly with newsletters and print media from myriad groups, that in many environments the value of a newsletter, hitherto a popularly accepted form of communicating with donors and prospects, has diminished as each newsletter has gotten lost in the crowd.

Conversely, the personal letter--brief, concise, and crisp--sent with a stamp on the envelope, has maintained its assurance of attention by the recipient. In the age of computer-dialed telemarketing, computer-generated letters, and e-mail SPAM, the singularity of the hand-written note on a note card with a stamped envelope has begun to be recognized again as the truly personal communication.   A few words on a hand-written note can be immeasurably more effective with key donor/prospects than any form of printed or electronic communication.

As will be discussed in the Chapter on Campaigns, significant impact can be achieved by not asking the questions: "What kind of letter (or newsletter, or video, or whatever media) do we need?   What information needs to go into it?"   Instead, ask the questions: "Who do we want to see/read this communication?   What do we want him to do after he has read/seen it?"

An excellent example of utilizing state-of-the-art communications to personalize a Case for Support is NetAid, an organization that uses the

Internet to connect volunteers and donors throughout globe to provide services in the most desperate corners of the developing world. NetAid's website (www.netaid.org) focuses on and highlights, first and foremost, the individual real-life stories of the people, especially children, who have benefited from the activities of the volunteers within its global network.   It is highly personal more than highly high-tech.

4. Personal Testimonials Work

In person, in print, and on video, personal testimonials motivate others to give. So do donor profiles.   They can be brief, visual, and crisp. They enhance the sense of satisfaction of the donor being featured, and they motivate non-donors to give out of a sense that the institution really appreciates its donors.   They bring the message "home."

"Here's what I did!   You can do it, too!"   is a message that should be replicated, peer-to-peer, in as many forms as can be imagined.

5. Include Some Piece of News on Gifts In Every Communication

Every brochure, newsletter, and other communication except for personal correspondence should contain some reference to the positive impact of giving to your Institute, expedition, or laboratory.

Every brochure, newsletter, and other communication except for personal correspondence should, somewhere, express the Case for Support.

Immediately when major gifts and commitments are made, bulletins should be sent to all major donors, fundraising committees, and key major prospects with which the cultivation process has already begun - the shorter the better.   A one-sentence bulletin in an urgency-evoking font such as "Impact" connotes action, vitality, and movement.

6. Balanced Variety Gets Attention.

A good communications plan to a prospect/donor contains a balanced variety of the above forms of communications.   This balance should include a combination of personal and mass-produced print media.   For the top-level donors and prospects, reprints of newspaper/magazine articles should be sent individually with a personal comment from the CEO or institutional director.

D. Cultivation strategies

The word "cultivation" in institutional advancement really should be supplanted with "relationship building." Cultivation is not something that begins with a prospect and ends with a gift from the prospect. It is an ongoing process that continues for the (hopefully long) term of the relationship between the donor and the institution. Cultivation continues after a donor has made a gift to the institution.

In fact, the post-contribution cultivation is the most important of all, because it is conventional wisdom that your best prospective donors are your existing donors, i.e. you are more likely to get an increased or extended contribution from your existing donors than you are from a new prospective donor.

In the cultivation of a prospective donor, it is our job to identify the key aspects of the prospective donor's values and experiences with which we can resonate as we acquaint the donor with our Mission and Case for Support.

Cultivation takes many forms, and, for the major prospect, is tailored to that prospect's individual values. There are many models for cultivation strategies. The authors have found the following to be useful:

1) Introduction: The prospect is introduced to the institution, its principals, and its Mission in a social setting such as a reception, to which s/he has been invited by a member of the Board or other already-involved person.

2) Engagement: A responsive chord is struck with the prospect, with a connection established between the prospect and an area of interest and/or rapport/interest in a person or group that is part of the institutional family.

3) Involvement: The prospect becomes involved in the Mission of the institution. Such involvement can take many forms, e.g. hosting a reception, participating on a program committee, providing expertise in an area of the prospect's competence, or evaluating prospective donors on an evaluation committee.

4) Commitment: At some point in this continuum, the prospect becomes committed to the Mission and work of the institution. S/he becomes a "stakeholder" in the success of the work of the institution. They share in the

success or failure of the institution's work, and they are committed to ensuring the success.   It is in this phase that a financial commitment is sought.

5) Stewardship: Ongoing donor relations are critical to the enduring success of an institution.   It is amazing how many institutions drop the ball at this phase and stop paying attention to the prospect when they become donors, taking them for granted after this point.   Regular communications in many forms, especially personal communication and reports to the donor on the progress of the program or area they support, are crucial.

Co-author Vartorella has written about the involvement phase of the cultivation of donors, specifically, on an archaeological excavation ("dig"). He has been through the drill many times himself and has learned what it takes to cement a donor relationship through a first-hand experience.   The principles described below work equally well with expeditions focusing upon paleontology, bioanthropology, coral reef monitoring, geology, polar planetary analogues, ethnography, remote rovers ("telepresence"), and projects involving young field scientists (European Union support of biota sampling at Iwokrama rainforest in Guyana).

Writing amusingly in *The Explorers Newsletter*, he observes:[30]

"Donors like to dig."

They want to see the fruit of their financial labors in supporting an archaeological expedition. They want fuel for the cocktail circuit when they return home.   "There I was, there I was uncovering ancient (you fill in the blank) holding a 2,000-year-old (necklace, pot, whatever)."

Before you cringe, consider this.   A donor who is part of the process is part of the solution. Such a donor neither wants nor expects six bone-crushing, diarrhea-surprise, sunstroke-and-sand-flea-filled weeks in the Sahara or mosquito and spider-laden Central America.

What s/he wants is a short, comfortable, educational, safe "adventure in paradise."   The more pith helmets, the merrier.   And--here's the good part--they are willing to pay well for that privilege, perhaps as much as U.S. $500 per day (or more).

Based upon my field experience in the U.S. and abroad, the successful donor-digger trip consists of the following all-important elements:

---

[30] William F. Vartorella, "Don your pith helmets, here come the donors," *The Explorers Newsletter*, Volume 31, Number 1 (January-March, 1999), 9-10.

"The Visible Accouterments":

>   1) an exotic landscape, complete with above-the-ground ruins
>   2) a traditional camp setting with all the 1920's amenities:

- white tent, steamer trunk, pressed linen, mosquito netting, cot (with a 1990's air mattress under sheets), personal wash basin with a never-ending supply of cold water, quinine to sip, extra starched expedition clothing, a pith helmet lurking nearby, classic reading matter fitting for the period (plus modern briefing paper about the site, its importance, catalogued representative pottery and other artifacts, etc.);
- classic camp chairs and folding table; old-time lanterns & insect coils, plenty of fresh, white tablecloths; the ubiquitous aged Land Rover;
- a first-rate bar: single-malt scotches, top-shelf gin, vodka, bourbon, plus brandy, cordials, and a good supply of fine cigars; local exotics including beer, wine, rum, etc.;
- "traditions":   "sundowners" (cocktails), followed by a pleasant repast, after-dinner drinks/cigars and a brief informal chat by the Expedition Leader and rotating presentations by staff;
- a personal trowel, which is given to each donor as a memento at the end of the dig; high-quality team T-shirts.

"The Invisible Accoutrements":
- Cell phones, first-aid kits, fire extinguishers, insect repellant;
- Medical evacuation insurance (and IAMAT list of highly-trained local physicians);
- Your basic release form covering everything from *force majeur* to earthquakes; a staff that understands, completely, that these donors are an important part of the political landscape and that they are underwriting staff's privilege to be in the field for long hours in the tropical sun; a sense-of-humor is *de rigueur*.

Positioning and marketing donor experience is key.   Sites with best potential for high-end donor-digs include the following components:

- the ubiquitous romantic ruins mentioned above (ancient Egypt and Mayan temples are magical examples)
- excellent opportunity for uncovering artifacts location in a country with a reasonably stable government

- relatively easy access (e.g., Central and South America offer good flights and infrastructure without significant "jet lag"); local drivers considerate of donor stomachs on hair-pin mountain roads
- a local cuisine that does not include monkey brains, fried rat, fruit bat or other delicacies; potable water (without iodine treatment, etc.) is critical
- closer to sea level, the better: altitude sickness inflicts not only a blinding headache, but is the precursor to a host of serious health threats; on the other hand, avoid Malaria and Bilharzias zones, and potential earthquake hazards, if possible
- an accessible language (e.g., donors can practice their Spanish, French, etc.) and--ideally--good English-speaking support team
- reasonable sanitation and the opportunity to wash one's hands; at least a warm shower available, daily
- finally, a "shopping opportunity" for that all-important souvenir.

The average day should not be average.   Mix it up; training, trench talks, etc.   The donor should learn the basics, perhaps exclusive of surveying and mapping.   Five straight days at the sifter will come back to haunt the Expedition.   Sometime mid-experience, get the donors off-site for some basic ethnography and photo opportunities.

Delegate tasks and give constructive advice and plenty of praise (hopefully, warranted). The phrase "you have quickly become an important member of this team" is helpful.

This may all seem arcane and perhaps a bit snooty.   So be it.   Yet, if you look at the history of archaeology and the Golden Age of Patrons, what appears above is more the rule, rather than the exception.   More importantly, it enables Donors to understand what it is that archaeologists do and why understanding and preserving the Past is so important.

E. Solicitation Strategies

Solicitation is ideally one component in the continuum of prospect-to-donor cultivation, solicitation, and stewardship.   Optimum solicitation should embody the following characteristics:

1) It is not an isolated or *ad hoc* occurrence.   It does not happen outside the framework of other contacts and communications with the prospect.

2) For any gift of significant size (an amount to be determined by size, level of development, and other organization or institution aspects - a "significant" ask could be U.S. $1,000 it could be U.S. $10,000, or any other amount deemed significant by the expedition/Institute at the particular point in its history and development), solicitation is in person, not by phone or mail.

3) It is not a *pro forma* exercise. The circumstances, participants, and presentation materials are tailored to the prospect's values and priorities as learned in the Introduction and Involvement phases of his/her cultivation.

4) If it is a major ask, the prospect's spouse may be present.

5) It embodies the communication principle of the "responsive chord." It is evocative of the values of the prospect that resonate with the Mission embodied in the presentation.

6) It is as formal or informal as the prospect would like it to be.

7) It is in a venue chosen according to the tastes of the prospect.

8) Other individuals are involved based upon the cultivation/solicitation plan, including the considerations in the Donor Focus Matrix.

9) The solicitor *must* always be a person who has already made a commitment, either at the level of commitment the prospective donor is being asked to make, or at a level that is recognized by the prospective donor as a "stretch" commitment for the solicitor to have made at his/her level of means.

10) The solicitation is challenging but not threatening. The challenge is in the realization of the vision of what the donor will be making a reality. The realization of that vision is "worth the investment."

11) In the spirit of Investment Philanthropy, the solicitation includes the articulation of what the return on the investment will be in terms of the values and priorities of the donor that have been learned in the Introduction and Involvement phases of cultivation.

12) There is closure. When the "ask" has been made, the person making the ask and the other participant(s) in the solicitation remain silent until the prospect has responded.

13) There is immediate follow-up in the form of a handwritten note from the principal in the institution and the volunteer solicitor.

14) If a pledge is made, there is immediate follow-up from others as designated in pre-designed gift acknowledgement procedures. For example, if designated that the Chairman of the Board will write to all givers over U.S. $10,000, a draft for the Chairman's signature reflecting pledge terms is on his desk the same day and signed and mailed the next. Acknowledgements should be sent within 24 hours of pledge. (One rule-of-thumb is there should be seven thank-you letters from different people for a major gift.)

15) If the prospect wishes time to consider his/her response (a good and common practice), follow-up visit or call (as determined by the cultivation/solicitation strategy) is made two weeks after the visit, or otherwise as determined in the solicitation visit.

 F. Recognition Strategies

1) Purposes of Donor Recognition: Recognizing donors' and their gifts has several purposes:

> a. It gives the donors a sense of personal satisfaction and achievement.
> b. It provides a feeling that they are appreciated for their gifts.
> c. It stimulates giving from other donors. They see the expressions of appreciation offered to the recognized donors and they say to themselves: "This organization really appreciates the people who support it. I would like to be a part of that."
> d. A long list of donors in a publication, listed by giving level, demonstrates to corporate and foundation funding sources that the expedition or Institute is a good investment that has the support of a lot of people.
> e. Donors names on field houses or labs and on donor walls in Institutes elevate the awareness of private philanthropy as a primary factor in the quality of the NGO.

2) Types of Donor Recognition:

There are four main types of donor recognition:

a. Permanent: Donors names on buildings, labs, rooms, gardens, and other facilities provide a special honor to the donors and the people whom they memorialize, and it provides a perpetual reminder to all passers-by that someone thought enough of the institution to make a major philanthropic commitment to it.

b. Print: Donor names appear on plaques on walls in giving categories or according to object of support (e.g. an academic department, an Institute, etc.), and in "honor rolls" published in alumni magazines, annual reports, and campaign reports. Standard plaques have become "tired," and there are now numerous companies who, utilizing current technology, have developed imaginative ways to place donors on walls in what could legitimately be called an art form.   Instead of the tired old bronze plaques with names that require an electron microscope to read, we increasingly see names on brass leaves of tree sculptures, on creative tile mosaics with dramatic colors that sweep across the wall in waves, or other images.

c. Social: Donors are fêted at special events such as campaign kickoffs and victory celebrations, donor society balls (e.g., U.S. $1,000-a-year donor societies), and other special events. These can become imaginative events that people look forward to.   They have also become competitive with each other, more and more elaborate, and expensive.

d. Take Home: Donors are given gifts recognizing their own philanthropic gifts.   In Capital Campaigns, the upper level givers are usually given their gifts at the donor recognition banquets.   Such recognition gifts vary widely with the tastes and budgets of the institutions, from Steuben Glass sculptures to institutional neckties to medallions with the metals of which they are made signifying the gift level.   At lower levels of giving, some institutions have a wedding cake of donor premiums with a different premium for each gift level (e.g., National Public Radio), while others have rejected the smorgasbord of premiums entirely and have a single symbolic gift that goes to all donors over a certain level.

3) Recommendations for donor recognition:
    a. Keep it simple.   The wedding cake of donor premiums
works for National Public Radio (NPR) because it is a radio
medium.   Having a host of giveaways can cheapen the
appearance of the program and motivate donors only at the
very lowest levels.   The institutions that have gone to only
one donor gift have found that doing so has added a certain
cachet to the gift.
    b. Meaning beats Extravagance: It is counterproductive to
give donor gifts that are obviously expensive.   Donors want
the institution to spend money on the programs they are
supporting, not on the donors.   A gift that is imaginative,
inexpensive, and embodies something of the institution itself is
far more appreciated by donors.   Examples include museum
quality *reproductions* of small dinosaur fossils or antiquities or
a limited-edition expedition patch generally only awarded to
field team members.
    c. Involve Donors in Event Planning but don't let them get out
of hand.   Events tend to take on a life of their own and can get
out of control in expense and the tastes of one or two dominant
people.   But managed properly, volunteer donors planning
and decorating for a major event can be highly creative and
save a lot of money.
    d. Get Donor Input in the creation of donor walls and other
permanent donor recognition pieces.   There will always be
someone who does not like whatever is selected, so it is critical
to have the positive input from your most prominent and
supportive constituents who have a high degree of credibility
among the rest of your constituents.

VI. The Future Is Now--Donors of the 21ˢᵗ Century:

    At the Annual Fund Raising Congress of the Association of Fund
Raising Professionals' Toronto Chapter in November, 2002, Michael
Adams made an exceptionally insightful and provocative presentation
characterizing donors of the 21ˢᵗ century.[31]

---

[31] Adams is president of Environics Research Group in Canada (http://erg.environics.net/). He is author of
Better Happy Than Rich and *Sex in the Snow*, which provide a unique view on social change in Canada.

His annual surveys, begun in 1983, focused on 2,600 Canadians 15 years of age and older. Three hundred questions measured more than a hundred values, motivations, and socio-cultural characteristics. His conclusions provide valuable insight into Canadian donors, and a tantalizing expectation of research to come in the U.S. and elsewhere.

His research found people grouped into quadrants characterized by the following "mental postures":

1) Social Success, Materialism, and Pride;
2) Security, Stability, and Exclusion;
3) Experience and Personal Development; and
4) Autonomy and Well-Being.

Interestingly, age groups did not congregate, as one might expect, homogenously into one or another quadrant, but were spread throughout the four quadrants of mental postures. They clustered into groups he characterized as "tribes" and described by their icons, their shibboleths, and sometimes irreverent characterizations of their giving priorities.

The context of social change and philanthropy in which these "tribes" demonstrate their priorities and shape their futures is one in which the dominant characteristics are 1) globalization, and 2) a more competitive society in which some of the "tribes" lose and some win - a society in which, as he puts it, "ethics have been privatized."   Within this context, Adams describes "socio-cultural mega-currents" as "increasing emphasis on money and celebrity, more everyday life stress, and a quest for meaning."

In the past, Adams observes, "philanthropy was motivated by guilt, *noblesse oblige*, and a Christian sense of duty."   And, he adds, "It was often conspicuous."

As for the future of philanthropic giving, Adams offers six factors that will motivate giving:

1) Personal choice and control:

Donors will be less prone to accept the values handed down to them and support philanthropically the institutions that perpetuate those values, notable traditional churches.   They will be more apt to support institutions focused on the development of a present and future world that is the type of world the donors would wish their children to inhabit.

The authors gratefully acknowledge his notes in preparing this section and that the materials are used with his express written permission.

2) Desire to make a difference:

Donors will not simply want to contribute "to a good cause."   Their giving
will be motivated by much more than the size of their income and the tax
deductibility of their gifts.   They will, in the mentality of Investment
Philanthropy, want to contribute to institutions that offer tangible evidence
of effecting positive change.

3) [Expectation of] measurable results:

The donors of the 21st century will expect more accountability from the
institutions to which they contribute.   Their satisfaction in giving will not
end with the gift, but will be dependent on the success of the institution
demonstrating a job well done with empirical evidence.

4) Quest for intensity, experience, and escape:

The vitality of the donor of the 21st century will be manifest in his/her
fundamental desire for a better experience.   As institutions and
organizations focused on exploration seek to strike the responsive chord and
resonate with these donors, this aspect of their mentality will be to such
institutions' favor.

5) More fun, more spontaneous, with immediate emotional gratification
   for the individual:

These donors will not be "all work and no play."   Across the age groups of
Adams' research, from the pre-Baby Boomers to the young, the old Puritan
work ethic as the dominant focus of one's life is clearly fading from view.

6) And it will be less ostentatious, although philanthropists still need
   recognition.

So in order to strike that responsive chord with these "tribes" of donors,
there will clearly be a shift from status to meaning in the presentations of
the Case for Support and in the recognition of donors' support. [32]

---

[32] Cf. Our Summary Chapter for comments on donor trends within a global context.

VII. Conclusion:

The simplistic stereotypes of donor motivations, the focus on institutional needs before the values and priorities of the donor, and sit-across-the-desk-and-ask-for-the-gift solicitation approach, are giving way to a cultivated institution-donor relationship that is

- more donor focused,
- more of a continuum than a series of steps leading up to an "ask" and then hitting a plateau, and
- more dynamic and interactive.

As donors seek both more meaning and more accountability, the institutions focused on scientific exploration are going to have to be more exploratory of their prospective donors' values, their priorities, and their aspirations, in order to strike the responsive chords in them that will result in sustained support.

With regard to donors, the challenge for institutions focused on exploration will be to be *exceptions* to the Confucian saying:

> The traveler to far off places
> Finds only what he brings with him.

***

Bibliography for Chapter 4

"Donors as Individuals - Investment Philanthropy and the Psychology of the Invitation"

Alpert, Mark. "Making Money in Space: Exploring the solar system turns out to be the easy part. The next great challenge will be creating profitable space enterprises." *Scientific American Presents The Future of Space Exploration Quarterly*, Volume 10, Number 1 (Spring, 1999), 92-95.

Argyris, Chris. "Good Communication That Blocks Learning." *Harvard Business Review*, July/August, 1994, pp. 78-85.

The Center on Philanthropy at Indiana University. *Giving USA.* Indianapolis, Indiana: AAFRC Trust for Philanthropy, 2001.

Interview. *New York Times*, November 18, 2002, p. 23.

Keel, Donald S. *"Chapter Three*: Investment Philanthropy & the Psychology of the Invitation," pp. 41-55 in *Into the Field: Strategies for Funding Exploration— Proceedings of the Conference held at Nesbitt Hall, College of Design Arts, Drexel University, Philadelphia, PA on 20-21 April 1996*, edited by P.J. Capelotti, Ph.D. Philadelphia: The Philadelphia Chapter of The Explorers Club, March, 1997.

Kelly, Kathleen S. "Commentary: The Top Five Myths Regarding Nonprofits." www.prsa.org/Publications/magazines/Tactics/0800comm1.html.

Panas, Jerold. *Mega Gifts: Who Gives Them, Who Gets Them.* Chicago, Illinois: Pluribus Press, 1984.

Prince & Associates. "Profile: Wealthy Donors to Environmental Organizations." *The Chronicle of Philanthropy*, April 5, 1994, p. 14.

_____. "Profile: Wealthy Donors to Museums." *The Chronicle of Philanthropy*, September 20, 1994, p. 12.

_____. "Profile: Wealthy Donors to Zoos and Aquariums." *The Chronicle of Philanthropy*, May 31, 1994, p. 10.

Schwartz, Tony. *The Responsive Chord.* New York: Anchor Press/Doubleday, 1973.

Shin, Elizabeth. "New Study Details Giving Habits, Preferences of High-Tech Millionaires." *The Chronicle of Philanthropy*, May 17, 2001, p. 29.

Vartorella, William F. "Don your pith helmets, here come the donors." *The Explorers Newsletter*, Volume 31, Number 1 (January-March, 1999), 9-10.

_____. "Exploring Inner Space: the Mind of the Donor." *Human Performance in Extreme Environments*, Volume 3, Number 1 (September, 1998), 113-116.

*****

Chapter 5: "Corporate Consciousness, Corporate Culture"

By William F. Vartorella

> *"My formula for success? Rise early, work late, strike oil."*
> *J. Paul Getty*

I. Introduction:

When corporate executives discuss "global warming," it usually concerns their business, rather than the natural environment. Their focus is growth of global "hot spots" that offer the best opportunities for commerce and the creation of wealth.

Where companies locate subsidiaries during the early 21st century could have a profound impact upon the ability of indigenous scientists to attract corporate volunteers, in-kind contributions (equipment and supplies), access to the Information Superhighway, and cash grants.[1]

Briefly, these regions of opportunity are categorized as "cool," "warm," or "hot" spots. [2]

Natural history museums--some 6,500 worldwide--and the diversity of their scientific research are a "sentry species" in terms of measuring the overall health of the funding climate globally.

In the cool zone, e.g., that with the least expected growth, is much of Africa and the Middle East. The existence of fragile economies, relative isolation, unstable governments, and high poverty means transnational companies will adopt a "wait-and-see" posture in terms of investment. Adapting a simple overlay using Professor Michael A. Mares table of "Demographic and Museum Data for the World" [3] indicates that--excluding South Africa--nearly 140 Natural History Museums have the potential for falling even farther behind in terms of *access* to funding partners--in this

---

[1] William F. Vartorella, "Creating Sustainable Funding for Natural History Collections in the New World Order--Foundations and Corporations: Old Allies, New Opportunities," *Museum Management and Curatorship* (England), Volume 15, No. 3 (September, 1996), 330.

[2] Chart--"Global Warming" in *"CIO* 100 World Leaders," *CIO,* August, 1996, p. 38.

[3] Michael A. Mares, "Natural History Museums: Bridging the Past and the Future" in *Int. Symp. & First World Congress on Pres. and Cons. of Nat. Hist. Col.--Vol. 3,* 367-404.

case, corporations.

Eastern Europe & the former Soviet Union fare a bit better as "Warm Spots," with Poland and Romania expected to experience strong multi-national business growth. In spite of the competition of other nonprofits and NGOs, some 350 Natural History Museums in strategic locations such as the port of Constanta, Romania could reap real benefits as transnational companies begin the process of improving infrastructure and employee amenities. Western Europe, Japan, and the United States also fall within the "warm" zone, as high deficits and mature markets offer only marginal investment incentive.

South America, on the other hand, is as hot as a chili pepper. Brazil, Mexico, and Argentina are the chief targets. The roughly 200 Natural history museums there could benefit markedly, depending upon the kind of industry and a museum collection's ability to meet specific marketing plans and corporate Visions.

In the "hot" regions, especially, a robust infusion of corporate investment philanthropy would mean the creation of "communities of interest"--a technical term meaning zones of philanthropy for local, regional, or national giving.

Many of the key indicators for such a trend were already in place, pre-September 11th in the United States.

According to a Conference Board report in 1993, much of the American corporate philanthropy was focused in Western Europe (42%) and Canada (22%). Africa (15%), South America (12%), and the Pacific Rim (9%) filled out the equation. "Education" was the central thrust with 33% of the donations. The biggest problem experienced by American companies, unlike their global counterparts, was an apparent inability to evaluate the impact of the overseas grants or to deal effectively with the cultural differences. (See the Conference Board, "Global Contributions of U.S. Corporations").

By the mid-1990s, American corporations had "begun to build up reserves in their company foundations." [4]

The year 2000 saw corporate gifts from 207 U.S. corporate giants to U.S. nonprofits totaling U.S. $3.9 *billion* and U.S. $2.8 *billion* offshore, according to the Conference Board.[5] Yet, detailed analysis indicated

---

[4] Anonymous, "Companies Forecast First Significant Increases in Giving in 5 Years," *The Chronicle of Philanthropy*, September 21, 1995, p. 12.

[5] David Whelan, "Corporate Giving Rose in 2000, Survey Finds," *The Chronicle of Philanthropy*, January 24, 2002, p. 11.

companies were giving just one percent (1%) of their pre-tax profits, [6] well *below* the long-standing "theoretical threshold" used by many in the nonprofit world to measure vitality of corporate giving. Regardless of the Conference Board's cautionary notes regarding less future growth and even a decline in corporate donations, the median international gift was **U.S. $1.1 million**--up 28% from 1999. [7]

In September of 2001, *CFO* reported its "Global Confidence Survey Results" from finance executives in the U.S., Europe, and Asia. Some 72% were "confident or very optimistic about the global economy during the next five years."[8] By region, 78% of European executives polled reflected this attitude, with some 59% in the Asian segment equally inclined. [9] The U.S. results mirrored the global outlook.

Then came September 11th, accounting scandals, and a roller coaster ride on the global stock market.

In October, 2001, Cone, Inc.--a Boston, Massachusetts/U.S. consulting firm--released a study centered on consumer attitudes toward corporate citizenship based upon the results of two surveys conducted by the research firm, RoperASW, during the pre- and post- September 11th periods. Perhaps most telling was the result in October, that some 63% of those polled believed "A company's commitment to causes is important when deciding which stocks and mutual funds to invest in," compared with 40% responding to the question in March, 2001. [10]

Other data aside, corporations are intent upon acquiring, retaining, and nurturing investors. Investor interest in a company being perceived as a "good neighbor"--as we shall see below--is an integral part of the marketing and promotion mix, especially with the growing interest in applying "social filters/lenses" as part of the investment decision by individuals.

So, what does this all mean and where are the opportunities for scientists to secure funding? In the 19th century, "Go West, young man," was America's advice. In the 21st century, our long-view is east to Asia (more on that next Chapter).

---

[6] *Ibid.*

[7] *Ibid.*

[8] M.L., "Newswatch--Global Confidence Survey: Legends of the Fall," *CFO*, September, 2001, p. 26.

[9] *Ibid.*

[10] Debra E. Blum, "After the Attacks: Consumers Choose Products Based on Corporate Philanthropy, Studies Find," *The Chronicle of Philanthropy*, November 29, 2001, p. 24.

Unlike American-based companies, for example, which are traditionally less "strategic" in their giving ("get-off-the-grass" grants to local nonprofits), truly global corporations see philanthropy as an extension of marketing. Cultural differences aside (primarily because global companies usually function within local subsidiary cultures rather than externally), global corporations tend to focus their efforts on the following:[11]

1) Roughly 90% are community-focused, looking at local institutions.
2) Educational institutions are a top priority with nearly one-third --primarily as a function of reaping the benefits of research related to their industry or their parent companies.
3) Nearly 7% of all donations have an **environmental focus**-- unlike American companies, which target only 1% of their total philanthropy within this category.
4) Employee volunteerism is highly encouraged and--at least within the U.S.--some 48% of foreign firms match charitable donations made by workers.

This is occurring at time when American companies are reexamining their philanthropic support offshore.

Today, we may expect a re-shift of these resources as American transnationals look at "Emerging Markets for U.S. Companies" and make contributions based on their decisions. While global companies are quick to adjust to these market opportunities, American companies have become more "reflective." As noted by Craig Smith, an expert on corporate giving, in the *Harvard Business Review* (see May-June, 1994 issue), "the strategic use of philanthropy has begun to give companies a powerful competitive edge."

Unfortunately, in an era in which American corporate profits range from solid to unstable, CEOs are attempting to pare their philanthropic budgets and downsizing staffs. American corporate "leadership" in the global philanthropy arena may well be on the wane. Who fills that vacuum in the short-term is uncertain.

---

[11] Vartorella, "Creating Sustainable Funding for Natural History Collections," 331-332.

II. It's a Vision Thing:

> "Mission statements are the operational, ethical, and financial guiding lights of companies. They are not simply mottoes or slogans; they articulate the goals, dreams, behavior, culture and strategies of companies."
>
> *Say It and Live It: The 50 Corporate Mission Statements That Hit the Mark* by Patricia Jones and Larry Kahaner [12]

According to Alan Farnham, writing in *Fortune*, by at least one estimate, more than half of the companies in the U.S. now have a Vision or Mission Statement of some description.[13] Moreover, in a survey reported in the *Journal of Business Strategy* of 500 people at 460 companies in all industries--one-third of which had corporate sales in excess of U.S. $2 *billion*--Bain & Company/Boston demonstrated that Mission Statements were the #1 tool used in corporate culture over a five-year period. It out-distanced customer surveys and total quality management and a host of buzz words and jargon.

While corporate honchos may not agree on which core values to espouse, *sharing* the stated values seems imperative. Gone are the halcyon days of the big-budget, staff-rich "Strategic Plan." In its place is the simple Mission Statement, which at least one isolated study (Charles A. Rarick and John Vitton) has linked with a 16.1% average return on stockholder equity for firms with them. For those without--the return was 9.7%.

Herein lies a cautionary tale for scientists: **the ability of a researcher to meet the goals and objectives of a donor company's Mission is first and foremost the best way to secure funding.**

Annual Reports are clearly the best source for getting a sense of Vision and also may disclose how many requests for corporate donations were received and the number funded (e.g., success rate of grant applicants). Yet, initial information often appears in the advertisements of global corporations or in special reports in publications such as *Fortune* magazine.

Beginning in the early 1990s, for example, some of the best, easily accessible summaries of corporate funding for science and education appeared in *Fortune*. Science educators could get a quick read and

---

[12] Alan Farnham, "Managing: Ideas & Solutions--Brushing Up Your Vision Thing," *Fortune*, May 1, 1995, p. 129.
[13] *Ibid.*

contact information for a host of companies including **Allied-Signal**, (then) **Amoco, Apple Computer, Atlantic Richfield, Bell Atlantic, Cray Research, Dow Chemical, Eastman Kodak, Ford Motor, General Electric, Monsanto, Shell Oil, Timken, Xerox**--and many others. [14]

The challenge is translating corporate iconography and Mission into fundable science.

Our stated viewpoint is simple.

If a corporation uses a specific scientific theme, image, or event (historic discovery, for example) in its advertising, promotion, or marketing, it should be prepared to support serious research consistent with that depiction.

Opportunities abound. Be creative in your approach to companies that choose to use your scientific specialty as "borrowed interest." Examples:

Anthropology:

"**Amazonas**. Fashion Capital of the World." Dramatic image of indigenous

Amer-Indian. "So if you're looking for the best in shoe products, remember the company that's named after a place where people wear no shoes." (Ad copy discusses Brazil, where the company apparently creates the base for its shoes.)

"It is a moment of triumph. When a treasure from the past, and the strength of your commitment to unveiling it, are thrust clearly into the light of day." (Female diver/archaeologist (?) with amphora.) **Omega Watches**.

"Are you having difficulty interpreting the choices in long distance communications?" (Close-up image of a petroglyph of two humans (?)

[one a shaman?] used by **Mitel**® **Enterprises**, which has a presence in Australia, Brazil, Germany, Hong Kong, Japan, Mexico, U.K., and U.S.)

---

[14] To get a sense of how *Fortune* provides specific information on science-related funding within an educational context, *begin* by looking at Susan E. Kuhn, "How Business Helps Schools, *Fortune/Special Issue*, Spring, 1990, pp. 93-94, 96, 98, 100, 102, 104, 106 and Nancy Ramsey, "How Business Can Help the Schools," *Fortune*, September 16, 1992, pp. 148, 150, 154, 156, 160, 162, 166, 168, 172, 174.

Biodiversity and the Environment:
"One small step for man, one giant leap for frogs, fish and turtles."
New Earth Wash Jeans™ are "made with low-sulfide dyes, biodegradable enzymes and less water to help protect our rivers and
streams." **(Wrangler**® Rugged Wear covers a number of bases --
biodiversity, conservation of resources, clean water.)

"In 25 years, we've never heard of a solar crisis. Bringing solar to over
160 countries. It's a start." **(BP**'s "beyond petroleum™" campaign
that also includes, "Take the time to stop and smell the reduction
of sulfur. Cleaner fuels in 40 cities. It's a start." See, also, **BP**'s
"Electric cars won't happen overnight. There's got to be a way
of making fuels cleaner," with image of writer Scott Takeda.
A rare, provocative campaign that focuses upon traditionally
"difficult-to-fund" science.)

"At **Wausau**, the programs we've developed protect all types of businesses--
from the most common to the rarest of breeds--against hazards in their
workplaces. The kinds of problems that could lead any company to
extinction." (Close-up photo of rhinoceros with a Wausau business
card stuck on its horn. Tagline is "What can we do to help you?"
Depending upon the species of rhino, a scientist's answer might be
"Plenty."[15] Address is Wausau Insurance Companies, 2000 Westwood
Drive, Wausau, WI 54401 U.S.A. Also, <http://www.wausau.com>.)

"Trust is not being afraid even if you're vulnerable." (Girl petting a
rhinoceros.) **The St. Paul** (property and liability insurance).

"There's a Better Breed of ASP. One you can trust." (Running rhino,
consistent with **Agilera**'s "Run with the swift. Stand with the
strong" campaign.)

---

[15] An example is the endangered desert black rhinoceros in Karoo National Park in South Africa. There, researchers cooperate with bushmen trackers, who use innovative handheld computer and software, CyberTracker (conceived by Louis Liebenberg), to record wildlife observations by touching icons of species/gender and animal behaviors on keypad. Fast, elegant, specific and system requires no "literacy" in the pencil-and-paper sense. Rhino images proliferate in advertising, unlike black rhino species. While corporations seem indiscriminate regarding which rhino species they chose for advertising ("borrowed interest"), the discriminating investigator such as Liebenberg--who sees CyberTracker as having broader monitoring applications worldwide--may want to leverage support from Ecofac, the EU conservation organization active in general region, with specific global companies using black rhino iconography.

"Sure, others fly south to Mexico and Latin America. Of course, we do it
over 340 times a week." (Migration of 11 avian species to countries
varying from Panama [American Kestrel] and El Salvador [White-
Faced Ibis] to Ecuador [Northern Waterthrush] and Colombia
[Scarlet Tanager]. This **Continental Airlines** ad is a rarity, with
illustrations befitting a field guide.)

"Every year, one of our investments has an average return of 15 million."
(Part of **Phillips Petroleum Company's** campaign on its
environmental partnerships, this one discusses its Playa Lakes Joint
Venture, U.S. where approximately 15 million migratory birds spend
their winters. In the fine print is contact information for the project.)

"(Breathtaking. Awesome. Incredible.) It's what people say about our
cruises. It's what agents say about our commission." (Image of
whale breaking the water in a *trade* publication ad for **American
Hawaii Cruises**®. This should resonate with cetacean groups
such as the Pacific Whale Foundation ["Adopt-a-Whale" Program]
or the coalition of scientists and the public involved in the Free Willy
/Keiko Foundation [Keiko of the "Free Willy" film   phenomenon].)[16]

"See them all." Few places support as much marine life diversity in such a
small space as the Caribbean" (26 marine species matched up (?)
with 25 Caribbean islands plus Mexico. Great chance to partner with
U.S. Airways *Caribbean* on a species or island-specific basis.)

Egyptology:
**2002 marked the 80th anniversary of Tutankhamun's tomb
discovery and the centennial of the founding of Cairo's Egyptian
Museum. Egyptology remains highly-fundable, if grossly under-funded.**

"If ancient Egyptians had had duct tape, the Sphinx would still have a
nose."   (**Miller Lite Beer**, U.S. Network Television Ad.)

---

[16] Often, it seems, donor information shows up in unusual places. See, for example, the detailed discussion of Keiko, the killer whale (*Orcinus orca*) in Susan Orlean's treatment, "Where's Willy? Everybody's favorite whale tries to make it on his own," *The New Yorker*, September 23, 2002, 56-63. Ms. Orlean names-names of key donors: **Warner Brothers, New Regency** (production company), **The Humane Society of the United States**, and the **Craig and Susan McCaw Foundation**. See, also, Doug Mellgren's report for The Associated Press, "'Free Willy' whale to winter in Norway," October 16, 2002.

"Are you all wrapped up in budgeting? **Comshare**® unravels the mystery."
(Throw-back to the old mummy films.) Comshare®: "ᵉBusiness
solutions for management planning & control."

"The Pharaohs knew how to keep their treasures safe and secure.
Shouldn't your company do the same?" (Pyramid, which is also
the stylized logo of **Epoch Internet**.ˢᵐ)

"Every once in a while a projector technology comes along that is so
monumental . . . it changes your point of view *forever*."
(Pyramids at Giza.) **JVC** Professional.

"If they could have called *Cold Spring*, they would have saved *face*."
(Sphinx, reference to missing nose.) **Cold Spring**: "quarriers and
fabricators of building stone and memorialization products."
(This is the kind of ad that should resonate with the consortium
working hard to Save the Sphinx.)

Image of hieroglyphic registers on packaging for **Pete's Wicked Red,
Amber Ale**. (One of the very, very few companies worldwide to
use ancient Egyptian language characters so dramatically. For
difficult-to-fund ancient Egyptian language research and related
conservation/preservation of the distinctive stone relief style,
this should be a prime candidate for focused discussion.)

"Once reserved for kings, Lapis now brings majesty to your writing."
(King Tut is the "borrowed interest" of this campaign for **Cross**®
and The Cross Townsend® Collection of fine, wide-diameter
writing instruments.)

"There are 7 Wonders of the World. But there's only one **Beefeater**.®
(Depiction of the Great Pyramid of Cheops, with "The 8th Wonder?
Beefeater and Tonic.")

"An irresistible package gets you through to the toughest customer."
(Image of Cleopatra rolled up in a rug for her surprise introduction
to Caesar.) **Westvaco** Envelope Division.

Basketball star Charles Barkley in an ancient Egyptian tomb setting for
U.S. television ad for **Right Guard**® Clear Gel, antiperspirant
deodorant.

"Announcing the most significant development in preserving bodies in the
last 3,000 years. The Simoniz system for preserving today's
precious bodies." (Play on mummification and the protective
qualities of **Simoniz** Non-Abrasive Car Wax for modern automotive
finishes.)

"How to Build a Pyramid." (Part of the long-standing, dramatic campaign
engineered for the financial services company, **Transamerica**:
"The power of the pyramid is working for you.")

"When the heat's on, you can trust us to perform." (Image of the pyramids
and the Matterhorn. Unusual juxtaposition, but excellent opportunity
for researchers in the European Union [EU] and, particularly,
Eastern Europe, where **Swiss Life** [employee benefit plans, etc.]
is active.)

Mountaineering:
"Nancy Feagin--World-renowned Rock Climber, climbing The Rostrum,
Yosemite Valley" and "Nancy Feagin--Training in Hunters Bowl,
British Columbia." (Comparison ad for **Tekware**, which reportedly
"dries dramatically faster than the cotton [T-shirt], making it
lighter and more comfortable." See "sponsorship" section, below,
re: high-profile team leaders and ability to secure sponsorship based
upon name recognition within market niche.)

"The next time you think about buying a tent that can withstand winter in the
Himalayas, ask yourself one question: When will I be spending
winter in the Himalayas?" (Ad for the Apollo™ tent by **Peak 1**®.)

"**Ford** Explorer. No boundaries." (Visually exciting television ad in 2002,
with what appears to be a horizontal Ford Explorer vehicle, which
actually is vertical, as demonstrated by rock climbers rappelling
alongside.)

"Xerox Chess Can Put You Here." (Close-up image of climber celebrating on mountain summit. **Xerox** Chess is a manufacturing support system that helps "market and manage" supply chain and inventory. Excellent opportunity to tie in Xerox, a global trademark, to a supply chain-"donor pool.")

Polar Studies:
"There's only one place tougher on tools than the North Pole. The South Pole." **Craftsman**® Makes Anything Possible®. (True business-to-Polar Studies connections are extremely rare. One approach: catalogue known suppliers to the various research stations active in Antarctica, create an overlay of local subsidiaries active in your "home town," and contact them with an urgent, compelling, and interesting case for support for three years' mentoring, in-kind gifts, and funding.)

Space:
"We know how to get you to the moon. **Fieldcrest Cannon** knows how to keep you comfortable while you're there." (An excellent example of two companies with global brands--**Lockheed Martin** and Fieldcrest Cannon--working together): "You don't have to be a rocket scientist to understand the strategic value of managing information."

"Helping NASA with its sensitive transportation needs . . . back on earth."
Mayflower® **International**. (More co-branding.)

"If it's in space, **Rockwell** probably put it there." (Plays upon name recognition with NASA and Rockwell's work with orbiters, the National Aero-Space Plane, GPS satellites, etc. Point here to explore is that industry leaders, like Rockwell, also have *other* divisions [telecommunications, avionics, automotive, etc.] that can participate in supporting your science. The obvious portal for approaching a company may not be the best one.)

"Where to find a 200-year-old company." (Part of a series, this **DuPont**® ad focuses upon Kevlar®, "the fiber that protects the International Space Station from space debris." Good entrée into projects that may need high-tech, special-applications fibers.)

Science and discovery are common themes in corporate advertising. They are harbingers of change and are an important adjunct to reference books and software on corporate funding trends [17] --which are snapshots of past funding.

Remember the anthropological dictum: "Absence of evidence is not evidence of absence." Just because funding does not seem to exist, based upon past corporate performance, does not mean that funding is not there.

Perhaps the greatest hidden opportunities lie within the ever-changing spheres of influence of the global automotive industry and its supply chain partners.[18]

Cars and rugged individualism, mixed with exotic locales and technological *machismo*, are the legendary "right stuff" of science and exploration imagery.[19]

A new breed of "captains of industry" has displaced colonial powers, which once carved up Africa or the Americas. As noted by Carlos Ghosn, **Renault-Nissan**, "Cultural clash does not exist only between two different countries. It exists between different companies, or even within the different departments of the same company." [20] Understanding this neo-colonialism

---

[17] A host of high-quality tools exist to assist scientists through the corporate funding maze. For example, see Aspen Publishers' latest edition of *Giving by Industry: A Reference Guide to the New Corporate Philanthropy* and its subscription newsletter, "Corporate Philanthropy Report." Electronic fundraising databases, which are available for purchase or on a fee/use basis, include GrantScape, *The Chronicle of Philanthropy*'s grants listing, and goods & services provided by The Foundation Center. Exotic, proprietary databases also exist, such as SPHINX--which provides a global view of funding for archaeology, bioanthropology, etc.

[18] "Hidden" may be the operative word here. Knowing how much money is ferreted away in the foundation accounts in Germany and the rest of Europe is difficult to gauge, as foundations there generally are not required to provide detailed disclosures of assets and expenditures. Foundations literally may often own controlling interests in companies. An example is Robert Bosch Foundation. It owns more than 90% of the shares in the electronics manufacturer (for automobiles, etc.) of the same name--a company that has annual revenue of easily U.S. $ 20 *billion*. The donor is as close as the dials on your Blaupunkt stereo, but as ethereal as the airwaves. The challenge is first, identifying the hidden wealth, and second, accessing it. See Vince Stehle, "European Philanthropy Experts Disagree on Rules for Giving in Era of Euro," *The Chronicle of Philanthropy*, May 21, 1998, p. 37.

[19] For insight into the Byzantine world of "angel investors," corporate shenanigans, and supply chain intrigue in the arena of cutting-edge automotive design, see Mark Christensen, *Super Car: The Story of the Xeno*. (New York: Thomas Dunne Books/St. Martin's Griffin, 2001). In it, Christensen and auto design genius Nick Pugh rush headlong against conventional wisdom in an effort to create a low budget, "perfect beast" with racecar handling and an environmental conscience. In the end, theirs is a cautionary tale of the perils and pleasures of radical design, the dangers of voodoo economics, and the lack of an identified constituency of donors/investors. The reader is left with "the cost of the car has nothing to do with its price" and other eternal automotive truths. This book is required reading for Big Idea engineers hell-bent upon raising serious project money. In short, it is a brilliant, edgy analysis of the three automotive pillars of form, function, and fundraising.

[20] Peter Nunn, "The New Automotive Universe 2000--The view from Asia," *Automobile Magazine*, July, 2000, p. 80.

and who-controls-whom is critical, as cars are ubiquitous--or crucial--in most land-based environments (including the moon).

Until **Daimler-Benz** swallowed **Chrysler** in May of 1998, the automotive industry, according to analyst Richard Feast, had evolved in a "Darwinian manner,"[21] with survival-of-the-fittest a constant challenge among weaker brands/marques. Then came sweeping evolutionary change, as **Bentley**, **Bugatti**, **Lamborghini**, **Land Rover**, **Rolls-Royce**, and **Volvo** changed hands.[22]

Of particular interest is Land Rover, which has assisted the Royal Geographical Society (with the Institute of British Geographers)--London, England--since 1977. The Society, which offers advice to some 500 young scientific expeditions annually, has received Land Rover support in a host of locales including Nepal, the Mkomazi Game Reserve in Tanzania, and the Bedouin communities of the semi-arid region of northwest Jordan.

Land Rover has made its reputation, perhaps, as the gutsy vehicle of choice by explorers and field scientists slogging through rugged, unforgiving terrain. That theme is the underpinning of various Land Rover campaigns, for example:

> "Sometimes you have to get out and push a Range Rover."
> (Image of an explorer poling a Range Rover on a raft across a
> jungle stream.) "And considering all that it has to offer, would
> you really want to be up the creek in anything else?"

Or, for the Defender 90, "Climbing down into the deep Copper Mines of Zambia, up the towering cliffs of the Hindu Kush, and bouncing across otherworldly savannas."

What Land Rover has done is transform its vehicles into a *lifestyle* of exploration and, consistent with this theme, has supported researchers at far-flung outposts of science.

Other car companies, such as **BMW** and **Mercedes-Benz** are equally active, albeit in different ways. BMW, with its U.S. presence in South Carolina, honors individuals in that State who have made "lifetime

---

[21] Richard Feast, "The New Automotive Universe 2000--as the dust settles, our stellar experts analyze the new order," *Automobile Magazine*, July, 2000, p. 76.

[22] Mark Dancey, "The New Automotive Universe 2000 (illustration)," *Automobile Magazine*, July, 2000, pp. 76-77. Up until July, 2000, this graphic (and article) may be the best general guide for the scientist trying to sort out how to best approach the automotive industry for funding.

contributions to protecting natural and cultural resources" with the BMW Conservation Award. BMW is recognized as an industry leader "in the production of environmentally sustainable vehicles."

Its ads include a spacesuit-clad scientist peering under the hood at BMW's 4.4-liter V8, extolled by the company as "possibly the best V8 in the universe. Or at least on this planet." Considering the financial needs of researchers intent upon creating the next generation of spacesuits-- "cat-suits" (lightweight, mobile suits whose joints do not accumulate lunar or planetary dust which render them useless)--and BMW's focus on driver ergonomics, this is an excellent example of how "borrowed interest" might be translated into a joint project. This is particularly true, as the BMW plant in the U.S. is situated within the midst of the U.S. textile industry's high-tech research and development (R&D) corridor, where world-class expertise in textiles abounds. (Add to this the DuPont example above, plus IBM's DB2® campaign with spacesuit-clad scientists and you can see how a creative fundraising effort could attract high-profile, world-class brands in several needed disciplines: ergonomics, textiles, computing.)

Mercedes-Benz U.S.A. is equally active in the sustainable future of automobiles, with work going back at Mercedes until at least 1991 with its very high-tech F 100 study automobile.

Plus, parent DaimlerChrysler ties into the spacesuit example above, with its long-standing aerospace interests, to wit:

"May 4, 1971: Yet another company creates an off-road vehicle by copying Jeep® technology." (Using a NASA image of the lunar rover, the ad reads, "The only 4x4s with the kind of inspired technology that not only excels off-road but off-Earth as well!." What stitches this ad nicely into our broader discussion is that **Boeing**, in fact, created the three Lunar Rovers that racked up a total of 55 "moon miles" for the three Apollo moon crews from July, 1971 to December, 1972.[23])

Specifically, Daimler-Chrysler's Department for Analysis of Vehicle Functions has a world-class virtual program that looks at simulated "events" (read: "accidents") in roughly 150,000 tiny time intervals that equal one-tenth/second in a real event. Furthermore, researchers can render opaque components transparent through animation, thereby revealing hidden part

---

[23] D.C. Agle, "Rover Boys: Three crews of Apollo astronauts experienced an out-of-this-world driving adventure," *AutoWeek,* July 30, 2001, p. 17.

deformation. By implication, scientists could overlay and develop spacesuit designs consistent with safety and crew comfort dynamics within the reduced gravity of lunar or planetary landscapes.

And do not discount the funding possibility that what may be good for the automotive manufacturers, like **General Motors (GM),** may well be good for the environment. The Tellus Institute, Boston, showed GM how to reduce chemical use in its 60 North American facilities by 30%, thereby saving the automaker U.S. $ millions of dollars and providing it a platform for discussion of its environmental record.[24]

In short, piecing together advertising themes consistent with hard science can pay dividends, especially if analysis of corporate funding environments (via Mission Statements, Annual Reports, grants software) indicates general or specific interest in your avenue of research.[25]

Jaguar Cars probably understands this viewpoint as well as anyone, and, as we shall see in the sponsorship section later this Chapter, is the Big Cat that helps the Big Cat in the rainforest.

III. Striking Oil in the New World Order:
Expeditions in the late 20th Century were confused.

---

[24] Former GM president, Charles E. Wilson, in his famous U.S. Congressional testimony some 50 years ago as part of his nomination for U.S. Secretary of Defense noted, "what was good for our country was good for General Motors and vice versa." Today, automakers like GM and Ford Motor Company are looking at the interface between cost-saving measures and environmental responsibility. Issues such as renewable energy sources and recycling, climate change, greenhouse-gas emissions, and hybrid strategies have changed the public dialogue about automobiles. From our perspective, scientists with interest and expertise in these issues should approach automakers with partnership proposals that include mentoring, technology-sharing, and cash--our standard scenario for support. Mercedes-Benz U.S.A., for example, actively supports student teams at universities who build and race full-size, open-wheel electric cars (i.e., e-Bobcat Racing--Ohio University) and share their data and technological tweaking in seminars. For a broader discussion across several industries, see the provocative article by Michael Anft, "Toward Corporate Change: Businesses seek nonprofit help in quest to become better citizens," *The Chronicle of Philanthropy*, September 19, 2002, pp. 9, 12, 10.

[25] Other car companies are equally intriguing as potential corporate partners. To name just a few: **Audi**--("The Eastern Desert, June 1. The first time I made my own road, spoke a language I didn't know, got lost on purpose, measured time in cups of mint tea."--Egypt, Giza Plateau.)--The choice of an unusual camera angle for the placement of the Audi all-road quattro coincides with the depiction by one of Napoleon's artists in *Description de l'Égypte* and should resonate with researchers interested in the smaller queens' pyramids. **Mazda**--("Is your car an invertebrate?")--Dinosaur display in a formal museum setting. Natural history museums take note. **Toyota**--("Today: A vehicle whose only emission is pure water. Tomorrow: Enjoy driving with the window down again.")--Very high-tech, with a discussion of an advanced fuel cell for "the world's first commercially available, hydrogen-powered vehicles." Separate from its regular corporate contributions efforts, on its 30th anniversary in the U.S. (1987), Toyota established its Toyota USA Foundation with "Pursuit of Excellence" as its central theme. Educational projects strong in mathematics and science have long interested this global company.

"*Derring-Do*" was the adventure-related Expedition model that probably died out as a viable fundraising approach with the discovery of the tomb of Tutankhamen in 1922 -- an act that bridged the gap between Discovery and the emergence of Expeditions as Science with a **truly global public following**.

From that day forward, it seems, companies have been intent upon scientific inquiry capable of providing them a platform for selling their goods and services to specific markets, complete with all the trappings of corporate good citizenship and image-building.

The model we advocate is one of "*daring deals*," in which Extreme Exploration or laboratory science is tied to entrepreneurship where return on investment (ROI) is, in itself, a potentially "peak experience" and may be measured as much in image-enhancement as raw cash.

With that said, it is appropriate to examine the Corporate Old World Order and emerging New World Order for the *Third Millennium*.[26]

21st Century Trends in Corporate Philanthropy

Terms	Old World Order	New World Order
Philosophy	Philanthropy at arm's length; business issues central focus	Synergistic link of public interest and business
Mission/Vision Statement	Nonexistent or marginalized	Crucial
Key Player	CEO; "founder"	Multi-layered: CEO, strategic marketing team
Causes	Viewed in isolation; formula: 40% education, 30% health and human services, 10% arts, etc.	Market-driven considerations: global/local, "green issues," "cultural values," and "access issues"
Science and Exploration	"Derring-do": combination of high adventure and science	"Daring Deals: central to core corporate culture and image building; science, patents, and layperson as consumer of products and images
	"Big Bang Theory of Giving:" high profile; big-bang-for-the buck invested	"Steady State Theory of Giving": evolving, Big Ideas, big picture vision, consistent with research and development (R&D)
Type/Support	80% cash & 20% other	60% cash, with rest split; gear, expertise -- all tied to corporate volunteers
The Giving Mechanism	Old United Way model in the U.S., *noblesse oblige* globally	Consortial, fluid, and reflecting cultural diversity

---

[26] William F. Vartorella, "Exploring Inner Space: the Mind of the Donor," *Human Performance in Extreme Environments*, Volume 3, Number 1 (September, 1998), 114. Our book's chart is an evolution of this earlier rendering and text.

Ƒᴜɴᴅɪɴɢ Ɛxᴘʟᴏʀᴀᴛɪᴏɴ | Cʜᴀᴘᴛᴇʀ Ƒɪᴠᴇ

Decision Process	"Reactive grant-making"	"Proactive opportunities
	"Where are problems?"	and Strategic Marketing"
	Unfocused, spontaneous	Focused; central to Mission/Vision Statement
Timing of Request	Quarterly or Annual Cycles	Entrepreneurial, opportunistic
Budgets	% of Pre-tax income	Benefit to business
Evaluation	"Hit-and-Miss"	Management by Objectives (MBO)
Average Grant	Less than $5,000 in *Fortune 500*	More than $30,000 in *Fortune 500*

Source: Vartorella's variation on Craig Smith with additional credit to Robyn J. Sole

The major points here are these:

1) While average cash amount may be rising, companies increasingly demand Management with Objectives (accountability), more consortial attention, participation by company executives as volunteers, and a return to core corporate and societal values in the public (and company's) vital interests.

2) Corporations worldwide are paying more than "lip service" to Vision and Mission Statements. Companies see these as defining moments, with the context the constituencies and niches they hope to attract in the global-local marketing wars of the 21st century. In the words of the late U.S. General George S. Patton, "A good plan executed right now is far better than a perfect plan executed next week." Companies are looking for "Steady State" opportunities--long-range, focused, and accountable.

3) *Noblesse oblige* and paternalism of a "company town" have given way to much more streamlined, entrepreneurial models. In the Old World Order and Economy, companies used "get-off-the-grass" grants of U.S. $5,000 as a minimalist approach to philanthropy. ("Here is $5,000-- best of luck.") That has changed, especially for scientists with potential patents, who can-- and should--enter funding negotiations with companies through both a traditional corporate giving portal *and* a marketing side of the company.

4) Further, the 2% giving ceiling has been replaced by more fluid, dynamic market-driven considerations in "communities of interest"--e.g., cities or countries where transnational companies have facilities and/or major customers. This means a combination of giving that emphasizes both social responsibility and market forces.

5) In the wake of corporate malfeasance and creative accounting practices,

shareholders who have suddenly seen their retirement plans vanish, now require company philanthropy to be part of the broader effort to improve the "bottom line" and dividends.

6) Finally, the company's founder and patriarch is taking a more consensual role, working with senior management to see how being a "good neighbor" through philanthropy is smart business.

How, then, do you **market** your science in this ever-changing, chaotic environment?

The answer is simple: Through a three-tiered request strategy.

1) Corporate Volunteers: the first step--engage the interest of company executives in the project; seek assistance with technical tasks; goal is for them to have a **personal stake** and interest in expedition's success; Asian companies increasingly require this step, prior to being asked for further assistance.

2) In-kind contributions of gear, supplies, or other infrastructure; goal is to secure *loans* of gear, donations of expendable supplies, and other kinds of infrastructure--lent vehicles, seats on corporate jets, offshore lodging, etc.

3) Cash: the "Final Frontier," and usually seen as the most important by expeditions, particularly for unusual costs and "bail-out" money "up-country" when the volcano erupts.

Clearly, the key is "positioning." Corporations expect Extreme Expeditions to come prepared with a financial prospectus, not a pith helmet. An expedition must know the relative *monetary* value of Discovery, especially as it translates into patents, new processes, and *access* to new markets or opinion leaders. It also must know the value of manageable risks.

Case Study #5-a: IBM

IBM's support of unusual, high-tech science in fields ranging from archaeology to historic preservation and use of that philanthropic iconography in advertising is an example of seamless global marketing and "good citizenship".

For example, in 1965, IBM helped spearhead what became the successful Akhenaten Temple Project that led to the identification, orientation, matching, and assembly of some 283 Karnak *talatat* into a wall in the new Luxor Museum. The *talatat* –(building blocks) depict a colored relief of offering-bearers and servants performing duties in temple offices. As noted by the late Egyptologist Cyril Aldred, some 40,000 *talatat*, "sculptured in sunk relief and often bearing traces of brilliant color, as well as a rather greater number of plain blocks of similar size" presented a jigsaw puzzle of enormous complexity.[27]

Essentially, using IBM technology over a period of six field seasons, investigators photographed each sculptured surface of the *talatat* and entered the specifics of each scene on IBM punch cards for matching by computer. The result: mosaics of scenes emerged, functionally reconstructing by computer selected "destroyed" reliefs of the Aten temples.

IBM's recent advertising campaign, "Solutions for a Small Planet™", continued this motif with evocative images of painstaking physical anthropology at Thomas Quarry, Casablanca, Morocco and a stonemason at Germany's Frauenkirche church, Dresden, which was destroyed during Allied bombing in 1945.

The advertisements read, in part--

"In Casablanca, a sliver of bone revealed a chunk of history when Dr. Jean-Jacques Hublin unearthed a few fossilized skull fragments. Then Hublin and a team of IBM scientists fed this shattered 3-D jigsaw puzzle into a unique program called Visualization Data Explorer.™ The tiny pieces helped form an electronic reconstruction of our early ancestor, the first *Homo sapiens*. This new IBM technology has turned time back 400,000 years, uncovering clues to the origins of mankind."

And,

"Where Bach and Wagner once performed, there now lies only broken rock. But recently, stonemason Franz Huber and a team of other artisans and architects began to painstakingly resurrect the city's symbol of harmony. Once IBM reconstructed the Baroque landmark in 3-D cyberspace, the team could begin to rebuild the ruins.

By 2006, the church will reach to the heavens once more, thanks to 18th-century craftsmanship and a powerful 21st-century tool."

In Italy, IBM joined forces with the Vatican Library and the Pontifical Catholic University of Rio de Janeiro in Brazil to reproduce digitally and electronically store selected works of the Library's more than 150,000 manuscripts and one million printed books. The pilot study phase (1994) copied some 20,000 images, including a 15th-century Latin manuscript about medicinal herbs and a 16th-century Aztec Indian

---

[27] Cyril Aldred, *Akhenaten: King of Egypt* (London: Thames and Hudson Ltd., 1989), p. 81.

manuscript--one of the few remaining written works from that pre-Columbian society.[28]

Once the images passed quality assurance (QA) checks at the Vatican and at IBM/U.S., they were sent to the Pontifical Catholic University in Brazil, which served as the Internet gateway. For copyright protection, the rare computer images each received a digital watermark ("video mark"). Only 2,000 scholars currently visit the 500-year-old Vatican Library, whose priceless holdings include Ptolemy's *Geography*, annually. Depending upon how the project ultimately progresses, selected works may be available to literally millions of viewers via the Internet.

In short, this brief Case Study reiterates that "access issues" --particularly to evolving technology and the Internet--resonate with corporate citizens in a global economy.

IV. Sponsorships:

American humorist Mark Twain is reputed to have once responded to a question about tainted money with "The money may be tainted, but it taint enough."

The daunting challenge for some scientists is to decide whether a sponsorship opportunity means accepting money from a corporation whose goods, services, or business practices may be perceived as controversial or socially irresponsible in some circles.

The stakes are enormous, as more than **3,500 companies worldwide** have more than a decade's experience with serious sponsorships and are seemingly always on the prowl for new opportunities that meet their corporate Missions.

Conservationist Jane Goodall, whose research has involved animal behavior/chimpanzees and the need to conserve their natural African habitats,took the trailblazing position in the early 1990s that contributions from controversial companies may well have a better chance of promoting change.[29] Specifically, the Jane Goodall Institute worked with sponsor **Conoco** to help establish a sanctuary for endangered chimpanzees. At issue was not only Conoco's reputation for environmental responsibility *vis-à-vis* other oil companies, but whether this sponsorship could be leveraged into broader change within the corporate culture of its parent company, **E.I. DuPont de Nemours**.

Reportedly, the result was increased dialogue on a host of issues, including the use of animals in pharmaceutical research.

---

[28] Vera Haller (with Hay Amicone), "Scribes in Cyberspace," *Beyond Computing*, October, 1995, p. 20.
[29] Holly Hall, "Joint Ventures With Business: A Sour Deal?," *The Chronicle of Philanthropy*, April 6, 1993, p. 21.

Other positive examples abound, not the least of which is **Royal Caribbean** Cruise Line's "Ocean Fund," which provides researchers financial support for studies involving coral reefs, effluent discharge from cruise ships, anchor "drag," and related "green issues."

Essentially, Royal Caribbean has positioned itself as a proactive, rather than reactive company in a symbiotic relationship with the coral reefs and sanctuaries in the Caribbean Basin.

In recent survey results released by The Pew Charitable Trusts (Sea Web Initiative), Americans indicated overwhelmingly,

- our oceans are deteriorating (60% of respondents)
- the destruction of the oceans is a threat to quality-of-life (85%)
- we are dumping too much into the oceans today in the form of "wastes, oil, and agricultural run-off" (80%).

Source: Mellman Group for Sea Web, 1997

The Caribbean Basin has nearly 100 protected areas and culturally and environmentally sensitive destinations/ports-of-call. As an example, St. Lucia's Maria Islands Nature Reserve marine park is ranked as a high regional priority requiring management support in a recent World Conservation Union (IUCN) report.

This is also consistent with the view of Seacology (Berkeley, California USA) that island ecosystems are biological catastrophes, in terms of biota extinctions. According to Duane Silverstein, Executive Director, in the last 400 years some 90% of plant extinctions and 50% of animal extinctions have occurred on islands. Worse hit have been birds--an astonishing 90% of bird species extinctions.[30] (Researchers take note: in the U.S. in 2002, **Shell Oil** ran a "Waves of Change" television ad that focused on an *island* and *bird species*.)

A fertile area of research, cruise data currently fail to present a systematic picture of market growth and usage patterns within the Caribbean Basin as they impact the biotic and cultural diversity of protected areas.

Royal Caribbean Ocean Fund's geographic interest, leadership in marine science education, and its realization that strong coral reef science maintains biodiversity and assists cruise lines in "treading lightly" near

---

[30] See "Islands at Risk," a letter from Duane Silverstein in "Airmail," *Condé Nast Traveler*, at <www.cntraveler.com>. Also, worldwide, the United Nations Development Programme estimates that 11% of the 9,675 bird species are at significant risk of extinction. See, Anonymous, "Matters of Fact," UNDP *Choices*, Volume 12, Number 2 (June, 2002), p. 28.

sensitive areas may ultimately lead to unified coral-friendly planning on a policy level. Plus, the long view of islands as genetic sanctuaries may evolve as productive dialogue. Regardless, islands and coral reefs are fundable icons, particularly with those companies whose livelihoods depend upon their preservation.

Consider this: tourism is *the* largest industry in the world and generates **U.S. $2 *trillion* a year** in spending. In most countries, tourism is the nation's largest industry. And, if you look specifically at the rapidly expanding adventure segment, ecologically friendly ("green") hotel chains and tour operators abound. They are poised to support science and discovery that protect the environment.

A partial list of "green" hotels, for example, includes

Accor
Canadian Pacific Hotels & Resorts
Conrad International Hotels
Forte Plc
Hilton International Corporation
Holiday Inn Worldwide
Inter-Continental Hotels Group
ITT Sheraton
Marriott Lodging Group
Omni Hotels International
Ramada International Hotels & Resorts
Ritz-Carlton® **Hotel Company, L.L.C.**
Societé des Hotels Maridien
Sonesta.

Sonesta, with its worldwide hotels (Curaçao, U.S., etc.), has long been a leader in supporting ecology and in featuring biodiversity and the relationship of their properties in their advertising. Sonesta's evocative moonlight ad about giant sea turtles "that come to lay their eggs outside our doors" is illustrative of the kind of commitment and opportunity that "green" hotels offer to scientists in specific specialties.

Hilton Taba Resort (Sinai, Egypt) provides visitors with a brochure, "How to Protect the Environment of the Red Sea." It details not only Hilton's commitment in the Sinai (desalination of sea water, use of solar energy, biodegradable products, etc.), but offers clear guidelines for visitors enjoying their properties ("do not touch coral which grows 1-8 cm per year," no spearfishing, respect the privacy of the native Bedouin population, etc.).

Others, like **South Sinai Travel**, take a broader perspective, supporting efforts to research and conserve the antiquities of Egypt, while developing environmentally sound properties near the Ras Mohammed National Park (and other ecotourism venues).[31]

Some hotels have teamed up with credit card issuers, donating a specific sum to an environmental NGO every time a guest used the card to pay her/his bill.

NOTE: unfortunately, there is no absolutely systematic standard for measuring "green" globally in hotels, lodges, and other visitor "way-stations." A number of monitors exist--Ecotel®, Green Globe (based on the standards drafted at the 1992 Rio Earth Summit), and regional "certifiers" such as Australia's National Ecotourism Accreditation Program, Scandanavia's Nordic Swan, and Costa Rica's Certificate of Sustainable Tourism. Yet, put in a positive light, this lack of universal guidelines opens the door for scientists to present cutting-edge sponsor opportunities that "stretch the envelope" for research and sustainable development at tourism facilities whose doorsteps are the rainforest, coral reefs, arctic tundra, deserts (Sahara), and serene mountain peaks of the world. [32]

Even the amenities in hotel rooms deserve more than a casual

---

[31] The Egyptian Environmental Affairs Agency--Department of Natural Protectorates has prepared an extensive, free, full-color environmental guidebook to the *Natural Parks of Egypt: South Sinai Sector*. Accompanying the expected maps and regulations, are sections on coral reefs, human impacts, resource management, Bedouin culture, and the linked coastal ecosystems. A small NGO, Sinai Wildlife Projects (SWP), is particularly active in the region with projects ranging from its Bedouin Assistance Program to a Wildlife Rehabilitation Centre. In addition to support by the Ghazala Hotel, SWP receives small grants from the **Federal Republic of Germany**, the **Canadian International Development Agency, Baraka-Eau Naturelle, Amoco/Egypt**, and private donors. Ecological ventures also exist West of the Red Sea, such as Tim Baily's efforts to save the Nile perch fishery on Lake Nasser through a combination of tagging, monitoring, and mapping via sport fishing, training of indigenous guides in the importance of creating a sustainable resource, and opening remote Jackal Island (Wadi Abyad), etc. to controlled ecotourism. From our perspective, these are indicative of the kinds of small scientific projects especially suitable for cross-cultural partnerships. The author acknowledges the kind assistance of Antoine Riad, who has introduced us to a host of NGOs in the region and Terry McKendree, president of Conservation Outdoors, Inc. (a U.S.-based NGO active in the Middle East, Caribbean Basin, and Central and South America).

[32] Scientists are encouraged to scan the multitude of works by Megan Epler Wood of The International Ecotourism Society (TIES) for regional ideas regarding projects involving the human-Nature interface. See, for example, editors Dr. Donald E. Hawkins, Megan Epler Wood, and Sam Bittman's *The Ecolodge Sourcebook for Planners and Developers* (North Bennington, Vermont: The Ecotourism Society, 1995). Another excellent source is *Conde Nast Traveler*. Both organizations offer timely updates on the status of ecotourism, its successes and failures.

glance, as shampoos extol the virtues of their safe, botanical formulae and whose research labs, *"Ne teste pas sur les animaux."* (**Laboratoires St. Ives, S.A.**, Genève, Suisse).

The same is true of tour operators, who are combining science, destinations, and philanthropy as part of their successful global marketing.

For example, tour operators can join the **Grand Circle Foundation**, a nonprofit that supports global cultural, community, and environmental causes. Past recipients of its grants have included The World Monuments Fund; The Foundation of Friends of the Museum and Ruins at Efes, Ephesus,
Turkey; and a monitoring station at LaSelva, Costa Rica, where eco-visitors to the rainforest may participate in bird species census.

With the rainforest and its biodiversity disappearing at an alarming pace, let's begin with a mini-case that demonstrates the sponsorship concept:

Case Study #5-b: Jaguar Motor Cars—the Big Cat Supports a Big Cat:

Perhaps one of the longest-running, shared solutions to a sustainable future for an endangered species involves Jaguar Cars--an upscale, British product of Ford Motor Company--and the Wildlife Conservation Society (WCS)--a global NGO--in establishing the Cockscomb Basin Reserve in Belize. There in the 1980s, Jaguar Cars/Canada worked with WCS and researcher Alan Rabinowitz to found the first area worldwide dedicated to protecting the big cat.

The key is understanding the linkage of a corporate logotype and commitment to quality, the environment, and customer sensitivity to "green" issues (which also mirrors the green, corporate livery of its Formula One™ racing team) to the very real plight of jaguars articulated by Wildlife Conservation Society. Furthermore, one can easily make the mental leap to appreciating Jaguar Cars' interest in a project that combines the speed, beauty, and agility of *both* big cats and the common research goal of innovation. In short, a classic "win-win" situation for sponsor and scientists.

The sponsorship did not end with the Cockscomb Basin Reserve. Rather, they explored unique ways in which both global organizations could raise public awareness consistent with the goals and objectives of each one's Mission/Vision Statement. For example, in March, 1999, Jaguar Cars joined forces with the Universidad Nacional Antonoma de Mexico and WCS to host "Jaguars in the Next Millennium." This workshop, held in Mexico City, brought together the world's jaguar experts--thanks to a generous U.S. $ 80,000 donation from Jaguar Cars. Specifically, the scientists compared datasets and constructed a geographic information system (GIS) database, mapping jaguar status, ecology, and distribution across the animals' range--from southern Arizona to northern Argentina.

In addition, Jaguar Cars made a U.S. $1 million donation to WCS over a five-year period for what WCS termed "a major investment in the future of its [Jaguar's] corporate symbol." [33] Apparently, this funding is earmarked for a *new* jaguar program for jaguar field surveys to determine current status of the species.

Embedded in a unique, compelling, and interesting Case for Support for jaguar research is both the mythology and the mystique of the largest cat in the Americas. Unfortunately, lack of systematic knowledge has led to more persecution than protection, as ranchers--in particular--have blamed the cat for missing livestock. The reality is much different, as jaguar depredation appears more likely to occur when human activities poach upon the cat's habitat. An important part of the educational focus will be a rancher workshop on how to minimize jaguar predation on livestock.

As we shall see in the importance of creating brand equity in field or laboratory research, shared corporate and scientific values are crucial to successful, long-enduring sponsorship. In the case of Jaguar Cars and WCS, corporate culture and research goals were *not* mutually exclusive. Instead, they provided a touchstone for discussion and a benchmark for setting in motion a fundable iconography that is as much visceral as it is intellectually imaginative. "Jaguar Helping Jaguars" is a model for success.

How, then, does a scientist proceed to attract sponsorships and long term strategic alliances and where are the "pitfalls"?

First, a reality check: ***Sponsorships are not altruistic in intent. Their goal is the achievement of commercial objectives.***

Second, a definition: a sponsorship is a cash or in-kind fee paid to your Institute or expedition in return for *access* to whatever commercial potential a company believes associated with your work.

Access, as we have said before, is fundable. In this case, the access may be to whatever perceived *brand equity*--reputation--your team enjoys, the unusual, high profile nature of your work, and the affiliated constituencies and venues. This comment about brand equity is important, because--like it or not--positioning your science in brand language is an often overlooked, under-utilized, critical tool for attracting money.

Third, the Internet has leveled the corporate playing field in terms of *global* branding. In the Old Economy, prior to the rise of *e*-Business,

---

[33] See the website of the Wildlife Conservation Society (WCS) at <http://wcs.org> for full information and how corporate and individual donors can participate in saving the jaguar. This Chapter's author also had the privilege to visit Iwokrama rainforest, Guyana, to see unrelated efforts there to survey the jaguar population, manage rainforest habitat, and develop sustainable solutions involving responsible ecotourism and the resident AmerIndians. A final example: The expanding role of the mass media in philanthropy is underscored in the recent (2003) U.S. $2 million grant by the *Florida Times Union* to the Jacksonville Zoo for an exhibit on jaguars.

companies had to navigate dangerous cultural minefields, creating a patchwork of strategies to cope with the nuances of product sales from the Himalayas to the hinterlands. This patchwork approach created confusion and led to a global brand battlefield, where the strong and *visceral* brands with a consistent strategy and symbolic content dominated.

More about "branding," later.

Let's go right to the "pitfalls" and get them out of the way.

The corporate jungle can be extreme. Deception and camouflage are part of the Natural Order of predator and prey. However, just as in the jungle symbiotic relationships not only exist, but also thrive, sponsorships can evolve into the same "win-win" scenario.

Understanding the "art-of-the-deal" is your first step.

Business is all about earnings and protecting the "bottom line."

With sponsorships, corporations are intent upon maximum exposure, maximum profits. This means they will attempt to leverage their support of your science to the nth degree.

At issue are the following--and these should be negotiated *first*, before your Institute or expedition begins celebrating any financial windfall:

1) How will your scientific team and logotype be portrayed in corporate advertising? **Strategy: your agreement should specify any and all uses--print, broadcast, on-line, annual reports, house organs, personal appearances, banners, website links –in short, the universe of marketing platforms and ploys.**

2) How will your Institute/expedition be remunerated? Are you licensing the use of your logo for a specific project? Are you realizing a percentage of the sales of a particular product for which the sponsor advertises this point in its advertising and/or on its product packaging and point-of-purchase displays? [34] **Strategy: avoid contingency deals, in which you get paid based upon the number of goods sold. Best approach is to negotiate a guaranteed fee for your logo use, *plus* some**

---

[34] See, for example, the Council of Fashion Designers of America's initiative, *Fashion Targets Breast Cancer* (FTBC), a partnership between and among selected U.S. breast cancer organizations, Saks Fifth Avenue, and Mercedes-Benz U.S.A., L.L.C. Based upon an annual shopping weekend at its 61 stores and a percentage of sales donated--both at the shops and of the Special Edition CLK 500 autos sold--some U.S.$ 6 million has thus far reportedly been raised. Science related to women's health has traditionally been very difficult to fund, especially within developing nations. These are global brands and serve as a simple, easy-to-implement-and-measure paradigm for smaller projects, worldwide.

graduated % based upon co-branded (your logo and theirs) sale of product. *Try* to establish benchmarks by which if the joint venture campaign exceeds expectations, your team derives additional % benefits, receives more product/ equipment support, etc. *Avoid* abstract, hard-to-measure deals in which the sponsor establishes a ceiling on sales-related donations or fails to specify the exact percentage arrangement in its advertising.[35] Furthermore, if personal appearances by scientists are required, insist in writing upon reasonable expenses *and* arrange for sharing of databases of those who attend these corporate marketing events. Your goal is not just cash--it's access to potential *new donors*.

3) What is the length of the sponsorship and how will it be evaluated, by whom, and when? **Strategy: set common goals and objectives that are easy to measure (number of product inquiries by consumers, for example) and have a small, joint team in place to monitor the sponsorship at the beginning, middle, and at the end. Remember: people give money to people, not to ideas. This is relationship marketing. If the sponsorship goes well, you may have a partner for life.**

Finally, a negotiating tip--a "killer ap(plication)." In the course of your discussions ask whether the sponsor's "supply chain" (supplier of key goods and services to your sponsor) is being considered in the deal process. A broader, more cohesive "business-to-business" (B2B) sponsorship means

    a) greater exposure for all parties,

    b) potentially greater revenues, and

    c) a broader, new corporate donor pool for your science team.

With this said, how does a scientist identify potential sponsors?

The answer is as close as your Mission Statement and today's news headlines, whether your science is based in the rainforests of Guyana, a research laboratory in Italy, a petroglyph site in Portugal, the deep oceans, or the prospects for asteroid mining.

---

[35] The Nature Conservancy® addresses this problem in its river restoration effort by embedding a sponsor's commitment and "click" at TNC's website. As noted on the packaging of **Nature Valley®** 100% Natural Crunchy Granola Bars: "Rescue the Rivers! Help Nature Valley support this [Spunky Bottoms] and other Conservancy freshwater initiatives. Go to The Nature Conservancy's website, *nature.org*, and participate in **Nature Valley's Rescue the Rivers** campaign. For every click registered, Nature Valley will donate [U.S.] $ 1 (up to $ 125,000) to the Conservancy." Excellent example of co-branding, with the potential for developing a database of donors (?).

Enter the realm of "socially responsible investing" (SRI), where individual conscience and corporate culture may part company. Essentially, this is a process by which private investors can apply social filters to mutual funds and individual stocks in an effort to ferret out those companies whose worldviews differ markedly from their own.

In the U.S., nearly one out of every 10 U.S. dollars under management is now part of some type of SRI portfolio.[36]

The common lenses include,

- alcohol
- discriminatory labor practices
- environment
- gambling
- human rights
- product testing on animals
- tobacco
- weapons/defense.[37]

The good news is that organizations such as Morningstar, Inc. and the Social Investment Forum are ready sources of information by which a scientist can create her own social screens for determining whether a company or family of companies is a good philosophical, as well as strategic business match.

In addition, both scientists and sponsors alike can turn to a new website (www.iegsponsordirect.com), which lists sponsorship opportunities and allows corporations to browse them at no charge. According to *The Chronicle of Philanthropy*, IEG SponsorDirect will generate revenue by charging nonprofits two to six percent of the amount they realize from a corporate sponsorship that results from the listing.[38] The press reports that the focus of attention will be upon lower-profile causes and events, where sponsor serendipity or chance has too often played a crucial role.

Earlier, we looked at **Jaguar Cars** and its branded approach to supporting its corporate symbol through cause-related marketing.
Brands are important and the brand (and its inherent equity)

---

[36] Bob Evans, "Personal Finance: Socially Responsible Investing: You Don't Have to Sacrifice Profits for Principles," *Self-Employed America*, March/April, 1997, p. 14.

[37] "A Guide to Social Investing," *My Generation*, November-December, 2001, p. 30.

[38] Anonymous, "Technology: New Approach to Linking Corporations, Charities," *The Chronicle of Philanthropy,* May 30, 2002, p. 31.

established by a research Institute or expedition is a crucial marketing step with long-ranging implications for funding and sustainability.

One example of a research Institute that understands branding basics is The Hawaii Institute of Marine Biology. **Motorola**, a global communications and technology innovator, recently ran an advertisement focusing upon shared goals ("borrowed interest") of dolphin sonar and Motorola's Power Class™ cellular modem--long-range communications.

The full-page, four-color piece discussed the work of Dr. Whitlow Au, Chief Scientist of the Marine Mammal Research Project and one of the world's authorities on dolphin sonar. Furthermore, the ad provided a platform for cooperative advertising (?) for seven retailers (with toll-free numbers for four of them). Simply put, all the parties were sharing the brand equities of both Motorola and Dr. Au's Institute.

Brands need to be simple, evocative, and capable of standing alone in translating your image to the global mind--both corporate and public. The Motorola/Dr. Au advertisement (complete with an inset photograph of the scientist at work and swimming dolphins) gelled with the caption, "The idea of sending and receiving wireless signals isn't new to everyone."

Specifically, your brand can be a simple name, an image, or as in the case of Jaguar Cars, the protected name "Jaguar" and a leaping cat, which is also carried over as their automotive hood ornament.

Everyone talks about "logotypes" or "logos" when discussing corporate marketing. A logo is the unique representation of a corporate trademark or name that embodies some essence of the company. The simpler the logo, the better. Brand and logo, in the global village, need to be synonymous and seamless. In today's world, creating a brand and embodying it with a strong logo are essential steps in developing a timeless, ethereal, *fundable* presence.

At the risk of heresy, your Institute or expedition is probably only as good as its logo.

Why? Think about it.

Whether emblazoned on your website, letterhead, or direct mail (DM) promotion--or on the side of your teetering expedition vehicle, balloon, or submersible--your logo is often a donor or the public's first impression of your organization. While researchers are serious about their science and protective of their data against all odds and the barbarian hordes, they are often careless or cavalier about something as deceptively simple and crucial as their corporate image. Multinational companies spend U.S. millions of dollars to create, upgrade, and protect their logos. "Infringement" means an attack upon the corporate identity, or to borrow from the slogan that evolved from C.C. Pinckney's response to the bribe demanded in the historic XYZ Affair, "Millions for defense, but not one cent for tribute."

You don't need to spend millions, but whatever you do invest with a professional logotype designer needs to be time and money well spent.

Three points of specific advice:

1) Be certain logo-creation process includes designer interviews with key science personnel to determine the focus (reflects Mission Statement), goods and services of the Institute or expedition, and its place within the broader, competitive global market.

2) Require that the logo, when completed, includes a *usage manual* that describes how the logo is to be displayed in a host of situation – including signage, product, letterhead, business cards, on- line, in

    miniaturization, in motion on a research vehicle, animation, etc.

3) Ensure that the logo "travels well" across cultures globally. Is the logo an abstraction or symbol whose shape or colors give offense?

As novelist Anthony Burgess noted in a different context, "The scientific approach to life is not really appropriate to states of visceral anguish." With a mixture of common sense, scientific team participation, and strong, sensitive design, your logo need not create "visceral anguish" in the unsuspecting public, [39] whether a donor or prospective corporate partner.

According to Scott Nelson, research director of the marketing knowledge and technology service at Gardner Group, Inc., the best brands are "global symbols that evoke visceral, emotional responses from consumers" [40] Further, he notes that the three top priorities of global branding are consistency, community, and customer service. [41] For our purposes, your community is one of stakeholders: donors, Boards (corporate and yours), and end-users of your laboratory science/patents, etc. Customer service crosses the same boundaries, driven by donor Mission.

Branding Extreme and Experimental Science (BEES) requires

---

[39] William F. Vartorella, "Doing the bright thing with your company logo," *Advertising Age*, February 26, 1990, p. 31.

[40] Carol Hildebrand, "Branding the Globe," *CIO Enterprise*, Section 2 (March 15, 1998), p. 38.

[41] *Ibid.*

creating a corporate culture with a lot of marketing buzz and a sharp point. Remember it as the 4 e's and 4 p's:

- **Establish** your science as a brand, with a simple, easy-to-recognize and-remember logotype.
- **Entrench** it and create a "bar-to-entry"--namely, make it difficult to poach upon, confuse with, or ambush your brand (ambushing is an effort by a competitor to make your constituencies think that the competitor is a sponsor of your event, for example).
- **Expand** it into new territories and customer bases as part of a consistent, robust global strategy.
- **Envision** it as

1) **preeminent** (yours is the science to support)
1) **pervasive** (global)
2) **persuasive** (donors, team, and other constituencies are passionate about your Institute, expedition, or laboratory research)
3) **protectable** (logos, trademarks, registration marks, patents, copyrights--in short, defend the realm).

The best logos suddenly appear everywhere, at once, seemingly overnight. That is precisely how it works. Corporate takeovers, for example, often mean a weekend of old signage being pulled down and new logos being erected in time for the opening bell at the New York Stock Exchange on Monday. In short, launch your image as if it were timeless, ubiquitous, and competitive.

Now that you have established your brand, run corporations through both social investing and Mission/Vision-statement-driven "filters," and identified the key "suspects" (a "prospect" is one with whom you actually develop a dialogue), it is time to jump into the sponsorship fray.

Again--some background, IEG data set the stage:

- Sponsorships total some U.S. $60 **billion annually**--and growing.[42]
- Roughly 15% of that amount goes directly to "arts" and "causes."

---

[42] For an excellent chart summarizing corporate sponsorships and charitable income in the 1990s, see Susan Gray, "Charities' Income From Sponsorships Up 10%--Chart: How Corporate Spending to Sponsor Events Has Grown," *The Chronicle of Philanthropy*, March 26, 1998, p. 20.

Nearly 70% has some sports focus.
- Top reasons companies sponsor--visibility, image creation/change or repair, niche marketing. (Others include client relations, merchandising, business-to-business/B2B, etc.)

The difference between a "cutting-edge" and "bleeding-edge" sponsorship is one of nuance and communication. Remember our earlier comment? "Adventure is the result of poor planning." The same rings true with sponsorship deals.

Why sponsorships fail with science and discovery projects:

- "Take-the-money-and-run" approach: scientists fail to recognize and provide appropriate donor recognition, access to new niches/databases or new markets, etc.

- One-year deals, rather than long-term relationship planning: myopic worldview, lack of understanding of the corporate "big picture."

- Inability to measure results in corporate-friendly terms, e.g., consistent with company's Vision/Mission language and marketing goals and objectives.

- Nobody-at-home at the Institute or expedition: sponsor relations are crucial, communications is key. Again, people give money to people, not to ideas. Developing cordial, friendly relations pays real dividends.

- Poorly created and executed sponsorship packages: "cherry-picking" by sponsors. Scientists need to think through which aspects of a sponsorship deal have the most and best chance for leveraging into "value-added" opportunities for which sponsors would be prepared to pay a premium. NOTE: these need to be embedded in specific sponsorship packages and *not* be available for "cherry-picking," e.g., corporations extracting the best ideas and attempting, *ad hoc*, to negotiate these at a reduced financial rate.

Now some advice on how to create a successful, win-win scenario with a sponsor:

Why sponsorships succeed with science and discovery projects:

- Fundamental understanding and copious research related to the potential sponsor's Vision/Mission and markets/consumers.

- Category exclusivity: no sponsor competitors. For example, if you attract **Gateway** computers as a natural history sponsor (an actual area of interest of the company), you will have to 1) ignore other direct competitors (or perceived competitors) and 2) be prepared to use Gateway products.

- Sponsor name, logo, etc. featured in news and promotion releases; mentioned during broadcast and print media interviews. Use world-class automobile racing as an analogue. When a driver exits a car after a victory (or narrow defeat), the first words he utters usually focus on sponsor names and their virtues. Drivers go to "charm schools" for training in sponsor and media relations. You may not need to go to that extreme, but getting used to providing donor recognition at every opportunity is important.

- Hot link to sponsor's website. Your web page should have an easily accessible link to sponsors' Internet sites. Reciprocity is extremely important, with your logo featured on sponsor websites in a hot-link-how-you (donor)-can-help format.

- *New, improved, and free entrepreneurial opportunities*, which provide bonus exposure ("free circulation") for sponsors. Again, think in *access* terms, particularly if the opportunity is a public event (cityscape archaeology; lab tour for an experimental, electric racing car; annual bird species census free lectures on the latest applications of human genome mapping to prevention or cure of specific diseases, etc.

- *Controlled & Secure* Access to Mailing List: your donor list is your life-blood; use a list broker as an intermediary and institute guidelines for content approval of any mailing made by the sponsor.

- Science and exploration, with its unusual apparatus, riveting tales of (mis)adventure, and the "right stuff."

- Final report by nonprofit property, re: attendance or news coverage.

One point needs to be driven home. Do not get lost in the minutiae of a bold sponsorship endeavor. While the "devil may be in the details," negotiate the main points above first as part of a broad, value-added package that is specific as to the sponsor and both your budgets. Different sponsorship levels should have clearly articulated *benefits*. Research should tell you what the "hot-buttons" are for each sponsor. Address these in dollars-and-*sense*.

Then, get into the "horse-trading" of the details. Know what things cost and what you are prepared to negotiate as free, additional exposure. (But do *not* cross over into the next sponsor level down and allow for cannibalization of those benefits, to the detriment of other sponsors and your endeavor to make money.)

Items of relatively low cost include,

-- Product sampling with attendees

-- Discounts on additional tickets to event; discount on food, etc.

-- A specified number of Very Important Person (VIP) passes, etc.

-- Opportunities for use of meeting facilities during event day for mini-seminars/networking for sponsor guests.

Hospitality suites for clients/supply chain tend to be high profile and costly. You cannot afford it--but you may be able to provide the thematic background, consistent with your science (e.g., an exhibit, complete with scientists capable of bringing the science to life in an exciting, unusual, and provocative way).

Now, some

Tips for Attracting that Key 1st, "Anchor" Sponsor:

- **Know your sponsors' market goals & objectives.**

- **Know how your audience reflects those goals and objectives. (Have you ever surveyed your Institute's donor base or membership in a scientific, reliable, and valid way?)**

- **Know the size of the event, its usual/expanded coverage, and potential delivery of the key geo-demographic segment desired**

by the sponsor.
Understand that your property (Institute, expedition, museum, etc.) or cause has its own inherent "brand equity." Exploit that brand equity with similar-minded, high-profile, high-quality sponsors.

Once you attract the lead sponsor, examine its "supply chain" or technology partners for other potential, B2B, second-tier sponsors.

- Understand that cash and in-kind can be the same thing and can be leveraged to attract other sponsors.

- Begin your sponsor screening process with local affiliates of the "heavy-hitters"--soft drinks, cars, telecommunications, banking, beer, airlines, packaged goods/food, credit & debit cards, retail (adults vs. children, male vs. female), and supermarkets.

- Keep your categories of exclusivity broad enough.

- Create a simple, systematic level of sponsorship that does *not* present a menu of options (e.g., various costs, etc.) which encourages a "choke-and-rob." The "choke" occurs when a corporation throttles off other potential revenue sources by taking the best benefits, thereby "robbing" you of additional revenue streams from other potential sponsors.

- Be specific, re: website content, number & kinds of signage, where posted, advertising credits, etc.

- Remember: he-who-writes-the-contract-controls-the payment schedule.

A word about pricing a sponsorship is important.

Basically,

- Goal is to cover all event costs with sponsorship--"profit" is in ticket prices, associate sponsors, in-kind goods & services, etc.

- Challenge is to leverage the sponsorship into broader support through business-to-business (B2B) and "supply chain" partners.

- Most expeditions, for example, try to target the *tangible assets* or aspects of a sponsorship. These include signage, event program guides, sponsor logos on tickets, media coverage (reach x frequency = gross rating points/broadcast media or column inches/print media), "goody bags" given to event participants, etc. True, these can be measured easily, but their overall value is less than *intangible assets*, such as

1) your Institute or expedition's prestige and brand equity
2) trademarks ™, registrations/rights $^{®}$, copyrights $^{©}$,
3) patents, slogans, jingles, etc.
4) name recognition of lead scientists, explorers
5) awards associated with your team (Nobel Prize, etc.)
6) media coverage potential, especially free or bonus circulation in multiple markets in which sponsor has subsidiaries or target consumer audiences
7) inherent interest of your science with specific geodemography (dinosaurs with children and adolescents, etc.; fishery research/habitats with sport fishermen/women, etc.)

Sponsorship pricing is less about absolutes, than attributes.

It is not a zero-sum game in which sides grapple for a single loaf of bread, winner-take-all. Pricing is a function of fair-market value, applied fairly.

Remember:

Sponsors want—

1) Clearly articulated proposals that demonstrate who you are your audience base, what you are prepared to deliver at a competitive price, and particularly--how this help s a company meet its marketing goals and objectives (either stated or implied)

2) "Value-added"--extra media exposure, larger crowds than expected, B2B networking, recognition for products/services, and branding opportunities

3) Exclusivity of product/service line and no "ambush marketing" in which brand/sponsor confusion exists as to whom, precisely, is supporting your event

4) Long-term relationships: "one-shots" offer virtually no chance for changes in approach, measurable long-term results, etc.

5) *Cost-effective*, unique events and venues that separate them from the clutter of day-to-day competitors

6) Role models, especially from traditionally underrepresented groups in science

7) No surprises. No controversy, scientists accused of falsifying data, grandiose and unsupported claims, or poorly managed risk. Plunging over Niagara Falls in a barrel--no matter how "hi-tech" the barrel--is a stunt, not science.

*Again, while it all seems to be about money, generally speaking **tax implications** for companies (and individual donors) tend to fall well behind more important corporate Mission or individual passion for a project.*

Furthermore, companies and individuals are bound by different cultural mores, political climates, and tax structures depending upon the country in which they legally reside.

For a detailed single source on *nonprofit* legal context, tax treatment, personal benefit restrictions, public obligations, business activity, etc. in some two dozen countries, see Lester M. Salamon's *The International Guide to Nonprofit Law.* [43] It puts into broader perspective development approaches we advocate in *Funding Exploration*, particularly if your nonprofit scientific team works or resides legally in Australia, Brazil, Canada, Egypt, France,

---

[43] Lester M. Salamon, *The International Guide to Nonprofit Law* (New York: John Wiley & Sons, Inc., 1997). Scientists actively engaged in projects in the listed countries may wish to use Dr. Salamon's book in conjunction with appropriate legal and tax counsel. For a specific example with an exploration focus, see Peter E. Hess, "Deep Shipwreck in High Courts," *Delaware Lawyer*, Volume 17, Number 1 (Spring, 1999), 16-19.

Germany, Hungary, India, Republic of Ireland, Israel, Italy, Japan, Mexico, The Netherlands, Poland, The Russian Federation, South Africa, Spain, Sweden, Thailand, United Kingdom, or United States.

V. Equipment, Supplies, and Free Travel:

Roughly U.S. $1,000,000 per *day* in equipment, supplies, and services are lent or donated to U.S. nonprofits (for example). Some estimates have placed fast-paced company gifts of products as high as 30% or more of total corporate giving.

Yet, scientists worldwide continue to spend money on gear.

Question is--"why?"

One of the best ways to save cash for critical, hard-to-get-donated services, such as Optical Stimulated Luminescence analysis (OSL-- @ U.S. $700 per tube sample) or radiocarbon suites (U.S. $600 per sample), is to develop an aggressive, systematic program of lent and donated goods and services. [44]

A powerful approach is a "lending," rather than "owning" strategy. Corporations are barraged with requests for free equipment. They rarely are approached by scientists with a plan for "borrowing" gear and returning it when the field season is over, complete with strong donor recognition, some free public lecture component, and an in-house briefing for corporate families, etc.

Why own the gear? It is eventually going to wear out, so why not use it, return it in good shape, develop the relationship with the donor, and borrow the *upgrade* next field season?

This is central to the concept we explained earlier, namely that the goal should be to attract 1) corporate volunteerism, then 2) lent or donated gear, and 3) often simultaneous with (2), cash.

So, how do you target a potential lender/donor?

An important first step is a

"Marketing Self-Analysis." [45]

If you can answer "yes" to the questions in this brief survey, you are well on your way to a host of equipment grants:

---

[44] William F. Vartorella, "The `Archaeology' of Finding Equipment, "*The Glyph,* Volume I, Number 13 (June, 1998), 11.

[45] William F. Vartorella, "An Insider's Guide to Getting Equipment Grants," *Nonprofit Management Strategies*, October, 1992, 7.

1) Our board has a written policy encouraging the solicitation of corporate gifts, including equipment and expertise.

2) Our board adheres to standard accounting practices, including audits and the participation of a recognized financial expert (a Certified Public Accountant--CPA or the equivalent internationally).

3) Our newsletter (or other written or on-line media) includes an easily identified section that features the accomplishments, goods, and services of firms that support our scientific efforts.

4) When we receive corporate gifts (even anonymous ones), we issue a news release, post the information on our website, and follow these guidelines:

- Articulate the basic who, what, when, where, why, and how of the donation or loan, emphasizing how it will be used.

- Feature a quotation from the corporate donor/partner.

- Share the media list of those receiving the public relations (PR) piece with the corporate donor for suggestions as to additions that reach her/his constituencies, including trade and professional journals, annual reports, etc.

- Arrange photo opportunities that include use of "house organs", such as employee newsletters.

- Use the products of corporate donors and their subsidiaries (very important for future, related requests) in our daily operations.

- Ask all corporate donors or targeted donors to include us on their mailing lists for annual reports and other public releases.

From there:

1) Create an itemized list of necessary equipment (including any specialized
   field clothing, boots, etc.), complete with an explanatory paragraph regarding its specific use and importance to the excavation's results.

(This will become part of your urgent, compelling, and interesting Case for Support.) Identify who manufactures the equipment and the contact person for Corporate Contributions. Also, locate the nearest distributor.

2) Create a marketing overlay for the region of the country (or the world) where the expedition will be active. In simplest terms, this means identifying which of the companies or their subsidiaries or joint venture partners noted in (1) is actively mining, manufacturing, or distributing goods and services in the vicinity of your field research or excavation.

3) Collect samples of advertising campaigns of (1) in order to get a sense of the "corporate culture" and missions of these companies. These will provide important clues, re: how to approach them in a manner which indicates you know the company and key corporate goals.

4) For broader corporate support, watch for advertising campaigns in *Fortune*, *Forbes*, *Business Week*, etc. and trade publications (especially for GIS/GPS) that have science and discovery themes.

    With these in hand, consider how the expedition can

1) assist the manufacturer with a rough-and-tumble field test of it gear under trying conditions (possibly even becoming part of the advertising campaign in a sponsorship arrangement)

2) help the corporation reach new niches/consumers in the U.S., indigenous, or global markets

3) improve name recognition of the equipment for professionals utilizing the gear for other field applications (especially true for emerging GIS and GPS companies);

4) serve as a training platform for the corporation, with expedition members actually teaching sales-related seminars for the company, post-expedition;

5) discover/create new uses for the equipment in the field.

    These should be articulated in a simple briefing paper/request, complete with an assessment of how this loan meets the corporate mission of the donor. Often the first step is to contact personally the nearest distributor, who may take the request up the chain-of-command. This is important, as "people give money to people--not to ideas." In other instances, a direct approach to the head of the Corporate Contributions Committee is appropriate.

Now for some advice & tips:

1) Ask for long-term *loans* of computers, copiers, and other expensive
> equipment. At the end of the lending period, request an upgrade.

b) Companies are often anxious, at the end of a model year, to write-off gear as a donation in order to clear inventory.

c) Recycle equipment/upgrades among consortial partners. Many U.S. Federal Agencies are ambivalent as to whether equipment must be returned at the end of a grant.

d) Develop strong Donor Recognition Programs for Corporate Partnerships. In newsletters and other media, photograph gear in use and name the corporate or foundation sponsors.

e) In general, beware anyone offering free, used (un-reconditioned) computers. These usually lack enough memory and are often incompatible with critical software. Worse, they breakdown in the field and, because of age, usually lack any semblance of technical support, warranties, etc.

f) Consider developing unusual consortial arrangements that offer lender/donors the opportunity to field test the gear under differing research situations (e.g., mapping of new roads in developing countries as well as archaeology applications, etc.) As most expeditions are not in the field year-round, this is an excellent opportunity to encourage gear use by indigenous scientists and engineers--an even stronger Case for Support with lender/donors that may yield cash infusions even in the short-term.

Travel support (and services) is another issue, as it may be more than

50% of an expedition's budget. Five power tips:

1) Try to schedule your expedition during off-peak/shoulder periods when airlines are not crowded. Much better chance for comp tickets.

2) Get your expedition's individual donors to give you frequent flyer miles which can be exchanged for tickets (now allowed under many airline programs). Rarely used strategy for getting your team into the field.

3) Entice an airline to be the official sponsor of the expedition.

4) For every PAID ticket, ask airline to match with a free or reduced price ticket.

5) In-country: Look to oil and mineral exploration companies for the loan of a good all-terrain vehicle (with a driver & petrol, ideally).

Telephone bills generally run 1-10% of an expedition's budget. No reason to pay for telephone calls, either (within reasonable limits of official use only). Get annual reports of **AT&T**, **MCI**, **Sprint** to see which global markets they are attacking (e.g., Sprint in South America). Create a plan whereby the company gets exposure and expedition gets, say; FREE U.S./Timbuktu calls for period of field stay.

Shipping your gear overseas? If you are shipping your gear via ocean, look to freight forwarders and shippers who are moving into the market in which you are exploring. The newcomers will be more apt to be responsive, as they need exposure and good will to attract market share and improve their own in-country exposure. Your gear will probably take less than a container, so consider contacting other explorers in the region to share the space & increase visibility for the shipper.

Finally, look at lent/donated gear as the critical first step in attracting long term expedition sponsors. Combine these with donor site visits and "trench talks" and companies become far more open to even bolder requests for support.

Now it's time to get the view from the summit:

Case Study #5-c: Telemedicine on Mt. Everest--Two Perspectives:

"We've knocked the bastard off!" is how (now) Sir Edmund Hillary characterized the first successful ascent to the summit on 29 May 1953.   Others, like John McPhee (*Basin and Range*, 1981) have been equally succinct: "The summit of Mt. Everest is marine limestone."

Since 1953, the cold reality has been a lack of oxygen at the mountain's extreme altitude has sometimes also meant a lack of judgment.   Estimates have placed the human toll at perhaps as high as one in four climbers. Yet, Mt. Everest continues to capture the imagination of serious scientists, climbers, and advertisers alike.

Advertising images and comparisons abound, such as this attention-getter from a computer-monitor company: "Cornerstone is just another big monitor. Like Mt. Everest is just another big rock." Even Sir Edmund has climbed into the act, with the "Mt. Everest teaches you humility" campaign for a new **Toyota** operating very close to Base Camp altitude.[46]

However, today research on climber physiology at high altitude and remote biomonitoring and locating each expedition team member by GPS is a far cry from trailblazing new routes and the machismo of mountaineering.

The 1999 Everest Extreme Expedition (E^3) is a case in point, as a research team from the Yale University School of Medicine tested the hypothesis of a "physiologic cipher"--"the concept of non-invasively identifying an individual's real-time physiologic status by monitoring vital signs, biochemical and other parameters with sensors worn by the individual." [47] In addition, they sought to validate "the technical feasibility of real-time vital signs monitoring and geolocation of individuals in an extreme environment." [48] Essentially, the E^3 vital signs monitoring (VSM) system consisted of a lightweight wearable system with sensors (heart rate, surface body temperature, gross body motion, and sleep time), a GPS receiver, and a radio transmitter. At Mt. Everest Base Camp (EBC, 17,800 feet), a laptop received and compiled the data and sent them by satellite to Malaysia, then via an Internet backbone to Yale University School of Medicine in Connecticut (U.S.).

As noted in the intriguing summary by Richard M. Satava, M.D., FACS and Thomas Blackadar, Ph.D. in *GPS World*, physicians at Yale could "see the signs of physical stress of hypoxia and strenuous activity in the overall elevated baseline heart rate as the climbers ascended." [49]

Important from the point of our discussion are two sets of acknowledgements at the end of the article. The first lists **FitSense Technologies**, **Trimble Navigation**, and

---

[46] "Everest at 17,262 Ft. Muscles Twitch. Nerves Fray. Engine Roars. The All-New 4 Runner. Larger. More powerful." Fold-out, gateway ad for the new **Toyota** 4 Runner, apparently photographed "testing" on the skree at elevation on Mt. Everest. Released in conjunction with Toyota's television spots in the U.S. (2002), which feature Sir Edmund Hillary.

[47] Richard Satava and Thomas Blackadar, "The Physiologic Cipher: Telemedicine on Everest," *GPS World*, October, 2001, p. 20.

[48] *Ibid.*

[49] *Ibid.*

Inmarsat (which was the satellite that transmitted EBC data to Malaysia) as manufacturers whose gear was used in the study. The second is a note of the other collaborative partners--an underlying theme of our book and a key strategy in getting funded: The Yale University-NASA Commercial Space Center for Medical Informatics and Technology Applications (CSC/MITA), Millennium Heathcare Solutions (MHS), and The Explorers Club.

A second perspective is provided by **Compaq Computers**, whose *NewsBytes* ("Compaq PCs assist Mt. Everest expedition," undated tear sheet) indicated that three Compaq Armada 7400 Series notebook PCs were also part of the effort and were expected to be used for duties including "data compilation, IP video conferencing, e-mail and other day-to-day tasks." Gear pre-tests included evaluation in a U.S. Army environmental chamber up to 18,000 feet (cf. Everest Base Camp altitude) and down to -30 degrees F.

The first perspective emphasizes the scientific results and, in a narrower sense, the related equipment. In the second, we see a global manufacturer viewing its participation as crucial to the success of E^3. Both perspectives are honest and focused. Taken out of context and *expanded*, E^3 may serve as a model for 1) consortial partners, 2) a mixture of corporate volunteering, equipment loan, and cash--in that order, and 3) applications of how scientific research in one extreme environment has commercial and strategic applications in another ("locating wounded soldiers and determining severity of their injuries" [50] or in extreme expedition settings). [51]

Nearly 30 years ago, Andrew Harvard and Todd Thompson perhaps set the benchmark--or at least raised the bar--for donor recognition related to climbing with a serious scientific component. Their book, *Mountain of Storms: The American Expeditions to Dhaulagiri, 1969 & 1973*, in addition to Drummond Rennie's "Note on Retinal Photography," includes a *five-page*, single-spaced "List of Sponsors and Suppliers." [52]

More recently, in 1989 climber Yvon Chouinard, founder of **Patagonia**, and Wally Smith, president of **Recreational Equipment, Inc. (REI)**, teamed up with **Kelty Pack** and **The North Face** to form the **Conservation Alliance**. Simply put, they and what now is an alliance of some 62 outdoor business partners, determined the best way to protect the environment and their own business interests was to work in concert.

---

[50] *Ibid.*

[51] Also, see the 1998 Everest Extreme Expedition's summary in "GPS Goes on Medical Mission to Everest's Heights," *GPS World*, July, 1998, p. 56. Interesting here is the observation on equipment at temperatures as low as -45 degrees C., "causing plastics to become brittle and batteries to stop working, and thin air pressure that causes laptops to crash. . . ." For a robust treatment of high altitude medicine, see Dr. Kenneth Kamler's *Doctor on Everest. Emergency Medicine at the Top of the World—A Personal Account including the 1996 Disaster (New York: The Lyons Press, 2000).*

[52] Andrew Harvard and Todd Thompson, *Mountain of Storms: The American Expeditions to Dhaulagiri, 1969 & 1973* (New York: Chelsea House, New York University Press, 1974), pp. 203-207.

Funding Exploration | Chapter Five

Since its founding, the Conservation Alliance has provided grants of more than U.S. $3 million to a host nonprofit efforts. These have included the Ice Age Park and Trail, Tatshenshini Wild, Lighthawk--The Environmental Air Force, River Conservation International, Mineral Policy Center, InterTribal Sinkyone Wilderness Council, Sierran Biodiversity Institute, Rivers Canada, the Sea Turtle Restoration Project, Grand Canyon Wildlands Council, Ancient Forest International, Save Our Wild Salmon, and a host of others--in the U.S. $15,000 to $55,000 grant range.

According to its website (http://www.conservationalliance.com), its goal (Mission?) is to "play a pivotal role in the protection of rivers, trails, wild lands--natural areas where outdoor enthusiasts spend their time." What makes the Alliance unusual is the grant proposal system is not an open one. Environmental nonprofits are required to contact member businesses, which in turn vet the proposals and nominate groups for consideration by the grants coordinator and the membership. All (100%) of the membership dues in the Alliance go toward grants--a fundamentally unique way of raising and awarding funding. While the entire membership is featured on the website, selected companies include **Bernzott Capital Advisors, Campmore, Inc., Climbing Magazine, Columbia Sportswear Company, Lowe Alpine Systems, Milliken & Company,** *National Geographic* **Adventure, Nike ACG, Pearl Izumi, Royal Robbins, Sierra Designs, The Timberland Company, W.L. Gore & Associates, Inc., and Watergirl.**

In short, funding does not have to evaporate "into thin air."

The gear-leads-to-cash model we advocate works.

Back to sea-level, you should also explore low-cash alternatives in the form of **government and private surplus** hi-tech equipment and supplies.

Two real-life examples:

1) A few years ago, before the general availability of night-vision technology, a field biologist investigating the nocturnal behavior of beaver, turned successfully to the **U.S. Army** for the loan of aging, first-generation night-vision scopes. This was an early example of now-continuing interest by the U.S. military in technology transfer/sharing to unusual scientific applications.

2) A U.S. women's college, as part of a new communications program, needed a broadcast-quality television studio, suitable for student productions and programming for the local cable outlet. With a "bare-bones budget" of U.S. $10,000, studio designers leveraged the cash into a six-figure, "Back-to-

Basics" studio by turning to the U.S.General Services Administration, "Federal Supply Service," for access to donations of surplus federal goods.[53] These included patch panels, audio racks, television monitors, frequency generator, and a host of much-needed, low-cost components.

Point here is that scientists too often think "cash" from their Federal Governments and overlook the obvious infrastructure needs that can also be met by Government in a non-competitive, casual way.

Private "surplus" groups can also assist scientists worldwide who are structured as nonprofits. Three that deserve your attention include

- **Gifts In-Kind International**, which works with 50,000 nonprofits worldwide, has also developed relationships with industrial trade shows (such as Comdex) to facilitate the donation of *exhibited goods*.[54] Tip: attendance at trade shows where high-tech gear and scientific equipment are displayed is an excellent strategy for making quick contacts that can lead to sponsorships and gear loans. Gifts In-Kind International receives contributions from more than 750 companies, half of which conduct business internationally.

- **The National Association for the Exchange of Industrial Resources (NAEIR)** redistributes donated corporate goods, which include office supplies, tools and hardware, and computer accessories.[55]

- **The East-West Education Development Foundation** is active in more than 70 countries and is designed to support nonprofits that "promote ecology, human rights, democracy, freedom of speech, and better understanding between peoples of the world," according to Foundation materials. Focus is revamping donated computers and transferring them to groups globally who need them.

For each of the above, surf the web for the latest programs, guidelines, and any fees. Other recycling programs have sprouted and some have died, so a timely web search is the best advice.

---

[53] Ronald W. Feeback and William F. Vartorella, "A `Back to Basics' Studio for $10,000," *Educational & Industrial Television*, Volume 13, Number 10 (October, 1981), 53.

[54] Anonymous, "Where to Donate (and find) Surplus Goods," *Successful Meetings*, June, 1996, p. 42.

[55] *Ibid.*

Finally, scientific suppliers themselves sometimes provide *free* grant-related services (identification of funding sources and professional review of draft grant proposals), *if* it is clear that a successful donor application includes the need for an equipment purchase from their firm.

VWR Scientific was an early innovator in the 1980s and 1990s, offering free database searches of foundations earmarking funding for scientific gear, *plus* supplying an in-house evaluation of draft grant proposals. Today, for example, **Sargent-Welch** offers a grant-match for science laboratory materials and equipment for schools, with the simple stipulation that "only materials cataloged and stocked by Sargent-Welch or VWR Scientific can be purchased with Grant Match awards on the GRANT MATCH 2002 program." [56]

VI. Power Proposals or "Who's a Player?"[57]:

In today's fast-paced, ever-changing corporate culture, you may have only minutes to make your pitch for company donations of cash, equipment, or volunteer services.

Sure, you've done your homework. Made certain your programs meet the company's marketing mission and corporate goals. Not requested more than the company's "average" grant/donation based on research and experience. Maybe even kept the request below U.S. $5,000, just to keep it out of the jurisdiction of a lengthy review process.

Problem is, whom do you approach for the final pitch?

Most firms have a "Corporate Contributions Committee," although they rarely seem to convene to hear personal appeals from the heads of Institutes or expeditions. More often than not, you will be directed to someone doubling as either middle management or special projects director.

And herein lies the problem.

There are two kinds of corporate types who may be involved. Both seem to be successful and opinion leaders. The fact is, they are not and you need to recognize quickly "Who can help, who cannot."

---

[56] Correspondence between the author (Vartorella) and VWR Scientific, 1990 ff. VWR Grant-It Program proved helpful in identifying funding sources--often little-known ones--for scientific equipment related to the analysis of wild and domestic yeasts from the archaeological site of the world's oldest-known brewery, plus the analysis of Egyptian mummy DNA and procedures for conservation of mummified human materials. In addition, for a colleague at a scientific foundation, VWR identified matching funding for grant funding already committed. For specifics on Sargent-Welch Grant-Match, please consult its website at <www.sargentwelch.com>.

[57] William F. Vartorella, "Corporate Fund Raising in Transition: Posers, Players, and Power Proposals," *Fund Raising Institute (FRI) Monthly Portfolio*, Volume 33, Number 7 (July, 1994), 1-2.

Scenario #1: The "Up and Out" Executive:

The "up and out" executive looks something like this: A male, late 50s or early 60s, this person has all the trappings of power -- corner office; lots of awards on the wall; newspaper clippings; clean desk. He fits the old-style profile of the traditional donor.

Yet, for reasons that are murky, he now is relegated to the position of "special projects director" or "corporate head of strategic planning." Responsibilities are vague; power is non-existent. Time for a reality check: At his age he should be vying for the executive suite -- CEO, CFO, etc. Instead, he's on the wrong side of the power curve. Much of his time, frankly, is spent on final preparations for his separation agreement -- benefits package, the gold watch--maybe early retirement, or the emergency "golden parachute."

The most you can expect from the "up and out executive" is a reasonably-enlightened "listen" to your proposal. Don't be surprised if you get a "get-off-the-grass grant" -- which is jargon for a corporate donation that has more to do with saving time than serving your science. You end up with small change (usually less than U.S. $5,000) and a deceptively dangerous short-term relationship. This executive is a "poser."

Scenario #2: The "Up and In" Executive:

The "up and in" executive looks like this: A new-style executive, perhaps female, Hispanic, Asian, or African, this person is driven by corporate objectives.

Napoleon's dictum, "Take anything but my time," has real meaning in this office. Awards are replaced by profit-and-loss statements, ringing telephones, and an airline ticket to Timbuktu.

In the first scenario, the executive sought praise and respect, while this executive seeks performance and results. She is looking for a big, bold, high profile idea that shows off her company and meets shareholder expectations in new, far-flung markets. She has never heard of a "get-off-the-grass grant" and wouldn't waste money on it if she had. Unlike the first executive, she is ready to take ownership of an idea and run with it. This executive is a "player."

Strategies for Scientists:

Naturally, the two types of executives need to be approached differently. In Scenario #1, ask the executive specifically whether others will play a role in the decision-making process. The answer is usually an unequivocal "yes." This is really an opportunity to build consensus and a relationship with the "movers-and-shakers" who will soon replace this executive.

The goal here is to look long term, to become part of the team.

Your proposal then, should be streamlined, with a three-year "fuse." Your objective is to carry your project beyond the tenure of this interloper.

In Scenario #2, carry two proposals in your briefcase. The first is the request at hand, namely a sustainable, easy-to-measure, short-term project (annual giving, etc.). The second is a one-page "blue-sky" summary of how her corporation can support your science through a bold initiative. Remember, she is being groomed for a corner office. Your success is her success. After you make your brief "pitch" (very brief, in her case) for the short-term project, test the water.

"We believe this meets your marketing goals (read: Mission Statement) today, but where do you see your company moving in the early 21st century?" If you have been shrewd, you have some inkling of what her answer might be. If so, part of her opportunity to participate is lurking in your briefcase. Thus, "I just happen to have a copy of our Vision Statement for the next decade. Its program(s) may interest you."

In each case, it is important to read between the lines. With corporate culture in transition (and barbarians at the gates), you must do everything in your power to position your Institute or expedition's support for the long haul. Be on the look-out for rising new-style executives who take a much more focused view of traditional values and how these will play out in terms of corporate philanthropy.

True, corporate contributions are flat or dipping slightly in comparison with 1987 dollars and as a percentage of pre-tax income. This is not to imply, however, that executives are not prepared to offer volunteer services or in-kind donations of equipment as part of an interim strategy.

How you evaluate corporate cultures on a case-by-case basis will have a fundamental impact on the well being of your team. Napoleon's dictum is timely in another sense: You have to move now to plan for the future, before it -- and your Institute or expedition -- becomes obsolete.

VII. Islands of Opportunity:

A study of 424 U.S. firms by Coopers & Lybrand, LLP disclosed--

- Faculty cultures are not receptive to business.

- Many universities lack interest in developing resources/programs for businesses.

- Universities have no experience working with growth-oriented companies. [58]

The indictment gets worse. According to Coopers & Lybrand, LLP, only 40% of growth companies have relationships with U.S. universities and only half of these function smoothly. While this "cautionary tale" may not apply globally, in our experience scientists lag well behind college infrastructure and endowment demands when it comes to getting an administration's attention to Institute or expedition needs and opportunities.

This accounts in part for our recommendation that scientists create free- standing "islands of opportunity"--Institutes--that take over some or much of the fundraising for their projects and long-term growth. Again, self-sustainability is the result of entrepreneurship.

A first step, consistent with this Chapter, is to begin the multi-tiered process of identifying, cultivating, and tapping corporate donors/sponsors.

When seeking corporate partners follow

Vartorella's Law of Concentric Funding Circles:

---

1) *The Inner Circle*: **usually local, these are corporations and foundations at your doorstep which respond to grant proposals in fewer than 60 days. These are the "mother lode" and include family and corporate foundations whose Missions may be the easiest to address. Also, often these are subsidiaries of global players and offer access to the broader funding pipeline. Best bet.**
2) *The Regional Circle*: **these are funders that cross State or Provincial borders. Excellent opportunities for consortial projects. Lots of cash--not much competition, generally. Good bet.**
3) *National Circle*: **lots of loot, lots of competition. Long shot, unless you can match target consumer niches, etc. Shared**

---

[58] Chart, *CIO*, September 15, 1995, 18.

solutions, high visibility, simple Mission are keys to success.

4) *International Circle*: this is the battleground of global NGOs, with extreme competition for new donors, new ideas, and new cooperative ventures that offer significant media attention. Think small and agile. Positioning your Institute or expedition as a global brand, with a strong Internet presence, is crucial. Choose your allies carefully and attack niches where you can compete. Expect an arcane, slow review process. Your Board is your strategic asset. You will need financial resources to succeed here, which means short-term sacrifice.

Remember: think globally (e.g., those multinational companies with local subsidiaries) and act locally (apply to them and to community and family foundations with a "doorstep focus.")

Think of it this way: essentially, it is similar to dropping a stone in the water, where the biggest waves formed are closest to the stone. The stone is your idea and your Case for Support. The biggest splash will be local, but the long-range ramifications (and opportunity for long-term funding) are farther out--internationally.

Again, the critical point for corporate donor and scientist alike is an understanding of the *enlightened self-interest* of each party. Foremost in the mind of the Corporate Donor are these questions:

If the project is truly new--

- How does this meet *our* long-term corporate Mission, re: market penetration, niches, new product launches, etc.?

- How will our company, products, services be showcased?

- What is the upside? Downside? Financially and in terms of corporate image.

- Who are the Players (e.g., are other corporations funding your efforts)?

- Are these costs realistic, competitive, *safety*-conscious?

- Can our support be infused in stages (see volunteer, gear, and cash recommendations, above)?

- Is your core team *qualified* in terms of experience, training, and risk-assessment?

- Worst-case scenario, what kind of human and equipment losses can you sustain and still be successful? And, what is your plan for *remedial public relations* (e.g., "damage control") if the "worst case" comes to pass?

- What is the plan for donor recognition? Internet, real-time?

- What kind of *intangible resources* are you providing, re: name recognition, reputation of team members, *institutional affiliations*?

- What kind of *tangible resources* are you providing (team members pay for transportation, part of training, etc.)?

- Do we understand the scope of the project, hypotheses in lay terms and the related scientific method?

Finally, is the Case for Support *urgent, compelling, and unique*?

But do **not** forget this "deal-killer":

- **Has this project been done elsewhere, better, and for less money?** Companies are *rarely* interested in retracing the steps of past explorers, especially as these ventures are every bit as *dangerous* as the initial efforts.

Positive answers to these questions and a visceral sense that the scientific team leader can keep his/her ego in check are a crucial first-step for a long-term relationship that translates into a *peak experience* for the corporate supporter and scientist alike.

But then, let's explore more deeply the corporate mind and what makes it tick.

VIII. The View from the Boardroom--A Grant Reviewer's Lament:

Behind closed doors in the cloistered inner sanctums of power, corporate executives dissect sponsorship and grant proposals quickly and efficiently. Additional, *real-life questions* include,

1) Who are these people and what is their reputation in the scientific community?

2) Do we know members of their Board? Any of our executives participating in their projects? Who?

3) Is the science in any way *controversial*? (Stem-cell research, ozone layer, population control, bio-prospecting in the rainforest, marine fisheries, laboratory studies involving animals, cloning, etc.) Are we prepared for robust public debate on the issue?

4) Who's their bank?[59] What do we know about their financial situation? Any audits available? Annual Report?

5) Who's running the Institute/expedition? What's s/he like? Dependable? Presentable at Board functions, media events, etc.?

6) Have we supported them before? When? How much? Any problems on the financial or publicity side?

7) Which other corporations in the community are being solicited? How much are they giving? Are any of our competitors involved? Does our bank support them?

8) OK, we know who they are. How does this project meet our Corporate Vision? Any marketing implications? What does our sales staff think? Any customer impact locally, regionally, nationally, internationally?

---

[59] Banks are perhaps the best and most underutilized global donors. Grants in the U.S. $ 5,000 range are common and "correspondent banks" active internationally are a goldmine of untapped resources, both cash and contacts. Set your filter at those bank holding companies with domestic assets of U.S. $ 10 *billion* or more. While bank mergers and acquisitions seem to be daily events, see "Hold On--There's More," *Entrepreneur*, September, 1998, pp. 128-129, for a starter-list of names and websites of the Top 50 that meet our criterion.

9) Do they understand our corporate culture? Can we coordinate the publicity and co-manage any problems before they become public issues? Who's their "sponsor" here?

10) Is the proposed project innovative? Positive, high profile? Good core values?

11) How are we/they measuring success with this project?

12) How/when will the outcomes be apparent? Are we going to have to micro-manage any of this?

13) Do we want to spread whatever risk there is around? Any other companies want to help us with this? Who should we/they call?

14) What is the potential for patents? What does our legal department think? Have we broached this issue with the scientists?

15) *Finally, the Big Question: What kind of bang for our buck are we getting here?* Are our shareholders going to support this? How about senior staff and Board of Directors? Does anyone see any downside?

IX. *Recommendations:*

When in doubt, follow the money, large *and* small.

Functionally, in terms of corporations you are looking at the "global warming" we mentioned at the beginning of this Chapter. Namely, you need to keep pace of which companies are moving where to produce what and why.

Plus, there are three other "overlays" you, as a scientist, need to create.

The *first* overlay reflects offshore giving as a percentage of total donations. In the U.S., for example, some 20 corporations annually give more than 10% of their total donations to nonprofits outside the U.S.

Some--like **ExxonMobil, Weyerhaeuser**, and **Alcoa**--give in excess of 20%--with pharmaceutical giant Merck at the astonishing 80% level (e.g., primarily in-kind donations of drugs, etc.).

The *second* overlay establishes a "gift plateau" for companies--say, at least 20% in-kind. For the U.S. example, selected players include **Dell Computer Corporation, Intel Corporation, UAL Corporation** (United Airlines), **3M**, and **Microsoft Corporation.**

A *third* overlay looks at total revenues for a company worldwide. If more than 50% of the revenues of a company based in your country are generated *offshore*, it should be on your target list of donors. (**Texaco**, which operates facilities in more than 150 nations, is an excellent example for U.S.-based scientists with overseas projects. Biomedical researchers might examine the model proposed by **Bertelsmann A.G.**, the German media conglomerate, whose Foundation has assets estimated at U.S. $10 *billion*.)

In an ideal world, several names would occupy all three lists, with these names central to the science in which you are engaged. These would be serious, serious targets for your fundraising efforts.

In real estate, the mantra is "location, location, location." It is true here, too. Functionally, you are planning an invasion. Ride in on the crest of the corporate wave and establish a beachhead. Dig in deep. Watch your rear, as other scientists will see your success and want to poach your donors. (More on this, later.)

In addition to small corporate grants (U.S. $ 30,000+ in the *Fortune* 500), two areas of opportunity exist--and they both need to be explored vigorously:

1) *Cause-related marketing*: food and beverage is usually thought of first here, as they often link their products with causes and carefully measure resulting sales. These "share-of-stomach" companies are aggressive, focused, and potentially generous. They also are deluged with proposals. Growth sectors include accounting (especially with the scandals in the U.S.), airlines (*global* code-sharing partners), banking/investments, chemical (200th anniversary of DuPont), and pharmaceutical entities. Opinions differ regarding media companies, but the consensus is they are crucial partners (especially in sponsorships). Remember: "customers like companies that support good causes."[60] Even in the early 1990s, when choosing products of equal quality and price point, 78% of survey respondents indicated they would buy those made by companies that contributed to medical research, education, and similar efforts. Two-thirds indicated they would switch brands, if a company supported a cause of particular interest to the buyer.[61]

---

[60] Justin Martin, "Good Citizenship is Good Business," *Fortune*, March 21, 1994, p. 15.

[61] *Ibid.*, p. 16. Cone Communications has long been a leader in charting corporate citizenship and consumer response to social activism.

2) Sponsorship: Brand entrenchment, equity, enrichment, and expansion are the core opportunities. Some U.S. $1 *billion* went to U.S.-based nonprofits last year, according to IEG, but sports continue to dominate sponsorships (70%). Taking advantage of the sports focus, particularly the high-tech and global aspects of industry-leader automobile racing, could pay dividends for innovative Institutes or expeditions active in key sponsor market areas.

Power Tip: monitor studies by Total Research Corporation, which examines the perceived quality, salience, and equity of world-class brands using its own proprietary EquiTrend methodology. While some brands are high-profile--**Craftsman Tools, Rolls-Royce Motor Cars** (and often under the microscope for sponsorships), others like **Waterford Crystal, WD-40 Spray Lubricant, Bose Stereo & Speaker Systems, Crayola Crayons, and M&M's Chocolate Candies** may be overlooked for novel funding partnerships.[62]

Lest anyone doubt the power of brand and the importance of tapping this power for your scientific endeavors, look no further than motor-sports. The global phenomenon of American-style "stockcar racing"--the NASCAR brand of motor-sports--demonstrates the power of brand loyalty to sponsors exhibited by die-hard automobile racing fans.[63] Some 72% surveyed indicated their loyalty to brands which sponsored racecars driven by their favorite drivers. It is this kind of passion that you need to instill in your sponsors, donors, and your own global brand.

Plus, the adage, "Think Small," should be embraced, enthusiastically.

---

[62] See *Quirk's Marketing Research Review* and its website at <www.quirks.com>.

[63] Simmons Market Research Bureau, Inc., Performance Research and ESPN Chilton studies released for 1999. In global marketing circles, NASCAR is often cited for its cutting-edge sponsorship programs, which should be viewed carefully by scientists interested in sponsorship from the automotive and other high-tech sectors as a funding analogue. For detailed information on the financing strategies of the premier motorsports series worldwide—F1-- see Russell Hotten's *Winning: The Business of Formula One* (New York: Texere, 2000). For funding implications and sponsorships in Central Europe, see William F. Vartorella, "Pod zltou vlajkou: Sponzorovanie timu F1 a boj o Strednu Europu" ("Under the Yellow Flag: F1 Team Sponsorships and the Battle for Central Europe"), *F1 Sport International/Slovenske Vydanie,* July, 2002, 24-25 and Vartorella, "F1 Racing at the Ragged Edge: Team Sponsorships and the Slovakia Connection," *Grand Prix Business,* February, 2004, pp. 30-33, with an English abstract, p. 88.

ℱUNDING ℰXPLORATION | ℭHAPTER ℱIVE

Pocket change can add up, as the Center for Ecosystem Survival discovered with its simple "Conservation Parking Meter" plan to help save the rainforests. In 1991, the Center began installing meters in aquariums, botanical gardens, zoos, and in stores of the **Nature Company** in an effort to raise money to purchase and protect land in tropical rainforests. The meters depicted leopards, hummingbirds, and gibbons in the area usually dedicated to the amount of parking time remaining. Selected venues raised U.S. $ six figures in the first three years of operation.

"Think Small" also refers to scientific projects with microscopic venues, such as malaria research, or other literal "islands of opportunity," such as Barbados--where science leads to informed environmental policy. In Barbados, scientists monitor 40 reef sites, plan a 10-megawatt "wind farm" with turbines, install buildings with solar-powered water heaters, and protect the 60-mile coastline with breakwaters and groins.

In island contexts, the interface of Nature, energy, and human issues is eminently fundable, particularly with at-risk ocean environments and growing pressure from tourism and coastal development.

The point is that your research or expedition may be most fundable when it combines science with positive policy and business implications (*not* to be confused with *advocacy*, which makes corporations shudder and raises legitimacy issues about the form and function of your nonprofit structure). Yet the line between constructive dialogue and controversy is a narrow one, from the corporate perspective.

In other words, science in a vacuum is rarely fundable: it must have context in people terms. For companies, people = consumers = profits.

Meet corporate Mission--first, the needs of your constituencies-- second, and your team's infrastructure--third. That is the formula for success.

If you are a museum or Institute-based scientific group:

- Canvas your Collection for both its strengths and its most unusual specimens. Think of how your Collection should evolve in terms of both its competitive components (strengths) and those that are most opportunistic (meteorites, ancient birds, minerals, etc.) in terms of attracting media visibility and funding.
- For those companies that seem the best targets, develop small revolving exhibits of your Collection which can be displayed prominently at a corporate facility. A sub-set of this exhibit should be created *specifically* for the office of the CEO. Your collection needs to be **visible** to potential donors and their

global supply-chain.

- Conduct special, behind-the-scenes visits for not only CEOs and the families of decision-makers at corporations but for company clients/suppliers, etc. who may be visiting the plant. Become an indispensable part of corporate culture as an ambassador of the natural history of your area/nation. You volunteer your services; get them to volunteer theirs--first step to gear and money.

- Become attuned to the sister companies of the subsidiary. Know a company's **4 M's: Mission, Mood, Motive, Markets**. Its "Mood" is a reflection of good times/bad times. And remember this: there's no "good time" to raise money. You need to be raising money **now**, both for immediate needs (next three years) and in perpetuity (endowment = self-sustainability).

- Don't just think outside-the-box, look inside. Whoever has *Velociraptor* should pick up the telephone and contact the NBA's Toronto Raptors. Dinosaurs, children, and sports personalities has global cachet. No telling what might emerge from a robust conversation.

- Create an atmosphere of dialogue and **life-long learning** between Collections and development professionals (as well as Board and Institute or Museum Director). The more they know about the   nuances of the Collection, laboratory, or fieldwork--the better. Include urgent preservation/conservation needs in each and every request for corporate or individual support for program-related   money. Preservation is difficult to fund in isolation. Make it part of the Big Picture.

Remember: global companies are searching for themes that have a direct bearing on some aspect of the corporate Vision--which includes penetration and exposure in new markets, new consumers, and *access* to governmental decision-makers *you* probably already know. But equally important, they are focused on their corporate image, "good corporate citizens," and leadership-by-example.

If you are an expedition--

1) Avoid the "Scott Syndrome." Robert Falcon Scott (1868-1912), the intrepid polar explorer, had a frustrating season trying to raise £ 40,000 for his final assault on the South Pole. In October, 1911, he informed his team that the expedition had run out of

funding. Regardless, he moved forward on that fatal rush to Pole, losing the race to Roald Amundsen--himself long beset with funding difficulties--and died in his tent with companions on the ice during the return trek. Point: being adequately funded is crucial to risk-management. Today's risks in extreme environments are no less daunting than those faced courageously by Scott, regardless of today's advanced communications and GIS/GPS technologies. Furthermore, expedition members also contributed finances to his team, much in tune with the model we have advocated. Scott perished. Therein lies a cautionary tale.

2) Retracing the steps of some famous explorer is more about nostalgia and adventure than fundable science, **unless** it
   * documents **sociological changes** along an ancient trade route over the millennia;
   * measures **environmental degradation** against some earlier benchmark;
   * conducts a systematic **census of some species** against earlier data;
   * presents a **discovery within some new context** (debunks the conventional wisdom, reveals important participation by indigenous peoples, leadership by women, etc.).

3) Get the infrastructure funded as in-kind donations of supplies, air travel, telephone, etc. and lent equipment. Most of the gear should be proven, field-tested, with a smaller percentage "cutting-edge and innovative." Managing the gear used is part of managing the risk, particularly in extreme environments. Make this point clear to manufacturers and suppliers. "Cutting-edge" can be "bleeding-edge" and the summit of K2 or a deep dive on mixed gases is no place to find out which is which.

4) Before signing any "film deal," seek expert legal advice from a *seasoned entertainment attorney*. What starts as a one-page "deal memo" can rapidly escalate into a 72-page contract. Film finance is secretive, counter-intuitive, and agonizingly complicated. It can involve "cross-collateralizing" and a host of other tricks-of-the-trade. It is an extreme environment in its own right.

Also, consider these: **Rolex Watches** and **The Charles A. and Anne Morrow Lindbergh Foundation** deserve a serious look, especially as their funding can attract additional support in an exponential way. The **Rolex Awards for Enterprise** is global and extremely competitive. From 1976 through 1996, for example, Rolex awards included the study of European cave paintings; the breeding of endangered bird species by developing methods for sex identification; testing the ability of gorillas to learn and use human sign language; Himalayan snow leopards; Mayan wall paintings; an extreme winter in tents at Antarctica's Brabant Island; the rainforest canopy; ground beetles in Nepal (and how biological species are formed); the use of lasers in museum conservation; an environmental education center in Indonesia; CFC-free refrigerators to help reduce depletion in the ozone layer; student operation of a network of telescopes by remote control; and humanitarian/surgical projects. **The Charles A. and Anne Morrow Lindbergh Foundation** offers equally prestigious grant awards with categories ranging from aviation/aerospace to exploration. Extremely competitive, with rigorous review procedures. **Breitling Watches**, sponsor of Orbiter 3--the first non-stop, round-the-world flight by a hot-air balloon (Bertrand Piccard and Brian Jones), is a generous donor to aerospace exploration. On the young explorer front, **Outside Magazine** provides "Outside Adventure Grants"--the talent search for the greatest explorers of the next generation. [64]

Final thoughts—

1) Diversify your fundraising efforts. Governmental monies are at-risk, globally. Your new strategy must be more market driven. What you have to sell is "information" in the global age. Create a "product advantage" ("unique selling proposition"/USP) for your project. What are its strengths? How can these be translated into joint projects with corporations?

2) Recognize that the Mission/Vision of the corporation is of *primary* importance, with your audience second and your goals, third.

3) Think "brand." Yours. Theirs. Revisit your Mission annually, with the goal of making it more responsive to global community needs and desires. More memorable.

4) Conduct an overlay, as suggested above, to determine which corporations (and foundations) are a) most active in your market now and b) are most apt to become active. Goal is to help them meet their Missions. Do not overlook "controversial" companies that may be linked to public

---

[64] See *The Best of the Rolex Awards for Enterprise, 1976 to 1999* for the wide-ranging scope of interests at Rolex. For further information, contact the Secretariat of the Rolex Awards for Enterprise, P.O. Box 1311, 1211 Geneva 26, Switzerland. For The Charles A. and Anne Morrow Lindbergh Foundation, the address is 708 South 3rd Street, Suite 110, Minneapolis, MN 55415-1141 U.S.A. Breitling Watches, world headquarters, may be reached at P.O. Box 1132, 2540 Grenchen, Switzerland. For young explorers, see "Outside Adventure Grants," *Outside Magazine*, 420 Lexington Avenue, Suite 440, New York City, NY 10017 U.S.A.

health or environmental issues. These often prove to be the best partners as it is in a company's best interest to be a "good neighbor" and to advocate for sustainable resources. Create a "clip-file" of ads that mirror your research. Donors are lurking everywhere. Be vigilant

5) Venture forth into Cyberspace. Home pages. On-line $$$ searches. (For companies, see The American Leadership Forum's website, which is providing corporations with advice, re: improving corporate-giving programs, equipment donations, etc. (http://www.alfsv.org/involve).

6) Get your financial reports in good order. Accountability is the shibboleth of the 21st century.

7) Begin the process early of identifying and soliciting joint venture/consortial partners. Choose those with a) a history of giving money or b) a track record for attracting money.

8) Use "volunteerism" as the first step in soliciting corporate partners. Then move to requests of in-kind contributions (equipment and supplies) and, finally, cash.

9) Promote your Collection or your expedition/science through your nation's tourism board, hotel chains, etc. Be visible.

10) Finally, provide *measurable results* for all projects. While corporations cannot be expected to provide all your financial needs, they open the door to increased giving from both individuals and government--even in recessionary times.

***

Bibliography for Chapter 5
"Corporate Consciousness: Corporate Culture"

Agle, D.C. "Rover Boys: Three crews of Apollo astronauts experienced an out-of-this-world driving adventure." *AutoWeek,* July 30, 2001, pp. 16-17.

Aldred, Cyril. *Akhenaten: King of Egypt*. London: Thames and Hudson Ltd., 1989.

Anft, Michael. "Toward Corporate Change: Businesses seek nonprofit help in quest to become better citizens." *The Chronicle of Philanthropy*, September 19, 2002, pp. 9, 12, 10.

Anonymous. "A Guide to Social Investing. " *My Generation*, November-December, 2001, p. 30.

_____. "Companies Forecast First Significant Increases in Giving in 5 Years." *The Chronicle of Philanthropy*, September 21, 1995, p.12.

_____. "Hold On--There's More." *Entrepreneur*, September, 1998, pp. 128-129.

_____. "Matters of Fact." UNDP *Choices*, Volume 12, Number 2 (June, 2002),
    p. 28.

_____. "Technology: New Approach to Linking Corporations, Charities."
    The Chronicle of Philanthropy, May 30, 2002, p. 31.

_____. "Where to Donate (and find) Surplus Goods." *Successful Meetings*, June,
    1996, p. 42.

Blum, Debra E. "After the Attacks: Consumers Choose Products Based on Corporate
    Philanthropy, Studies Find. " *The Chronicle of Philanthropy*, November 29, 2001,
    p. 24.

Chart--"Global Warming" in *"CIO* 100 World Leaders." *CIO*, August, 1996, p. 38.

Chart. *CIO*, September 15, 1995, p. 18.

Christensen, Mark. *Super Car: The Story of the Xeno.* New York: Thomas Dunne
    Books (St. Martin's Griffin), 2001.

Evans, Bob. "Personal Finance: Socially Responsible Investing: Your Don't Have to
    Sacrifice Profits for Principles." *Self-Employed America*, March/April, 1997,
    pp. 14-15.

Farnham, Alan. "Managing: Ideas & Solutions--Brushing Up Your Vision Thing."
    Fortune, May 1, 1995, p. 129.

Feeback, Ronald W., and Vartorella, William F. "A `Back to Basics' Studio for $10,000."
    Educational & Industrial Television, Volume 13, Number 10 (October, 1981),
    52-54.

Gray, Susan. "Charities' Income From Sponsorships Up 10%--Chart: How Corporate
    Spending to Sponsor Events Has Grown." *The Chronicle of Philanthropy*,
    March 26, 1998, p. 20.

Hall, Holly. "Joint Ventures With Business: A Sour Deal?" *The Chronicle of
    Philanthropy*, April 6, 1993, pp. 21-22.

Haller, Vera (with Amicone, Hay). "Scribes in Cyberspace." *Beyond Computing*,
    October, 1995, pp. 18-21.

Harvard, Andrew and Thompson, Todd. *Mountain of Storms: The American
    Expeditions to Dhaulagiri, 1969 & 1973.* New York: Chelsea House, New York

University Press, 1974.

Hawkins, Donald E.; Wood, Megan Epler; and Bittman, Sam. *The Ecolodge Sourcebook for Planners and Developers*. North Bennington, Vermont: The Ecotourism Society, 1995.

Hess, Peter E. "Deep Shipwreck in High Courts." *Delaware Lawyer*, Volume 17, Number 1 (Spring, 1999), 16-19.

Hildebrand, Carol. "Branding the Globe." *CIO Enterprise*, Section 2 (March 15, 1998), pp. 34-35, 38-40, 42.

Hotten, Russell. *Winning: The Business of Formula One*. New York: Texere, 2000.

Kamler, Kenneth. *Doctor on Everest. Emergency Medicine at the Top of the World—A Personal Account including the 1996 Disaster*. New York: The Lyons Press, 2000.

Kuhn, Susan E. "How Business Helps Schools." *Fortune/Special Issue*, Spring, 1990, pp. 91-94, 96, 98, 100, 102, 104, 106.

M.L. "Newswatch--Global Confidence Survey: Legends of the Fall." *CFO*, September, 2001, p. 26.

Mares, Michael A. "Natural History Museums: Bridging the Past and the Future" in *Int. Symp. & First World Congress on Pres. and Cons. of Nat. Hist. Col.--Vol. 3*, 367-404.

Martin, Justin. "Good Citizenship is Good Business." *Fortune*, March 21, 1994, pp. 15-16.

Orlean, Susan. "Where's Willy? Everybody's favorite whale tries to make it on his own." *The New Yorker*, September 23, 2002, pp. 56-63.

Quirk's Marketing Research Review and its website at <www.quirks.com>.

Ramsey, Nancy. "How Business Can Help the Schools." *Fortune*, September 16, 1992, pp. 147-148, 150, 154, 156, 160, 162, 166, 168, 172, 174.
Salamon, Lester M. *The International Guide to Nonprofit Law*. New York: John Wiley & Sons, Inc., 1997.

Satava, Richard and Blackadar, Thomas. "The Physiologic Cipher: Telemedicine on Everest." *GPS World*, October, 2001, 20.

Stehle, Vince. "European Philanthropy Experts Disagree on Rules for Giving in Era of

Euro." *The Chronicle of Philanthropy*, May 21, 1998, p. 37.

Various Authors. "The New Automotive Universe 2000." *Automobile Magazine*, July, 2000, 76-80, 82, 84-85. Richard Feast, "As the dust settles, our stellar experts analyze the new order," pp. 76-77. Georg Kacher, "The view from Europe," pp. 78-79. Peter Nunn, "The view from Asia," pp. 80, 82. Paul Lienert, "The view from America," pp. 82, 84-85.

Vartorella, William F. "An Insider's Guide to Getting Equipment Grants." *Nonprofit Management Strategies*, October, 1992, 1,7,11.

_____."Corporate Fund Raising in Transition: Posers, Players, and Power Proposals." *Fund Raising Institute (FRI) Monthly Portfolio*, Volume 33, Number 7 (July, 1994), 1-2.

_____. "Creating Sustainable Funding for Natural History Collections in the New World Order--Foundations and Corporations: Old Allies, New Opportunities." *Museum Management and Curatorship* (England), Volume 15, No. 3 (September, 1996), 328-333.

_____. "Doing the bright thing with your company logo." *Advertising Age*, February 26, 1990, p. 31.

_____. "Exploring Inner Space: the Mind of the Donor." *Human Performance in Extreme Environments*, Volume 3, Number 1 (September, 1998), 113-116.

_____. "F1 Racing at the Ragged Edge: Team Sponsorships and the Slovakia Connection." *Grand Prix Business*, February, 2004, pp. 30-33. English abstract, p. 88.

_____. "Pod zltou vlajkou: Sponzorovanie timu F1 a boj o Strednu Europu" ("Under the Yellow Flag: F1 Team Sponsorships and the Battle for Central Europe"), trans. by Peter Fritz. *F1 Sport International/Slovenske Vydanie,* July, 2002, pp. 24-25.

_____. "The `Archaeology' of Finding Equipment." *The Glyph,* Volume I, Number 13 (June, 1998), 11, 13-14.

Whelan, David. "Corporate Giving Rose in 2000, Survey Finds." *The Chronicle of Philanthropy*, January 24, 2002, p. 11.

See the website of the Wildlife Conservation Society (WCS) at <http://wcs.org> for full information and how corporate and individual donors can participate in saving the Jaguar. See "Islands at Risk," a letter from Duane Silverstein in "Airmail," *Condé Nast Traveler*, at <www.cntraveler.com>.

Chapter 6: "The Asia-Pacific Century--Plucking Fruits from the Money Tree"

By William F. Vartorella

> *"All men can see the tactics whereby I conquer, but what none can see is the strategy out of which victory is evolved."*
> *Sun Tzu (ca. 400-320 B.C.), Art of War [6: 27]*

I. Introduction:

According to John Naisbitt, author of *Megatrends Asia: The Eight Asian Megatrends That are Changing the World* (1996), Asia is the hottest of the hot and is positioned to dominate the world's economy in what many have termed the arrival of the Asian Century.

Scientists with projects in The People's Republic of China (PRC), Indonesia, India, Malaysia, and Vietnam take note, as software engineering, the rush for upscale consumer goods, and improvements in health care will mean an influx of technology and consumer subsidiaries.

As "Nature abhors a vacuum," money and opportunity will vie for these new markets. Scientists need to be poised to be beneficiaries of this onslaught to Asia.

First, let us examine the "strategic environment" for business.

By the late 20th century, in terms of measuring world competitiveness relative to *domestic economies*, six of the 10 best performers were in Asia. According to the International Institute for Management Development (IMD) in Lausanne, Switzerland, these included,

* People's Republic of China (2nd)
* Singapore (3rd)
* South Korea (4th)
* Japan (5th)
* Malaysia (7th) and
* Hong Kong (8th).[1]

---

[1] Richard Zelade, "Leading the Pack," *International Business*, December 1996/January 1997, p. 6.

IMD has created a "World Competitiveness Scoreboard," which weighs 225 criteria divided into eight factors--with some two-thirds of those based upon global statistics. Essentially, by definition IMD is examining a country's ability "to increase national wealth, based on a variety of economic, social and geographic factors."

An analysis of the Top 30 discloses eight Asian economies:

* Singapore (2nd)
* Hong Kong (3rd)
* Japan (4th; the U.S. has displaced it as #1)
* Taiwan (18th)
* Malaysia (23rd)
* People's Republic of China (PRC, 26th)
* South Korea (27th)
* Thailand (30th).[2]

Additionally, in the decade that ends in 2005, East Asia will require about U.S. $1.5 *trillion* to meet its huge demand for infrastructure. As noted by World Bank in 1996, private investment projects and privatization drive infrastructure developments in transport, power generation, and telecom-munications[3]--particularly in Latin America, East Asia, and Central Europe. Domestic economies, poised for rapid growth, are globally competitive.

Yet, we must avoid putting too much of a gloss on this seeming globalization. The short-term reality is that Asia-Pacific--like North America and the European Union (EU)--is a *trading bloc*, an economic engine shifting gears from standardized to customized economies. This engine is fueled by pent-up demand for new consumer products, most of which are driven by the Information Age and software innovation.

Toshiro Shimoyama, **Olympus Optical's** chairman and CEO, has characterized tomorrow's corporate leaders as the "2.5" companies. The global economy, according to an interview in *Fortune*, has evolved from the agricultural stage (#1) to the manufacturing stage (#2) toward a high-tech, information-based economy driven by service (#3).

What today are *niches* tomorrow will be full-blown *markets*. Yet it is in this transition between trading bloc and freewheeling global economy

---

[2] IMD, *World Competitiveness Yearbook*, Chart, "World Competitiveness Scoreboard: Top 30, 1996" in Richard Zelade, "Leading the Pack," *International Business*, December 1996/January 1997, p. 6.

[3] World Bank, *Private Infrastructure Project Database, 1996*, "Private Investment Projects, 1984-1995" in "Let's Make A Deal," *International Business*, December 1996/January 1997, p. 6.

where opportunity beckons. The old saying, "money never sleeps," is especially true for Asia and the Pacific Rim. [4]

Plan; muster your forces and Mission; attack.

But remember this: just as most corporate projects in Asia-Pacific Rim are capital intensive and virtually beyond the single capability of most companies, so too your scientific ventures. Asia-Pacific is perhaps the best analogue for creating partnerships that address specific aspects of your shared Missions, while maintaining balance and the potential for growth.

Imagine your scientific endeavor in terms of a technology-driven, "S-curve." It takes your Institute the same amount of time to develop and capture 10% of a market, as it does to move from that point to 90% on the continuum. In other words, a competitor enters with an equal product (or one "superior" in terms of marketing capability) and in, say, five years grabs 10% of the market and five years later your Institute finds itself out-flanked and out-of-business.

Now we turn to the second part of the equation: Asian consumers and geo-demography. In mid-1990s, the U.S. Department of Commerce named the People's Republic of China (PRC), Indonesia, India, and South Korea (in no particular rank order) as the four world's 10 biggest emerging markets. Simultaneously, The Futures Group identified the PRC, India, Indonesia, South Korea, and Thailand in its Top 10 of selected countries with a growing Middle Class "based on purchasing power parity, $ 10,000 to $ 40,000."[5] Similarly, *The Kiplinger Washington Letter* reported that by 2025, there would be some 700 million *new* Middle-Class consumers in Asia.

Yet, as these nations industrialize and consumerism takes hold, their birthrate falls and the *median* age rises. By 2010, Japan's projected median age is 42 years, the Koreas--34, and the PRC--34. By comparison, according to the private Population Reference Bureau in Washington, D.C., the U.S. average age in 2010 will be 37 years. This impacts the kind of consumer products, their niche markets, and pricing.

New prosperity. New markets. New opportunities for scientists, both domestic and foreign, to get funded as subsidiaries locate in adopted "communities of interest" and supply-chains develop accordingly.

So, how does one proceed?

---

[4]   In October of 2002, The International Monetary Fund (IMF) launched a web site related to the foreign direct investment (FDI) practices of 55 countries. It was designed specifically for financial analysts, researchers, and journalists. The web site address is www.imf.org/external/np/sta/di/mdb97.htm.

[5]   See Chart, "Number of Middle-Class Workers," in *Fortune*, May 30, 1994, p. 76.

II. *East Meets West--Understanding the Asian Business Mind:*

In 1989, the business world was abuzz. Akio Morita, the co-founder of **Sony,** had teamed up with politician Shintaro Ishihara to write a business treatise entitled, *The Japan That Can Say No.* The book, which quickly became a sensation in Japan and immediately sold some 60,000 copies, makes three points, which are important in our current context:

1) Perhaps because of Confucian influences, the Japanese find it difficult to say, unequivocally, "no." They use silence in its stead, which is easily misunderstood by global outsiders.

2) The Western (and particularly, American) business outlook is rather myopic (evidenced by the remarks of a currency trader in New York whose global timeframe is 10 minutes), while the Japanese think in 10-year terms.

3) Predictions abound that the service sector will overtake manufacturing--leading to a post-industrial society in which innovation and creativity are lost.[6]

Japanese companies and Asian companies writ large are enigmas disguised as conundrums.

Part of the key to unlocking the mystery is to understand the underlying business behavior of the Asian behemoth corporations.

Staying with the Japanese example, a few words about the *kaisha*--the large Japanese corporation--are in order.

1) Unless you are Japanese, you are a *gaijin*--a foreigner. You will be treated differently, but do not be misled. The context of a business situation is everything and tends to dictate the insider-outsider relationship, which can be very fluid. Your goal is to bring to the table opportunities that are consistent with the corporate culture and the overall goals and objectives in such a way as to position your project and its brand equity as an "insider."

---

[6] Anonymous, "Competition--A Japanese View: Why America has Fallen Behind," *Fortune,* September 25, 1989, p. 52.

2) Fear of embarrassment--what the West simply glosses over as "losing face"--runs deep in Japanese culture. This means individual business executives are reluctant to take risks, *unless* their company's reputation *vis-à-vis* a competitor is in jeopardy. Knowing the "pressure points"/competitive disadvantages faced by a company in the market place can help move executives to action, even if reluctantly.

3) Appearances can be deceiving. The *kaisha* looks egalitarian, acts egalitarian, but is not egalitarian. It is a highly hierarchical organization of workers who do not wish to stand out.[7] In dealing with Japanese business leaders and Asian corporate executives generally, look beyond the obvious, including who is leading the discussion with you at the bargaining table.

Understand this. Until 1990, tax advantages for Japanese companies involved in philanthropy did not substantively exist.

For perspective, one needs to turn to the creation of the Council for Better Corporate Citizenship (CBCC) in Japan on 4 September 1989. According to its own "press kit,"

> Responding to the changing international business environment, Japanese companies continue to increase the investments abroad. . . . However, there is concern that a lack of awareness of local business practices, social values, and cultures will adversely affect the economic, social, and political fabric of local communities as well as national economies.[8]
> **Akio Morita, Chairman, CBCC Chairman, Sony Corporation**

The CBCC drafted and distributed a "Proposal for Better Corporate Citizenship" to its membership, which had swelled to 330 companies by April, 1991. Fundamentally, it proclaimed,

---

[7] Advice abounds on business dealings with Japanese and Asian corporations. Start with Noboru Yoshimura and Philip Anderson's *Inside the Kaisha: Demystifying Japanese Business Behavior* (Harvard Business School Press). Also recommended is Boye De Mente's *Made in Japan* and Sondra Snowdon's *The Global Edge: How Your Company Can Win in the International Marketplace*. Ms. Snowdon's book offers concise advice on proper negotiating techniques in 25 venues, including Japan, the PRC, Hong Kong, India, Singapore, South Korea, and Taiwan. Roger E. Axtell's *The Do's and Taboos of International Trade: a Small Business Primer* is also useful, especially Chapters 11 ("Communication") and 12 ("Dealing with the Japanese Mystique").

[8] See, Council for Better Corporate Citizenship, Keidanren Building, 1-9-4 Otemachi, Chiyoda-ku, Tokyo 100, Japan. This brief Chapter section is drawn from initial CBCC materials in "press kit" form. Without delving into the intricacies of the tax issues, in order to be tax exempt, Japanese companies made donations to the CBCC, which were then distributed by the CBCC. The stated goal of these "overseas contributions by Japanese companies" was "to benefit local communities and contribute to improved understanding of Japan."

It has become increasingly important that investing companies should be recognized as important contributors to each local economy and be accepted by the local communities as good corporate citizens.[9]

To that end, Japanese companies were advised to adopt some simple guidelines for philanthropy in new communities of interest: [10]

1) One Percent Volunteer Activities: ". . . the employees or representatives of Japanese companies will take the initiative to use at least one percent of their time during the year (approximately 90 hours) to join in local volunteer activities.

2) Donations that Meet Local Needs: ". . . it is necessary for the home offices of investing companies to understand the importance of local donations, show the greatest respect for local decisions concerning these donations, and respond to the importance of financial contribution by meeting community needs with funds and other kinds of support."

3) Understanding Social Problems and Cooperating to Find Solutions: "As a part of society, investing companies should increase their understanding of social problems and issues related to minorities, education, crime, and poverty and work for their solution."

While much of this was framed for Japanese investment in the U.S., generally speaking these *simple guidelines* continue to resonate with Japanese companies active worldwide.

By keeping the above simple corporate philosophy and guidelines in mind, scientists can probe local Japanese subsidiaries with the goal of acquiring corporate mentoring (request for 90 hours of company expertise), equipment ("other kinds of support"), and cash (solution-based; Japanese philanthropy has expanded significantly to research and development/R&D programs at universities and Institutes; note interest in Japanese support for minorities--and women).

The Chinese business culture is equally murky to Western eyes. In the PRC, relationships follow individuals, not organizations.[11] The phrase

---

[9] *Ibid.*

[10] *Ibid.*

[11] Arnold Pachtman, "Getting to 'Hao!', *International Business*, July/August 1998, p. 25.

"old China-hand" merits remembering, as a scientist dealing with a potential corporate donor/partner needs all the help she can muster.

She is going to be in the dark on several levels:

- The Chinese are not going to proffer information regarding their company, its assets, strategic plans, etc. Invisible stakeholders and unarticulated interests are going to be the greatest stumbling blocks --"hidden agendas" are of significant importance to the Chinese.

- Chinese negotiators seldom can bring any deal to a conclusion--the power often resides with some hidden authority at the Central Government. Worse, according to Arnold Pachtman, writing in *International Business*, these negotiators will attempt to dominate a deal in such a way as to make it more palpable to their superiors. Pachtman's advice: take care with your own disclosures.[12] The goal is to move the dialogue and information-gathering to the point where those who can close the deal actually participate.

- Precedent for supporting the science or expedition is extremely important to the Chinese. For example, Financier J.P. Morgan played a central, if behind-the-scenes role, in assisting Roy Chapman Andrews in securing permission from the Chinese nationalists to search for human fossils in the Gobi Desert. Joint projects and scientific exchanges are traditionally well received in the region and set the stage for long-term, bolder efforts. Witness the 1991 expedition in which a joint team of paleontologists from the American Museum of Natural History and colleagues from the Mongolian Academy of Sciences ventured into Mongolia's Gobi Desert in search of fossils and unrecorded historical sites.[13]

With both the Japanese and the Chinese, the concept of "shared solutions" mirrors their own worldviews. The key is to understand how striving for consensus often breaks any appearance of an impasse. Partial

---

[12] *Ibid.*

[13] Consortial examples in paleontology abound. See, for instance, P.J. Currie, Dong Z.-M., and D.A. Russell, 1993. "Results from the Sino-Canadian Dinosaur Project," *Canadian Journal of Earth Sciences* 30: 1997-2272.

deals are also possible--use, for example, the equation of mentoring, first; then equipment and supplies; and, finally, cash. Consider your request a bundle of alternatives, which can be reassembled in new and creative ways, without sacrificing your major goals--or, importantly, theirs.

In Sun Tzu's *Art of War*, feints and strategic use of deception were highly prized elements of the arsenal. Worse case planning (WCP) is essential, as is knowing the pressure points of the competition. To avoid emboldening a trapped enemy, Sun Tzu urged military strategists to leave a controlled escape route. In your case, leave some room for saving face. In short--know, utilize, and control the strategic business landscape, but allow room for compromise.[14]

While Japan and the PRC can hardly be presented as symptomatic of all of Asia, they do offer insight into the challenges and opportunities presented to scientists who are committed to the "long view."

In seeking grant funding from Asian companies, scientists need to keep the following basic rules in mind:

1) In the West, we tend to be quick to *agree*, yet slow to *implement*.

2) Asians often work by consensus and, therefore, are *slow* to agree, yet *quick* to implement.

3) In the West, we see time in short intervals of high activity. ("We need the $$$ *now*!")

4) In Asia, generally, the Big Picture is key, with long intervals for generations of growth. (Example: Takenaka, a construction and engineering company, is led by a 17th-generation descendant of the founder. As we go to press with *Funding Exploration*, Bok Im Hwang, a South Korea citizen, has announced plans to establish the Hwang Global Foundation, whose assets may exceed U.S. $1-*billion*. The reported Mission is to "support medical research, educational programs that focus on Korean history and culture, and economic projects." Again, understanding the "long view" is important: The Hwang family is descended from 16th Century Korean prime minister and admiral of 10th Century Silla Dynasty.)

---

[14] While the fine art of negotiating is well beyond our purview here, see the classic work by Chester L. Karrass, *The Negotiating Game: How to get what you want* (New York: Thomas Y. Crowell, 1970).

5) Your business card (translated into the native language) has a serious role in determining your level of access to Asian executives. Heads of nonprofits can deal with heads of Asian corporations, depending upon the title on a business card. "President and CEO" is an excellent title, as it offers at least the potential for access to the president of an Asian firm.

With this said, proposals to Asian funders should be carefully crafted to incorporate core cultural values and to imbue a sense of tradition and respect for both *their* and *your* corporate culture. Showing respect for your own Institute or expedition is a serious issue. Men: keep your business cards in your breast pocket, not in the bulging wallet in the seat of your pants. A crumpled business card extracted from that nether region says volumes to an Asian executive of how you regard your Institute or expedition.

Finally, when in Asia follow the Chinese principle of *guanxi*: Asians generally do not like to conduct business with strangers. A mutually known and respected contact is your best source of introduction. Other sources include your correspondent bank, law firm, embassy, trading company, or official trade mission.

The opportunity for scientists worldwide is enormous. In the U.S. alone, some experts estimate that early in the 21st century, one in every 20 foundations will most likely be that of an Asian corporation.

American Honda, Brother International, Canon, Daiwa, Matsushita Electric, NEC, Nikon, Ricoh Electronics, Sony Corporation, Subaru, Toshiba, Toyota Motor Sales and a growing host of others have specific interests in science, mathematics, and projects close to their corporate Missions and areas of research, development, and marketing.

III. Beneath the Cloak of Secrecy:

Funding Exploration, like Sun Tzu's *Art of War*, focuses upon strategic and tactical advantages. In the quest for funding, the difference between victor and vanquished often comes down to which side has the better field intelligence and allies.

For scientists working on projects in Asia-Pacific or seeking support from Asian multinational corporations, gaining insight is crucial.

Keeping abreast of Asian marketing and advertising is one way.

The second, published surveys on corporate philanthropy and nonprofit directories.

Third, corporate site selection data.
Let's begin with your ongoing effort to monitor science-related advertising.

For years, Fortune magazine has run an annual "Special Advertising Section" which focuses on global companies--primarily in Asia--with a common underlying theme ("Global Management Strategies for the 1990s," "Global Alliances," etc.). In addition to providing insight into the corporations and their CEOs, sometimes one gets a rare glimpse into how these companies are applying emerging technologies to what the Japanese call kyosei--*"creative shared existence" or "the common good."*

For instance,

Hino Motors: Japan's largest medium and heavy-duty truck manufacturer, Hino developed the HIMR system--the first of its kind to combine diesel and electric systems in one engine. This reduces emissions of smoke, CO^2, and NOx gases, plus improves fuel efficiency. Hino trucks have featured prominently in international off-road racing, like the Paris-Dakar Rally. Truck manufacturers generally are underutilized as funding sources for atmospheric science.

Japan Airlines (JAL) was the first airline to use commercial flights to gather data related to global warming and the endangered ozone layer. Essentially, JAL collected high-altitude air samples over the Pacific as part of a five-year study to measure the amounts of gases causing atmospheric pollution, such as carbon dioxide and methane. This is another example of an unusual funding source for the complicated and often controversial issue of the degradation of the ozone layer.

Mazda Motor's: 75% of Mazda's cars--mostly the metal--are recyclable. Mazda has developed the world's first repeatedly recyclable, plastic composite. It can be used to re-form other automotive components such as dashboards and interior molding. For scientists interested in unusual composites and the implications for 100% recycling, this company may be an appropriate starting place for donor dialogue.

Other, equally intriguing information is embedded in evolving corporate Mission/Vision activities such as **Mitsubishi Motors'** creation of a special "action council" to address global warming, recycling, and energy conservation.

Plus, Asia-Pacific companies have a penchant for evocative environmental projects, the human-machine interface, and marketing:

"How to teach a plant self-defense." **(Mitsubishi Kasei**'s ad for creating new strains of insect and disease-resistant rice notes that the crop is a staple for billions of people. Genetic engineering is the focus, as indicated in the copy, "You'll see how we're helping to feed a world that's hungry for more than just new ideas.") "Unfortunately, a hole in the ozone layer may be coming to a town near you." (Provocative and unusual, to say the least.) "And if you think these holes are just over the South Pole, you're wrong. They may be forming right over your head." (The ad focuses upon **Matshushita Electric**'s satellite-mounted ozone sensor that reportedly can "simultaneously measure concentration, temperature and pressure in the ozone layer.") At Matsushita, "we're not only concerned about our products, we're concerned about our planet."

"Symbiosis: ism." (A bee, white flowers, and **Nippon Steel**.) "Symbiosis is one of the natural world's truly beautiful systems. In reality, this principle of dynamic natural relationships exists not only among plants and animals; it also applies to animals and humans, humans and humans, companies and companies, companies and the environment, humans and the earth." (Protecting the environment has been touted as an "essential element" in the company's management strategy. Heavy industries often seek environmental partners to underscore corporate commitment to earth's preservation. Botanists take note.)

"More green for less green." (**Toyota**'s television ad campaign for its hybrid fossil fuel / electric vehicle--"Prius"--uses the great outdoors and great promised fuel mileage as well as tax advantages for U.S. consumers in 2002.) Then, thhere is the *print* campaign for Prius, to wit:

"Hybrid Fact #3: Prius has been honored by the United Nations, Sierra Club and the National Wildlife Federation (no wonder our competitors are turning green). Prius | genius." (Co-branding in a truly global sense.)

"The latest development in advanced technology: Back to Nature." (This ad for **NKK Corporation**--steel--has a recycling theme.) "Furthermore, 99.5% of all waste products are recycled, saving resources and underscoring NKK's commitment to clean air and water." (NKK's "Clean and Green" program emphasizes "greater harmony with the environment." Ad also mentions its subsidiaries in U.S. and Europe, plus it principal overseas offices in Vancouver, Beijing, Hong Kong, Bangkok, Singapore, Jakarta, Taipei, and Al-Khobar.)

"In the Chin Dynasty, They Built a Wall. Now They're Using AST Computers to Add a Highway." (Ad for **AST® Computer**, which elivers computer systems "pre-loaded with Chinese software as far away as Manchuria." (Excellent candidate for computer needs for scientific projects in China.)

It may prove true that the last wholly biological generation of humans will be the one reading this book. In 1987, the Japanese announced a bold project called "The Human Frontiers"--heralded as the largest international collaboration of scientists ever conceived. Taking a holistic approach, investigators began to look hard at the nature of thought and consciousness, the living cell, immune systems and implications for designing the next generation of Artificial Intelligence (AI) projects.[15]

Subsequently, scientists worldwide have converged on sentient research[16] with the ultimate goal of a biological computer--the marriage of carbon- and silicon-based technologies. Estimates by 2030 put genetic engineering in "full-swing," with the distinction between carbon and silicon-based platforms blurring, as robotics and miniaturization attack human frailties in ever-smaller contexts. During the Roman Empire (275 B.C.), the average lifespan was 26 years. By 2200, futurists believe the average lifespan will be some 200 years longer.[17]

Honda has not only been a leader in the overall research effort, but has incorporated its work into its 2002 advertising campaign:

> "We're building a dream, one robot at a time. The dream was simple. Design a robot that, one day, could duplicate the complexities of human motion and actually help people. An easy task? Hardly. But after more than 15 years of research and development, the result is ASIMO, an advanced robot with unprecedented human-like abilities   . . . . Honda: the power of dreams™. (Take note: in the next section, we shall discuss "dream documents" and their importance in the funding equation.)

Some companies such as Tokyo-based **Canon, Inc.** approach international environmental arena differently, eschewing military projects--for instance-- as international understanding and war do not mix. So, too, any research that harms the global ecosystem is systematically avoided.

Then, there are the somewhat more familiar advertisements for the region:

---

[15] F. David Peat, *Artificial Intelligence: How Machines Think* (Rev. ed.: New York: Baen Books, Distributed by Simon & Schuster, 1988), p. i.

[16] By "sentient," we mean the capability of computers to mimic (?) at least rudimentary consciousness. Prototype software has been tested in Kenya (giraffe habitat study, Sweetwaters Reserve) and in Spain (field archaeology, Iberian and Roman periods at el Gandul, southeast of Seville) that "takes note of its environment--observing time, weather, and companions and ascertaining position using GPS." See Jason Pascoe, *et al.*, "Context Aware: the Dawn of Sentient Computing?", *GPS World*, September 1998, 22.

[17] *Knight-Ridder Tribune*, "Chart: Average life expectancy," June 28, 1992, n.p.

"Waking up at 16,000' is amazing anywhere in the world. But there's something special about looking off toward central Asia and remembering the yak yogurt you had a few days before with Genghis Khan's children." (Quotation from and photograph of Alex Lowe, alpinist, from the summit of "The Bird," Ak-Su, Kyrgyzstan. Ad for **The North Face**®, with a testimonial flavor and equipment-in-extreme-use.)

"The New Marco Polo Business Class. Built to help the corporate body arrive in better shape." (Ad for **Cathay Pacific Airlines**.)

"At **Sunkyong**, we are not awaiting the 21st century, we intend to shape it." (This Korean multinational firm is a leader in the fields of energy, telecommunications, engineering, and construction. Of particular importance is the ad's emphasis upon global alliances, which "reflect the focused application of time, energy, and resources required for a shared understanding of objectives--a shared vision of economic globalization.")

Finally, a point not often made is that just as the West is looking east at new markets, so, too, is the East looking east. The tradition of well-established trading companies is paying huge dividends to those who have planned and prospered. **Samsung**, the oldest of the Korean *chaebol* and one of the largest corporations in the world, realizes more than half of its sales revenues from either exports or its overseas subsidiaries.

Published surveys on Asian philanthropy are also important resources.

The Japan External Trade Organization (JETRO) occasionally issues reports based upon a "Survey of Corporate Philanthropy at Japanese-Affiliated Operations in the United States."
Key findings have included,

- Approximately 80% of Japanese-affiliated operations in the U.S. responding to the survey said they engage in corporate philanthropy.
- Cash donations remained the most common form of philanthropic activity (91%).
- More than 40% encourage employee voluntarism.[18]

---

[18] Japan External Trade Organization, *Survey of Corporate Philanthropy at Japanese-Affiliated Operations in the United States* (New York: JETRO, June, 1995), p. 2.

By the late 1990s, it was becoming clear that for two-thirds of Japanese companies operating in the U.S., their parent companies in Japan no longer had direct involvement in U.S. philanthropic decision-making.

Still, financial donations tend to be greatest among largest Japanese corporations. Companies with 1,000 or more workers are most active (97%), while facilities with fewer than 50 employees are least active (64%).

A piece of advice: Japanese firms tend to share the risk and the opportunity for projects with their supply chains. Identifying the key 200 or so suppliers for a Japanese automotive facility, for example, may pay dividends as you forge a long-term, strategic alliance.

Yet, embedded in all of this is a cautionary tale, as critics of Asian philanthropy--and Japanese giving in particular--maintain that high-profile giving has more to do with trade deficits in countries like the U.S., where competitors cry foul of restrictive Japanese import policies. In short, the Japanese may be looking to quash criticism by academics, journalists, politicians, and business competitors. [19] This is just another piece of strategic information in the funding puzzle. The Japanese can be generous, particularly if cultural icons, such as rare Samurai armor, are involved.

One rarely employed strategy is for scientists to form joint ventures with one or more of the roughly 200 Japanese non-governmental organizations (NGOs) active both domestically and in some 100 nations. The time is ripe, as the "Law to Promote Specified Non-Profit Activities," which took effect in 1998, has significantly weakened the Japanese government's control over a broad range of activities--including bank accounts in the names of NGOs. Of particular interest is the fact that these same potential partners are looking to the U.K. and U.S. for governance, funding, tax-treatment of donations, and other charitable models.

For instance in Japan, Global Village is active in recycling and environmental projects in 16 countries. The Association to Help Chernobyl is focused on the plight of children in the Ukraine who suffer from radiation sickness. As we shall see in our Chapter on foundations, such consortial efforts open the funding door exponentially to such synergistic projects.

Regardless, staying abreast of developments via JETRO, The United States-Japan Foundation, *The Asian Wall Street Journal*, corporate Annual Reports, and other sources is critical. [20]

---

[19] *The Japanese Power Game* by William J. Holstein is one such "cautionary tale." A decade ago, he wrote a high-profile opinion piece, "We're Naïve About Japanese Philanthropy," in the January 14, 1992 issue of *The Chronicle of Philanthropy*, pp. 38-39.

[20] See, for example, issues of *Joining Hands: News of Japanese Philanthropy in the United States* (JETRO, New York, U.S.), *Directory of Japanese Giving* and *Consultants in Japanese Philanthropy* (contact,

Corporate site selection also provides competitive advantages for the scientist keen on Asian support.

This is especially true for extremely difficult-to-fund projects, such as *coral reef research*--which has traditionally had to depend upon

- **private regional foundations (Pew Charitable Trusts, Curtis & Edith Munson Foundation, Charles Darwin Foundation, etc.)**

- **scientific institutions (South China Sea Institute of Oceanography, Marine Science Institute of the University of the Philippines, Silliman University--a leader in village-based coral reef reserves, University of Singapore, the Thai research facilities in Phuket, The Smithsonian Institution, etc.)**

- **governmental entities (Governments of Japan, Australia, Indonesia, U.S. Agency for International Development (USAID), U.S. Peace Corps, etc.), and**

- **individual donors and NGO memberships for financial support, including the royal family of Thailand.**

We urge a micro- rather than macro-view and analysis--for funding, like the World Conservation Monitoring Centre (WCMC), which measures reef locations based upon four-kilometer-resolution grid data.

The key is to create overlays (including GIS mapping) that disclose patterns of corporate investment in a city or region that can be used to your strategic advantage.

Corporate Philanthropy Report, Seattle, Washington, U.S.), occasional reports by corporate-foundation partners (IBM and the **Asia Foundation**, for instance), and even *free* language guidebooks from the Japan National Tourist Organization in your country. For women trying to unravel Japanese business practices, see Christalyn Brannen and Tracey Wilen's book, *Doing Business with Japanese Men: A Woman's Handbook* (Stone Bridge Press, Berkeley, California U.S.).

Case Study #6: Rainforests of the Sea--Coral Reefs, Biodiversity, and Threatened Pharmacopoeia in East Asia:

Coral reefs exist in 109 countries, with perhaps 30% of the world's mapped reefs in Southeast Asia.[21] According to the World Resources Institute (Washington, D.C.), more than 80% of the reefs in the region are at risk--with more than half (56%) at high risk.[22]

With some 70% of the region's population clustered within the coastal zone, pressure from fishing, sedimentation, and pollution combine to endanger the coral reefs which flourish at less than 100-meter depths. According to the United Nations Environmental Programme, World Conservation Union Global Coral Reef Monitoring Network Strategic Plan, and the Intergovernmental Oceanographic Commission, at least two-thirds of the world's coral reefs are on the verge of collapse. While coral reefs are estimated at 2% of the seafloor (approximately 600,000 sq. km.), they may account for 25% of all marine species.

Methodologies and maps developed by the World Resources Institute (WRI) depict a coastal sea of red, high-risk reefs, particularly around Indonesia and the Philippines. These two nations each account for some 2,500 species of reef fish--but only 30% of their coral reefs are in good or excellent condition.

Indonesia is particularly perplexing, as its 17,000 islands and 81,000 km. of coastline represent the region's most significant reef resource. The Philippines is the largest source of the illicit trade in coral for displays and aquariums, despite strict prohibitions in-country and by tourist nations. Malaysian reefs are expected to decline demonstrably during the next 20 years. Construction of port and oil-processing facilities have degraded reefs of Singapore and off the islands of Japan, coral bleaching is a problem.[23]

---

[21] Stephen C. Jameson (National Oceanic and Atmospheric Administration--NOAA), John W. McManus (International Center for Living Aquatic Resources Management), and Mark D. Spalding (World Conservation Monitoring Centre), "International Coral Reef Initiative Executive Secretariat Background Paper: State of the Reefs--Regional and Global Perspectives," <www.ogp.noaa.gov/misc/coral/sor/sor_asia.html>.

[22] World Resources Institute, "Status of the world's coral reefs: East Asia," <www.wri.org/reefsatrisk/reefasia.html>. Of particular interest for our discussion is the map, "Estimated threat to coral reefs." It provides a graphic depiction of coral reefs in East Asia classified by the World Resources Institute's (WRI) "Reefs at Risk Indicator," which WRI developed based upon four risk factors: Coastal Development, Marine-based Pollution, Over-exploitation, and Inland Pollution and Erosion.

[23] Stephen C. Jameson, John W. McManus, and Mark D. Spalding, "International Coral Reef Initiative Executive Secretariat Background Paper: State of the Reefs--Regional and Global Perspectives, May, 1995," <www.ogp.noaa.gov/misc/coral/sor/sor_asia.html>. This is an excellent summary and review of the situation and offers Recommendations for Regional Action.

As the problem intensifies, so does the Case for Support for funding.

Coral reefs, like the rainforests, may offer important pharmacological benefits for the prevention or cure of human diseases. In the Indian Ocean, near Seychelles, researchers are evaluating the sponge, *Plakinistrella*, which has a defense compound with intriguing properties for killing microorganisms related to certain lung and skin infections.[24] Another approach is synthesizing rare compounds, as chemists at the University of Illinois-Chicago did with an anticancer drug--laulimalide--isolated in a few, select species of South Pacific sponges.

Private biotechnology companies, such as **Diversa**, are looking at selected coral reefs off other regional venues--like Bermuda--for compounds and applications for pharmaceutical and other purposes.

"Bio-prospecting" can be a sensitive issue with indigenous populations, who know the therapeutic applications of selected flora and fauna--yet fear economic exploitation and threats to their cultures.

Regardless of the fact that many Southeast Asian countries have created legislative protection and designated marine preserves, research and coastal zone management funding is as at-risk as the coral reefs themselves.

Or so goes the conventional wisdom. These--and village-level capacity building--are fundable within the context of Asian companies (and offshore multinationals) actively engaged in business in the region. Preserving the resource enhances brand equity, global visibility, and is an important aspect of being a "good neighbor."

In the Western Hemisphere, the analogue is **Phillips Petroleum**. Witness its advertisement,

> "To understand our concern for the environment, sometimes you have to look beneath the surface." (Ad for an artificial reef and the hundreds of fish species it has attracted, "created from a former Phillips Petroleum production platform." What makes this ad unusual is Phillips Petroleum's creation of a "Rigs to Reefs" program as part of its broader environmental initiatives. Example of funding at the interface of the natural and built environments.)

Asian companies also recognize the point of "green brands," such as:

---

[24] Lance Frazer, "Threatened pharmacopoeia: The world's coral reefs," *The Rotarian*, October 2002, p. 12. Frazer's article underscores a point made throughout our book--that ideas, resources, and fundable perspectives abound in unexpected places. His article suggests further information is available at The National Oceanic and Atmospheric Administration's Coral Reef Online (www.coralreef.noaa.gov), U.S. Coral Reef Task Force (www.coralreef.org), Ecological Society of America (www.esa.org), and Harbor Branch Oceanographic Institution (www.hboi.edu).

"Steering Toward Excellence in Engineering." (This ad for **Hitachi Zosen**, Japan, features a school of fish above a coral reef. The focus is upon the company's completion of Japan's "first double-hull VLCC. Double-sided and double-bottomed . . . its superior design greatly reduces the risk of spillage.") Hitachi Zosen Corporation "plays an increasingly assertive role in projects to protect the environment. After all, we won't have it tomorrow if we don't take care of it today."

We have already noted selected hotel chains with an ecological focus (see Chapter 5). An overlay of these--and others such as the **Marco Polo Hotel Group** (Hong Kong, the Philippines, PRC, and Vietnam)--should be juxtaposed with nearby coral reefs and the resulting hotels approached with dramatic, high profile, easy-to-measure projects.[25]

Other companies who have been generous in funding island biodiversity and related projects include **Chevron Research & Technology Company, Esso, Shell Oil, Occidental, Container Ship Management, Ltd., AAC Saatchi & Saatchi, Australia Japan Cable (Management), Ltd.,** and **Roche International, Ltd.** These, too, should be part of the mix, depending upon whether they are active within a particular regional market or nation. (Our coral reef example applies worldwide. The International Coral Reef Initiative points out that damaged or destroyed reefs can be found in 93 countries, with coral reefs in East Africa and the Caribbean also at great risk.)

A venerable resource is *Owen's Worldtrade: Africa and Asia Business Directory*, which provides vital industrial and trade insight into Brunei, Indonesia, Malaysia, and Sri Lanka. Banking, shipping, hotels, marine and port service providers, automotive companies (and supply chains), chemical companies, construction firms, environmental equipment, fishing and aquaculture, pharmaceuticals--the possibilities are enormous. Do your homework. Look at who is doing business, where.

Penetrate the corporate veil. Remember this: while the U.S. (for instance) exports mostly *ideas* to Japan (royalties and licensing fees), U.S. companies quietly established research and development (R&D) beachheads beginning by the early 1990s in Tokyo (**IBM**/computers, **Hewlett-Packard**/photonics, integrated circuits), Chitose (**Medtronic**/medical

---

[25] In marketing, we often speak of SWOT Analysis: Strengths, Weaknesses, Opportunities, and Threats. In the case of coral reefs, their ecosystems are threatened on two main fronts: Nature (climate, sediment, etc.) and Humans (sewage—often from hotels—leads to algae growth; divers and anchor drag inflict physical damage; dive boats sometimes pollute with engine/combustion by-products, etc.) Each of these Threats can be changed into a funding platform as a Strength and Opportunity, especially if consortial win-win projects target not only the overall coral reef condition, but sustainable solutions at the beach, lagoon, reef flat/crest, and slope.

devices), Tahara (**American Cyanamid**/agricultural chemicals), Osaka (**Procter & Gamble**/soaps, etc.) Nagoya (**Pfizer**/pharmaceuticals), Atsugi (**W.R. Grace**/new materials), Gotemba (**Dow Chemical**/chemicals), Kakegawa (**Corning**/new materials), Tsukuba (**Upjohn**/pharmaceuticals, **Texas Instruments**/semiconductors, **Intel**/semiconductor design, **DuPont**/agricultural chemicals, **Monsanto**/agricultural chemicals), Narita (**Applied Materials**/semiconductor manufacturing equipment), Yokohama (**Dow Corning**/new materials, **IBM**/computers, **DuPont**/new materials, **Bristol-Myers Squibb**/pharmaceuticals, **Digital Equipment**/computers, and **Eastman Kodak** (electronics).[26] The players and partners may have changed, but the intensity of competition and opportunity has not.

Your country's Chamber of Commerce contacts in a selected coral-reef nation, embassy personnel, trading companies--all offer unparalleled access and opportunity.

Finally, remember Sun Tzu's advice at the beginning of the Chapter and think, position, and act in a quiet, strategic manner.

IV. *Shogun Strategies for Plucking the Asian Money Tree:*

In the West, the *money tree* is viewed as a largely mythological image, with no real basis in reality -- so much for Western thinking.

Actually, metal molds in the shape of a simple vertical tree with branches and coins--as fruit--were created in the East for the "minting" of coinage. An excellent example is an intact Japanese money tree, circa 1850, used in advertising by **First Union**®--a provider of investment banking services. Essentially, the nine coins would be plucked, polished, and then spent. The trunk or stem of the money tree would then be melted down and recast as more coins.

In Middle East *souks*, gold merchants believe that some gold jewelry they sell has been melted down and re-sold since Pharaonic times -- so, too, with the money trees of Asia. How to plant the seeds that lead to the harvest of these venerable trees is the point of this Section's discussion.

A Successful Grant Proposal to an Asian-Pacific Funder will have

- **An emphasis upon high visibility, public projects**
- **Projects with the potential for strong, positive media coverage**

---

[26] "Where the U.S. R&D Is," Chart, *Fortune*, March 25, 1991, p. 85.

- Global issues, especially environmental issues; the oceans
- Colleges and universities, Institutes as consortial partners
- Science, technology, and/or mathematics focus
- A public component (free public lectures, training for young scientists, etc.).

With this said, Asian-Pacific companies generally avoid projects with

- deficit spending
- goals which are difficult to measure, too complex or controversial
- and, *especially*, projects in which Boards do not have a clear financial stake (annual giving, capital campaigns, etc.). (In the U.S., see, for example, the grant application for Toyota USA Foundation, which requires a detailed Board Roster and their business affiliations.)

Tips for securing long-term Asian-Pacific financial support--

1) Listen carefully to what companies are saying about their long-term Community and Corporate Goals.

2) Learn as much as possible about the Company's *philosophy* and specific *Corporate Culture.*

2) Research the background and interests of the Company's *founder* and the current CEO.

4) Move slowly--educate the partner, re: your Institute or expedition's history and goals.

5) Always move toward Consensus: as the executives are usually rotated, your relationship must be broadly-based, between your scientific team and the Company.

6) Practice patience, tolerance, and extraordinary discretion.

7) Develop all your concepts in terms of *dream documents.* Generally, arrive at meetings with two one-page summaries:

one for the project-at-hand; the second, a broader, bolder, long term scenario for support. Be prepared, at some point in the relationship, for being asked what your dreams are for your scientific endeavor, long-term.

8) Understand the "1-5-40 Rule," which is shorthand for how Asian-Pacific companies sometimes fund. In Year One, they may give ¥1, £1, $1 (or a multiple thereof, for our example); by Year Three this may increase to ¥5, £5, $5 (or multiple). With a *dream document*, this funding could easily skyrocket to ¥40, £40, $40 (or multiple). Note: in this final extrapolation, the funding may be a shared function among the company's supply chain or traditional trading partners.

9) Show no weakness; respect and consistency are prized values.

10) Think "technology," strategically. The best sources are at your fingertips. Interested in Japanese biotechnology, semiconductors, superconductivity (see, U.S. Department of Commerce's National Technical Information Service and the U.S. National Science Foundation)? JETRO makes introductions to business people exploring technical exchanges with Japanese companies. English-language publications such as *The Japan Economic Journal* and *Japan Times*--which cover R&D and new products--are available through Nikkei Telecom. For abstracts and translations of 500 Japanese scientific and business journals, see Scan C2C. The *Samsung Newsletter* details the company's new global strategic alliances, its key industries (electronics, engineering, and chemicals), and unusual product research (biophotodegradable resin, a "Bio TV," etc.). Japan and South Korea are generally accessible in terms of information that can lead to a successful alliance with your Institute. The PRC requires more sleuthing, with trade organizations in Hong Kong and traditional trading companies, good ports of entry. Your nation's "China Desk" for trade is a logical first stop. The U.S.-based Asia Foundation also informally keeps track of NGO presence through its global offices and contacts. Important, as cooperation rather than competition is an excellent strategy as donors often are increasingly interested in consortial projects.

At the risk of overstatement, Asia-Pacific companies tend to cluster, once one has established a "beachhead" in a community. Depending upon nationality, they also tend to view each other as primary suppliers. Imagine them as a wheel, with--say--an Asian automotive manufacturer as the hub and Asian suppliers as the spokes. Each supports the other and therein, is your opportunity for funding.

To be successful in the Asian-Pacific Century, an Institute or expedition must marshal its resources (trustees), be fiscally responsible, high-profile, understand corporate culture, and prepared to *seize the day*. Simultaneously, it must be creative in developing long- and short-term funding strategies that lead to endowments and significant planned gifts.

V. *Preparing for the Asian Century--Donor Prospecting, Direct Marketing, and Defending the Realm:*

If we look at how the modern "West was Won," the answer may be through *direct marketing (DM)*, particularly through the "Old Economy" mechanism of *direct mail*. The reality in the 21st century is that DM (supported by aggressive e-mail strategies) may be more a way of developing lists of "suspects" (possible donors) than "prospects" (narrowly-targeted donors). This is a subtle, but important distinction, as scientists and other non-profits look globally for financial support, amidst an apparent cacophony of cultures and voices.

Saturation is already reaching extremes in the U.S., for example. A medium-sized business can average as many as *300* pieces of unsolicited mail *per day*, especially during the key DM "mail drops" from August through November. For fundraisers in the U.S., November tends to be the most popular month for sending appeal letters. [27] (Scientists take note: it also represents the most clutter. An alternative strategy is to mail appeals during *least* congested months, such as May or June. Remember: tax consideration ranks rather low as a reason for donors to support your project.)

Internationally, the Pacific Rim is the hot growth area for direct marketing *generally*. Global NGOs are already fishing donor pools worldwide and are tightening the nets in the Pacific. Direct marketers know that tightly-held mailing lists for Japan are closing the gap quickly on Germany, the United Kingdom (U.K.), and Canada in terms of overall

---

[27] The Kleid Company, a New York firm, monitors "seasonality" trends for direct mail, based upon purchase orders from nonprofits and others who rent its extensive mailing lists. *The Chronicle of Philanthropy* traditionally publishes the results as they pertain to fundraisers, looking at individual years and comparing them with five-year averages.

profitability (measured, in part by the percent of respondents to a particular DM package--outer/envelope, lift letter, response device/order form). The Pacific Rim ranks third, regionally, behind North America and Europe in terms of the "profitability profile."[28]

In short, the long-range view is to the East. In addition to corporate support, you need to be casting your nets *now*, as growth in individual affluence in the region needs to be harvested--carefully, strategically. Excellent initial sources to test include professional and trade associations with membership in the region, as well as major technical publishers. Australia, Japan, Singapore, and New Zealand have excellent internal postal services. Good citywide mail service is available in Indonesia, Malaysia, Taiwan, and Thailand.[29] And direct-mail appeals tend to get opened and read, particularly in Hong Kong, Malaysia, and Singapore, where rates exceed 50%.

Large global NGOs know this and are acting according.

Three tips can save you cash when mailing DM pieces for the region:

1) Watch your weight. This is the big cost in international DM. Use a lighter paper stock and reduce your "trim-size." Small is beautiful.

2) Consider printing *in-country* (which can be expensive). Remember: the cost-savings of mailing *locally* may overshadow the initial DM package costs.

3) A little-known fact: postal services compete aggressively against each other for *international* mail delivery. Your local post office may not be the least expensive *or* the most efficient.

As usual, there is a downside: international mail disruptions. Check your nation's version of the *Postal Bulletin* and via the Rapid Information Computer Bulletin Board System (RIBBS).

---

[28] *Direct* magazine is an excellent source for continuous monitoring of the global marketplace, providing insight into geo-demography, successful appeals, and trends.

[29] One of the best, obscure, *free* sources on international mailings is the U.S. Postal Service's *International Marketing Resource Guide*. In more than 300 pages, it provides overviews to international markets by region, offers insights into individual nations (Japan; macroeconomic data, direct marketing infrastructure, buying habits, etc.), details strategies to obtain "quality international lists," supplies examples of foreign government regulations for "bulk mail," and a host of other, high-quality, unexpected statistics and bits of useful advice. Regardless of where your Institute or expedition is working worldwide, this readable paperback is an important reference.

But remember the sage advice of Sun Tzu in *Art of War*:

Do not repeat the tactics that have gained you one victory, but let your methods be regulated by the infinite variety of circumstances. [6:28]

Just as Sun Tzu had acuity for gleaning important military intelligence from the apparently mundane, much of the conventional wisdom about what works in direct marketing is under fire. Numerous books have been written on the creation of direct mail packages and the importance of free offers, "live" stamps (rather than *indicia*), post-scripts ("P.S.--"), and negative appeals in generating a magic 2% response rate (considered excellent, especially for "new acquisitions" of donors/members).

Yet, there is disquieting evidence in this "post-literate age" that things are not as they appear. In 1998, *Direct* reported a study by Sigma (a New York database firm), which took the conventional wisdom to task:[30]

- One-third of respondents were so suspicious of a free offer that they discarded the DM piece without opening it.
- Third-class stamps fared as well as first-class stamps in impacting a prospect's behavior.
- Eighty-eight percent (88%) did not notice the "P.S.," whose intent was to have the reader revisit the letter after skimming through it.
- Positive messages elicited stronger responses than negative messages. Pieces disguised as official-looking governmental envelopes did not increase response rates.

However, the study did confirm, "a letter from a well-known return address was more likely to be opened than one with an unknown return address." (Post-September 11, this may be even truer, as postal authorities in the U.S. and elsewhere have urged caution on the part of patrons in opening unknown mail.)

With these caveats in mind, scientists should test the donor waters with direct mail that emphasizes the following:[31]

---

[30] Jonathan Boorstein, "P.S.--Think Again: Survey shows postscripts, first-class stamps and free offers aren't necessarily what the people want," *Direct*, March 1, 1998, pp. 38-39. According to *Direct*, "The research methodologies were developed in conjunction with professors and students at the William E. Simon Graduate School of Business in Rochester" (NY).

[31] William F. Vartorella, "Some Common Errors and Misconceptions about Direct Mail," *Fund Raising Management*, April, 1991, pp. 24-25.

1) a clear, easy-to-understand appeal

2) an urgent, compelling, and interesting Case for Support of the Institute or expedition

3) concrete examples ("precedent," see earlier comments) of recent successes brought about by members/donors

4) a personalized appeal and sense of *esprit de corps*

5) a credit-card option (*if* applicable law so allows); this option can improve donations by as much as 25%, and

5) good quality paper texture--in some cultures, subtle response is as much tactile as it is intellectual and emotional.

List rentals need not be a "shot-in-the-dark."

Some simple advice:

1) When renting lists and testing within your *own* country, the fact that a particular list has an inordinate number of names on it (disclosed by a name "merge-purge") that are your members (duplications or "dups") is a sign that the list has an "affinity" with your "house file" (e.g., your internal member/donor list) and, therefore, may perform ("pull") *better*.

2) When testing an offshore list, note that the direct mail sophistication of "suspects" in Japan (or Australia) is much different than in Indonesia or most of the rest of the Asian region. Also, do not be misled by the raw consumer numbers of India, which marketers tout as a Top 10 growth market with its one *billion* population, largest English-speaking concentration outside the U.S., and well-educated middle and upper classes. As **Bertlesmann A.G.,** Europe's largest media company, discovered, only one million households of an upscale target niche "sort" spoke English. Worse, India's stagnant Middle Class and the political climate combine to form at least a short-term "bar-to-entry." The only upside seemed to be that lists exist which allege they can reach

CEOs who open their own mail.[32] For the "rest" of Asia-Pacific, rent names based upon random n[th] draws in specific cities, rather than nationwide. (This advice also has salience for the European Union [EU]. Germans, who traditionally respond extremely well to "green"/environmental and endangered species, etc. appeals, prefer to see donor benefits listed.[33] The "Latin" countries respond to a more emotional approach. Germans expect direct debit or invoices. Some European donors elect money orders or credit cards --which proliferate. In short, the general advice is to begin with larger countries in both regions and not to consider one country representative of Asia-Pacific or the EU.)

3) Mail a list until it "dies"--e.g., is no longer profitable. The concept of "profitable," like beauty, is in the mind of the beholder. "Unprofitable" may be defined as any list that does not at *least* pay for the related creative and mailing costs. Experts differ.

4) Test lists and donor packages constantly.

You can build an enormous library just on the skills necessary to create successful mailing pieces. A *better approach* is to 1) collect DM pieces that arrive in your own mailbox, *especially* those you feel compelled to open; 2) many of the list rental companies specializing in high-tech, rich lists, or specific offshore markets offer excellent tips and glossaries within their *free* catalogues; order them and get a thumbnail sketch, free education; 3) monitor how successful scientific organizations (competitors?) solicit, acquire, and renew donor/members. Let your own membership expire and see what kind and how many "dead ex" (expired) appeals you receive to renew. Ultimately, you *should* get a new acquisition letter that ignores the fact you ever belonged.

Perhaps the best way to begin writing successful appeal letters to donors is to follow a form of Asian *reverse-engineering*. In short, mimic and modify appeals that work within a specific culture. However, translations can be troublesome.[34] English is an accepted *lingua franca* of both business and science. You may want to test English-language lists first.

---

[32] Len Egol, "Endnote on Book Club India," *Direct*, January, 1996, p. 67.

[33] Klaus Piske, "The 10 Most-Common Mistakes Americans Make When Direct Marketing to Europe," *Target Marketing*, March 2002, p. 61.

[34] Roy Jurdak, "Do's & Don'ts of Translation," *The Source Blue Book--1997 Edition* (*Atlanta International Magazine*), n.d., pp. 31, 37.

Our core advice: forewarned is forearmed. Do some serious background reading, now. [35]

Japan is the critical outpost on the New Donor Frontier for several reasons: [36]

1) As noted by **Pricewaterhouse-Coopers** in Hawaii, the Asian recovery is strongly tied with the lead economy of Japan. An NGO's donor foothold in Japan can translate to access to Asia on the coattails of Japanese businesses locating throughout Thailand, Singapore, South Korea, and Indonesia.

2) Japan has led the way in demonstrating to Asian nations that the best way to defuse anti-Asian sentiments globally (trade barriers, etc.) is through highly visible philanthropy. Witness the number of business chairs established at U.S. universities.

3) Japan has long been fascinated by the West and its robust

---

[35] Direct marketing and advertising are thorny issues under the best of circumstances. Add a global component--particularly non-Western donors--and generalizations can easily become hyperbole. Yet make no mistake. Charles Darwin (*Origin of Species*, 1859) said it best: "namely, multiply, vary; let the strongest live and the weakest die." In the words of Masaru Ibuka (Sony Corporation), "We worked furiously [to realize our goals]. Because we didn't have fear, we could do something drastic." For your Institute or expedition not just to survive, but endure, you must compete with DM. See, for instance, Roland Kuniholm's *The Complete Book of Model Fund-Raising Letters*. Although not globally or science-focused, it covers the landscape with some 350 sample letters for acquiring new donors, nomination-to-membership, front-end and back-end premiums, survey approaches (note: popular with and successful for the space science community), special events, protect/petition (always useful within the endangered species or oceans specialties), renewal series/upgrades, major donor, monthly sustainers, lapsed donors, and a host of special purposes and non-monetary assistance appeals. (Selected letters include appeals from the Center for Marine Conservation, Center for Science in the Public Interest--a complete renewal letter series, Memorial Sloan-Kettering Cancer Center, National Wildlife Federation, WETA/Washington, D.C., World Wildlife Fund, and Worldwatch Institute.) See also, Pat Friesen's "25 Ideas for Getting Your Envelopes Opened" at <www.targetonline.com>, who addresses the issue within the context of the post-anthrax-in-the-mail-scare. While the focus of *Funding Exploration* is centrist, advocating clear "win-win" scenarios with business, industry, foundations, and individual donors, the DM success of groups such as Greenpeace cannot be overlooked. Greenpeace uses simple, evocative promotions including, "Wanted: One Person to Save the World," which quickly covers the landscape from drift nets (a threat to dolphins, whales, and turtles) to the rainforest (80% of ancient forests destroyed or degraded) to the need for offshore wind, wave, and solar energy. (Example is from Greenpeace/U.K.). Print and electronic advertising, which are not treated specifically in our book, often are beyond the resources of most scientific Institutes and expeditions. Yet, single copies of "Why Bad Ads Happen to Good Causes and How to Ensure They Won't Happen to Yours" (underwritten by **The Edna McConnell Clark**, **Robert Wood Johnson**, **David and Lucile Packard**, and **Surdna** Foundations) are available, free, from Andy Goodman at <www.agoodmanonline.com>.

[36] William F. Vartorella, "Preparing for the `Asian Century': Donor Prospecting in Japan through Direct Mail," *Taft Monthly Portfolio*, Volume 38, Number 4 (April, 1999), pp. 1-2, 7.

consumerism. Regardless of the strength of the $, £, or DM against the ¥, the Japanese are anxious to become less insular, more global, in a sense--more Western.

While the Japan Direct Marketing Association (JADMA) presents a mixed picture of mail order sales growth from 1988 to 1995, several trends are significant.

First, the Japanese have moved from low-priced daily consumables to high-end accessories, women's fashion, and world-class brand-name products.

Second, joint ventures are in vogue, especially with upscale, trendy catalogues such as the U.S. firm, **Eddie Bauer**. Another, **Patagonia International, Inc.,** has established a strong foothold in Japan, particularly through its emphasis on environmentally friendly innovations, such as producing fleece sweaters and jackets from the polyester recovered from PET bottles.[37]

Third, in the business sector, leaders such as **Mitsubishi Corporation** have embarked on experiments with the Internet aimed at business consumers interested in everything from discounted airfares to office supplies. **Gateway** and **Dell**--strong entrepreneurial U.S.-based companies--are actively engaged in direct sales of personal computers in Japan. "Personal imports" (one term used for international catalogue sales) crested U.S. $ 1 *billion* by 1995.[38]

So what does all of this mean for philanthropy and the potential for direct mail?

Plenty. Databases of stratified consumers and corporations are slowly becoming available for rental. Increasingly, list intelligence is emerging in such lead categories as travel, finance, and up-scale goods and services. This, combined with more positive tax implications in Japan, means that philanthropy as we know it in the West is becoming institutionalized.

Moreover, as noted recently in *Focus Japan*, "compared to markets like the U.S., where mail order is an enormous industry, there is still plenty of room for expansion in Japan." JADMA has reported U.S. DM figures that indicate the average household receives some 66 DM letters/catalogues and other promotions per day, with the average company--300. In Japan,

---

[37] Anonymous, "Patagonia in Japan: U.S. Outdoor Gear Catches On," *Focus Japan*, April, 1998, p. 11.

[38] Anonymous, "Catalog Sales in Japan," *South Carolina World Trader*, Volume 4, Number 8 (October, 1996), p. 9.

the averages are 1/10 of these. According to JADMA, direct mail response in Japan is relatively 3 percent--more than twice that in the U.S. Less competition. Better response rates. Excellent opportunity for donor prospecting *if* combined with an incentive that carries a discrete U.S. logo.

Asahi Bank Research Institute predicted nearly ¥ 3 trillion would be spent on mail order sales by the year 2000. Annual growth rate: 5 %. That translates into an enormous data warehouse of rentable names and geo-demography of people/corporations with cash.

Simply stated: a test package, when mailed to an entire list (e.g., say 150,000 targeted households), may pull better or *worse* than the test. Yet, if we assume for the sake of argument that a scientific NGO can achieve average response rates in Japan comparable to U.S. DM consumer goods there, clearly there is enormous opportunity, especially considering that Asian color separations for DM pieces--in addition to being high quality--are also less expensive, especially *now*.

Moreover, "bar-to-entry" (e.g., competition from other global NGOs) is not particularly an issue. For example, it is an open secret that the mega-environmental and biodiversity NGOs are in a donor feeding frenzy, as saving endangered species--from a DM perspective--is an "impulse buy," with membership renewals and conversions (a second and subsequent renewal) increasingly at-risk. Europe is a strong donor target (see earlier comments) and Asia is next. However, in order to penetrate Asia, their best bet is to enter through Japan--again for reasons of the Japanese influence in the region and Japan's experience interlocking philanthropy and long-term relationships in communities of interest.

Experience, particularly with donor campaigns with a museum and conservation focus, leads us to the following advice:

- Japanese donors are interested in clean environment, the human-Nature interface, and projects demanding a novel, high-tech solution (e.g., a metallurgical analysis, restoration, and conservation of an historic Samurai suit of armor).

- A sizable expatriate market exists in Japan for which an urgent, compelling, and interesting Case for Support has immediate salience. Separate market, admittedly, but an often-overlooked opportunity, with implications for approaching Japanese companies directly.

- Any corporate DM campaign in Japan should be constructed in such a way that the company donor there is tied into the activities of its subsidiary in your country or its general manufacturing or service sector.

- If you are going to create a DM piece in Japanese, it should be written in Japanese **first**--not written in your native tongue, then translated into Japanese. (After the draft is completed in Japanese, hire an independent translator to render it in Italian, Spanish, German, French, English, Dutch, Slovakian, Arabic, or Swahili, etc. for comparison.) You also must be extremely careful regarding choice of colors of promotion pieces. Generally, bold colors should be avoided.

- Text: the goal is harmony, what the Japanese call *wa*. Controversy and extravagant claims are to be avoided. Also, in Japan, style is as important as substance. Even in writing, avoid putting the Japanese donor in a potentially embarrassing situation--e.g., lack of support would mean the death of an endangered species, for example.

Investing in direct mail in Japan may seem cumbersome, but offers the reward of a beachhead on the shore of Asia--the largest untapped donor landscape on the globe.

But Japan and Asia-Pacific also offer a dark side, as donor companies may see philanthropy as access to detailed scientific intelligence, patents, and the lifeblood of your Institute or expedition: *your mailing list*.

In *Art of War*, Sun Tzu wrote,

You can ensure the safety of your defense if you only hold positions that cannot be attacked. [6:7]

Splendid advice. And herein lies another of our heretical views:

Defending the Realm:
  How to Protect Your Donor Mailing List from 'Fund Raiders'

Your donor list is perhaps your most important strategic asset.

Properly managed and protected it will get your non-profit Institute or expedition through the best and worst of times. Unfortunately, many non-profits treat their donor lists with a cavalier attitude.

That is a formula for disaster.

Our ironclad rule is to NEVER sell, rent, lend, or provide unrestricted access to your donor list. That includes both the barbarians at the gates eager to raid your donor treasure-trove and the spies within who insidiously poach the list for friends, misguided Board members, and outright enemies of the realm.

Several observations:

1) List rentals by catalogue companies are often one of their two most profitable revenue streams. The other? Shipping and handling. Actual catalogue sales may be a distant third. That is how important lists are in the corporate community and why many, many successful catalogue/direct marketers never, ever rent or trade names, amounts of average sale (equivalent to your average donation), or disclose their direct mail strategies (when they mail, how many pieces, tests of direct response packages, results, etc.).

2) Successful catalogue companies that do rent lists, rent them through their own in-house letter shops. Why? They want total control over who uses their list, how, and how often.

3) These same in-house list rentals are tightly controlled, internally. List segmentation by average order size, zip code analysis, and information on which direct mail (DM) package pulled best and when are all highly-proprietary. List access by employees is often controlled by the most Draconian of rules and pass codes.

4) Even the list itself has its own Machiavellian guises, tricks, and traps. Names are seeded in the list (more on this below) that is monitored for any misuse (e.g., unapproved text of mailing pieces, outright list theft, multiple offers mailed, etc.).

5) Unlike most nonprofits, catalogue companies require employees to sign confidentiality and non-compete agreements, plus routinely change the pass codes when employees with list access leave their shops.

With this said--and the ironclad rule NEVER to rent, sell, trade, or provide unauthorized access to donor lists--**nonprofits which choose to risk the realm for short-term cash flow** can take steps to protect themselves and, more importantly, their donors from both external and internal threats.

First, *infrastructure*:

All list control should be internal. Lists are potential "cash cows" if used properly in combination with successful donor appeals. List access should be limited to selected employees, using pass codes, and ALL nonprofit staff and Board should be required to sign confidentiality and non-compete agreements. "Steal the list and risk jail" is the mantra. Written, codified policies (employee and Board handbooks) should state categorically that donor lists are out-of-bounds for any use not mandated by the formal Mission Statement of the nonprofit and approved by the Board.

Translation: your Board members cannot "borrow" the list and staff cannot lend it to their cousins. In fact, list use--how, for whom, how much in fees, etc.--should be a formal part of nonprofit corporate culture with Board minutes to support it. No gray areas for interpretation. An insidious problem is the Board member or Executive Director who casually requests a copy of the donor list for review: "I need to see who is on this list so I can match it with their friends who may become donors." Printed copies become pirated copies. If you print a copy, number it, attach a cover sheet that requires another confidentiality and non-compete signature and state in boldface type that the viewer agrees not to remove the copy from the office and not to make any additional copies. Sign it out and sign it back in.

Second, the *list itself*:

Never provide access to the entire list, to anyone. Segment the list by geodemography (average donation size, where donor lives, how many years as an active donor, etc.) for your OWN use, but be extremely careful about renting the list based upon average donation size. These are your donors and deserve privacy. (You may actually want to isolate your best donor names--including those who can be targeted as "Anonymous" by anyone who takes the time to review the list--and keep them out of the general rental mix.)

Set guidelines that only 5,000 names are available for testing. Remember, a test package, when mailed to an entire list (e.g., say 150,000 targeted households), may pull better or *worse* than the test. For example,

Test mailing	Response %	If Whole List Mailed Response Will Be
5,000	1%	0.72% to 1.20%
5,000	3%	2.52% to 3.42%

In other words, a rental of 5,000 names provides a reasonable, predictable response rate, while keeping total list control under your surveillance.

Also, these guidelines should detail that the non-profit controlling the list must approve the letter/offer. The actual pre-stuffed envelopes must be presented to the non-profit for affixing addresses/Cheshire labels to the mailing. This represents a lot of additional work that must be part of the rental price, but worth it in terms of protecting the realm. Once the mailing is complete (labels would have been pre-sorted by zip code, counted, etc. to meet nonprofit bulk rate in the U.S.--for instance), the non-profit controlling the list physically takes the mailing to the Post Office and gets a receipt for the mailing. The list, in short, never leaves your sight.

Regardless of these protections, the list should be atypically seeded with names that are virtually undetectable by the most wily "fund raider."

Here's how:

A smart list thief will know that the list is seeded, meaning that selected people on the list report any-and-all direct mail appeals from other non-profits to the Executive Director of the group that owns the list. A raider will usually remove the names of known Board members and staff and will purge the list of names in the immediate zip code of the non-profit. Usually, that will clear sentries or at least reduce the possibility of detection.

That is, unless the non-profit seeds the list atypically using a simple, but hard-to-detect strategy. A few suggestions (excluding a few trade secrets!):

1) Seed outside your non-profit's main zip code.
2) No staff, no Board members recognizable by name.
3) Three people who are passionate about your Mission and like getting mail. You want sentries who open everything that hits their mail boxes.
4) Use of the maiden name of a key, trusted staff member outside the main zip code. Misspell the maiden name as per this staff member.
5) Add "M" (for mailing) or "R" (for rental) as an incorrect middle initial for a sentry.
6) The sentries are moles, secret moles.

Finally, at the head of every donor list have a cautionary tale that the list is client-protected, seeded in an unusual manner by experts, and subject to aggressive prosecution for any misuse.

Third, *mailings*:

Rent your names based on contracts that stipulate one-mailing use, who is mailing what, to whom, when, with what kind of approved content. (Get a legal opinion on how to structure this and affiliated issues.)

At the point when your labels are about to be placed on the envelopes, open five random (obviously un-addressed) envelopes and check the contents carefully and thoroughly to be certain they meet agreed use. The renter might be testing different offers or lift-letter copy (A-B splits) surreptitiously and you MUST check the variations carefully for "fair-use" under your agreement.

Avoid renting your list continuously to groups in the same area. This increases the number of mailings your donors are receiving. Plus, any non-profit which understands direct mail knows to rent and test a successful list until it finally stops "pulling" responses. Generally speaking, any promotion piece that pays for itself is considered successful in the acquisition of new names. Another way to evaluate a mailing is the rule-of-thumb response rate of 1% or 2% as successful.

Do not rent your list during the same time frame as your own donor mailings ("mail drop"). You do not want to compete against yourself.

Non-profits who rent your list will want to know how it pulled in the past (% response to a similar appeal) and who has been using your list. Be circumspect. Talk trends, but not specifics, as it may get to the core of how your own donors respond. Catalogues, for example, may provide information on average purchase amount, but often are reticent when it comes to discussing the purchase patterns (number of orders per year, seasonality, etc.). Also, just as non-profits are asking you how the list performed, try to get a sense of their experience with your list. Regardless of what you may be told, if a particular non-profit continues to rent your list (or requests greater access than you normally provide), it is probably because the list is pulling well. Deception is a widely used and time-proven business tool.

Fourth, *"vulnerability"*:
Your donor list is most vulnerable under the following scenarios:

1) The entire donor list can be copied to one diskette or can be copied and sent as one e-mail attachment. Get expert advice so this can be prevented.

2) The list has easily understandable codes at the top of the list or directly adjacent to a specific donor (e.g., dates of donor gifts, amounts, upgrades, special gifts--capital campaigns, endowments, etc.). These usually show up inadvertently on the non-label master.

3) Co-mingling of your list with names acquired by YOUR rentals. This leads to a host of seeding problems, not the least of which is the rental group can "capture" your direct mail strategy through monitoring your list use by its own sentries.

4) Your non-profit finds itself in a "cash-flow-crunch" and is desperate for revenue. The temptation is to rent or even SELL your list willy-nilly.

5) The non-profit renting your list is a stranger. The last thing your donors need are unsavory mailings that may be fraudulent or have "sound-alike" names similar to high-profile, very reputable health care or disease-research facilities.

6) You rent the list to a weak non-profit with lofty goals, but whose intention is the "battering-ram" approach to getting donors, by hook-or-crook.

7) You have a momentary lapse and decide that "expired" members (known as "dead-exs" in direct mail) no longer should be included on the main list and you rent their names as cast-offs. The rule is simple: once "expired" members fail to respond to, say, three renewal letters, treat them as a "new acquisition" and send them a new member appeal as part of the test of a membership package. "Dead-exs" have value. Environmental groups, especially, have problems with renewals, if the initial appeal was visceral. Member acquisition is very expensive, so keep "dead-exs" at the ready.

8) Your corporate sponsor needs your list quickly to mail an "invitation" to the VIP reception or to send a gift or product sample. Your donors will be mined, massaged, and managed in a new database and, if somehow deemed unworthy, may be traded or sold through list shops or via cyberspace.

Final Thoughts:

Again, the ideal is never let your donor list out of your sight. If you must rent for reasons of sheer economics, every non-profit must weigh the long-term implications. These include:

- donor sensitivity to appeal letters from non-profits/commercial interests other than those you send
- the potential of negative "fall-out" and unwanted publicity for some mailing that includes your non-profit by NAME as the source of the donor name, plus a sleazy or inappropriate offer or promotion
- pricing--narrowly-focused, niche-specific lists can demand competitive fees on a cost-per-thousand (CPM) basis and add to the non-profit's revenue stream
- "donor-flight" to another cause; erosion of your donor base
- emergence of list rentals as a serious revenue-generator
- costs and aggravations affiliated with direct mail list management, including NCOA processing (U.S. Postal Service National Change of Address records), "merge/purge" operations (various forms of de-duplication of names), establishing list hierarchies (top performing vs. worst performing lists, for example, in the merge/purge process), affinity files (high rates of name duplication = greater response rates), Zip+4 postal pre-sorts, cleaning and updating your list, etc. In Singapore, for example, you are likely to run into names from three cultures: Chinese, Malay (Islamic), and Western. In addition to the issue of cultural nuances in the appeal letters, Chinese names appear as last/middle/first order; Islamic names as last/first (usually); and Western in first/middle/last sequence (in short, a merge-purge nightmare).

With top lists renting for more than U.S. $150 per thousand names, your list is clearly a strategic asset. While no one seemingly knows the total number of lists available systematically worldwide, more than 10,000 are a conservative "best guess" within the industry.
Remember: the list is the most cherished coin of the "realm." In a successful direct mail campaign, it is more important than the offer, copy, seasonality/timing, or the overall package.

VI. Summary and Recommendations:
Some of what we have explored this Chapter may seem contradictory, counter-intuitive.

On the one hand, Asia-Pacific may be a money tree, but the fruit may not be easy to pick or to digest.

The conventional wisdom is "think globally, act locally," but the emergence of global brands has restructured marketing efforts based upon customer needs and affinity, rather than location. [39] We have written of Asia-Pacific as a region, but it is just as likely described as a group of emerging, interrelated (and separate) markets. Donor prospecting in Indonesia is much different than in Japan. The business triad of petty fiefdoms--North America, the European Union (EU), and Asia-Pacific--appear as strategic units (at least on paper), but business executives are at a loss to develop and implement strategies based on common assumptions about market structure or critical skills necessary for capturing and holding markets before the "S-curve" claims their profits.

Asia is moving so rapidly toward modernity that the true answer to the puzzle may lie in the past, whether with ancient master strategist Sun Tzu or the CBCC's "Proposal for Better Corporate Citizenship" a mere decade ago.

Our message is to follow elegant, reasoned simplicity.
1) Look to the Mission and Vision Statements of companies. Appeal to their core values with simple narratives that speak eloquently of your science or your exploration in human terms.
2) Begin modestly. Build the relationship and trust, life-long. Think in terms of consensus, rather than winning. Leave room for face-saving, whether in person or in print.
3) Understand that secrecy, deception, and silence have both corporate and cultural meanings that are difficult to decipher in Western terms. Knowledge of the actions of competitors can be a useful bargaining tool. Know when to be circumspect, when to defend the realm.
4) Pay attention to precedents and use them as building blocks in your Institute or expedition's Case for Support.
5) Recognize that Asia-Pacific, too, is looking East and inward. New business constructs are being created--including a more global view of philanthropy--and you can help.
6) Respect the "Old (China, India, Japan, etc.) Hands" and seek their guidance and contacts. The access and influence of the old "trading companies" and generations of business families may be invisible, but it remains stalwart.

---

[39] E.B. Baatz, "Business Strategy: The Big Picture," *CIO*, August 1996, p. 24.

7) Monitor outside philanthropy as part of your strategic assessment. Actor Richard Gere established the **Gere Foundation** to promote awareness of Tibet and its endangered culture (but he is also interested in 19th-century Japanese vases).

8) Use coral reefs as a funding platform analogy, as business in Asia-Pacific involves shipping, environmental concerns, the ocean as a replenishable resource, regional cooperation, high-technology (the potential for bio-prospecting), trade, eco-tourism, and at-risk indigenous cultures.

9) Experiment with direct mail/marketing as a donor tool. Lists exist that claim they include CEOs and other decision-makers who actually open their own mail. Create overlays for markets and companies whose donor Missions are relatively easy to match--and your science consistent with the needs of their customers and/or supply chain.

10) Remember that it is generally less expensive to keep a current donor than to acquire a new one. It is all about "relationship marketing" and understanding that donors have financial lifetime values to your NGO, Institute, or multi-year expedition. The easiest way to "relationship market" is via a *membership program* for your donors (using Direct Mail, etc.).

A final example, from Point # 10 above:

Let us say your NGO or Institute has 5,000 members @ U.S. $50/year and that the renewal via DM of this original group is never more than 50% per year. (We are not talking about acquiring new members here, just renewals.) Do the math:

Year	Membership Renewals	Totals
Year # 1:	5,000 @ U.S. $50	U.S. $250,000
Year # 2:	5,000 x 50% renewal X U.S. $50	U.S. $125,000
Year # 3:	2,500 x 50% renewal x U.S. $50	U.S. $ 62,500
Year # 4:	1,250 x 50% renewal x U.S. $50	U.S. $ 31,250
Year # 5:	625 x 50% renewal x U.S. $50 (slight rounding error)	U.S. $ 15,625
Total Five-Year Value of Donor Pool		U.S. $484,375

And that assumes that you have done virtually *nothing* on any other front--

endowment, special events (galas, donors-as-diggers, etc.), planned giving, etc. You started off with 5,000 donors and ended up with 312. *Still*, the poor retention effort generated nearly U.S. $ 500,000 over five years. In short, Asia is at the door, and you need to open it with Direct Mail.

Yet, remember the words of Mohandas K. Gandhi, "There is more to life than increasing its speed." Deal making in Asia-Pacific is an art form, as much calligraphy as choreography.

***

Bibliography for Chapter 6

"The Asia-Pacific Century"

Anonymous. "Catalog Sales in Japan." *South Carolina World Trader*, Volume 4, Number 8 (October, 1996), p. 9.

_____."Competition--A Japanese View: Why America has Fallen Behind." *Fortune*, September 25, 1989, p. 52.

_____. "Patagonia in Japan: U.S. Outdoor Gear Catches On." *Focus Japan*, April, 1998, 11.

_____. "Where the U.S. R&D Is" (Chart). *Fortune*, March 25, 1991, p. 85.

Baatz, E.B. "Business Strategy: The Big Picture." *CIO*, August 1996, p. 24.

Boorstein, Jonathan. "P.S.--Think Again: Survey shows postscripts, first-class stamps and free offers aren't necessarily what the people want." *Direct*, March 1, 1998, 38-39.

Council for Better Corporate Citizenship. *Untitled Press Kit*. Tokyo, Japan: Council for Better Corporate Citizenship, 1991.

Currie, P.J., Dong Z.-M., and D.A. Russell. 1993. "Results from the Sino-Canadian Dinosaur Project. "*Canadian Journal of Earth Sciences*, 30: 1997-2272.

Egol, Len. "Endnote on Book Club India." *Direct*, January, 1996, p. 67.

Frazer, Lance. "Threatened pharmacopoeia: The world's coral reefs." *The Rotarian*, October 2002, pp. 12-13.

The Futures Group. "Number of Middle-Class Workers" (*Fortune* Chart). *Fortune*, May 30, 1994, p. 76.

Holstein, William J. "We're Naïve About Japanese Philanthropy." *The Chronicle of Philanthropy*, January 14, 1992, pp. 38-39.

Jameson, Stephen C.; McManus, John W.; and Spalding, Mark D. "International Coral Reef Initiative Executive Secretariat Background Paper: State of the Reefs— Regional and Global Perspectives (May, 1995)." <www.ogp.noaa.gov/misc/coral/sor/sor_asia.html>

Japan External Trade Organization. *Survey of Corporate Philanthropy at Japanese-Affiliated Operations in the United States.* New York: JETRO, June, 1995.

Jurdak, Roy. "Do's & Don'ts of Translation." *The Source Blue Book--1997 Edition (Atlanta International Magazine)*, n.d., pp. 31, 37.

Karrass, Chester L. *The Negotiating Game: How to get what you want.* New York: Thomas Y. Crowell, 1970.

Knight-Ridder Tribune. "Chart: Average life expectancy," June 28, 1992, n.p.

Kuniholm, Roland. *The Complete Book of Model Fund-Raising Letters.* Englewood Cliffs, New Jersey: Prentice Hall, 1995.

Pachtman, Arnold. "Getting to `Hao!'" *International Business*, July/August 1998, 24-26.

Pascoe, Jason; Ryan, Nick; and Brown, Peter. "Context Aware: the Dawn of Sentient Computing?" *GPS World*, September 1998, 22-29.

Peat, F. David. *Artificial Intelligence: How Machines Think.* Rev. ed.: New York: Baen Books, Distributed by Simon & Schuster, 1988.

Piske, Klaus. "The 10 Most-Common Mistakes Americans Make When Direct Marketing to Europe." *Target Marketing*, March 2002, pp. 61, 64-65.

Vartorella, William F. "Preparing for the `Asian Century': Donor Prospecting in Japan through Direct Mail." *Taft Monthly Portfolio,* Vol. 38, Number 4 (April, 1999), 1-2, 7.

_____. "Some Common Errors and Misconceptions about Direct Mail." *Fund Raising Management*, April, 1991, pp. 24-25.

World Bank. *Private Infrastructure Project Database, 1996.* "Private Investment Projects, 1984-1995" in "Let's Make A Deal." *International Business*, December 1996/January 1997, p. 6.

World Resources Institute. "Status of the world's coral reefs: East Asia." <www.wri.org/reefsatrisk/reefasia.html>

Zelade, Richard. "Leading the Pack." *International Business*, December 1996/January 1997, p. 6.

***

Chapter 7: "Foundation Funding -- 'Final Frontier'"

By William F. Vartorella

> *"Nothing in life is to be feared. It is only to be understood."*
> *Marie Curie*

I. Introduction:

Foundations are like illegal whiskey stills: they brew up a batch of projects, which may taste like ambrosia, but can have the effect of arsenic. And, like the producers of "white lightning," foundations can elude the most diligent of investigators, as a *single* reference source for all the world's foundations, trusts, and related donors does not exist.

Unlike corporations and individual donors, where long-term relationships can be fostered, foundations usually have a different purpose: the narrowly defined "project."

This "project" may be one or three or five years in duration, but make no mistake. The support is *short-term* and comes with its own morning-after reality: when the project funding runs out, how can the research (read: Institute) be sustained?

With this revelation (?), what is the role of foundation support in an Institute's or expedition's long-range Strategic Plan?

The answer, according to Joel J. Orosz, is probably back at the liquor still--the "Skonk [sic] Works" of Al Capp's *Li'l Abner* comics, where something was always gurgling and brewing.[1]

In his thought-provoking commentary in *The Chronicle of Philanthropy*, Orosz called for the largest foundations to create their own "Skunk Works"--a "small, loosely run group that promotes creativity and innovation" among a fund's brightest thinkers.[2] Modeled loosely after the famous "Skunk Works" developed some 50 years ago by then-Lockheed Corporation ("stealth technology" for the most advanced fighters and bombers, as well as America's first production jet planes, etc.), these new "Skunk Works" would aim at the creation of transformative ideas--the basis for new or remodeled Strategic Plans at foundations.

---

[1] Joel J. Orosz, "Opinion: Big Funds Need a `Skunk Works' to Stir Ideas," *The Chronicle of Philanthropy*, June 27, 2002, p. 47.

[2] *Ibid.*

Essentially, Orosz argues that strategic thinking becomes a point of diminishing returns: less flexible, less creative, less receptive to the outside world. On the one hand, he seemingly advocates the analogy of returning to the woodsy still, which by its nature is secretive (witness the work at **Lockheed Martin Aeronautics Company's** "Skunk Works"). On the other, he touts advantages of the modern cant, "thinking outside the box," resplendent with more contact with grant seekers and other visionaries.

This may seem paradoxical, but it isn't. The best "bootlegger" (e.g., the producer of illegal liquor--"moonshine") has to have a distribution system to be successful. The same is true of the grants system, as we know it. Yet, the difference is that most Institutes or expeditions are already "Skunk Works," with distinct new ideas, a flavoring of old standards, or weak distillations that they are hawking to the folks with the money. They have to work with the foundations (corporations, individual donors) --or go to the government ("the revenuers") for help. No one wants to go to a government--which has its own problems, regardless of where worldwide you are reading this.

So, how then, does your Institute or expedition approach and work with foundations without, in American vernacular, "getting skunked" (e.g., not funded)? That is the point of this Chapter.

First, let us look realistically at foundation support value and potential for leveraging additional cash and in-kind donations. Then we shall examine critical trends and finish with ingredients for a successful grant proposal.

Dictum: Foundation support is more about creating a community of donors (corporate, individuals) than about the financial support itself.

The average grant proposal takes roughly 125 hours to produce—most of which is comprised of research and planning. In terms of Return on Investment (ROI) and chances (7%--hopefully much better after you read this Chapter), grants do not seem to be cost-effective.

Yet, they definitely are useful and here is why:

> **High-profile foundation grants**
> - **attract other money through a foundation's brand equity**
> - **offer creative match for other donor requests**
> - **bolster an Institute's or expedition's reputation (brand)**
> - **are perfect for the Special Initiative, and**
> - **anchor the other legs of the funding platform: individual donors, corporations, government.**

Furthermore, they establish a *trend*, as donors prefer to participate in successful endeavors--what Don Keel has termed "Who-else-is-going-to-the-party-and-what-are-they-wearing?"

In short, while tomes have been written on the process of attracting foundation funding, our point here is that foundation support is more about cash flow, easing government support, and--especially-- adding the smell of success to an Institute or expedition's efforts.

II. *A Glimpse at the Global Landscape:*

We have already explored the paradox "Think globally, act locally," which means, simply, that while funding is ultimately local, its strategic purpose may be entrenchment, enrichment, or extension of a global brand.

If we examine the 100,000 or so foundations worldwide, several facts and trends immediately emerge:

At present, fewer than 2,000 foundations "cross" international borders to support projects.[3] Of these, roughly 600 are American-based and—in 1998--were focusing their efforts in [4]

Western Europe:	22.0%
South America:	21.6%
Asia-Pacific:	18.9%
Sub-Saharan Africa:	18.7%
Former Soviet Bloc:	6.4%
Canada:	5.7%
North America, Middle East:	5.6%
Caribbean:	1.1%
Total:	100.0%

Of the "Causes Funds Support," the "Environment" (8.4%) and "Science" (1.5%) fell well behind "Health" (for example) at 14.8%.[5]

---

[3] William F. Vartorella, "Creating Sustainable Funding for Natural History Collections in the New World Order--Foundations and Corporations: Old Allies, New Opportunities," *Museum Management and Curatorship* (England), Volume 15, No. 3 (September, 1996), 329.

[4] Debra E. Blum, "American Foundations Increase Giving to Support International Projects," *The Chronicle of Philanthropy*, January 11, 2001, p. 23. See especially, Chart, "International Giving by American Foundations," whose source is Foundation Center.

[5] *Ibid.* See Foundation Center chart, "Causes Funds Support."

While these data, based upon the report by the Foundation Center (NYC) and the Council on Foundations (Washington, D.C.), are *pre*-9/11, the faster giving paces of corporate foundations and often-overlooked *community foundations* were trends deserving notation. Also, the growing interest in Western Europe edged out Latin America as the "hot spot," albeit only slightly (yet, cf. our earlier comments, re: corporate regionalism).

In the late 1990s, a number of foundations--**The John D. and Catherine T. MacArthur Foundation**, the **McKnight Foundation**, the **Rockefeller Brothers Fund**, and the **Ford Foundation**--went into "a period of reflection" ("donor-speak" for reassessing funding allocations, Mission interpretation, etc.) to redefine priorities. The result at Ford Foundation, for instance, was resurgence in offshore giving.[6]

In 2001, a declining stock market saw foundation assets plunge by an average estimated 10% for the largest U.S. foundations. Regardless, U.S. foundations awarded some U.S. $29 *billion* in 2001--an estimated 5.1% increase over the previous year.[7] Hardly a rallying cry, but no reason for total "gloom and doom" either. The jury is still out relative to the long-term impact or focus of international grants since September 11th, although several foundations--including Ford Foundation--are creating initiatives aimed at conflict resolution within the borders of countries.[8]

In the fall of 2002, philanthropist Ted Turner announced curtailment of his own funding, precipitated by a sharp decline in the price of **AOL Time Warner** shares. Reportedly, the plan at the **Turner Foundation** for 2004 is to begin awarding grants to selected organizations, but will no longer solicit applications from other groups.[9] This is a blow to scientists involved in conservation or curbing population growth. The **David and Lucile Packard Foundation**, whose major holdings are in Hewlett-Packard stock, has also slashed its funding. While the Packard Fellowships for Science and Engineering seem reasonably intact, the science and conservation programs

---

[6] Ford Foundation has gone well beyond just funding projects, including strategic advice through a free website called "GrantCraft." See, for example, its *free report*, "When Projects Flounder: Coming to the Rescue When Good Grants Go Astray" at <http://www.grantcraft.org>.

[7] Ian Wilhelm, "Foundations Gave $ 29-Billion Last Year, a 5.1% Increase, Report Says," *The Chronicle of Philanthropy*, April 18, 2002, p. 16. For the full report, "Foundation Growth and Giving Estimates: 2001 Preview," see <http://fdncenter.org>. For an interesting perspective on why U.S. foundations may wish to consider giving away only the minimum amount required under U.S. federal law--5% of their investment assets--see Marina Dundjerski, "To Live Forever, Foundations Should Give Away the Minimum, Reports Say," *The Chronicle of Philanthropy*, November 18, 1999, p.12.

[8] Ben Gose, "Terrorist Attacks Did Not Cause Major Shift in Focus of Most Grant Makers," *The Chronicle of Philanthropy*, September 5, 2002, p. 18.

[9] Stephen G. Greene, "Belt-Tightening at Two Foundations Puts the Squeeze on Charities," *The Chronicle of Philanthropy*, October 17, 2002, p. 11.

are being combined. The ripple effect of both foundation plans impacts groups such as **The Global Fund for Women**.[10]

In May of 2002, financier and founder of the Open Society Network-- George Soros--announced to non-profits and friends in some 40 countries that, while current commitments would be met, his new **Open Society Network of Networks** would be global in impact with a new emphasis on advocacy and public policy. This is a sea change, but perhaps not unexpected. Regardless, however, a Foundation Center analysis of 2002 data from the U.S.'s nearly 62,000 foundations indicated that foundation giving "remained steady," despite a struggling economy and volatile stock market. Early results from a study by the Association of Small Foundations (U.S.) indicated their membership may have lost an average of nearly 5% of their assets in 2002, but awarded an average of 9.4% in grants that year. And for 2003, estimates reported by *The Chronicle of Philanthropy* had individual foundation forecasts wildly veering from feast to famine. Go figure. In spite of an economic downturn, the **Carl C. Anderson, Sr. and Marie Jo Anderson Charitable Foundation** provided U.S. $1,500,000 as part of a challenge grant to underwrite museum exhibits featuring the history, art, and science of hot-air ballooning.

Yet, unlike the **Soros Foundations**, which may have felt the turbulence of international markets, **The Bill & Melinda Gates Foundation**'s endowment is largely self-sufficient because of its shrewd financial diversification.

The message here is the same as that of *Funding Exploration*.

"Diversification" of donor sources (individual, corporate, governmental, and foundation) is critical to long-term sustainability.

This same diversification is evident in the slightly shifting focus of foundations active in the countries that often make the *most-granted list*, as reported by the Foundation Center. Researchers in venues such as South Africa, Brazil, Mexico, PRC, India, Kenya, Costa Rica, and Thailand take note. Using this list and the regional analysis give us a reasonable picture of the global opportunity. (Ditto for our earlier comments, re: "hot" zones of global activity by corporations.)

But there is more to the picture than immediately meets the eye.

---

[10] *Ibid.*

A rarely used indicator is that of *volunteerism* on a global scale. Simply put, annual spending by non-profit groups in 22 nations monitored by researchers at Johns Hopkins University (U.S.) now exceeds **U.S. $1.1-trillion**. In its report released at the annual meeting of the European Foundation Centre in 1998, that aggregate sum "eclipses the national economies of all but seven countries in the world."[11] The authors attribute the trend to growing doubts about the ability of governments or market forces to respond effectively to Society's pressing problems in arenas such as health, social services, and education.[12] When one compares non-profit spending in the 22 countries (which include Argentina, Australia, Belgium, Ireland, Israel, Japan, Slovakia--for example) against baseline national economies, the PRC, Germany, and Italy--among others--come off well, with Brazil, Russia, and Spain outpacing even Canada.

Russia, for instance, has undergone explosive growth in the non-profit sector. In 1987, the number of non-profits there totaled approximately 40. By the late 1990s, the total skyrocketed to roughly 35,000 groups.[13] Everyone there is scrambling for money, not the least of who are scientists displaced or under-employed as the result of the apparent demise of the "Cold War" and the resulting "New World Order." Opportunities for consortial projects with established scientific Institutes throughout the Newly Independent Countries (NICs) abound, although the "Digital Divide" (access to Internet technologies and ever-spiraling computer innovations) is a "clear-and-present-danger" in the race to parity in the Information Age.

While no one likes to admit it, this explosion of non-profits in the region has led to renewed concern about corruption and the handling of donations, plus the potential for illicit technology transfer that de-stabilizes not just the region. Three large-scale concerns are the perceived legitimacy of non-profits there, governance, and issues of capacity building.

Yet, environmental groups in the Black Sea region, for example, were among the first non-profits organized there and have a strong, useful presence for scientists intent upon finding shared solutions to freshwater pollution. And research involving "Closed Systems" (biospheres, lengthy bed-rest studies, prolonged exposure to micro-gravities, etc.) should almost by definition include former Soviet Bloc scientists and be fundable on a

---

[11] Stephen G. Greene, "A World of Difference: Spending by non-profit groups in 22 nations exceeds $1-trillion--and is growing, says a global team of researchers," *The Chronicle of Philanthropy*, November 19, 1998, p. 31.

[12] *Ibid.*

[13] Olga Alexeeva, "The Taste of Pineapple," *Foundation News and Commentary*, January/February 1996, 14.

shared basis. Other consortial possibilities include "sword-to-ploughshares" technology-transfers from military-industrial complex to broader scientific and public sectors, theoretical mathematics, ancient mummy bio-anthropology,[14] high-altitude physiology, and polar research. Even the automotive industry is looking to unusual test-beds for break-through technologies. According to *Business Russia*, the Moscow City Government has already contracted with MIG, the fighter-jet specialist, to design a Formula One racecar.[15]

For detailed discussions of philanthropy and the role of foundations in Central and Eastern Europe, two benchmark books should be consulted: Tom G. Palmer's *Philanthropy in Central and Eastern Europe: A Resource Book for Foundations, Corporations, and Individuals* and Daniel Siegel and Jenny Yancey's *The Rebirth of Civil Society: The Development of the Non-profit Sector in East Central Europe and the Role of Western Assistance.*[16]

Unfortunately, the Johns Hopkins study did not cover three important regions--Africa, Asia, and the Middle East. For the nation of South Africa, for instance, officials at Civicus (which promotes citizen activism worldwide) are not even certain of the number of non-profits/NGOs operating in-country.

---

[14] E.J. Farkas, "Preliminary Report of the Human Remains from the Theban Tomb No. 32 (Season 1991)," *Acta Archaeologica Academi*ae *Scientiarum Hungaricae*, 45 (1993), 29. Farkas comments upon Osteoarthritis as a "common condition among the ancient Egyptians" and puts it within the context of osteoporitic pathologies as perhaps "environmental or dietary aberrations." For a contemporary discussion of the potential funding for Egyptology in the Eastern and Central European regions for mummies and other projects, see William F. Vartorella, "Global Funding for Egyptology in the 21st Century: An Appraisal and Recommendations for Change" (paper presented at the 43rd Annual Symposium of the American Research Center in Egypt [ARCE], Seattle, Washington: Spring, 1992), p. 4. Specific examples included the palaeopathology of mummies in Czechoslovakia and the status of collections in Poland (Jagellonian University and the Archaeological Museum, both in Cracow).

[15] William F. Vartorella, "Pod zltou vlajkou: Sponzorovanie timu F1 a boj o Strednu Europu" ("Under the Yellow Flag: F1 Team Sponsorships and the Battle for Central Europe"), trans. by Peter Fritz, Editor, *F1 Sport International/Slovenske Vydanie,* July of 2002, p. 25.

[16] Tom G. Palmer, *Philanthropy in Central and Eastern Europe: A Resource Book for Foundations, Corporations, and Individuals* (Fairfax, Virginia: The Institute for Humane Studies at George Mason University, 1991). See, especially, pp. 19-21, "Organization of Intellectual, Academic, and Policy Life," and the telling statement on p. 19, "The most notable thing is the parallel system of universities and institutes. Unlike the United States, the various national academies of science play a very large role in the intellectual, professional, and political lives of the ECCs." This is often still the case in the former Soviet Bloc and provides an excellent base for joint projects. Daniel Siegel and Jenny Yancey, *The Rebirth of Civil Society: The Development of the Nonprofit Sector in East Central Europe and the Role of Western Assistance* (New York, New York: Rockefeller Brothers Fund, 1992). While this seminal work dealt primarily with the challenges facing a nascent nonprofit sector ("brain drain," etc.), it also underscored the state of the environment in the region, noting (p. 23), "East Central Europe is now stricken by almost every conceivable ecological malady; some areas are among the most damaged in the world." Furthermore, "The environmental movements of ECE--some of which were officially tolerated by the previous regimes--preceded and in many ways precipitated the political sea changes of 1989." In the view of *Funding Exploration*, environmental science in the region remains a promising avenue for fundable shared research agendas, with an urgent and compelling Case for Support.

Estimates range from 20,000 to 55,000. Scientists interested in vector-borne diseases, etc. may wish to consult Michael R. Sinclair's *Hope at Last: A Guide to Grantmaking in South Africa* to glean a broad sense of what NGOs faced in the early 1990s and the issues at hand.[17]

In short, according to the Johns Hopkins authors, what remains is a non-profit world that is the "lost continent" on the modern social landscape.

Our assessment is more far ranging, relative to foundations. We see it as a "lost world," with enormous opportunities in the Caribbean Basin, the rainforests of Northern South America,[18] remote at-risk coral reefs, the malarial battlegrounds of the tropical latitudes,[19] high mountain peaks, and

---

[17] Michael R. Sinclair, *Hope at Last: A Guide to Grantmaking in South Africa* (Washington, D.C.: Henry J. Kaiser Family Foundation, 1990). See, especially, pp. 58-62, re: "the deeply-nuanced" situation that traditionally faces South Africa. This book may be somewhat dated, but it is a provocative, sweeping view of possibilities.

[18] Scientists worry that the greatest extinction since the death of the dinosaurs may be underway in the rainforests, as habitat is under attack by humans. Estimates for annual rainforest destruction range to 20.2 million hectares (50 million acres) worldwide. While they may cover only 5% (five percent) or so of the Earth's surface, they are home to an estimated 50% (fifty percent) of the world's flora and fauna. Highly-fundable consortial initiatives to foundations might include bio-prospecting (a mere 1% of tropical plants have been evaluated for their medicinal potential), naturally-occurring pesticides, and the experimental practice of "pharming"--the growth of "drugs" in surrogate plants to increase the amount of antibodies. Medicinal advances associated with the rainforest include the bark of the cinchona tree (quinine for malaria), curare (vine extract used by indigenous peoples to poison darts and arrows, used as a muscle relaxant during surgery), and secretions of the Amazonian frog, *Phyllomedusa bicolor* (with applications for seizure, stroke, etc.). Some estimates place 25% of all pharmaceuticals used in the U.S. as rainforest-originated. See, for example, the preview for the home-video version of the film, "Medicine Man," starring Sean Connery. The preview details the efforts of the **National Arbor Day Foundation** ("Rain Forest Rescue") to raise global awareness and activism of the plight of the rainforests. This is an unusual consortial educational approach, with the assistance of **Cinergi Productions**.

There are foundations that are coming to the rescue. Witness the 10-year, U.S. $ 261-million grant to Conservation International by the **Gordon E. and Betty I. Moore Foundation** (he was the co-founder of Intel Corporation). Focus: protect large expanses of tropical wilderness and prevent species-at-risk from extinction in 25 regions of the world. Ultimately, this donation may be leveraged into a multi-billion-dollar, consortial effort.

[19] Malaria research has one of the most powerful Cases for Support this author has ever seen: "50% of all humans who have ever lived on earth may have died of malaria." According to World Health Organization (WHO), malaria is worsening or barely contained in many parts of the world. Some 40% of the world's population--two *billion* people--are at risk. Some 300 million people carry the parasite and 120 million cases of clinical malaria are diagnosed annually. (These figures range widely, depending upon source: agreement is that 1.5-2.7 million deaths occur annually.) In the early 1960s, only 10% of the world's population was at risk. This rose to 40% as mosquitoes developed resistance to pesticides and malaria parasites developed resistance to treatment drugs.

Most malaria infections occur in Africa. Sub-Saharan Africa is estimated to account for 80% of all clinical cases and about 90% of all people that carry the parasite. Outside Africa, 75% of the cases are concentrated in nine countries, according to WHO: India, Brazil, Afghanistan, Sri Lanka, Thailand, Indonesia, Viet Nam, Cambodia, and China (in decreasing order). High-risk groups are young children, women during pregnancy, non-immune travelers, refugees, displaced persons and laborers entering endemic areas. Malaria kills one child every 30 seconds. The direct and indirect costs of malaria in sub-Saharan Africa exceed U.S. $2 *billion* annually. Consider this: Randomized control trials conducted in the Gambia, Ghana, Kenya and Burkina Faso show that about 30% of child deaths ("child survival") could be

deep ocean troughs--as well as the laboratories, Institutes, observatories, and Natural History museums that dot our planet.

Developing a cogent, concise, and cohesive plan involves a global vision and the ability to recruit partners and donors who share that vision.

III. Strategies and Tactics for Securing Foundation Underwriting for Laboratory and Field Exploration:

In terms of traditional funding for science and discovery, Natural History museums may be a "sentry species."

With their expeditions, planetariums, and focus upon biodiversity and public education, they are the models for Institutes and field researchers active on the frontiers of science.[20]

They are also endangered, with billions of specimens at risk and the "Digital Divide" passing them by for *perceived* lack of funding.

---

avoided if children slept under bed nets regularly treated with recommended insecticides such as pyrethroids. Unlike early insecticides such as DDT, pyrethroids are derived from a naturally occurring substance, PYRETHRUM, which is found in chrysanthemums and will remain effective for six to 12 months. (Cf. the footnote above.)

The International Organization for Chemical Sciences in Development (IOCD) Working Group on Plant Chemistry recently convened a global symposium in Mali on "Plants Used in African Traditional Medicine." Dr. R. Brun (Basle, Switzerland) described the evaluation of African medicinal plants for their "activities against *Trypanosoma, Leishmania* and malarial parasites." See, IOCD, "International Symposium: Chemistry and Pharmacology of Plants Used in African Traditional Medicine," *IOCD Update*, Fall, 2002, p. 4.

Current funding levels are appalling. In 1996, *Nature* reported that malaria research is severely under funded, cf. other diseases, when relative incidence and global death toll are taken into account. About 50% of all malaria funding comes from U.S. sources. [Problem: skeptics point out that the disease offers little potential for long-term pharmaceutical profits or even recouping the costs of research (source: *The Washington Post*, 1998)]. The Bill & Melinda Gates Foundation awarded U.S. $50 million to a group working on developing vaccines for **malaria**--a high-profile foundation grant that should have attracted other global donors. Hope is that an effective vaccine will be available within the next seven to 15 years.

Malaria research is fundable on a number of levels, ranging from remote sensing of micro-environments (marshes with the same spectral signals), geo-demography of patients, to GIS correlation between habitat and level of malarial risk.

For an intriguing article on malaria, latest GIS modeling, and the inherent sparse funding, see Kevin P. Corbley, "Identifying Villages at Risk of Malaria Spread," *Geo Info Systems*, January 1999, pp. 34-37. For a comparison of how little malaria affects outsiders venturing into the tropics, who have taken the proper precautions, see the work of Professor Robert Steffen, University of Zurich, whose travel-risk charts are published by WHO.

[20] See, for example, the unpublished seminar materials provided by John Rorer, Executive Vice President at The New York Botanical Gardens and Trudi Hayden, Director of Foundation and Government Support for the American Museum of Natural History (NYC), at the 14th Annual Meeting of the Society for the Preservation of Natural History Collections, "Finance and Funding Workshop," Ripley Center, The Smithsonian Institution, Washington, D.C., 28 June 1999. Also of potential interest is William F. Vartorella's "From 'Denizens to Dinosaurs': Entrepreneurship and Collections Management--A Workshop," from the same two-day session. The author acknowledges the generous support of Delta Designs, Ltd., which sponsored the Workshops.

Looking specifically at U.S. foundation funding for Natural History museums during the 1990s, in two-year segments, some 350 grants of U.S. $10,000 or more seemed the norm--about 3.5% of all the grant dollars within the category "Arts, Culture and the Humanities". Not "Science," you will note, but "Arts, Culture and the Humanities."

It is all a matter of positioning, and Natural History museums have been *mis*-positioned as *repositories* rather than *resources*.

In their case, the difference between "bleeding-edge" and "cutting-edge" is razor-thin. Repositories ("passive" institutions) are difficult to fund, as their Missions take on the mantle of "dusty antiquarianism." Resources ("active") are more vibrant, as the Collection becomes more central to the science as a living organism. It is as fundamental as the difference between digression (the museum as collected ephemera) and dialogue (skill-based teams interacting in a synergistic mode). Dialogue implies access. Access is fundable.

This is true for Natural History Collections, whether they are in the Global South (the Caribbean Basin, Central and South America, Africa), the ex-Communist Countries (ECCs), or the richer nations of the Global North (North America, industrialized Europe, and selected Asian economies).

The New World Order has turned foundation thinking upside down, with a move toward traditional values (here, democratization) and away from traditional institutions (museums, etc.). Plus, the competitive environment has changed. Now, Collections are even competing against governmental bodies for foundation dollars as decentralization and a reframing of civil society mean downsizing and new assumptions about what is valued within a culture.

Consider this: grant awards by foundations (in the U.S.) account for *less than 1%* of the budgets of most non-profits. Yet, it can be argued that a 1% increase in funding for a Natural History Collection in a developing nation could mean the addition of a part- or full-time conservator or, better yet, a Principal Investigator (PI) who can encourage consortial projects.

POINT: as an Institute or expedition, these same museums hold collections that may be central to your research. Furthermore, they provide broad contacts and infrastructure within a global Natural History community that can lead to funding. The solution lies in "thinking outside the box."

The Natural History Museum, London, for example, holds a world-class collection of meteorites. Other museums and Institutes around the globe have specialists (and Collections) in esoteric areas of microbiology, paleontology, arctic and Antarctic exploration. A novel proposal might emphasize an unusual point of convergence: "exobiology."

Case Study 7: Mars, Meteorites, and Microbes (?):

The search for Life, either fossilized or extant, will be the highest priority for early Mars explorers. At stake is a deceptively simple question: "Is Life a unique or universal phenomenon?" While the debate of Life on Mars has long been the focus of public interest, among the post-*Viking* planetary scientists "exobiology"--the search for and study of extraterrestrial living organisms--was far secondary to Mars seismology, meteorology, and geochemistry.[21]

The Mars meteorite found in Antarctica--ALH84001--changed that in 1996, with what then NASA administrator Dan Goldin called a "startling discovery" that raised the possibility that "a primitive form of microscopic Life may have existed in Mars more than three billion years ago." The release of an article in *Science* unleashed a maelstrom of debate.[22]

The fundamental argument is that the combination of carbonate, magnetite, and pyrrhotite present in the Mars rock could not have formed non-biologically.[23] As noted by NASA, these residues "left open the possibility that organisms might still exist in some cryptic environment--yet to be discovered."[24]

The possibility of such a cryptic environment--an "Oasis"--was enhanced by the apparent discovery by the Mars Odyssey spacecraft in 2002 of vast quantities of water-ice just below the surface of what the BBC termed "great swathes of the planet Mars."

This has re-ignited the debate of whether Life may still exist on Mars and opens the path for renewed NASA interest in a human expedition within 20 years.

If primitive Life existed on Mars, was it able to respond to evolutionary pressures for self-preservation that allowed it to retreat into "special environmental niches" where "metabolism, growth, or simply survival is possible"?[25] Scientists have been inclined to believe that Life on Mars was rare, if it existed at all.

Now exobiology and exopaleontology--the search for and study of planetary fossils--have gained momentum. To find fossil beds or to drill deep into the Martian landscape to bring up subsurface water in which Life may yet exist will take human prospectors and drill-rig teams working out of a permanent Mars base.

Moreover, as NASA is discovering with its Mars analogue experiments with new spacesuits, rovers, and other equipment at Haughton Crater on remote Devon Island in the High Arctic,[26] the procedures for and processing of Mars samples will likely need to

---

[21] Robert Zubrin with Richard Wagner, *The Case for Mars: The Plan to Settle the Red Planet and Why We Must* (New York, N.Y.: Simon & Schuster/Touchstone, 1997), p. 322.

[22] Paul Raeburn, *Uncovering the Secrets of the Red Planet* (Washington, D.C.: The National Geographic Society, 1998). See Chapter 5, "Is There Life on Mars?" for a cogent discussion of the work of David S. McKay, Everett K. Gibson, Jr., *et al.* in *Science*, entitled, "Search for Past Life on Mars: Possible Relic Biogenic Activity in Martian Meteorite ALH84001."

[23] Zubrin with Wagner, *The Case for Mars*, p. 318.

[24] Exobiology Program Office, NASA HQ, "An Exobiological Strategy for Mars Exploration," January 1995, p. 17.

[25] *Ibid.*, p. 29.

[26] See, for example, Pascal Lee, "From the Earth to Mars--Part One: A Crater, Ice, and Life," *The Planetary Report*, Volume XXII, Number 1 (January/February, 2002), pp. 12-17. Dr. Lee, a planetary

take place on Mars, rather than shipping samples back to Earth. Reasons? Potential for biological contamination and cost.

Our views of evolution, the biochemistry of primitive organisms, hydrothermal biology (hot-water vents, etc.), the process of fossilization--of change itself, are undergoing change.

Herein lies an incredible opportunity for Natural History museums and high-tech Institutes to integrate their collective expertise and access-to-specimens in a fundable context that taps individual, corporate, *foundation*, and governmental sources. Coalitions of such funders have existed before, relative to the challenges of planetary exploration. In Chile's remote and foreboding Atacama Desert, scientists from NASA Ames Research Center, the Field Robotics Center at Carnegie Mellon University, and the University of Iowa (Iowa City) tested a 1,600-pound robotic vehicle--"Nomad"--in a Mars (and Lunar) analogue experiment that included simulations for the search for Life on Mars.[27]

What we suggest in this Case is the creation of a "planetary tool kit," which we shall call DEMOS (dormant, extinct, metabolic operational search)--a compact, self-contained laboratory capable of storing, processing, and transmitting data gathered via a portable field kit to determine whether past or present primitive life forms are extant on the Red Planet.

Such a kit would require protocols for sample acquisition and analysis. And here is where the experience of paleontologists and a host of other unique skills (ice-coring, geochemistry, mountaineering, etc.) would bring to bear state-of-the-art technologies with sheer human ingenuity.

Knowing where to look, how, and with what kinds of inexpensive *proven* technologies (Mars tools), is crucial to success.

While all the components of such a kit may clearly lie beyond the capability or scope of interest of Natural History museums, a proposal might emphasize partnering with corporations, foundations, and NASA at Devon (or other sites) to

1) develop an on-line Virtual Collection of Natural History samples consistent with fossils, microbes, etc. found in analogue environments (polar, desert, etc.) at varying depths. (This whole *depth* issue is important, as some scientists believe that 10 meters is an appropriate drill-sampling depth--clearly beyond the lunar experiments by the Russian Luna and Lunokhod spacecraft with their one-meter capability.[28])

    This Virtual Institute, particularly for countries/Collections in important analogue locales, provides an instant "Field Guide" across several disciplines, while providing (fundable) access and potential upgrading of technology for the indigenous host institutions. Moreover, it brings to bear a wide range of institutional specialties, which exist at most Natural History museums, from

---

scientist, is the project lead and principal investigator (PI) for the NASA Haughton-Mars Project on Devon Island in the Canadian High Arctic.

[27] Deepak Bapna, *et al.*, "Nomad's Land: Robotic Rehearsal for the New Frontier," *GPS World*, June of 1998, p. 23.

[28] *Ibid.*, p. 40.

botanists to paleontologists, etc. These Field Guides could be accessed remotely from a laptop computer via the Internet (in the analogue simulation).

2) characterize Earth-analogue microenvironments ("Oases") and methods for investigating them.

3) apply and refine current (exo) paleontology to identifying potentially fossil-bearing strata (and those suggestive of habitats of extant life-forms).

4) test new strategies and tactics for utilizing proven technologies to search for chemical and biological signatures on the Red Planet in widely-varying analogue microenvironments that mimic Mars on Earth.

5) (based upon extensive field experience worldwide) advise on the creation of explorer-friendly hand tools ranging from modified rock hammers and simple climbing gear, to snap-on coring devices, etc. The goal of all field researchers is light-weight, easily-portable, energy-efficient tools suitable for collecting samples, whether in polar, sedimentary, etc. microenvironments as small as one-meter-diameter "Oases."[29]

6) advance clear, concise protocols for Mars explorers in the search for evidence of Life on Mars. Experience with biodiversity in extreme environments is fundable.

A very real part of the challenge of a DEMOS lab would be *in situ* methods for identifying and exploring micro-environments, which may provide data regarding dormant, extinct, or metabolic life forms.

With a surface area of 144 million square kilometers, the Red Planet has as much land to explore as all the continents and islands of Earth combined, with no fewer than 31

---

[29] Much of the infrastructure for the Case we are proposing here already exists. For example, scientists at The Paleontological Research Institution in Ithaca, New York already have experience in the Atacama Desert of northern Chile, working with colleagues from the University of Florida, the New Mexico Museum of Natural History, and Western State College in Colorado "as part of ongoing research on the biological consequences of the formation of the Isthmus of Panama." The trip included collection of fossil samples and was sponsored by the U.S. National Science Foundation. See, The Paleontological Research Institution, "Research," *Fiscal Year 1996-1997: Annual Report* (Ithaca, New York: The Paleontological Research Institution, October, 1997), p. 11. Also, the Antarctic Search for Meteorites Project (ANSMET) is now working with GPS at the one-meter ("Oasis") level and, since 1976, has collected roughly 7,400 meteorite specimens. These represent some 2,000-5,000 separate meteorite landings during the past one million years. See, John Schutt, "Searching for Meteorites," *GPS World*, August, 1996, p. 13. Columbia University's Biosphere 2 Center in the Sonoran Desert between Phoenix and Tucson, Arizona could bring a wealth of data to any project, particularly in the realm of atmospheric gas concentrations and their impact upon coral reef, tropical rainforest, desert, and temperate forest habitats--e.g., simulated climate changes over time. Plus, all of these could bring a consortium of funders together. For instance, about half of Columbia's Biosphere 2 Center's U.S. $17 million annual budget comes from foundation (e.g., the David and Lucile Packard Foundation), corporate (e.g., Ford Motor Company), and individual (e.g., Houston billionaire Edward P. Bass) donors. The approach we are advocating is one of holistic science and tinkering with existing, proven technologies. See, Stephen G. Greene, "Fund Raiser Aims to Cultivate Support for Living Laboratory," *The Chronicle of Philanthropy*, April 18, 2002, p. 58.

types of Martian terrain (ranging from volcanoes to ice fields, etc.). With the ultimate loss of its "greenhouse," climatic deterioration likely would have driven any life forms into sub-surface "Oases" and possibly into extinction.[30]

Nevertheless, microscopic organisms can leave macroscopic fossils (re: the debate over ALH84001). On Earth, these bacterial stromatelites date back 3.7 billion years, making them contemporary with Mars' tropical era.

By targeting specific microenvironments, scientists could search for extinct life forms by focusing on any biomarkers and morphological evidence. For chemical evolution, others would look for organic compounds.

As noted by NASA in its *Exobiology Strategy for Mars Exploration*,

> experience on Earth tells us that *if we know where to look*, finding evidence of ancient life is not particularly difficult, especially when one considers that such evidence can be relatively widely disseminated in the form of chemical or isotopic signatures.[31]

In short, the protocol advanced in exobiological investigations is a combination of proven paleontological methods, identification of key microenvironments (thermal-spring deposits, evaporates, etc.), chemical, and isotopic observations. These fall within the purview of existing Natural History museum Missions.

To borrow the view attributed to the late Dr. Carl Sagan, "extraordinary claims require extraordinary evidence."

In the case of a planetary tool kit, with components including virtual access to Natural History Collections and expertise, the opportunity for consortial funding is limited only by the imagination.[32]

With this said, a strategy based upon partnering with a Natural History museum is three-fold:

1) Identify those Natural History Collections in the rich nations who, because their own museums and foundation funding sources are at-risk (governmental cut-backs, etc.), are seeking innovative solutions and *new* consortial partners capable of attracting significant financial support, ideally over at least a three-year period.

---

[30] Zubrin with Wagner, *The Case for Mars*, pp.139-140.

[31] NASA, *An Exobiological Strategy for Mars Exploration*, p. 5.

[32] As a separate example, The Lunar and Planetary Lab, University of Arizona, Tucson is currently involved in the NASA Mars Surveyor program and ESA Mars Express Mission. In support of the team's camera design activities, the scientists also initiated a comprehensive education and public outreach program, particularly through their connection to a growing network of 43 Challenger Learning Centers located worldwide. For lander cameras, the team plans to "return vistas of the Martian surface, unprecedented microsope images of the soil, pictures of spacecraft digging and storing samples. The orbiter camers will image Mars with mid- and high-resolution." P.H. Smith, in addition to being in the vanguard of optical solutions for space exploration, is on the cutting edge of the highly-fundable interface of delivering world-class science to the lay public and, in particular, school children. See Agnieszka Przychodzen and P.H. Smith, "Challenger Flies to Mars" (paper presented at the Third International Mars Society Convention, Ryerson Polytechnic University, Toronto, Ontario, Canada, August 10-13, 2000.

2) Develop consortial proposals that *combine* public education, some staff training, *and* related infrastructure development (Internet connection, preservation technology, perhaps limited HVAC--if the project involves an exhibit). Be clear that you request part of the institutional overhead that the consortial partner will build into the proposal. **Institutional overhead translates into operating funds, for which everyone is clamoring, but few foundations care to provide.**

3) Focus on creating a personal relationship between your Collection and foundations, beginning with local funders, moving regionally (Europe, or Asia, Oceana, etc.), and finally to longer-term global sources. Remember: your Mission Statement is key to this relationship, as it defines your Collection and is the # 1 source of ideas for foundation grant support.

With an estimated 6,000 expeditions in the field annually worldwide, plus countless laboratory investigations, the successful field team or Institute must begin to reexamine what it is that makes it unique and how to market this uniqueness to foundations.

Here, we shall focus on strategies for successful grant funding, as well as some insight into the decision-making process at foundations.

A. Seven Power Strategies for Winning Grant Funding: [33]

1) The Reverse Needs Assessment:

Simply stated, this strategy analyzes ***donor*** needs and aspirations and articulates them within the framework of the expedition's goals and objectives. Essentially, an Institute or expedition's primary task is to match its Mission Statement to meet that of the foundation, corporation, individual, or governmental agency. Remember, the needs of an expedition rank *third* in importance to those of the potential donor, the client base (e.g., host country), and, finally, the expedition itself. A major question that funders will demand you address is this: "What is the reputation of your Institute or expedition, its leader, consortial partner(s), etc. and how do you know?" Being the best-kept secret in your field is hardly an appropriate response.

2) Board Documentation:

Two resolutions passed by your Board may dramatically increase your chances of getting significant foundation (and corporate) support. These are:

---

[33] William F. Vartorella, "*Chapter Five*: Strategies & Tactics for Securing Money (and Equipment) for Exploration," in *Into the Field: Strategies for Funding Exploration--Proceedings of the Conference held at Nesbitt Hall, College of Design Arts, Drexel University, Philadelphia, PA on 20-21 April 1996*, edited by P.J. Capelotti, Ph.D. (Philadelphia: The Philadelphia Chapter of The Explorers Club, March, 1997), pp. 62-72.

a) Resolved, the Board of Trustees of the [fill in name] Expedition completely supports and endorses the efforts and leadership of the Development Committee of the Board to identify and to solicit financial resources necessary to fulfill the important and growing Mission of [group's legal name]. Furthermore, the Board is committed to 100% participation in terms of each member's financial support in the form of annual giving and for those special and campaign projects that may arise from the Mission Statement. [Note: the Development Committee mentioned above is actually a Long-Range Planning and Development Committee whose primary responsibility is the long-term sustainability of the Institute or expedition and its umbrella organization--if one exists.]

b) Resolved, the Board of Trustees of the [fill in name] Institute or expedition completely supports and endorses the efforts and leadership of the Executive Director/Expedition Director of [group's legal name] to identify and solicit foundation, corporation, trust, and other donor grants specific to our growing Mission, whether in the form of cash or other in-kind support. [Note: bank trust officers should be included on an Institute's mailing and suspects/prospects list, as they are attuned to the interest by bank customers in creating named special funds in perpetuity.]

The point here is that your Board is taking *ownership* of the Project(s) and is *accountable*. These resolutions are very important in dealing with transnational corporations--especially, the Japanese.

3) Donor Pool Analysis:
After determining how the expedition's or Institute's goals can be fine-tuned to best address and meet the Mission Statement of a Targeted Funding Source, call and ask these critical questions:

- For a project such as ours, with whom should I speak? (Person at foundation most apt to handle/administer such proposals). Goal: make an early ally (remember: people give money to people, not ideas).
- How many proposals did the foundation receive last year?
- How many were funded (e.g., the *percentage* of the total submitted)?

If the ratio is worse than 1 in 5 (20%), look elsewhere for funding. The U.S. national average is 7% of all proposals will be funded this year. To beat that average, an expedition or Institute must choose its funding targets carefully and not waste time, money, and energy in needless competition.

4) Consortial Partnerships:

The day of the outright gift of money to a single group is virtually over. Consortial partners, especially those offshore or high profile institutions such as research universities, provide a strong Case for Support for funding.

Look for these assets when choosing a non-profit partner:[34]

a) Strong financial accountability

b) A Board that contributes and raises money

c) Clearly defined Mission Statement that is concise, concrete, fundable, and consistent with your Institute or expedition's global view

d) Strong, positive public identity

e) Record of success in attracting grant and in-kind gifts

f) Larger, approved Institutional Overhead Rate (e.g., Indirect Costs formula) than that of your expedition or Institute

g) Synergy through unusual combinations (medical schools, art museums, etc.)

h) Non-competition in terms of current or anticipated donor bases.

However, *avoid* these pitfalls in creating consortial appeals:

1) Proposals that duplicate efforts. Donors talk. They know who is doing what and being funded by whom.

2) Projects that are too grandiose, promising too much in too short a time period.

3) Concepts that require a massive increase in staff or infrastructure resulting in a fundamental change throughout the two groups that negatively impact daily activities and your "corporate culture."

4) Ideas that are controversial on the Board policy level, whether for your Institute or the donor foundation--you are trying to build consensus, not confrontation.

---

[34] William F. Vartorella, "Cooperation, Not Competition: Beating the Odds in the Grants Game through Consortial Projects," *FRI Monthly Portfolio,* May, 1993, 1-2.

5) Programs that force constituencies to make major changes overnight concerning how they interact with you--especially in cross-cultural contexts.

Aggressive, cost-effective, innovative consortial projects are the wave of the future. Ride the wave.

An expedition's goal is to improve its position and visibility with funders by shoring up its reputation through "borrowed interest" and its potential finances via an institutional linkage in which Indirect Costs may account from 40% to *400%* of direct costs (salaries, etc.). In addition, unusual consortial partnerships underscore uniqueness, especially if a host country's institution is involved.

5) Matching Grants:

As more and more foundations go on-line and interactive, pressures will build for greater financial accountability, primarily through in-kind matches by the potential awardees (expedition or Institute). This enables the roughly 62,000 foundations and Corporate Giving Programs in the U.S. (for example) to maximize their resources and deliver more "bang for the buck."

In general, *avoid* matching programs that demand "hard matches," e.g., *cash*.

Often overlooked Matching Strategies for *non-Federal grants* include,

a) Volunteer Time: Keep a log and assign fair-market $$$ values (but time spent by Board members in Board meetings is *not* part of this equation)

b) Use of dedicated equipment for project

c) "Forfeiture" of Institutional Overhead (e.g., provide heat, lights, square footage of office space as an in-kind donation); some universities are mandated to request these monies, so negotiations may be necessary.

Try to choose foundations, etc. that allow for creative matching funds. Never spend your valuable dollar resources on Grant Matches unless you absolutely must. Always structure a grant proposal as a Matching Grant-- regardless of whether the funding source demands it. This tactic puts your expedition or Institute is a less-competitive funding pool and thereby improves the chances for funding.

6) Independent Evaluations:

Regardless of whether a foundation requires it, build into the proposal a round of *independent* evaluation at the beginning, middle, and end of the grant. Issue is accountability.

Several tips:

a) Get the evaluator(s) to *donate* time and use its $$$ value as part of the expedition's Matching Grant Strategy.
b) Choose evaluators with experience with consortial partnerships and in the Institute or expedition's area(s) of expertise.
c) Multi-cultural and gender representation in Evaluation Teams is an advantage with foundation reviewers.
d) With corporate grants, build the company executives into the Evaluation Team.

Evaluation is one of the most overlooked and most useful of the competitive tools for securing funding. It implies confidence in the Mission, the Expedition's Leadership, and in the Project's Goals and Objectives.

7) Free Equipment:

As pointed out by the International Organization for Chemical Sciences in Development (IOCD),

Lack of funds and lack of functioning scientific equipment are the two major constraints to scientific research in developing countries, where technical infrastructure and well functioning instrumentation, which play a crucial role in the successful execution of research projects, are often less than optimal at universities and research institutions.[35]

While self-evident, such a viewpoint is too often overlooked by scientists in their quests for research funding. In developing settings such as Africa, consortial projects with Western colleagues offer the opportunity to secure not only much-needed project underwriting, but new or upgraded equipment as well.

---

[35] International Organization for Chemical Sciences in Development (IOCD), "Meeting in Western Africa: Purchasing, Servicing and Maintenance of Scientific Equipment," *IOCD Update*, Fall, 2002, p. 1.

Yet, the goal should not be to use scarce funding, particularly within a developing context, to buy equipment. An ideal scenario would be to approach a corporation that provides both cash and lent/donated gear, rather than encumber an already tight budget with expensive instrumentation that could raise the stakes (average grant size) beyond the donor's comfort level.

As a general rule, conserve money and do not buy gear. With some *U.S. $ 1 million per day* in equipment and supplies donated to non-profits in the U.S. alone, remember our earlier tips about equipment loans, year-end strategies, recycling to other NGOs, strong donor recognition, and the trap of free, used (un-reconditioned) computers.

Now, for an interior view of foundations--

B. *Sub rosa*--Breaking the Silence of Foundation Decision-Making:

Of the 100,000 or so significant foundations worldwide, probably fewer than 2% offer any realistic funding for Expeditions. To use archaeology as a simple example, far less than 1% of all grant monies worldwide are awarded in this field. Yet, some of the world's finest, little-known, small funders are active in this niche, to wit:

- **The Bioanthropology Foundation** and the **Bingham Trust** support the application of DNA technologies in the fields of anthropology and archaeology.

- **The Langworthy Foundation** supports marine archaeology.

- **The Michela Schiff Giorgini Foundations** have supported more than 40 archaeological projects and awarded more than 80 grants in the field of Egyptology, particularly in traditionally under funded specialties such as Egyptian prehistory. Founded by philanthropist/banker Mme. Gilberte E. Beaux, the Swiss and U.S. foundations honor the memory of the young Italian archaeologist, Michela Schiff Giorgini, and encourage the work of young professional Egyptologists worldwide.

The point is research, research, research. *The Chronicle of Philanthropy*, published in the U.S., reports the latest round of foundation funding in its pages and on its website--often in the U.S. $100 million range. Also based in the U.S., The Foundation Center has a host of materials in its

New York City repository (and affiliated libraries) and proffers a wealth of directories and guidebooks. Unfortunately, these often detail the activities of funders with a U.S. $10,000 threshold for grant reporting. (See our "Abbreviated Donor Bibliography" for more on this.) Many opportunities exist below U.S. $10,000 and they often take less time, decide quicker, with less rigmarole (and competition) than the larger, more public foundations.

At the time of this writing (late 2002), the impact of adoption of the euro (€) and the uncertainty of tax laws and incentives on philanthropy within the European Union (EU) mean that foundations are struggling with projects that beckon at the borders. Pluralism is the problem. Germany, for instance, has more than 7,000 foundations, with each of the country's 16 states struggling with governance of those within its borders.

Do not be misled by the relatively small number of foundations as compared with the U.S. As noted earlier, German tax law offers family businesses significant advantages if they are channeled into charitable foundations. And best estimates are that the generational transfer of wealth in Germany during this decade may approach U.S. $ 3 *trillion*.[36]

With that said, an expedition's overall funding strategy depends on what it is trying to accomplish, where, how, why, and with whom.

Earlier, we detailed a funding strategy/budget for field research.

It is by no means the only way to view the broader formula of

Individual + Corporate + Foundation + Governmental Support = Expedition or Institute Success.

Over the years we have advocated a number of scenarios for financial well being, including 70% individual, 10% corporate, 10% foundation, and 10% governmental. This is perhaps closest to Don Keel's models, which are structured with long-term growth in mind, particularly for Capital Campaigns and Endowments (both of which are *crucial* to self-sustaining strategies).

Vartorella's approach advocates a closer balance, to wit:

Individual (40%) + Corporate (30%) + Foundation (20%) + Governmental (10%) = Success.

---

[36] Vince Stehle, "European Philanthropy Experts Disagree on Rules for Giving in Era of Euro," *The Chronicle of Philanthropy*, May 21, 1998, p. 37.

We agree on the lesser balance of foundation and governmental funding in overall financial security. Vartorella fundamentally sees foundation underwriting as a "magnet" for other sources and crucial cash flow. Keel tends to advocate foundation funding as a "capstone"--final, high profile piece--to a successful campaign. Both models work.

Still, if approached properly, foundations offer an excellent source of funding for very specific, unusual projects.

Examples abound for scientific Institutes, NGOS, and expeditions working in exotic fields, which follow the power strategies and model(s) above:

- The Shark Research Institute (SRI), which has projects worldwide, uses microlight aircraft in the Seychelles, South Africa, and Mexico for monitoring whale sharks as part of SRI's tagging program. SRI is particularly known for its global educational efforts to bring attention to the plummeting populations of many shark species, including the basking shark and whale shark. (Point of reference: singer Olivia Newton-John is President of the Basking Shark Society, U.K. and supermodel Lauren Hutton is a supporter of SRI--examples of "celebrities" helping conservation.) SRI enjoys the generous support of the PADI Foundation, Project AWARE Foundation, as well as corporate, eco-tourism, and individual donors.

- Scientists, donors, and corporate partners working with NGOs in Brazil have rapidly made that country of 158 million people the world's foremost producer and consumer of alternative energy. Solar, biomass, and hydroelectric account for 96% of the nation's electricity. Similar success stories abound in Argentina and Costa Rica (wind farms), Chile and Peru (geothermal generators), and Honduras (biomass)--with solar power springing up everywhere. With the cost of alternative energy decreasing and peak demand increasing in many venues worldwide, South and Central America are the proving grounds of shared solutions to just, sustainable futures. NGOs there are ripe for energy-research partnerships, using the power strategies we have discussed.

- On 8 August 2000, the Confederate submarine, the *H.L. Hunley*, rose out of the murky waters off Charleston, South Carolina's harbor, secure in custom steel truss and slings, some 136 years after its fateful encounter with the Union warship, *U.S.S. Housatonic*. On 17 February 1864, the Confederate submarine rammed its spar torpedo into that ship's hull sinking it and, soon thereafter, the *Hunley* itself slipped from view, the first submarine ever to sink an enemy vessel. Located in 1995, the *Hunley* brought together a remarkable coalition of six U.S. state and 12 U.S. federal agencies, the U.S. Navy, the *Hunley* Commission, the South Carolina Institute of Archaeology and Anthropology (SCIAA), South Carolina Archives and History, the U.S. General Services Administration, the U.S. National Park Service (NPS), the Smithsonian Institution, the National Oceanic and Atmospheric Administration, the U.S. Army Corps of Engineers, and the President's Advisory Council on Historic Preservation,[37] plus corporate and individual donors spearheaded by the Friends of the *Hunley*, Inc. (a non-profit whose overall goal included raising "the funding needed for the recovery and conservation of the *H.L. Hunley* submarine.") [38] Best estimates of the cost for the recovery and conservation effort have ranged between U.S. $ 12 and $20 million. Thus far, costs have been borne by the State of South Carolina (U.S. $ 4 million), the U.S. Department of Defense (U.S. $ 3 million, with another U.S. $ 900,000 expected), businesses and individuals (U.S. $ 4 million), plus time and gear from NPS and SCIAA. An undisclosed sum has been donated by **The National Geographic Society**, which is documenting the process in still photography and film.[39] The next step: a proposed U.S. $40 million *Hunley* museum.[40]

As we have identified funding sources for specific kinds of projects in the *Donor Bibliography*, perhaps the best single piece of advice, once a Mission Statement "match" has been made, is this:

Never ask for more than the average amount awarded per grant during the past three years.

---

[37] Joseph Flanagan, "Raising the *Hunley*," *Common Ground: Archaeology and Ethnography in the Public Interest*, Summer/Fall, 2001, p. 18.

[38] Friends of the *Hunley*, Inc., *Celebrate the History. Solve the Mystery. Raise the Hunley!* (Charleston, South Carolina: Friends of the *Hunley*, Inc., n.d.), p. 4.

[39] Flanagan, "Raising the *Hunley*," p. 18.

[40] John Monk, "*Hunley* price tag rising for S.C. taxpayers," *The State* (a newspaper, Columbia, South Carolina U.S.), October 27, 2002, p. 1. As explained by Monk, the *Hunley* Project is an unusual Public/Private venture. "Unlike a normal state agency, the *Hunley* project is set up so public money flows first to a state agency, the *Hunley* Commission, then to a private foundation called the Friends of the *Hunley*. Under this arrangement, the project is exempt from various state regulations" (see p. A 16). For a Chart that details this fundraising model and resulting cash infusions, categories, and expenses, see "How Public and Private Money Flowed to *Hunley* Project in 2001," p. A 16). This model has its own inherent challenges, which *The State* attempts to address.

This is known as the "ease-of-fit" rule and is followed by many private, public, and corporate foundations. Generally, if one sees inordinately high grant awards (e.g., above the calculated average--see below), they fall within the realm of "Trustee Discretionary Grants." These rotate on an annual basis and have more to do with Foundation Board dynamics than your expedition. Often, a Foundation Directory (Foundation Center, NYC, and other companies) will provide the average $$$ grant for a particular funder.

If it (or the Foundation's *Annual Report*) does not, follow this rough chart in U.S. dollars:

Assets	Average Grant Size
If U.S. $10 million	U.S. $20,000
If U.S. $1-10 million	U.S. $4,000
If less than U.S. $1 million	U.S. $2,000

Remember: the average U.S. foundation has assets of less than U.S. $1 million. And, if you focus on the smaller--plentiful--family foundations, you can expect grant amounts likely to run in the U.S. $2,000-5,000 range.

Before you despair, remember that Family Foundations are less competitive, require simpler proposals (often one page plus budget and copy of IRS non-profit status), and can often respond within 90-120 days. They are an excellent source of small, relatively-easy-to-secure grants. Plus, if the request is less than U.S. $5,000, the proposals may not require full Board review--rather just the decision of the Executive Director (trust officer, etc.). And with U.S. IRS changes that make overseas giving easier from a tax standpoint, the door is open to tapping these underutilized sources.

Several recommendations:

- The best time to apply for review is the *last quarter*. Most proposals are submitted at the beginning of the cycle (e.g., for January consideration). Competition gets progressively less keen during the final three quarters, with the last quarter, the best chance for funding.
- Generally speaking, foundations do *not* like "planning" grants. They prefer "implementation" grants. Use the planning phase as a creative "match" in your budget and request the implementation money. *IF* you have succeeded in the past in attracting plan funding from a specific foundation, do not be surprised if that foundation, when asked for your implementation funding, declines.

- An expedition's proposal should be a) consortial, b) matching, c) (ideally) *three years* in duration, d) have strong financial oversight, e) include an evaluation component, and f) have a woman or minority as either the principal or co-principal investigator. The goal is for the proposal to stand out as meritorious, offer real value for the funder, meet its Mission, and provide an opportunity for women and minorities to lead expeditions or secure funding for their Institutes.

- The most difficult question to address is how the expedition, at the end of the funding period, will become *self-sustaining*. The answer, in part, is Board participation and the move toward creating an endowment. Another possibility is for publications, films, etc. that emerge as a result of the expedition to contribute financially to the overall well-being of the expedition, its host country, Institute, consortial partner, etc.

A final point: foundation support adds value to your expedition in terms of your ability to attract other kinds of funding (corporate, individual, governmental). It also adds name recognition to the expedition and imbues it with part of the brand equity of the foundation itself. A cluster of small grants (e.g., the U.S. $5,000 variety) has greater value than the mere sum of its parts, re: total raised. It provides a platform for the next level of funding, usually within the U.S. $25,000 to $75,000 range.

C. Going for the "Gold" with a Simple Proposal:

After you have read the funder's annual report, tracked a foundation's funding pattern, begun the process of making friends, identified the specifics of its Mission and how your Institute or expedition can meet that Mission you are ready for

The Letter of Inquiry

> *Tip: Many times a simple three-page letter serves as a formal proposal and saves funder and applicant considerable time. It also allows you more flexibility in keeping a proposal in front of funders as the response time usually is 90 days or fewer.*

This mini-proposal usually consists of the following:

1) 1-3 pages in length (especially when approaching family foundations)

2) Narrative Abstract: 25 words

3) Benefits to Funder and Mission, clientele, your Institute

4) No jargon --"people give $$$ to people, not ideas"

5) Cost, Duration, Type of Funding Sought (Matching, as team
   members, *et al.* are putting up time, cash, or in-kind)

6) Accountability: How evaluated?

7) Public Relations Value to Funder

8) Previous grants, recognition programs, and who else is participating

9) Request for Meeting

10) Copy of 501(c)3 (or similar non-profit status, depending upon
    country)

11) Budget Summary.

Follow the KISS formula--Keep It Short and Simple.

Now for A few more often overlooked tips on Proposal Submission:

1) An estimated *one-third* of all proposals submitted *today* will either have
   the *wrong signature* or *no signature at all. Check and double-check
   to make certain the signature is correct, complete, and--if a budget
   narrative is present--matches that signature as well.*

2) Submit all proposals on *good quality stationery--ideally paper with
   texture.* People are tactile. Good paper is a subtle commitment to
   quality and reflects well upon your organization, without being costly
   (or obvious). Avoid colors other than white, as these tend to be
   perceived as "off-beat" and, frankly, copy poorly--which detracts
   from your proposal.

3) Sign the *original proposal in blue ink (ideally with a fountain pen--which is perceived as more personal)* The "blue ink" copy is then easy to distinguish from all duplicates, which photocopy in black.

4) Unless specifically dictated by the funder, do *not* bind your copies with anything other than a paper clip (or staple, in the case of short Letters of Intent). Have the name of your organization (contact information) on top of each page and abbreviated name of proposal, just in case the pages get separated). Each page should have a number.

5) Deadlines: a submission is not a submission until the specific funder's office receives the document. For an "overnight submission," the front desk at the funder is not the office of record. Get a receipt whenever possible.

6) Keep a copy of the entire proposal--including attachments--both in hard copy and diskette formats.

IV. Foundations, "Global Tool-Kits," and the Internet:

If the only constant is "change," the Internet is changing everything, constantly.

Foundation and donor information are now available seemingly everywhere, at once, with an avalanche of data.

What follows are sources you, as a scientist, may not have consulted.

They include pertinent discussion groups, regional and country listings of funders, "tool-kits," and other useful and arcane websites. As it is difficult to parse out foundations from the broader donor milieu, overlap occurs, Missions change, and websites vanish.

Examples,

Africa:
Africa: Pambazuka: http://www.pambazuka.org
(To subscribe, send an e-mail to <pambazuka-news-request@pambazuka.org> with only
the word 'subscribe' in the subject or body of the e-mail. This is perhaps the premier entry site for African-related issues and opportunities.)
Africa, bulletin board: http://www.kabissa.org/members/bb
Africa, technology: "Kids for Africa," Hippo Water Rollers. Access to potable water is one of the most pressing needs in rural South Africa. Traditionally, the task of obtaining water daily falls to women, children and the elderly, who trek for hours in its pursuit. Containers sometimes weigh 45 pounds, which causes long-term physical injuries. The Hippo Water Roller, which costs approximately U.S. $60, resembles an old-fashioned lawn mower with a long, clip-on steel handle. It can be easily pushed, even by

children. The result is less-frequent trips to collect water using the "Hippos," since they hold more water than the traditional containers. Excellent example of fundable technology-transfer as part of addressing the global fresh-water crisis. "Kids for Africa" is a program of The Africa Foundation and shares the foundation's U.S. 501(c)(3) non-profit registration status.

Archaeology:
The Quinque Fellows Program offers conservation/preservation professionals based and working in either Scotland or the U.S. the opportunity to undertake a six- to ten-week fellowship with mentor-counterparts in their specialty. The program is a collaborative effort by the Quinque Foundation, a U.S.-based non-profit whose Mission includes the conservation and enhancement of natural and built heritage, and Historic Scotland, an agency of the Scottish Executive charged with safeguarding Scotland's archaeological and built heritage. For guidelines and an application form from the Historic Scotland program, contact <susan.brown@scotland.gov.uk>.

Awards and Prizes:
International Associations: http://www.uia.org/prize/prizndx.htm
Rolex: http://www.rolexawards.com
Rotary: http://www.rotary.org.foundation

Endangered Species:
Animals, protection: Pegasus Foundation: http://www.pegasusfoundation.org/RFP_Island_Nations.html
"Conservation Action Network": World Wildlife Fund "action alert" on issues such as the protection of tigers. See, <http://takeaction.worldwildlife.org>

Civil Society:
Charities Aid Foundation (Main Office, U.K.): <http://www.cafonline.org> and <http://www.allaboutgiving.org> (descriptions vary, but perhaps, a venture-capital fund or bank for civil society, is apt)

CIVICUS: http://www.civicus.org

For State-Civil Society relations in a specific country, see <http://www.ids.ac.uk/ids/civsoc>

Funded by the Ford Foundation and based at the Institute of Development Studies, U.K., the Civil Society and Governance Programme is a three-year research project involving researchers in 22 countries across six international regions: Africa, Asia, Eastern Europe, the Middle East, South America, and the U.S. Excellent insights for scientists interested in Institute-building, joint ventures.

Coral Reefs:
See the new World Wildlife Fund and The Nature Conservancy report which provides scientists, policy makers, and park managers with suggestions for managing protected coral reefs, helping reefs survive and recover from coral bleaching incidents, and guidance for the location and management of marine sanctuaries: <http://pnnonline.org/foundations/reefs120401.asp>
Also, National Fish and Wildlife Foundation grants which, "help build public-private partnerships to help reduce or prevent the degradation of coral reefs and associated reef habitats." *Funds globally.* See <http://www.nfwf.org/programs/coralreef.htm>

Corporate Databases:
Electronic newsletter, includes unusual information such as an extensive inventory of "business lists" entitled, "From Fortune 500 to Handelsblatt's European 500" (http://www.freepint.com).

Country Corruption Indices:
See the 2002 Corruptions Perceptions Index, published by Transparency International in Berlin. http://www.transparency.org/pressreleases_archive/2002/2002.08.28.cpi.en.html

Also, see *The Economist*: http://www.economist.com/agenda/displayStory.cfm?story_id=1301406

And the Cato Institute's 2002 Economic Freedom of the World: http://www.cato.org/economicfreedom/

Country Development Gateways, plus Selected Foundations:
Armenia: http://gateway.am
Australia, Mumbulla Foundation: http://www.mumbulla.org
Azerbaijan: http://gateway.az
Finland: http://www.varainhankinta.net (fundraisers interested in Finland)
Georgia: http://www.developmentgateway.org/node/94442
India: America India Foundation: http://www.aifoundation.org
(For information on resource/development organizations all over the world, primarily for the benefit of the India-based NGOs, contact <da_india@hotmail.com>.)
Israel: Give Wisely: http://www.givingwisely.org.il
Israel: Public Service Venture Fund: http://www.israel21c.org
Japan, news in English: http://www.asahi.com/english/english.html
Kazakhstan: http://kazakhstan-gateway.kz/index.php
Kyrgyzstan: http://eng.gateway.kg
Moldova: http://www.gate.md
Pakistan, investing: http://pakistan.lead.org/crpt.htm
Russia: http:// www.russia-gateway.ru/en/index.adp
Scotland: Scottish Council of Voluntary Organisations: http://www.scvo.org.uk
Tajikistan: http:// www.tajik-gateway.org
Ukraine: http://www.e-ukraine.org
Uzbekistan: http://www.uzbekgateway.uz

"Digital Divide":
Internet: http://www.internetworldsummit.org
Digital Divide Network/Radio and One World: http://oneworld.net/radio

Digital Opportunity Channel highlights uses of information and communication technologies for sustainable development, particularly among marginalized and poor communities. Its Mission is to educate a global audience on the use of information and communication technology (ICT) as a tool for promoting digital access for everyone, leading to sustainable development and improved quality of life.

http://www.digitalopportunity.org

European Union (EU), European Philanthropy, and the U.K.:
Welcome Europe: http://www.welcomeurope.com
E.U. (and the U.K.): http://www.access-funds.co.uk
Grants E.U. and U.K.: http://www.co-financing.co.uk
Grants E.U. and U.K.: Grants On-line: http://www.mycommunity.org.uk
Government grants (U.K.): http://www.Volcomgrants.gov.uk
Publication, Philanthropy in Europe: http://www.ourcommunity.com.au
U.K., e-mail forum, U.K. Fundraising: http://www.fundraising.co.uk

Fellowships and Scholarships:
Research: http://www.loc.gov/loc/kluge/kluge-fellowships.html
Scholarships, environmental, Francois Fiessinger Scholarship Fund: http://www.erefdn.org/scholar.html
Scholarships, William Grant Foundation: http://www.wtgrantfoundation.org
Ireland, Scholarships: http://www.erefdn.org/scholar.html

NSF-DAAD Collaborative Research Grants (National Science Foundation, U.S.):
This program provides support for travel and living expenses for scientists and scholars at U.S. universities and affiliated research Institutes, who wish to carry out joint research projects in the natural, engineering

and social sciences with colleagues at German universities and Fachhochschulen. Goal is to foster the advancement and specialization of young scientists within the framework of a proposed collaboration. http://content.sciencewise.com/content/index.cfm?objectid=11678

Health, Global:
United Nations: http://www.developmentgateway.org/pop
Global Health Council: http://www.globalhealth.org

The Gates Award for Global Health (U.S. $ 1 million) goes to an organization that has made a significant contribution to global health. Nominated organizations can be non-profit, a private company, or a public body anywhere in the world. Also, see the Howard Hughes Medical Institute (U.S.) and its initiatives to shore up biological research in Eastern Europe and the former Soviet Union.

Haemophilia http://www.bayer-hemophilia-awards.com
Bayer Biological Products (< http://www.bayerbiologicals.com>) has set up the Bayer Hemophilia Awards Program, a U.S. $ 2.75 million annual grant initiative to fund hemophilia research and education programs worldwide.

The Baxter International Foundation, the philanthropic arm of Baxter International Inc., supports more than 200 organizations in 15 countries and on four continents.
http://www.pnnonline.org/foundations/baxter031902.asp

HIV/AIDS: UNITeS (http://www.unites.org), an Information & Communications Technologies (ICT) volunteering initiative managed by the U.N. Volunteers Programme, (http://www.unv.org) is tracking success stories of NGOs using ICT to educate, prevent, and treat HIV/AIDS. Goal is to promote and share good practices and resources--particulaly those involving volunteers--from existing efforts to other organizations. Contact Jayne Cravens <jayne.cravens@unvolunteers.org>.

Research: http://www.aupha.org/baxter.htm
Parkinsons Disease: http://www.michaeljfox.org

Human Origins:
Leakey Foundation: http://www.leakeyfoundation.org/grants/g2.jsp

Islands and Inland Seas:
Pegasus Foundation
To understand and, if possible, resolve animal overpopulation in the Bahamas and the Caribbean, the Pegasus Foundation seeks proposals.
http://www.pegasusfoundation.org/RFP_Island_Nations.html

The International Research & Exchanges Board (IREX) continues its support of the Black and Caspian Sea Collaborative Research Program. The program is aimed at researchers in Armenia, Azerbaijan, Bulgaria, Georgia, Iran, Kazakhstan, Moldova, Romania, Russia, Turkey, Turkmenistan, and Ukraine. Projects should focus on issues of practical relevance to academic, corporate, and policy-making sectors. See, <http://www.irex.org/programs/black-caspian-sea>. You can also download an application form from the site and review applications that were funded in the 2001-2002 funding cycle.

Also, The Georgian Research and Development Foundation (GRDF) and the U.S. Civilian Research and Development Foundation (CRDF) have launched the Georgian-U.S. Bilateral Grants Program, a joint grants competition to support collaborative Georgian-U.S. research in basic and applied sciences. The program reportedly marks the beginning of a larger series of GRDF science and technology development activities to be carried out with CRDF funding. At least 80 percent of project awards must be designated for the Georgian component of the research team, including institutional support. Highest priority are proposals that involve former defense scientists and young scientists, advanced undergraduates at Georgian universities, graduate students, and those scientists who have received their Ph.D. or Kandidat within the last six years. All awards are for collaboration between researchers of the Republic of Georgia and U.S. colleagues.

For complete application guidelines, see the CRDF Web site:
RFP Link: http://www.crdf.org/News/grdfbgp02.html
E-mail: georgia@crdf.org

Libraries:
Bill & Melinda Gates Foundation.: http://www.clir.org/fellowships/gates/gates.html
http://www.clir.org/fellowships/gates/gates.html
Journals, Rare and Obscure: If you need a 17th century reference from *Philosophical Transactions*, published by the Royal Society in London, see JSTOR (a online project of the Andrew W. Mellon Foundation) at <http://www.jstor.org>. The latest issues of scientific journals are *not here* (by design), but if your college, university, or Institute subscribes to the service, some 218 scholarly journals in 24 disciplines (including business, etc.) are.

Non-profit Guides:
Capital Campaigns, Endowments, Operating Funds, Annual Support:
(To download your free directory: http://www.donordata.com/free_directories.htm)
Contact Directory to Non-profits on the Internet: http://www.contact.org
Grant Writing Tools for Non-Profit Organizations: http://www.npguides.org
Grants: Global Service Institute: http://gwbweb.wustl.edu/csd/gsi
Grants, Technology: web site that provides a searchable database, re: technology, software donations, computer-recycling, etc. See <http://www.techportal.org>.
List Rentals, "Chaperoning": An alternative to selling or renting e-mail lists between Institutes, NGOs, expeditions, etc., an Institute approaches another entity and asks IT to e-mail a free promotion, etc. (Form of co-branding.) For an illuminating article: http://news.gilbert.org/clickthru/redir/4361/2916/rms
Management: http://www.mancentre.org
News, Gilbert Center (01): http://news.gilbert.org
Publication, Pew Partnership for Civic Change: *Coming of Age in the Information Age*, available onlline at <http://www.pew-partnership.org/pubs/pubs.html>.
Research: http://www.nonprofitresearch.org
Technology, "Circuit Riders": if you are engaged in research or ecological monitoring in remote, extreme environments (like EcoBolivia at <http://www.ecobolivia.org>) see the technology "Circuit Rider" project at the W. Alton Jones Foundation (<http://www.circuitrider.net>) that describes their initiative.
Technology Tip Sheets: advice on building databases, web sites, etc. and the Internet, re: members, donors, volunteers. See <www.coyotecom.com>
U.S., Guidestar: http://www.guidestar.org
GuideStar is the resource for non-U.S. NGOs that need free information about a U.S. non-profit. It has collected program and financial data for some 850,000 U.S. non-profits, plus contact information. The GuideStar database also includes more than 730,000 digitized 990 forms, the financial returns that U.S. non-profits must file with the Internal Revenue Service.
http://www.guidestar.org/search/report/press.jsp?ein=54-1774039
U.S., e-mail fora, CharityChannel: http://www.charitychannel.com
Volunteers, management: www.energizeinc.com
Volunteers, Virtual: volunteers who provide *pro bono* services via the Internet. See, http://www.serviceleader.org/vv

Peoples Republic of China (PRC):
See, CANGO (China Association for Non-Governmental Organization Cooperation).
CANGO has a membership of 76 Chinese NGOs and cooperates formally with NGOs throughout the world. Programs include Community and Gender Development, Environment in Focus, and Microfinance and Capacity Building in Tibet. CANGO has active consortial partners and funders worldwide including Australia, Canada, France, Germany, Japan, Netherlands, Norway, U.K., and U.S.

http://www.cango.org

Population, Global:
Johns Hopkins University: http://www.jhccp.org
For information about the German Foundation, DSW's work in developing countries, see
<http://www.dsw-online.de>

Space Exploration:
A five-year project will take advantage of efficient, well-established modern digital technologies to save
some early star plates from deterioration and damage. See,
http://www.pnnonline.org/fundraising/stars031802.asp

Quantum Physics, Astronomy: W.M. Keck Foundation: http://www.wmkeck.org

Sponsorships:
Europe: http://www.sponsorship.co.uk
For a free newsletter via e-mail, contact <webeditor@sponsorship.co.uk> or visit
http://www.sponsorship.co.uk

Sustainability Index:
The 2001 NGO Sustainability Index for Central and Eastern Europe and Eurasia, March 2002, 168 pages.
USAID. Bureau for Europe and Eurasia, Office of Democracy and Governance:
http://www.dec.org/pdf_docs/PNACP212.pdf

"Think Tanks":
NIRA (National Institute for Research Advancement), based in Tokyo, has provided a comprehensive
directory of web sites from Think Tanks for several years. A new, updated version contains links to Think
Tank web sites, a short briefing about the groups, and where the Think Tank is located. Links for
organizations in some 75 countries are provided. NIRA's Web Directory to Think Tanks and Other Policy
Research Resources:
http://www.nira.go.jp/linke/tt-link/index.html

See the electronic newsletter, The Virtual Acquisition Shelf and News Desk
(http://resourceshelf.freepint.com/), which includes a pointer to a comprehensive
web-based directory of "Think Tanks" worldwide.

Universities Worldwide (potential consortial partners):
Searchable database of 6287 universities in 169 countries.
http://geowww.uibk.ac.at/univ

V. The View from Mt. Olympus--A Grant Reviewer's Lament:

Grant proposals often fail for a host of reasons, the primary one of
which is the inability of the requesting non-profit or NGO to meet the
Mission Statement of the donor organization.

Unfortunately, most Institutes pay little attention to donor "needs."

Equally troubling is their inability to anticipate the critical questions
and evaluation process employed by foundations and corporate givers.

As someone actively engaged both in raising money and serving on
foundation boards over the years, the view from the mountaintop depends
where you sit.

Here are just some of the checklist questions raised by Foundation Reviewers as they reflect upon a request for funding:

1) How does the proposal meet the specifics of our Mission Statement?

2) Would our original donors have supported this project? Why?

3) Does the proposal meet a real need with a convincing, cost-effective solution?

4) What is the role of the non-profit's Board in this project?

5) Is the project consistent with the non-profit's own Mission?

6) Who else is participating in the project--especially in terms of financial support?

7) Does the project really need our help or is money available elsewhere, much more easily?

8) If we support this project, which other projects we will be forced not to fund? Is this the best use of our scarce resources?

9) Will the project overwhelm the Institute's ability to deliver its traditional services?

10) Are we convinced that good fiscal responsibility is a hallmark of this non-profit/NGO?

11) Is this project easy to evaluate? If so, by whom?

12) Is the project inclusive or exclusive? Which underserved populations are getting real help?

13) Is the budget and the staging of expenditures feasible? How much cash/expertise is the potential grantee bringing to the table? Is there an annual financial audit in place?

14) Is the amount requested consistent with our usual policy (e.g., within our average range of support)? If not, what are the compelling reasons for us investing more $$$ in this proposal as opposed to others under review?

15) At the end of our funding, what kind of guarantees do we have that the project will continue on its own?

16) *Semi-Final cut:* Are the abstract, budget, and narrative consistent in terms of goals and objectives?

17) *Final Cut: OK, Staff--you have recommended funding for 10 proposals. We have the cash to support five this round. Of the 10--all of which have high marks--WHO DO YOU LIKE?*

(This last question addresses the point that "people give money to people, not ideas." It is all the difference between approved and funded and *approved but not funded.*)

A final comment: again, there exist foundations and corporations which fund one in every five legitimate proposals that meet their donor Mission Statements. That is a 20% chance. U.S. national averages are 7%. If you are going to climb the mountain, you have to be prepared.

Now that you know how foundation Boards "think," here is a

Checklist of Key Questions to Ask a Private Foundation

before you Apply for a Grant (and *after* you determine that you meet *their Mission*):

1) **Who is the best person on the foundation. staff with whom to discuss our *concept* and how it meets your Mission?**

2) **How many proposals do you get each year?**

3) **How many proposals are funded?** (*Do the math: if worse than 1 in 5 look elsewhere.*)

4) **During the past three years, what was the *average grant amount? One-year or multi-year grants?***

5) **Am I eligible to apply as an individual or as an organization?**

6) **Are there any *unpublished restrictions* in terms of geography, types of funding, special interest areas, etc.?**

7) Generally, do you fund *planning grants* **or** *implementation grants?*

8) Does a funding trend exist at your foundation that we can track?

9) What is the foundation's policy on matching or challenge grants?

10) Does it pay institutional overhead (administrative costs)?
   If *yes***, what is the average IO percentage allowed?**

11) Truly, when is the best time to apply for funding?

12) Do you prefer a telephone call, Letter of Inquiry, or the full-blown proposal as the initial contact?

13) How does your "peer review" process work?

14) Are smaller grant requests handled strictly in-house?

15) May our grant be considered for renewal?

16) Will you fund a project that is also getting public or corporate $?

17) How long will it take the foundation to consider our proposal?

If appropriate, please try to get a sense of the following:
- **Who were the donors and what were their interests (see: Annual Report, if one exists)?**

- **Who serves on the foundation's board? What are their interests?**

- **Is there a proposal already in "the pipeline" that is similar to ours and under active consideration?**

- **"Gut feeling:" what are our chances for getting funded?**
After assembling the above information, I believe my chances are:

___*excellent*   ___*average*
___*poor*   ___*zero*

Identifying the source and planning the dynamics of the proposal are about 70% of the battle. The writing is the other 30%.

VI. Summary and Recommendations:

We began this Chapter suggesting that foundations begin their own "Skunk Works" to brew up new ideas, new scenarios to meet the needs of evolving constituencies worldwide. We finished, looking at how foundation Boards think and the questions you, as a scientist, need to ask.

There's more and we offer this advice with trepidation.

Worldwide, liberal foundations and liberal donors are a vanishing breed.

While "Ideology Indexing" (our term) is beyond the purview of this Chapter or book, studies exist ("Giving for Social Change," for example) which suggest that a plurality of foundation leaders view themselves as "Conservative." The counterpoint to this is in the public policy arena, where the evidence indicates a far more liberal bent.

The upshot, based upon a lot of data and personal experience, is this:
1) If your science has implications in the public policy realm, look to those foundations that are more entrepreneurially-based and have a reputation for seed money and special projects (e.g.,"Liberal").
2) If your Institute is engaged in controversial, cutting-edge investigations such as cloning or stem cell research or is an expedition that focuses on evolutionary trends that advocate, for instance, that birds are living dinosaurs, look to the more liberal donor pools.
3) If your Institute or expedition is involved in engineering technology, a more centrist approach is probably best, as it is capable of attracting foundation interest from across the political spectrum.
4) If your science has the potential for immediate patent-related applications, explore the more conservative, industry-based or family spin-off related foundations.
5) If your expedition is involved in serious science with a more conservative bent (such as Biblical archaeology), look to those foundations that espouse science using traditional values.

This is not meant to imply any differences among the quality of the review process, the determination and commitment of outstanding Boards, or the sheer will and vision of dedicated donors. Foundations are living, breathing bodies with their own personalities and quirks. *Caveat emptor.*

With the more conservative foundations, Boards tend to pay more attention to the "Reverse Needs Assessment" we mentioned earlier, looking for close Mission-matches. Also, they are donor-focused ("What would

Miss Millie have us do?"). Tip: if in doubt after looking at a foundation's most recent round of grant awards, take a glance at where the foundation's assets are invested. Use your own "ideology filter".

More liberal foundations tend to use criteria that look at the long-range scientific impact on society. They tend to be less donor-focused and require evaluation strategies and rigorous academic "objectivity" (whatever that means). Again, if in doubt, examine the foundation's investment portfolio.

Regardless of philosophical orientation, your smaller family foundations are an often-overlooked gold mine. While their average assets are U.S. $ 1 million or less, they can be quick to provide smaller grants (U.S. $ 5,000 variety) that can help put an expedition in the field ("petrol") or provide an Institute with radiocarbon dates, etc. Furthermore, these family foundations sometimes join forces to leverage their modest resources for a grander purpose. In 2001, the 30 members of the **Sustainable Forestry Funders Collaborative** contributed U.S. $15 million in their effort to promote timber practices that are more "environmentally benign."[41]

Yet, regardless of these summary remarks, certain kinds of scientific projects can galvanize donors across the spectrum. Witness the Public Broadcasting System's (PBS) "The Secret of Life" series and, in particular, the broadcast that discussed the 1/3rd of the Human Genome (30,000 genes) that make up the human brain. Selected donor/underwriters included **Carnegie**, **Alfred P. Sloan Foundation**, **Lucille P. Markey Charitable Trust**, **George C. Smith Fund**, the **National Science Foundation**, the **Upjohn Company**, and the **U.S. Department of Energy**. The only common denominator here is a commitment to excellence.

Consensus building and the creation of consortia are crucial components of a successful grant proposal, no matter how esoteric the subject. Consider the perceived plight of "papyrology," with its 400,000 examples in collections worldwide, where one in 10 papyri is literary in focus. Arcane knowledge, to say the least. Yet, papyrology is the leader in the humanities in applying advanced information technologies. Columbia, Duke, Princeton, Berkeley, University of Michigan, Bruxelles, and Yale participate in the Advanced Papyrological Information System. **Phoebe Apperson Hearst** funded the important collection at Berkeley (Demotic Egyptian, no less) and the philanthropy of David Packard provided funding for the Databank at Duke.

---

[41] Stephen G. Greene, "Grappling With Social Needs," *The Chronicle of Philanthropy*, February 21, 2002, p. 16.

So much for the common complaint among scientists that their projects are too esoteric to attract serious funding.

Remember what inventor Thomas Edison said: "A genius is a talented person who does his homework."

Again, the goal is to see the landscape through new eyes.

Never request more than the "average-grant-size."

If a foundation funds less than one-in-five proposals, look elsewhere.

Think like a donor. Evaluate like a foundation's Board member.

Do not compete needlessly. Pick your targets.

While foundations cannot legitimately be expected to provide more than 20% of funding for your Institute or expedition, that 20% provides niche-specific cash (and, ideally, institutional overhead) for projects lasting three years (or five) and, more importantly, can serve as a magnet for other high-profile donors.

Finally, stir the pot at the foundations' Skunk Works.

You might raise more than a stink.

***

Bibliography, Chapter 7

"Foundation Funding -- 'Final Frontier' "

Alexeeva, Olga. "The Taste of Pineapple." *Foundation News and Commentary*, January/February 1996, 14.

Blum, Debra E. "American Foundations Increase Giving to Support International Projects." *The Chronicle of Philanthropy*, January 11, 2001, p. 23. See, also, Chart, "International Giving by American Foundations," whose source is Foundation Center.

Bapna, Deepak; Maimone, Mark; Murphy, John; Rollins, Eric; Whittaker, William; and Wettergreen, David. "Nomad's Land: Robotic Rehearsal for the New Frontier." *GPS World* (June, 1998), pp. 22-28, 30-32.

Corbley, Kevin P. "Identifying Villages at Risk of Malaria Spread." *Geo Info Systems*, January 1999, pp. 34-37.

Exobiology Program Office, NASA HQ. *An Exobiological Strategy for Mars Exploration.* January 1995. 62 pages.

Farkas, E.J. "Preliminary Report of the Human Remains from the Theban Tomb No. 32 (Season 1991)." *Acta Archaeologica Academi*ae *Scientiarum Hungaricae*, 45 (1993), 15-31.

Flanagan, Joseph. "Raising the *Hunley.*" *Common Ground: Archaeology and Ethnography in the Public Interest*, Summer/Fall, 2001, pp. 12-23.

Friends of the *Hunley*, Inc. *Celebrate the History. Solve the Mystery. Raise the Hunley!* Charleston, South Carolina: Friends of the *Hunley*, Inc., n.d.

Gose, Ben. "Terrorist Attacks Did Not Cause Major Shift in Focus of Most Grant Makers." *The Chronicle of Philanthropy*, September 5, 2002, pp. 15-16, 18.

Greene, Stephen G. "A World of Difference: Spending by non-profit groups in 22 nations exceeds $1-trillion--and is growing, says a global team of researchers." *The Chronicle of Philanthropy*, November 19, 1998, pp. 31-33.

_____. "Belt-Tightening at Two Foundations Puts the Squeeze on Charities." *The Chronicle of Philanthropy*, October 17, 2002, p. 11.

_____. "Fund Raiser Aims to Cultivate Support for Living Laboratory." *The Chronicle of Philanthropy*, April 18, 2002, p. 58.

_____. "Grappling With Social Needs." *The Chronicle of Philanthropy*, February 21, 2002, pp. 15-16.

International Organization for Chemical Sciences in Development (IOCD). "International Symposium: Chemistry and Pharmacology of Plants Used in African Traditional Medicine." *IOCD Update*, Fall, 2002, p. 4.

_____. "Meeting in Western Africa: Purchasing, Servicing and Maintenance of Scientific Equipment." *IOCD Update*, Fall, 2002, p. 1.

Lee, Pascal. "From the Earth to Mars--Part One: A Crater, Ice, and Life." *The Planetary Report*, Volume XXII, Number 1 (January/February, 2002), 12-17.

Monk, John. "*Hunley* price tag rising for S.C. taxpayers." *The State* (a newspaper, Columbia, South Carolina U.S.A.), October 27, 2002, pp. 1, A 16-A 17.

Orosz, Joel J. "Opinion: Big Funds Need a `Skunk Works' to Stir Ideas." *The Chronicle of Philanthropy*, June 27, 2002, p. 47.

The Paleontological Research Institution. "Research. " *Fiscal Year 1996-1997: Annual Report.* Ithaca, New York: Paleontological Research Institution, October, 1997.

Palmer, Tom G. *Philanthropy in Central and Eastern Europe: A Resource Book for Foundations, Corporations, and Individuals.* Fairfax, Virginia: The Institute for Humane Studies at George Mason University, 1991.

Przychodzen, Agnieszka, and Smith, P.H. "Challenger Flies to Mars." Paper presented at the Third International Mars Society Convention, Ryerson Polytechnic University, Toronto, Ontario, Canada, August 10-13, 2000.

Raeburn, Paul. *Uncovering the Secrets of the Red Planet.* Washington, D.C.: The National Geographic Society, 1998.

Schutt, John. "Searching for Meteorites." *GPS World*, August, 1996, p. 13.

Siegel, Daniel and Yancey, Jenny. *The Rebirth of Civil Society: The Development of the Nonprofit Sector in East Central Europe and the Role of Western Assistance.* New York, New York: Rockefeller Brothers Fund, 1992.

Sinclair, Michael R. *Hope at Last: A Guide to Grantmaking in South Africa.* Washington, D.C.: Henry J. Kaiser Family Foundation, 1990.

Stehle, Vince. "European Philanthropy Experts Disagree on Rules for Giving in Era of Euro." *The Chronicle of Philanthropy,* May 21, 1998, p. 37.

Vartorella, William F. "From 'Denizens to Dinosaurs': Entrepreneurship and Collections Management--A Workshop." Paper presented at the 14th Annual Meeting of the Society for the Preservation of Natural History Collections, "Finance and Funding Workshop," Ripley Center, The Smithsonian Institution, Washington, D.C., 28 June 1999.

_____. "Global Funding for Egyptology in the 21st Century: An Appraisal and Recommendations for Change." Paper presented at the 43rd Annual Symposium of the American Research Center in Egypt (ARCE), Seattle, Washington: Spring, 1992.

_____."*Chapter Five*: Strategies & Tactics for Securing Money (and Equipment) for Exploration." *Into the Field: Strategies for Funding Exploration-Proceedings of the Conference held at Nesbitt Hall, College of Design Arts, Drexel University, Philadelphia, PA on 20-21 April 1996.* Edited by P.J. Capelotti, Ph.D. Philadelphia: The Philadelphia Chapter of The Explorers Club, March, 1997.

_____. "Creating Sustainable Funding for Natural History Collections in the New World Order—Foundations and Corporations: Old Allies, New Opportunities." *Museum Management and Curatorship* (England), Volume 15, No. 3 (September, 1996), 328-333.

_____. "Cooperation, Not Competition: Beating the Odds in the Grants Game through Consortial Projects." *FRI Monthly Portfolio,* May, 1993, 1-2.

_____. "Pod zltou vlajkou: Sponzorovanie timu F1 a boj o Strednu Europu" ("Under the Yellow Flag: F1 Team Sponsorships and the Battle for Central Europe"). Trans. by Peter Fritz, Editor. *F1 Sport International/Slovenske Vydanie,* July, 2002, pp. 24-25.

Wilhelm, Ian. "Foundations Gave $ 29-Billion Last Year, a 5.1% Increase, Report Says." *The Chronicle of Philanthropy,* April 18, 2002, p. 16.

Zubrin, Robert with Wagner, Richard. *The Case for Mars: The Plan to Settle the Red Planet and Why We Must.* New York, N.Y.: Simon & Schuster/Touchstone, 1997.

***

Chapter 8—"Art and Science of the Capital Campaign"

By Donald S. Keel

> *"Never doubt that a small group of thoughtful, committed citizens can change the world, indeed, it's the only thing that ever has."*
> *-Margaret Mead*

I. The Context:

Serendipity has played an essential role in science.

In Horace Walpole's *The Three Princes of Serendip*, the faculty of making unexpected discoveries by accident rose to an art form and, hence, the term. Yet, there is a difference between adventure (which has been defined earlier as the result of poor planning) and advancement (here, in the United Nations sense of "shared solutions to a sustainable future"). To borrow from the words of Jean Riboud, if you want to innovate, to change the approach of your Institute or expedition, you must find donors willing to do the unexpected.

In this Chapter, we shall attempt to harness the unexpected, to make serendipity more commonplace among donors.

In short, we shall explore the most prevalent vehicle for intensified fundraising: *The Capital Campaign*. We shall describe what a Capital Campaign is and how it works, and "get under the hood" to take a closer look at its components. We are also going to analyze the variables within these components, so that you will be able to assess your own campaign situation and be able to ascertain what needs adjusting. Finally, we have created a ***model campaign plan*** for you to use as a template to create your own campaign initiative.

Capital Campaigns are normally organized to build buildings; hence, the term "Capital" campaigns. The term "Capital" in this regard refers to "capital" expenditures, e.g. "bricks and mortar." The model campaign we have designed in this Chapter, however, follows the Capital Campaign format, but it is a paradigm for a campaign to raise "endowment" for exploration.

We have chosen a campaign to raise endowment rather than "capital projects" for two reasons:

First, most people who are struggling to raise funds for exploration are generally not thinking about raising funds to build buildings.

Second, we wanted to focus the concept of endowment for exploration because it is so ideally suited for meeting the ongoing challenge of funding expeditions, each on an <u>ad hoc</u> basis.

An "endowment" is like a savings account in which only a percentage of the interest investment income is spent each year, with the unexpended balance of the investment income put back into the fund so that the endowment grows with inflation. So if endowment funds can be raised for your exploration, it would provide a regular annual cash flow on which to build, in perpetuity. So we have chosen to create a model, which focuses on raising funds for endowment and introduces the issues related to it, such as the policies necessary to maintain and manage an endowment.

A. What is a "Capital Campaign?"

A "Capital Campaign" is an exercise in mobilizing people.

If you have even a few people excited about what you want to achieve, you have the potential beginnings of a Capital Campaign. One of the most successful campaigns we were ever involved in began with two people and an idea about which they were enthusiastic. That institution raised more than U.S. $150 million in two consecutive campaigns.

Kent Dove, in perhaps the most comprehensive book on capital campaigns ever written, *Conducting a Successful Capital Campaign*, describes a capital campaign as "an organized, intensive fundraising effort on the part of a third-sector institution or organization to secure extraordinary gifts and pledges for a specific purpose or purposes during a specified time."[1]

A "Capital Campaign" is a way of organizing for fundraising that intensifies and narrows the focus of fundraising efforts and elevates the visibility of the objective in the eyes of prospective donors. It provides

---

[1] Kent E. Dove, *Conducting A Successful Capital Campaign--A Comprehensive Fundraising Guide for Nonprofit Organizations* (2nd ed.; San Francisco: Jossey-Bass Publishers, 2000.), p. 5.

- a context in which to mobilize prospective donors
- a forum in which to disseminate information about the objective of the fundraising.
- And a timetable that creates deadlines and, hence, enhances the urgency of the Case for Support.

A campaign is a "manufactured" enterprise in the sense that we create the goals, timetables, and Case for Support. The most critical variable is **people**, the people we must motivate to meet the goals and timetables and invest in the Case for Support.

We are limited only by our imagination, our energy, our persuasiveness, and our ability to organize and motivate people to share in our sense of Mission.

The best thing about a campaign is that it is whatever we make it.

B. Changes in "Campaigns" Over The Years:

The term "Campaign" has become like the term "Jazz." Many different types of music are referred to today as "Jazz," and many different types of fundraising and public relations efforts are referred to as "Campaigns." Capital Campaigns began to proliferate in the 1950s and 1960s as ways to raise money for specific capital purposes, i.e., a new science wing of a building. Campaigns have undergone a number of changes over the years.

1) The Ascent of the "Comprehensive Campaign":

In recent years, the term "Comprehensive Campaign" has come into being. These "Comprehensive Campaigns" include not only funds raised for capital purposes, but also funds for annual operating expenses, endowments, and anything else that the organizations' presidents and Directors choose to include. In other words, "Comprehensive Campaigns" are umbrella campaigns in which the totality of an institution's fundraising is addressed in a comprehensive strategy, to reach all prospective donors for virtually all needs of the institution. It is now relatively commonplace among major educational institutions to see "comprehensive campaigns" totaling not U.S. millions, but U.S. **billions** of dollars in their goals. It is also relatively commonplace to see "Comprehensive Campaign" timetables of *10 years* or even more.

In this book, we are focusing on the "Capital Campaign," a campaign that is raising funds for specific purposes for an independent not-for-profit organization classified by the U.S. Internal Revenue Service as 501(c)(3) or its equivalent worldwide. To illustrate what a Capital Campaign is, how it works, and what the strategies involved in it are, we shall create a fictitious organization, the "**American Exploration Institute,**" and we shall develop a model campaign plan for it.

While our reference point may be "the Americas" (based in the U.S., but engaged in active science in Central and South America), the reality with global fundraising is the model can be relatively easily adapted within the European Union and other venues, as scientific NGOs are increasingly active worldwide.[2]

2) The Evolution of "Investment Philanthropy":

One of the fundamental changes in philanthropy itself entering the variables of Capital Campaigns has been the emergence of "Investment Philanthropy" (see Chapter 4). In the days of the "Great Society" of the early 1970s, "investment" and "philanthropy" were mutually exclusive territories. "Return on Investment" was not part of the lexicon of "Charitable Giving." But "Giving" and "Investment" came closer and closer together through the years until they eventually overlapped. "Enlightened Self-Interest" in corporate giving became a recognized and acceptable motivation for financial support of not-for-profit organizations (even though it had been in practice for years). The idea that "a rising tide raises all ships" became more widely accepted as corporations developed charitable giving policies that unabashedly augmented their corporate objectives. Philanthropic individuals and families not only gave to causes to which they were ideologically, religiously, or otherwise attached, but they also gave in ways that provided additional tax benefits to themselves and their families.

With the steep rise in the stock market in the 1990s, "Deferred Giving" (bequests, charitable remainder trusts, etc., whereby donors pledge assets to be given to institutions after their deaths, with most forms of deferred gifts enabling tax benefits for the donors and their heirs) came into its own as a specialty, as donors learned at an accelerated pace how to take

---

[2] The I.R.S. recently ruled that U.S. foundations intent upon giving money overseas need only exercise "expenditure responsibility"--essentially, grantee accountability on how the money was used and, at year's end, whether any of the grant remained unspent. Yet, post-9/11, global giving practices and procedures have become a bit clouded. Consult your tax and non-profit attorneys.

advantage of tax benefits of deferred gifts and reduce their own taxes and the taxes of their heirs.

So the mentality of investment and of philanthropy merged into a concept under which not-for-profit organizations increasingly had to demonstrate to prospective donors that a gift to them constituted "a sound investment" to the future of the world in which the donor had an interest, and progressively more often, to the donor's own financial situation and/or that of his/her heirs.

In comprehensive campaigns, endowments more and more appeared in campaign objectives, and certain kinds of deferred gifts became acceptable and countable toward campaign goals.

3) Entrance of Tax-supported Institutions Into Fund Raising Milieu:

In years past, Capital Campaigns were entirely the domain of private not-for-profit institutions. It was generally believed that tax-supported institutions like "state universities" in the U.S. did not need to raise funds in the private sector because they were the responsibility of the public sector. In the 1970s and 1980s, however, tax-supported institutions, becoming alarmingly aware that tax-based funding alone was not going to enable them to keep up with the pace of advancement necessary for them to be competitive in their fields, began to mobilize fundraising efforts in the private sector to "bridge the gap" between what public funding would provide for and what they really needed.

Private foundations for public institutions proliferated. A term widely used in Capital Campaigns among public institutions to describe the purpose of their Capital Campaigns raising funds in the private sector was the "margin of excellence." In the evolving parlance of education, as private sector fundraising accelerated at public institutions, the "state schools" became "state-supported" schools, then "state-assisted" schools as we refer to them today in the U.S. Concomitant with the evolving vocabulary was the ever-growing role of private philanthropy in the budgets of tax-supported institutions, as the portion of institutional budgets supported by private philanthropy grew faster than the portion of their budgets supported by state appropriations.

4) Increased Role of Staff in the Solicitation of Major Commitments:

In earlier days of Capital Campaigns, volunteer campaign leaders did all solicitation. The rationale was that volunteers, not being paid to raise funds but rather contributing their personal time as well as financial resources, carried a more persuasive and difficult-to-decline message than would be possible for a paid staff member or consultant. It was explicitly stated in campaign plans that staff and consultants would not solicit commitments, and that solicitation was entirely the domain of volunteers.

Times have changed.

In recent years solicitation by staff has become more prevalent, especially at major institutions with large and sophisticated fundraising staffs. The norm in such an institution is to have a cadre of major gift development professionals each of whom has a "portfolio" of 200 to 300 prospective donors. Each of these staff members develops a cultivation and solicitation plan for each of his/her prospects, involving their superiors and volunteer campaign leaders along the way. The strategy is for the staff member to develop a relationship with the prospective donor and, in the process, raise the sights of the prospect so that, by the time of the formal solicitation by a volunteer, and/or a senior staff member, the prospect's sights have been raised sufficiently to motivate a commitment at the level at which the prospect had been evaluated.

5) The Constant Presence of Capital Campaigns:

Campaigns are virtually seamless in transition from one campaign to another, with an appropriate "non-campaign" interval in between during which the planning for the next campaign is taking place, while donors are paying their pledges, the organization (Institute, expedition, NGO) is looking for leadership for next campaign, and the organization is preparing the infrastructure for the next campaign.

6) The Ever-Increasing Plethora of New Not-For-Profit Organizations:

I.R.S. data tell us that there are 3,000 new not-for-profit organizations created every month in the U.S. Worldwide, it is anyone's guess of the growth of this sector, particularly for countries such as South Africa or on the far-flung frontiers of exploration. Particularly in smaller communities worldwide, this means increased competition for the philanthropic dollar and increased pressure to attract and retain volunteer leadership on Boards and campaign committees.

C. "To Plug In Or Not To Plug In, That is the Question":

Many individuals and organizations exploring new ways to obtain funds for their Institutes or expeditions are attached to larger entities, usually universities. The internal politics of these institutions mirror ancient Greece. Like "city-states" with their own constituencies, political clout, and resources, Law School, Medical School, and other University components vie for influence, donor access, and priority in institution-wide campaigns.

Plugging into a larger institutional campaign has the advantage that you do not have to worry about the execution of your fundraising effort and the expense of it. The disadvantage is that you do not have autonomy to determine your organizational fate, your fundraising strategy, and your access to prospective donors or the priority of your projects or institutes in the context of the parent institution's fund raising priorities.

If your expedition is a component of a larger institution such as a university or Natural History museum, it is doubtful that you would be able to obtain permission to conduct a campaign independently on your own. If the institution of which you are a part embarks on a campaign, your component will be or will not be a part of that campaign to the extent that your organizational component figures into the priorities of the institution.

However, it is possible in some institutions to gain a sufficient measure of this autonomy to conduct independent fundraising campaigns (if there is not an institution-wide campaign underway). There are foundations that--while they are part of or attached to universities--are permitted to do their own fundraising, albeit coordinated with the priorities, timetables, and politics of the host institution.

Since the purpose of this Chapter is to describe and explore the strategies of a Capital Campaign and not the navigation of intra-university political white-water, we are keeping it simple and positing the "American Exploration Institute" as a 501(c)(3) foundation which is subsidiary of a university or other larger organization with its own Board of Directors and has the blessing of the parent institution to embark on a Capital Campaign.

II. Requisites of a Capital Campaign:

There are four primary requisites necessary for your organization to conduct a successful Capital Campaign:

- A Case for Support
- A cadre of Volunteer Campaign Leadership

- A cadre of Prospective Donors with an existing or potential connection to the organization; and
- Basic Infrastructure to enable the campaign conduct.

Each of these requisites is critical to the success of the campaign.

A. The Case for Support:

As discussed earlier in several contexts, the Case for Support is the basic statement presenting why your campaign merits philanthropic investment.

The Case for Support is contained in the fundraising mail you receive in your mailbox many times each week.

It is contained in the United Way pitches during America's National Football League (NFL) games or as part of the charitable solicitations by Formula One (F1) race car drivers for children's hospitals, etc. worldwide. It is also contained in the endless spiels from telemarketers who call all too often at suppertime.

But most pitches we receive through various media do not strike home with us, the recipients of the message, because they fail to meet one or both of the basic requirements of a successful Case for Support.

The Case for Support, to be successful in attracting philanthropic investment, must meet the following two requirements:

- It must be perceived as Valid.
- It must be perceived as Urgent.

Validity--Connectivity and Resonance:

You are passionate about your specific field of science and have perhaps spent your whole life in it. So there are many things that are self-evident to you which may not be self-evident to a prospective investor in your project who is not as familiar with the subject matter as you are, and for whom there may be nothing whatsoever self-evident about the validity of what you propose to do. To articulate your Case for Support effectively then, you are going to have to do so in terms which connect with your prospective donor/investor, and which resonate with his/her own personal value system. This means knowing your prospective donors and being able to articulate what is important to you in terms of what is important to them.

Urgency--A Window of Necessity:

If your Case for Support is not perceived as Urgent, your prospective donors will defer action on supporting your campaign in favor of others which demonstrate a time window in which they must be supported. So your Case for Support must demonstrate not only that your campaign should be supported, but it must also demonstrate that it must be supported NOW, or something of importance to the prospective donor will be lost.[3]

Consider the events of September 11, 2001 as an illustration of the role of the Case for Support. The events of that day were so horrifying and so globally visible, that millions of dollars were contributed from people throughout the world, spontaneously, without being asked at all. The validity and urgency of the Case for Support of the families of the victims of 9/11 was so self-evident, so profoundly persuasive that no campaign whatever was needed to raise many millions of dollars from thousands of donors around the world.

B. Volunteer Campaign Leadership: "Who Else Is Going, And What Are They Going to Wear?"

The psychology of the invitation, described in Chapter 4, is central to Capital Campaign strategy and is implemented by Volunteer Campaign Leadership. In Chapter 4, we examined the similarity between the psychology of the invitation and the psychology of fundraising. When we receive an invitation to a party and see at whose home the party is, two questions immediately come to mind: "Who else is going?" and "What are they going to wear?"

Likewise in campaigns, donors want to know who else is involved and what is the extent of their commitment.

---

[3] Urgent and Valid (and Compelling) Cases for Support *abound*, but are often not articulated as such. See, for example, "William Spain, "Spoils of Aphrodisias: A legendary archaeological site's uncertain future," *Art & Antiques*, June, 1997, pp. 45-46, 48 for the plight of some of the world's finest and best-preserved examples of Greco-Roman statuary at the site in Turkey. For the endangered cheetah, see <www.wild.org> for a discussion of loss of habitat, competition with large predators and commercial ranchers. On another front, best estimates are that 1.3 *billion* people in developing countries lack safe drinking water. Researchers at the Environmental Engineering Division of Leicester University in the U.K. are working with the seeds of the Moringa tree (*Moringa oleifera*), which when pounded into a powder and combined with water, produces an effective water coagulant capable of removing most of the suspended solids.

They gauge their level of support and/or involvement largely on their view of relative participation with others already involved.

Hence, a campaign will be successful to the degree that it enlists volunteer leaders that inspire the involvement of others, and that will raise the sights of prospective donors by virtue of the level of their own commitments.

The degree of success of a campaign is directly in proportion to the caliber of volunteer leadership in terms of corporate rank, personal wealth, and record of philanthropic generosity. It is also dependent upon the sequence in which major donors' pledges are made.

Charles Fazio, principal of Fazio International, a global fund raising consulting firm, used to say that there are two kinds of people in the world:

"those who like to create a winner, and those who like to back a winner"

It is critical, in this context, to identify and solicit first the recognized leaders whom others will follow.

While it is true that staff has been increasingly involved for a number of years in the solicitation of commitments in Capital Campaigns, the role of Volunteer Campaign Leadership continues to be critical to the success of any campaign. Such volunteer leadership provides access to prospective donors who would otherwise be inaccessible to staff members. **This access to individuals controlling personal and corporate wealth provides the margin between four- or five-figure commitments and seven-figure commitments.** With such access, an organization can often raise literally U.S. millions more than would be possible without that access.

Kent E. Dove describes the necessary characteristics of volunteer campaign leadership as follows:

- A strong identification with the institution
- History of association and active involvement with same
- Connections with colleagues and friends who are also leaders
- A substantial record of major gifts to same
- Immediate name recognition with groups served by the institution
- The ability and willingness to be forceful, dynamic leaders.[4]

---

[4] Dove, *Conducting a Successful Capital Campaign*, p. 36.

These characteristics can be condensed into what our colleague Nisia Hanson has dubbed: "The Three C's:" Connectedness, Capacity, and Clout.

- *Connectedness* refers to the strength of pre-existing connection with your organization.
- *Capacity* refers to the capacity to make a substantial financial commitment. And,
- *Clout* refers to the access and influence a leader has in enlisting other leaders and obtaining major commitments from them.

Dove's description is an ideal scenario, and the unfortunate reality is that it is unlikely for any but the most developed and sophisticated institutions to have campaign leadership in which everyone exhibits all the characteristics described by Dove (whose subject institution is the University of Indiana in the U.S.). In the real world of smaller institutions and organizations, we find that the plethora of major campaigns among the larger institutions has "cornered the market" on top volunteer leadership, particularly in smaller U.S. cities where there is a finite number of philanthropically active leaders who are all well-known within the community. Hence, top leadership is more difficult to involve for smaller institutions and organizations when the top leadership is siphoned off for the larger, sophisticated institutions.

Fundraising and campaign textbooks often focus on the Board of an institution as the primary source for volunteer campaign leadership. If you are with a small NGO, Institute, or expedition, however, or a subsidiary of a larger entity (such as an Institute within a College within a University), your access to top volunteer leadership may be limited, and more creative ways to identify, approach, and enlist top volunteer campaign leadership will be necessary.

In the next section of this Chapter, we examine the relationship connections between an organization and its prospective donors, i.e. the ways donors are connected to the organizations they support. It is also helpful to use the relationship categories to identify prospective campaign leaders and to develop enlistment strategies based on those relationships.

C. Prospective Donors:

Donors and prospective donors are best identified and defined in terms of the existing or potential relationship they have with the fundraising organization. For an Institute seeking to identify and involve prospective donors and campaign leaders, the terms of these relationships also indicate the approaches to take with them. These donor categories and the nature of their primary connection with organizations they support are listed below and were detailed earlier in connection with communications development, solicitation strategies, and donor recognition best suited to the nature of their relationship with the recipient organization.

Donor Relationship Categories:

Organizational relationship = The donor is a Member. The nature of the connection is Belonging. Examples include alumni of schools, colleges, and universities and members of religious organizations.

User relationship = Donor avails himself/herself of services of the recipient organization. Examples include members of cultural organizations such as symphony associations, museums, and arts groups. A sub-group of this donor category, one that applies to funding for exploration, is the "Would-Be User" group. These are the donors who have such affiliations as social memberships in riding clubs, memberships in adventure-related associations, and other groups in which they identify with the participants but do not actively participate in the activity themselves.

Issues Relationship = Donor supports issue(s) that an organization addresses. The nature of the connection with the organization is support of the issue. **These donors are often passionate in their support of the issue first, the organization second.** If there is an organizational relationship (membership), it is secondary. Examples include environmental and conservation groups (Save the Rainforest, Black Rhino, Great Barrier Reef, the Sphinx, Venice, etc.); right-to-life groups; women's rights organizations (micro-enterprise in India, etc.); and the National Rifle Association.

Former Patient Constituent relationship = Donor was cured or helped by a medical organization such as a hospital. The nature of the relationship is often gratitude: "XYZ Hospital saved your life, now you can give to save someone else's." This donor category also applies to the loved ones of former patients. With this donor category, cultivation and solicitation is often done entirely by staff. This category also pertains to organizations such as social service organizations like YMCA's and Boys and Girls Clubs, children's homes, schools for the handicapped, and such, where former constituents feel a sense of giving back to the organizations that helped them realize fulfilled lives.

Approaches to these different prospective donor groups differ in presentation of the Case for Support and in solicitation strategy, as described in our Chapter on donors.

D. Infrastructure:

A Capital Campaign needs basic infrastructure proportional to its size in order to be successful. Often organizations, especially smaller NGOs mounting modest campaigns, neglect the up-front capitalization of a campaign. This hampers basic organization and, most important, poor donor relations, slowdowns in providing volunteer leaders with needed presentations, and poor follow-up.

The usual rule of thumb is that campaign cost is approximately 10 (ten) percent of the goal of the campaign. This amount can be more in the case of start-up situations where the organization must spend two years or more to set the climate for the campaign, or less for larger, sophisticated organizations with a full complement of fundraising staffs and a well-cultivated donor constituency.

All but the very smallest campaigns should have a *full-time* campaign director (for the duration of the campaign), at least one support person capable of handling correspondence, preparing proposals and presentations, and tracking the progress of cultivation and solicitation of prospects, and adequate hardware and software to record and track the numerous initiatives and personal contacts that are made during the course of a campaign. The software should have the capacity to record campaign commitments, automatically produce pledge reminders, signal the proper donor recognition for each donor, and track the path of cultivation and solicitation of each prospective donor.

"Making Do" is the reality of most small organizations mobilizing campaigns. It is always best, however, to determine what the minimum requirement for organizational infrastructure is to mount a campaign and do what is necessary to obtain that minimum level of capitalization.

Campaigns often go off track because they have not been capitalized, up front, with the basic infrastructure to maintain the level of communication and volunteer support necessary to build and keep up the momentum necessary to motivate volunteers.

Front-end costs of a campaign are some of the most strategically important, as will be discussed in the next section, because they are related to the development of the strategy for the whole campaign (e.g. feasibility study costs, Case Statement materials production, etc.). Hence, front-end capitalization is of critical importance to the development of sound campaign strategy.

Hand-to-mouth campaigns -- which pay their campaign costs out of campaign contributions as they come in -- have difficulty in three ways.

- First, they stress having to support ongoing expenses from the beginning with capital pledges.
- Second, they explain to their donors that not all contributions are going to the capital project for which they are designated because a portion of their contribution is going to operating expense.
- And, third, donors feel that their contributions are being "taxed."

Hence, it is immeasurably preferable to have the campaign capitalized from the beginning.

Front-end campaign capitalization normally comes either from a commitment from the parent institution to underwrite campaign costs either *in toto* or for a period of time, or from a lead donor who recognizes the criticality of adequate funding to get a campaign off on solid footing.

III. Campaign Phases:

There are three phases to a capital campaign:

- Preparatory Phase
- Quiet Phase
- Public Phase

The Preparatory Phase:

The Preparatory Phase of a campaign is the most critical phase; because it is here that the dominoes are set up which will ripple throughout the rest of the campaign to determine its level of success. G. Otis Mead, IV, founder of the Virginia Horse Center and a meticulous planner, used to say, "You can over-rehearse, but you can never over-prepare." A campaign is a truly cause-and-effect enterprise in which "one thing leads to another." Thus, the preparatory phase can be described as the point at which the initial stone is dropped into the water, creating the ripple effect that will continue through the end of the campaign.

In the Preparatory Phase, the following tasks are undertaken, pouring the foundation for a successful campaign:

1) Articulate the Case for Support:

For the smaller Institute or NGO, articulation of the Case may involve one or two people taking the time to think through exactly what it is they are trying to accomplish and relating it to their known or prospective constituencies of donors. In the larger, sophisticated institution, it may involve obtaining the input from different campuses and multiple organizations, and it may include focus groups among constituent groups. Across the spectrum of size and complexity, however, the following questions must be asked to arrive at the persuasive articulation of the Case for Support that will be perceived as Valid and Urgent:

- What is it we must do?
- Why must we do this?
- What will be the result of our doing this successfully?
- What will be the lasting benefit from our successfully meeting our objective?
- On whom will this lasting benefit have impact?
- When do we need to do this?
- Why must we do it in this time frame?
- What resources are needed for us to accomplish our Mission? i.e., How much will it cost for us to do this?

Again, it must be emphasized that these questions must be answered, and articulated in terms of knowledge and interests of prospective donors.

In the Preparatory Phase, the Case for Support should be produced not in any "slick" mass produced form, but rather as a loose-leaf notebook which carries the connotation that it is in "draft" form and can be changed after input from key people such as prospective campaign leadership and prospective lead donors. This is because a key strategy in the development of the Case for Support is to seek input for the Case from those who will be asked to invest in it. If future donors have input into the Case for Support, they will be "stake-holders" in it and will be more likely to make significant investments in it.

2) Recruit A Campaign Steering Committee:

Your Campaign Steering Committee is the "Brain Trust" of your Campaign. It is not itself a fundraising committee, although members of the Campaign Steering Committee will, no doubt, be members of the fundraising committees of the Campaign. The Campaign Steering Committee is your sounding board and the group to help you determine and validate your campaign strategy. It is this group that will evaluate and approve campaign strategies, goals, and organization charts.

You should recruit the very top leadership you can to your Campaign Steering Committee. It is often less difficult to enlist high-powered individuals to the Campaign Steering Committee for the very reason that it is not a fundraising committee.

3) Develop A Gift Acceptance Policy:

If your organization does not already have a Gift Acceptance Policy, you should develop one in the Preparatory Phase and get it approved by the Campaign Steering Committee and your Board of Directors (or Directors). Donors sometimes want to "gift" (e.g., give) items that an organization is ill equipped to accept, or they want to take credit for gift values whose value is, at best, questionable. In our experience, such gifts include a sailboat that was sunk (yes, sunk), a life insurance policy on the donor's infant grandson, a landfill, and a seven-figure gift to create an Institute at a university (with a donor specifying what would be taught and who would teach it).

A gift acceptance policy ensures that you are not put in the position of appearing arbitrary if a donor proposes to give a gift that is unacceptable for a variety of reasons. [5]

---

[5] A Gift Acceptance Policy is a critical tool for every Institute, NGO, and expedition. Essentially, it creates an institutional framework for maintaining and preserving the fiscal integrity of the non-profit entity. Specifically, it memorializes the terms and conditions of donor options regarding gifts, and establishes clear guidelines and procedures for staff and volunteers to follow in discussing and negotiating donor gifts. Liability issues aside, your Gift Acceptance Policy goes beyond definitions of "gift vehicles" (an overview of Revocable Living Trusts, for example) to the important nuances of the gift approval and acceptance process. The best examples we have seen address who has the authority (President, Vice-Presidents, Campaign Steering Committees, etc.) to accept gifts ranging from cash to the ever-problematical artwork and collectibles category where valuations may be a point of robust debate. In a global-giving economy, advice from tax and legal specialists is critical.

4) Determine The Goal Size:

A goal should initially be set that reflects real needs to accomplish the objective that the Campaign has been created to underwrite. If a Campaign is to underwrite a series of expeditions, then all the costs related to those expeditions should be included in the initial goal. If the goal is determined to be unrealistic or improbable by the feasibility study (to be discussed subsequently), then costs can be cut across the board, an expedition can be dropped, or other measures can be taken. It is important, however, to begin not with an extravagant goal, but with a realistic goal that does not leave out components that may be critical. Often organizations try to foretell what is feasible to raise in setting their initial goal and compromise their outcomes before any external testing of goal feasibility is done.

The worst-case scenario is to complete a campaign successfully only to find that you have not raised enough money to do what you had set out to do.

As previously observed, it is not necessarily "easier" to raise less money than to raise more. It is more difficult to raise less money for a non-compelling case than it is to raise more money for a compelling case.

5) Pledge Period:

The pledge period must be factored into the size of the Campaign goal. Most Capital Campaigns have pledge periods of three to five years. This enables the campaigning organizations to realize gifts that are much larger than they would be if they were one-time gifts.

Multi-year pledges, however, bring into focus the cost of money itself. If funds are going to be expended in two years for the organization's campaign purposes, but the pledge period is five years, then the cost of money borrowed to enable the expenditures before the pledge payments are made must be taken into account and added to the total campaign goal. This factor is all too often not taken into account by not-for-profit enterprises.

Consider a five-year campaign with a five-year pledge period. If a five-year pledge is made on the last day of a five-year campaign, it will be ten years from the inception of that campaign that the final dollar of the pledge will arrive. Thus, this factor must be taken into account in the initial calculations of project costs to be funded by the Campaign.

6) Create the Prospect List:

A master list of prospective donors to the Campaign must be prepared and entered into a database. The master list will include,

- Individuals and families
- Businesses and Corporations and
- Foundations

These should be entered into the master list so that they can be sorted by constituent type. Further, the prospect list should contain at least the following fields:

i) Name
ii) Address
iii) Constituency
iv) Contact (for corporations)
v) Solicitor (to be entered later)
vi) Target Ask
vii) Commitment, and
viii) Notes.

These are the basic features of the simplest of prospect lists for a grass roots campaign effort. If the organization is of a size that is able to purchase (or access) fundraising software, this information will be contained in the software's format (See section following). Such software has sophisticated reporting capability. Some have campaign modules, special event planning modules, prospect tracking capability, and other features.

The prospect list should be sorted into two tiers: The Quiet Phase Prospect List, and the Public Phase Prospect List.

The top 110 donors should be culled into the Quiet Phase Prospect List. These are the top prospects that will make or break your campaign.

The Public Phase prospect list is everyone else. It should include prospects such as local businesses (local subsidiaries of transnational corporations may actually fall into the top 110 donors), which may invest in your organization out of civic involvement, but which may not be involved with your organization at present.

7) Develop Campaign Infrastructure:

A campaign director will be hired (or designated from existing staff if the organization is in a position to do so.

A campaign assistant will be recruited or appointed to support the campaign director.

Development software will be procured if the organization is not already equipped with it. There is a variety of such off-the-shelf software, and it is highly advisable to purchase one of these, as opposed to attempting to cobble together something from one of the database softwares that are bundled with PC's. This may be necessary, however, depending on budget constraints.

8) Evaluate Prospects:

When a list has been assembled of prospective donors and the basic infrastructure of staff and software has been installed to manage it, prospects must be evaluated for capacity to give and readiness to do so.

The prospect evaluation process involves enlisting a prospect evaluation team of connected people who are familiar with the constituency and are reasonably aware of their capacity to make philanthropic commitments and their potential willingness to do so for the Case for Support of the campaign. This team convenes (as many times as necessary to cover fully the entire prospect list), discusses, and rates each prospect for potential. It should be noted that this evaluation team is focused primarily on the individuals, families, corporations, and foundations that are within the constituency of the organization or its host institution. Professional foundations and major corporations that have a potential interest in your project based on historical giving patterns are usually identified directly by the campaign director or support staff, or by the host institution's research staff. The purpose of the Evaluation Team is to evaluate prospective donors with whom there is an existing or potential personal contact and posit a reasonable target ask on each of those prospects.

The "reasonable" target ask is predicated on a combination of the prospect's giving capacity (potential) and his or her "readiness to give."

Determination of consensus on these factors, especially in an organization with little or no prospect research, requires discussion among members of the prospect evaluation team. There is no shortcut for this process.

The prospect evaluation process has another purpose. Whenever possible, it is advantageous to enlist prospective major donors to the prospect evaluation team. When individuals get engaged in the process of evaluating the gift potential of others, it causes them to consider themselves as donors also and often to raise their sights with regard to their own potential support.

9) Identify Prospective Campaign Volunteer Leadership:

Campaign leaders at the top levels get involved in campaigns primarily because they are inspired by the dynamism, enthusiasm, and passion of purpose of the CEO of the organization and because they believe in the objective of the Campaign.

There are some secondary motives that come into play. For example, corporate chief executive officers in a community periodically accept a visible charitable leadership position in the interest of visible community involvement. Often, "rising stars" in the corporate community get involved in leadership positions in campaigns to elevate their visibility and demonstrate community involvement and to demonstrate success in the civic arena. Where explorations are concerned, as Vartorella points out in his discussion of corporate support, product identification with an expedition, as personified by the visibility of the CEO or other top executive, serves a corporation's marketing objectives as well as their more generic community-service-visibility objective.

10) The "Three C's" of Campaign Leadership:

In identifying potential campaign leadership, it is important to remember "The Three C's:" Connectedness, Capacity, and Clout. (See section II.B.)

It often works out that you have to choose between one or two of these "C's." Your most Connected prospective campaign leaders – those who know you and your Mission the best and are supportive of it – are often those with less of the other two "C's," i.e. Capacity to give and Clout, i.e. access and credibility. Further, it often is the case that a Capital Campaign constitutes both an opportunity and a necessity to upgrade your organization's Board in terms of Capacity and Clout in order to achieve your goals. Often, those who "have been with you from the beginning" do not have the Capacity or Clout to exert the volunteer leadership in terms of Capacity and Clout for you to meet your goals. They may feel "upstaged" and even have hurt feelings if you bring into the organization other individuals with greater Capacity and Clout.

So if you happen to be in such a situation, enlisting campaign leadership of "higher caliber" than is present on your Board can be a very politically and personally delicate situation requiring adroit diplomacy.

We have been in situations where the founders of organizations had to be supplanted in order for the campaigns to realize the visions of the organization to succeed. If they had not been "upstaged" by others, the founders' own visions of the organizations they founded would not have been realized.

11) Develop a Campaign Volunteer Leadership Organization Chart and Position Descriptions:

A. Blending Vision with Realism:

Your Campaign Leadership Organization Chart and Position Descriptions, and your prospective campaign volunteer leaders, constitute a "chicken-and-egg" situation. The individual you recruit for Campaign Chair (or other volunteer leadership position) will be determined by the campaign position description you have developed. **But the reality is that your position description will be determined by the attributes of the individual whom you can recruit to that position, more than the position description will determine whom you recruit to the position.** This is because the pool of available volunteer campaign leadership available to you will be the driving factor in how you construct your Campaign Leadership Organization Chart.

For example, if you have the possibility of motivating a pace-setting commitment (i.e., the largest financial commitment you will be able to secure from anyone) from someone who will be motivated to make such a commitment if he/she is named Chair of the Campaign, then you should consider enlisting that person for the position, even if that person is not likely to exert continuing, energetic hands-on leadership and in the execution of your campaign. You will adjust your Campaign Leadership Organization Chart to reflect this reality by creating two Vice Chair positions for "Doers" who cannot make a similar level of commitment but whose Connectivity and Clout compensate for the Capacity. Thus, the construct of your Campaign Volunteer Organization Chart (except for the organization with a cultivated stable of predictable volunteer leadership – a "deep bench" in sports parlance) is a "work in progress" in which you maximize the productivity of your volunteer leadership by adjusting your campaign volunteer position descriptions to accommodate the best volunteers you have a realistic possibility of recruiting. Your organization chart should be structured with The Three C's balancing each other.

This concept is NOT to be confused, however, with the mistaken notion that you should obtain permission just to use some prestigious person's name as part of your volunteer campaign organization just because of the prestige of his or her name, on the assumption that somehow her name will attract financial support from others. The utility of visible volunteer leadership is the knowledge that a person with some combination of Capacity and Clout (regardless of whether they were Connected before they were enlisted) is applying that Capacity and Clout to your campaign to meet your objectives. Your objectives have become their objectives. The substantive demonstration of support from prominent, credible leaders -- through their financial support and exercising their access and credibility -- is what gets prospective donors' attention and results in their support of your campaign.

B. Test the Case for Support:

A critical component of the Preparatory Phase of the Campaign is the testing of the Case for Support. This process is begun in the convening of the Prospect Evaluation Team. You will get a good idea of how the Prospect Evaluation Team reacts to the Case, and which aspects of it are most compelling for them.

C. The Campaign Feasibility Study:

If your organization has the budget to pay for a Campaign Feasibility Study by an outside consultant, it is a good investment to make. Such a study may cost between U.S. $10,000 and U.S. $40,000 or more, depending on the firm conducting it and the format in which it is conducted and the number of people interviewed.

In a Campaign Feasibility Study, a consultant interviews a number of major prospective donors, usually prominent philanthropists in the organization's constituency or territory, and key Board members and other individuals (usually 30 to 50), and asks a number of questions that relate to each interviewee's perception of the organization, its leaders, its Mission, and its value. The consultant also asks a few questions related to what the interviewee would consider contributing to the organization if asked now. These interviews are confidential, and only sample non-attributed comments and observations are contained in the report from consultant to organization.

Included in this report also is a recommendation of what the goal of the campaign should be.

A Feasibility Study is not a survey, as it does not represent a statistical sample of your potential donor constituency. Some Feasibility Studies do, however, include direct-mail questionnaires or telephone interviews with larger numbers of people.

The Feasibility Study is intended to do the following things:

- It brings the Case for Support for your organization to the attention of prospective donors who could have a major impact on your reaching the campaign goal. In so doing, the Feasibility Study is, in this aspect, a marketing tool exposing your potential major supporters to your Case for Support. Hence, the interview is almost a "sales call."

- It demonstrates to your major potential investors that you do your home-work, your "due diligence," before embarking on a project in which you are going to be asking them to invest. It communicates good planning.

- It presents a snapshot of the perceptions that major potential investors have of you and your organization, enabling the consultant to project a realistic but challenging goal for your campaign.

- It provides an insight into what range major prospective donors would consider an investment in the organization.

Carl Shaver, founder of a New York City consulting firm, used to say that, at the very bottom line, a feasibility study would answer thoroughly four questions:

1) Is the organization perceived as effectively managed?
2) Is the Case for Support perceived as Valid and Urgent?
3) Is there a cadre of constituents with the resources to
give enough to meet the organization's goal? And,
4) Are they willing to do so?

Of course, Feasibility Studies should tell much more than the answer
to those four questions, but one has to be careful that amidst all the issues,
these four questions much be answered.

Feasibility Studies should guide you in the development of your
campaign strategy, recommend prospective campaign leaders, and provide
insights into the perceptions of your organization so that you can articulate
your Case for Support in the best way possible.

D. Choosing a Firm:

If you are choosing a firm just to conduct a Feasibility Study, to
provide on-going counsel in the development and conduct of your campaign,
or to provide full-time campaign direction, there are basically three types of
firms:

First are the small firms in which the principals may be the only full-
time staff members. In such firms, the principal(s) in the firm will provide
whatever client service you receive.

Second are the large firms with a staff of account executives. In these
firms, the principals or vice presidents make the sales calls and presentations,
and the client service is provided by the account executives. The American
Association of Fund-Raising Counsel is the association of primarily this type
of firm, which are the largest and most prosperous of fundraising consulting
firms.

Third are the firms that have a principal or two, perhaps some partners,
a small number of full-time employees, and a stable of free-lance campaign
directors who are tapped to direct campaigns on an as-needed and as-
available basis.

With all three of these types of firms, the quality of service provided
to your organization is going to be only as good as the individuals who
actually work on your campaign. Your campaign director or campaign

counsel will be involved with you and your major investors and will deal with the confidential matters related to ask amounts and solicitation strategies. After the principals and vice presidents depart the sales presentations, no matter what they say about their ongoing supervision of your campaign, you must be comfortable with the person who is going to be on the scene working with you in your campaign. Your Board chair, your Campaign Chair (if enlisted) and any other key individuals in your organization should also interview that person prior to finalizing the engagement of the firm.

E. How the Process Works:

Prospective interviewees are agreed upon by and set a Campaign Timetable.

i. Prospective interviewees are identified by the organization, usually a special committee, and the development officer. The interview list is agreed upon by the Campaign Chair, the CEO of the organization.

ii. A letter is written for the signature of the Campaign Chair, Board Chair, or other prominent volunteer. The letter is a letter of introduction for consultant. It explains the purpose of interview, that interviewee's comments will remain confidential, and that the consultant's visit will not be a fundraising call.

iii. The letter is sent out and followed by phone calls from the organization scheduling the interviews.

iv. A set of questions (usually not a "questionnaire" as this is not, strictly speaking a "Survey" but rather a probing in-depth conversation): The questions are discussed with the key people in the campaign and the list is agreed upon. It includes questions regarding how much the interviewee would consider investing in the campaign if asked to do so now.

v. Consultant conducts interviews (usually 30 to 50).

vi. Consultant prepares a report that includes sample non-attributed comments, discusses key issues, and recommends a campaign goal. Some feasibility study reports from some firms include an assessment of campaign readiness in chart form.[6] The consultant presents the report first to the CEO and development officer and then to the Campaign Steering Committee and other groups, including the governing board, as deemed appropriate.

vii. Sometimes feasibility study reports recommend not embarking on a campaign immediately, but rather taking a period of time, a lengthy preparatory phase, to set the climate and educate prospective donors on the case for support. Feasibility studies make recommendations based on projections of what key people might do. They are not infallible.

Example: After a feasibility study conducted by one major fund raising firm concluded that The VMI Foundation (Virginia Military Institute) could raise around U.S. $10 million, the Foundation decided to attempt a goal of U.S. $30 million. Under the leadership of its Executive Vice President, Harry Warner, the Foundation went on to raise U.S. $36 million in its first campaign, and over U.S. $100 million in its second campaign, achieving pre-eminent status as a state-assisted institution with one of the highest per-student endowments in the U.S.

Preparatory Phase:

The preparatory phase can take anywhere from six months to two years, depending on the amount of work that has to be done to get the organization and its leadership into a state of readiness.

For the purposes of our American Exploration Institute (based in the U.S., but with research labs and expeditions working, say, in Central or South America) we are making the assumption that it is an organization that has never embarked on a Capital Campaign before, and we are projecting a year for the Preparatory Phase.

---

[6] A particularly good example is Jerold Panas' "Campaign Readiness Profile" which examines and ranks several key issues in campaign readiness.

Quiet Phase:

The Quiet Phase usually takes six months to a year before the Public Kickoff, again, depending on the state of readiness of the organization and its leadership. For the purposes of our American Exploration Institute, we are projecting that the Quiet Phase will go nine months prior to the Public Kickoff, and the solicitation of major commitments will continue until the end of the campaign.

Public Phase:

The Public Phase can be timed for as little as three months to as long as a year. Considering that there will be a limited broad-based constituency for the American Exploration Institute, we are projecting a nine-month public phase from October to June.

Let's get some other basics in place:

1) Develop a Gift Range Table:

A Gift Range Table is a tool used to indicate to prospective donors what level of support will be necessary in different size gift categories in order for the goal to be met. Many times, people inexperienced in fundraising strategy will say something like: "We have to raise $100,000, so let's get a hundred people to give a thousand dollars each." As anyone who has been in a fund raising campaign knows, it doesn't work that way.

Harold J. Seymour, in his classic, *Designs for Fund-Raising*, articulated "The Rule of Thirds," a widely practiced rule of thumb that, in capital campaigns, you must get the first third of the goal from the top ten gifts, the second third from the second 100 gifts, and the final third from everyone else.[7]

The idea is simply that in most donor constituencies, you have a small number of prospects that are capable of doing much more than most of the rest of the prospects are capable of doing. By giving "*pace-setting gifts*," they provide the credibility in the success of the campaign for subsequent donors, encouraging them to do, proportionately, the most they are able to do (the "Who else is going and what are they going to wear?" principle).

---

[7] Harold J. Seymour, *Designs for Fund-Raising* (2nd ed.; Rockville, MD: Fund-Raising Institute, 1988), p. 32.

So a Gift Range Table is a way of providing a framework for a prospective donor to put his or her potential commitment in perspective. It is a way of saying, "If you commit X, others will give Y."

Gift range tables in practice are a forecast of what we believe we can raise, based in part on the information provided in the feasibility study.

Below is an example, an actual case of a Gift Range Table constructed for a U.S. $3.4 million campaign. We'll say it's for our "American Exploration Institute."

No. of Gifts	Gift Range	Range Total	Cum. Total
1	$ 1,000,000	$ 1,000,000	$ 1,000,000
2	$ 500,000	$ 1,000,000	$ 2,000,000
3	$ 100,000	$ 300,000	$ 2,300,000
4	$ 50,000	$ 200,000	$ 2,500,000
10	$ 25,000	$ 250,000	$ 2,750,000
20	$ 10,000	$ 200,000	$ 2,950,000
25	$ 5,000	$ 125,000	$ 3,075,000
50	$ 2,500	$ 125,000	$ 3,200,000
100	$ 1,000	$ 100,000	$ 3,300,000
200	$ 500	$ 100,000	$ 3,400,000

Notice that in the Gift Range Table, there is one gift projected at U.S. $1 million, and two projected at U.S. $500,000. If these three gifts are realized, they will constitute almost two-thirds of the goal. This does not fit "The Rule of Thirds." Why? Because it fits into what we believe is the potential from three donors.

The million-dollar prospect is known to be able to make this magnitude of gift, and he was a principal in the founding of the American Exploration Institute. The second gift is one that has actually already been made. The third gift is projected for the person who has agreed to solicit the million-dollar gift. That person has recognized that in order for his solicitation to be successful, he will have to demonstrate to the million-dollar prospect that he, the solicitor, has made a commitment in proportion to what he is asking the million-dollar prospect to do.

Thus, in this case, The Rule of Thirds has taken a back seat to the reality of the donor pool. Why not go for more than U.S. $3.4 million if we

can raise almost two-thirds of that goal from three people? Answer: because
the American Exploration Institute's constituency is a small constituency.
Again, in sports parlance, it does not have a big "bench" of major prospects.
There is only a small prospect pool, and behooves us to cultivate and solicit
each one as effectively as we can, because we do not have many alternatives.

2) Conceptualize the Print Media for the Case for Support:

With your Case for Support tested in the completed feasibility study,
your goal set, and your campaign organization laid out (recognizing that it
can change depending on the specific strengths of the individuals you recruit
at the top levels), you are now in a position to conceptualize your campaign
media, especially the print media for the next phase of the Capital Campaign,
the "Quiet Phase."

As will be seen in the description of the Quiet Phase, you will need
print media that do not have the look of mass production. You will need
creative and graphic media, but they will be in a format that connotes
"custom-made." You will need materials designed for one-on-one visits and
small-group gatherings.

a) The Case Statement Brochure

The cornerstone of your print media will be your Case Statement Brochure
or booklet itself. The function of this piece is as 1) a promotional tool to
graphically depict your Case for Support, and 2) a reference for your
volunteers, prepping for visits to major prospects.

The primary Case Statement document can take several forms,
depending on the nature of the Campaign, tastes of the leadership and
constituency, and the Campaign Strategy. Some organizations, especially
larger institutions mounting large campaigns, draft a large comprehensive
document, which exhaustively describes purposes of the Capital Campaign
in great detail, with floor plans of buildings to be built, charts and diagrams
detailing various aspects of the Campaign. At the other end of the spectrum,
the simplest of documents is used: a simple brochure.

A major determining factor in your Case Statement format is the
degree of complexity of your Case for Support. For example, we recently
saw a Case Statement Brochure for a multi-million-dollar campaign that was
a simple five-by-eight booklet of 8 pages. It wasn't slick, it wasn't fancy,
and it had few words. But it poignantly conveyed the Case for Support of
the organization whose campaign it represented. It was a Capital Campaign

for a breast cancer center in a hospital. The reason it could be so simple is that 1) everyone knows what a hospital is; and 2) everyone knows what breast cancer is. So what this Case Statement Brochure did *not* do was re-hash what everyone already knows about a hospital and about breast cancer. It conveyed the potential impact of the center on breast cancer victims in the region where the hospital is located.

So a major factor in conceptualizing your Case Statement document is **how much your constituency knows about what your organization does and what your Campaign is going to do**. The more explaining you have to do, the larger your primary Case Statement piece will have to be.

However, the rule of thumb in developing your print media should be to **keep the verbiage to an absolute minimum**. One university president we know equated the value of a brochure or speech or video presentation with the quantity of information in it. Consequently, the university produced print media that were voluminous and gorged with *words* -- words that were read only by the president of the university and the staff that produced the university's media for that president.

b) The Print Media Package

The Case Statement brochure is the centerpiece of a package of print media to be used in a variety of situations. Best bet: a modular package of components that can be used interchangeably depending on the venue and purpose of its use.

The most versatile and simplest package is one that contains the following basic elements:

i)   The Case Statement brochure or booklet.
ii)   A folder to hold the campaign materials, including the Case Statement.
iii)   Inserts with photos and bios of the campaign leadership. Use inserts as it seems that there are always latecomers to the campaign volunteer organization chart that would be excluded from mass-produced brochures printed before their involvement.
iv)   A Question-Answer insert for campaign volunteers.
v)   A pledge card. The pledge card is most often under-designed as a sales piece. It is the final point of contact when a prospect becomes a donor. It should be an attractive, and, in itself, persuasive graphic piece.
vi)   Individualized presentations.

vii)   Copies of articles, features, Op-Ed. pieces, etc., which have
       appeared in newspapers and magazines.

c) Campaign Video

The power of video is immense, especially for exploration.
Harnessing the drama of an expedition can get the attention of a prospect or
campaign volunteer and convey emotion that no print media can convey.
The key to powerful video that gets results is to avoid the question: "What
kind of video do we need?" Instead, ask, "Who do we want to see the
video?" and "What do we want them to do after they have seen it?" Design
your video on this premise and you will surprise yourself with your results.

We offer the following advice with regard to this medium:

i)   Ignore the "rules" about how long you can hold the attention of a
       viewer. You will be told that: "You can't hold anyone's attention
       longer than 10 minutes." That's an excuse for not producing an
       engaging video. (Example: The video I wrote and produced which
       received the most national recognition was 18 minutes long.)
ii)   Convey emotion, not information. You can back up your video
       with print media that will contain the information.
iii)   Don't be fancy. Be simple. Electronic acrobatics and fancy
       graphics don't win the hearts of prospective donors. People telling
       their own story honestly wins hearts. The drama of nature itself
       wins hearts. The look on a person's face wins hearts.

3) Conceptualize Your Major Special Events:

Your two main campaign events are like bookends. They are:
       a) your public kickoff event, and
       b) your victory celebration.

Your public kickoff event occurs at the end of the "Quiet Phase,"
discussed in the next section. At this event, major donors to date are
recognized, the goal is announced, and the amount raised toward that goal is
announced. It is after the public kickoff that your broad-based solicitation
begins. **The main purpose of the public kickoff is to pose a deadline to
major prospective donors to make their commitment in order to be
recognized at that event.** This is not an exercise in vanity on the part of

major donors. They want to help the organization as much as they can, and they know that the larger the total which has been raised, the more powerful the message to donors who have yet to step up to the plate.

The victory celebration occurs, obviously, at the end of the Capital Campaign. Its main purpose is to pose a second deadline for donors who did not step up before the public kickoff. It provides a final opportunity for donors to be recognized for their participation in the Campaign's success.

a. Conceptualize Donor Recognition

Donor recognition accomplishes two purposes. First and obvious, it gives the donor a sense of personal satisfaction at having done something worthy of such recognition, and a sense of personal gratification at the visibility of what he or she has done among his or her peers. Second and of more importance, recognition of a donor motivates other donors to invest proportionately in comparison to the recognized donor's gift. In other words, if a prospective donor considers him/herself a peer of a donor who is being recognized at a certain level, that prospect is motivated to be recognized at the same level by giving a gift at the same level. So donor recognition creates a kind of domino effect among subsequent donors.

i. Forms of Donor Recognition

There are five forms in which donors are recognized for their support:

1. "*Name-On-The-Wall Recognition*" is the visual recognition a donor receives by giving at a certain level and has his or her name entered on a donor recognition wall-listing donors at the various gift levels of the Campaign.

2. "*Naming Opportunities Recognition*" refers to major donors who are awarded the right to name a facility, endowed program, endowed faculty chair (or other type of position) in recognition of their major gift. This type of recognition is only applicable in a Capital Campaign for which the purpose of the campaign is to build facilities, such as an

expedition house or research lab, which then bears the donors' name(s).

3. "*Event Recognition*" is the announcement of a donor's gift at an event the organization has to recognize donors' support.
4. "*Take-Home Recognition*" refers to a plaque, scroll, or engraved bowl, etc., that the donor is presented with in recognition of a gift. At the other end of the spectrum of this Take-Home recognition are coffee mugs and tee shirts, such as those that National Public Radio listeners are offered for their phone-in pledges in the U.S.
5. "*Publication Recognition*" refers to recognition a donor receives in organization's publication, e.g. in an "Honor Roll of Donors," or in a full-page "Thank You" in the regional newspaper.[8]

What you are able to offer your donors in recognition depends on your organization's circumstances. If you do not have the physical locus of your own building in which to dedicate a wall to recognize donors or name rooms in honor of major donors, then obviously that option is not open to you.

A. The Quiet Phase

The "Quiet Phase" is the name commonly used to describe the Major Gifts Phase of a Capital Campaign. It is during this phase that the lead gifts are cultivated and solicited, quietly, without any public fanfare or publicity. A great deal of attention is given to the cultivation and solicitation of each of these gifts, because they set the tone and the pace for subsequent donors to gauge where they should be proportionately on the Gift Range Table.

The prevalent rule of thumb is that 50 percent of the goal of the Campaign should be pledged in The Quiet Phase. Why? Like "The Rule of Thirds," it is just one of those rules of thumb that has been handed down for nearly 40 years. Some organizations announce at one-third of the goal

---

[8] The Oriental Institute (OI), for example, produces an *Annual Report* that is a combination of Research Reports from its scholars--"Middle Egyptian Text Editions for Online Research " (Janet H. Johnson) or "Giza Plateau Mapping Project" (Mark Lehner), a report from the Development Director, and an Honor Roll of Members and Donors. OI is an excellent example of recognizing a donor within the context of the research "sponsored," or galleries upgraded, etc.

pledged. Fifty percent is a good rule of thumb. Countless campaigns have applied it, and it appears to work. So it continues to be practiced.

Again, it depends entirely upon each organization's constituency. In the case of the American Exploration Institute where we have three donors who will give nearly two-thirds of the goal, that constituency understands that this is the optimum scenario for that organization. However, in another organization, announcing at the public kickoff that two-thirds of the goal had been raised might signal to the rest of the prospective donors: "Oh, well, they are so far along already, I guess they don't need *my* support."

So determining the appropriate level of support to be raised in the Quiet Phase is a subjective matter ultimately to be determined by the campaign committee and the Board of the organization.

1) Convene the Leadership Team to Assign Prospects.

It is at this point that the actual fund raising in the Campaign begins. The Leadership Gifts Team (or Committee – we prefer the action orientation of the word "team" to the bureaucratic connotation of the word "committee") convenes to review the prospect list and assign prospects to each committee member. Prior to convening this committee for this purpose, you and your campaign director meet with your Campaign Chair and other key leaders to discuss the very top prospects and determine a cultivation/solicitation strategy for each. Part of this cultivation/solicitation strategy will be to determine who the best person will be to make the "ask". So the top prospective donors will have been assigned prior to the convening of the Leadership Team.

In the assignment of prospects, it is important to control the process so that no one on the Leadership Team volunteers to take too many prospects. The Chair of the Team must specify at the beginning of the process that no one is to take responsibility for more than *four* prospects. He or she must emphasize that a successful solicitation of top prospects will require more than one visit by a team of people hand-picked for that purpose based on private discussions with the Team member. It is usually the case that at least one exuberant team member will get caught up in the moment and end up leaving the meeting with 10 or more prospect assignments. What follows is usually procrastination and last minute low-quality solicitations. This is precisely what must be avoided in the Quiet Phase. All focus must be on the development of solicitation scenarios in which the right person is visiting the right prospect at the right time.

The object is not to get all prospects solicited; the object is to have each prospect solicited in the best possible way by the best combination of people. Each prospective major prospect, then, constitutes a "mini-campaign."

> 2) Conduct Informational/Cultivation Sessions for Major
>   Prospects.

During the Quiet Phase, and in some cases before in the Preparatory Phase, the "climate" should be set for major gift fundraising. In some cases with major campaigns, this period may take a year or two. In order to set the stage for visits leading to the ask for a major investment, it is effective to create occasions for small groups of major prospects to convene for a "sneak preview" of the project(s) made possible by the Campaign. These occasions take several forms. The most effective of these, in my opinion, are the small evening reception for no more than 20 people in a private home, and the breakfast or luncheon executive briefing for three to five people held in a private room of an appropriate eating club.

These venues provide for an intimate atmosphere in which to engage in conversation and dialogue about the project(s) envisioned, their potential impact on society, and the excitement of involvement in it.

These occasions are best done with a minimum of presentation materials. Too much in the way of presentation materials, fancy computer graphics, etc., creates the atmosphere of a formal presentation when what is desired by these occasions is the opportunity to develop personal chemistry with prospective donors and to imbue them with your enthusiasm about what you are about to undertake.

> 3) Obtain Strategic Media Placements.

While you are in the process of attracting the attention of major prospective investor/donors in your project, it can enhance your situation to have unpaid (i.e. not paid advertising) media placements in the form of feature articles and editorials on the Op-Ed. pages of the major newspapers in your organization's territory. Such placements are valuable long after they have appeared, because reprints can be included in the campaign folders, in proposals and presentations, and in the home receptions and executive briefings. Strategically timed articles in professional journals would probably not be noticed by prospective donors because they are not subscribers, but they could be re-printed and included in the folders and informational pieces shared with prospects in the receptions and briefings, thereby conveying validation of your credibility by virtue of the fact that publications in your field have recognized the significance of what you are doing in the field.

To obtain such strategic placements, it is necessary to make personal contact with the reporters and editors or your regional newspapers and magazines. If an organization is not staffed with professional media relations professionals to do so, then the principal in the organization must do so. This provides another opportunity to involve key campaign volunteers, and even to recruit the publishers of the regional media to the Campaign Team.

4) Cultivate and Solicit Major Gifts.

Prospects should be sequenced so that those who are the recognized trendsetters make their commitments first, so that they can be cited in subsequent solicitations of other prospects for which what the trendsetters have done will be a factor in their consideration of their own commitments. It is a rule of thumb in the cultivation and solicitation of major commitments to try to involve in some way as many people respected by the prospective donor. This means that a prospective donor may be visited by a team of two people whom the prospect respects, receive a follow-up phone call from another, a follow-up letter from a third, and receive "I hope you'll join me in support of this campaign," from a fourth on the golf course. This process must be orchestrated carefully so as not to constitute too much "pressure" on the prospect. How much is "too much" will be determined in the development of the cultivation/solicitation plan for the donor.

That having been said, however, it must be recognized that much of the fundraising and fund giving that goes on is a simple matter of "I contributed to your cause, now you contribute to mine." This is a basic reality of fundraising, and much of what we talk about with regard to the Case for Support and campaign materials and campaign organization ends up as means to mobilize this process of *"Philanthropic Reciprocation,"* prevalent in the business community.

B. The Public Phase

In the Public Phase, the goal and the amount raised is announced, and a broad-based solicitation of all the organization's prospects is launched.

This is not to say that **all** the major prospects have pledged or even been solicited by the time of the public kickoff. Remember that in the Rule of Thirds, two-thirds of the goal comes from the top 110 prospects and the rest from everyone else. So, if the announcement is made when 50 percent of the funds are pledged, that means that there are still a significant number of major prospects to be solicited.

While you want to raise as much as possible in the Public Phase from prospects being solicited in that phase, remember that many prospects are going to be giving U.S. $25 or U.S. $50. So the total value of the Public Phase is more than the dollars raised from prospects solicited in that phase, because the Public Phase of a campaign really has more than one purpose.

The Public Phase is really a campaign within a campaign, and it is organized much like the larger campaign of which it is a component.

In addition to raising dollars from contributors of small amounts, the Public Phase:

    c) Demonstrates to major prospective donors who either have not yet made their commitments or have not been solicited, that the Campaign has support at the grass roots level.

    d) Motivates major prospective donors who either have not yet made their commitments or have not been solicited to make a pledge so that they can be counted recognized at the Victory Celebration.

    e) Enlarges the donor pool of the organization, and, in so doing,

    f) Creates a circumstance in which **new** prospective major donors surface.

1) Public Phase Steering Committee

The Public Phase Steering Committee parallels the Campaign Steering Committee for the overall campaign. It is your "Brain Trust" for the broad-based solicitation of pledges of lesser amounts. It is they who will provide feedback on your strategy and approve it. They will recommend key people for key volunteer leadership positions, and most of them will serve on the fund raising committees of the Public Phase.

2) The Public Kickoff Celebration

As observed earlier, the Public Kickoff Celebration is one of the two "bookends" of the Campaign, the other being the Victory Celebration.
Its purposes—

i)   To raise the visibility of the Campaign to the public level.
ii)   To provide a platform to recognize individually the major donors to the Campaign.
iii)   To motivate other major prospective donors to join those who have already pledged and make their own pledge prior to the Victory Celebration.
iv)   To encourage new major prospective donors to surface.

Public kickoffs vary in scale and venue as much as not-for-profit organizations in America vary in size and scope. We have been involved in a campaign kickoff in the finest hotel in town culminating with waiters bursting in the ballroom doors with trays of glasses of champagne for all 600 guests at the moment that the Campaign Chairman proposed a toast to the goal and the amount raised while 6,000 balloons float down from the ceiling. We have also been involved in a campaign kickoff celebration which was a private affair for the constituents of an organization that shunned "public" affairs, considering themselves a special organization appreciated only by those associated with it.

Regardless of the size and venue of the public kickoff celebration itself, at least three months in advance of the event, personal contacts (which would hopefully already exist) with the regional media should be made to alert them to the event and what it means, and to the importance of the campaign it is celebrating. The amount of the campaign goal will not be news, in an era where comprehensive campaigns are being announced with goals in the U.S. $ billions. A campaign for exploration will, however, attract the attention of the media because it is not the usual campaign to build a sports arena or a hospital wing or endow a scholarship program. The public announcement of the campaign will provide an opportunity for Op-Ed. pieces (perhaps the most effective form of exposure, because it gets the attention of the opinion makers in the publication's readership, and they are often the most philanthropically active in any given region). So the announcement of the campaign in the media will provide an opportunity to focus on the **issues** associated with the campaign's purpose. Since the donor pool for exploration is most likely going to support it because of the "Issues Connection" (Section II C.), the focus of attention on the issues associated with the Campaign's purpose will likely attract new donors and raise the sights of existing donors.

3) Public Phase Solicitations

The solicitations in the Public Phase are divided into two tiers. The first tier is the in-person solicitation of pledges from individuals and businesses for a certain minimum amount. In the case of the American Exploration Institute, we shall say, U.S. $1,000 over five years. This campaign tier parallels the Quiet Phase solicitation in the sense that a Public Phase Campaign Chair is recruited, campaign divisions are created, prospects are assigned, and personal solicitations are conducted. Amounts solicited, however, are far less than the amounts solicited in the Quiet Phase.

a) Public Phase Division Organization

Division Teams reporting to the Public Phase Campaign Chair will conduct the actual fundraising in the Public Phase. These Teams will be focused primarily on constituencies in the community of the location of Institute and among its former donors.

For the purposes of our American Exploration Institute, we will have five Divisions. Each of the Chairs of these Divisions will recruit five Team Captains, each of whom will recruit five team members, each of whom will personally obtain commitments from at least five donors.

Thus, the total number of gifts to be obtained by these five divisions (including all the team members who it is understood will make pledges) is 780. Considering that every team member will not be 100 percent productive, this number of possible donors should yield a net number of pledges to meet the requirements of the Gift Range Table, which projects approximately 400 donors.

The second tier of prospects is the "suspect list" derived from your local Chamber of Commerce membership list, individuals on your mailing list who have never contributed and whom you may not even know. This is your "fishing" list, i.e. your list of "suspects" from whom you hope to generate a few new constituents. You will solicit them by direct mail. Any donors who surface from this list will be put into your database for follow-up. While a minimum result is expected from this direct mail solicitation, it will add to the Community visibility of Institute's Campaign.

4) The Victory Celebration

Like the Public Kickoff, the Victory Celebration provides an opportunity to thank and recognize donors to the Campaign. At this event, the donor recognition is unveiled, the top donors are called to the stage to receive special gifts and make a statement. ***Overall, it should be as large an event as the organization can afford.***

Of course, coverage in the local newspapers should be arranged ahead of time for the Sunday edition after the celebration. In addition to the feature coverage provided by the newspaper, a full-page advertisement should be bought (by the campaign or by a sponsor) thanking all the donors to the campaign and publishing their names in the campaign gift levels.

Now let's see how all this fits together.

IV. A Model Campaign Plan—"The American Exploration Institute":

Globally, with some 6,500 Natural History Museums, 6,000+ expeditions, countless labs, and a growing bevy of scientific Institutes--all with potential campaigns of different sizes and scopes--a generic campaign plan that would fit all situations would be so generic as to be meaningless. The authors of this book recognize that its readership will comprise a broad spectrum of readers -- from individuals with a dream of achievement with no organizational infrastructure, to principals of institutes, institutions, and organizations with evolved organizational infrastructures. It is written with the intent that members of this diverse readership will extract those components of the following plan to fit particular fiscal and organizational realities. Therefore, we shall draw some parameters around our American Exploration Institute and construct a campaign plan to fit its circumstances.

The American Exploration Institute is an organization classified as 501(c)(3) by the U.S. Internal Revenue Service. It is linked to, but not an internal part of Metropolitan University in an affluent medium-size Mid-western city. It was founded 50 years ago by a member of the Geography faculty at Metropolitan, in order to finance the expeditions she and a member of the botany department planned to make to the Amazon region to venture into uncharted places and to obtain specimens of local vegetation found only in that region, to bring them back for research into their medicinal qualities.

The two professors succeeded in obtaining foundation support for their expeditions, which yielded such findings in both geography and biomedicine that the Institute attracted something of a following. It now has 500 members who contribute annually, a full-time director and a staff of five, a board of directors of 25, and a U.S. $3 million annual budget.

The Institute has never had a Capital Campaign before, and the Board has determined to launch a U.S. $3.4 million campaign to create an endowment that will generate U.S. $150,000 to $200,000 per year to underwrite its research and expeditions.

A consultant was retained to conduct a feasibility study, which yielded the conclusion that a goal of U.S. $3.4 million was feasible. The following is the campaign plan that has been put before the Board for its approval.

<u>The Campaign for Exploration</u>

A Plan for a
Campaign
For
The American Exploration Institute

I. Introduction:

This plan, submitted herewith, for a campaign at the American Exploration Institute is the result of a campaign feasibility study commissioned by Institute's Board of Directors and three months of consultation with Institute's staff and Board.

II. Current Status:

The estate of John H. Doe provided Institute with U.S. $350,000 for expenses for the campaign. Hence, the Board approved proceeding to develop a campaign plan and to begin conversations with prospective campaign leaders. Jane Smith has agreed to serve as Chair of a Campaign Steering Committee to begin to revise and implement these plans pending the approval of the Board of Directors.

III.   Type of Campaign:

The Campaign for Exploration is a campaign to raise U.S. $3.4 million, primarily to create an endowment fund to provide underwriting in perpetuity for the expeditions of the Institute and the research emanating from it. During the Campaign period – January of 2003 through June of 2005 – annual support solicitations will continue, coordinated with the strategies and prospect contact of the Campaign for Exploration.

IV.   The Campaign Goal, and the Objective of the Campaign:

For 50 years, the American Exploration Institute has been contributing to the knowledge in a number of scientific fields through the significant findings of its expeditions. Yet to underwrite each expedition has required the leadership of the Institute to begin anew to seek *ad hoc* funds. In times of difficulty and economic downturn, this continuing necessity has jeopardized critical expeditions where travel windows are limited by weather and climate conditions.

For these reasons, the Board of Directors, supported by the findings of a campaign feasibility study, has determined to raise U.S. $3.4 million to create the **Exploration Endowment Fund**, an endowment whose interest in perpetuity will provide a reliable source of continuing funding for Institute's expeditions.

To realize this goal, five-year commitments will be necessary in the gift levels represented in the following Gift Range Table:

No. of Gifts	Gift Range	Range Total	Cum. Total
1	$ 1,000,000	$ 1,000,000	$ 1,000,000
2	$ 500,000	$ 1,000,000	$ 2,000,000
3	$ 100,000	$ 300,000	$ 2,300,000
4	$ 50,000	$ 200,000	$ 2,500,000
10	$ 25,000	$ 250,000	$ 2,750,000
20	$ 10,000	$ 200,000	$ 2,950,000
25	$ 5,000	$ 125,000	$ 3,075,000
50	$ 2,500	$ 125,000	$ 3,200,000
100	$ 1,000	$ 100,000	$ 3,300,000
200	$ 500	$ 100,000	$ 3,400,000

A first step has been to create the policies necessary to conduct such a campaign. These include a "Donor's Bill of Rights," an "Endowment Policy," and a "Permanently Restricted Endowment Policy"—each of which protects both the donor and the Institute's long-term financial integrity.[9]

Consistent with the endowment policy contained therein, five percent of the equivalent of the endowment's assets each year will be expended to underwrite the Institute's expeditions. The balance of earnings over and above the five percent will be returned to the corpus, which will thereby grow in perpetuity.

V. The Premise of the Campaign:

Strategy of the Campaign for Exploration is based on the following premise:

Campaign leaders, and other members of the Campaign Team who invite others to invest in the Campaign, will themselves be investors in the

---

[9] We have resisted the temptation to proffer examples of these policies, primarily because this book is intended for a worldwide scientific audience subject to an endless regime of legal and tax restrictions and opportunities, depending upon national residence. *However*, in general terms you can expect that the policies summarized below may take as long as *six months* to develop in close coordination with the President and CEO of your Institute, its development officers, and the Resource Development Committee of the Board of Directors. These documents are indicative of the issues that should be addressed by such policies, and the completeness with which they should be approached. Such policies should be developed with the full involvement of the appropriate individuals on the appropriate committees of the governing board of your Institute, NGO, or expedition. Let's begin with a "Donor Bill of Rights," which will reflect cultural mores, but overall is committed to building donor trust within your corporate culture. At the core is what Vartorella has described earlier as "access issues," here meaning donor access to 1) your Institute's Mission, 2) identities of Board members, 3) financial statements, 4) information on gift usage, and 5) and legal/tax compliance. Other issues revolve around "confidentiality" (anonymous gifts, protection from mailing list sales and rentals, etc.) and "donor recognition." Examples abound, but you may wish to consult the Association for Healthcare Philanthropy (AHP) for a science analogue or the Council for Advancement and Support of Education (CASE) for the perspective of institutions of higher education. A second document—"Endowment Policy"—is focused on the issue of long-range self-sustainability. A key point of this Policy involves investment income and the amount of the annual distribution (say, 5% in our Chapter's example) for support of annual operating revenues. Donor-imposed stipulations are also central to this document. Finally, there is the "Permanently Restricted Endowment Policy," which, while encouraging unrestricted donor gifts to the Endowment, establishes benchmarks for the creation of donor-endowed funds. Your attorney specializing in non-profit law (and taxation) will be a close ally in sorting out these thorny, but important, questions and creating the necessary documentation for Board review and action. Also, see Theodore J. Hopkins, Jr., "Commercializing the Third Sector: Public Benefit and Private Competition," A Paper Delivered at the Fifth International Conference of the International Society for Third Sector Research, July 8, 2002, University of Cape Town, South Africa. In particular, Hopkins offers a lucid legal summary in the realms of Capital Campaigns ("Role of 501(c)(3) Bonds . . . .") and Endowments ("replacement proceeds include pledged funds" both from p. 21 of his paper), which are beyond the purview of our remarks here, but critically important, nonetheless.

Campaign. Thus, **<u>Campaign Team members will not ask others to do anything they have not done themselves</u>**.

A. Campaign Phases

1) Preparatory Phase:

During the Preparatory Phase, campaign staff is recruited, basic infrastructure of prospective donor information is compiled and researched; gift counting policies, endowment establishment policies, and other administrative policies are established, development/campaign software is acquired and installed; a donor recognition program is created; and the Case for Support is creatively articulated and produced in formats suitable for use by Institute staff, and campaign volunteer leaders.

Institute has never embarked on a campaign of this magnitude before, and, hence, a year's time has been projected to fully prepare Institute with the resources necessary to conduct the campaign successfully.

Preparatory Phase Time Frame: January, 2003 – January, 2004

2) The Quiet Phase:

The Quiet Phase is that phase during which a cultivation and solicitation of major commitments to the Campaign will commence and continue for the duration of the Campaign.

    This phase will be conducted intensively during the nine-month period from February, 2003 through October, 2003. The cultivation and solicitation of major gifts, however, will continue after the kickoff of the Public Phase and will remain ongoing to the end of the campaign.

Quiet Phase Time Frame: February, 2003 – October, 2003

3) Public Campaign Phase:

The Public Campaign Phase is the phase of the Campaign during which the business community and all Institute's constituents are solicited. In this phase, not all solicitations are made on a person-to-person basis. Mass appeals, including direct mail, will be used to develop lesser gifts from a broader base of donors. This phase is not anticipated to generate major commitments, but it does generate new donors and provide a focal point for major donors who have not yet made their commitments. This phase is projected for nine months' duration.

Public Phase Time Frame: October, 2004 – June, 2005

VI. Campaign Organization

The Campaign Volunteer Organization Chart is found in the Appendix.

- Ms. Jane Smith has graciously consented to serve as Chair of the Campaign Steering Committee. She will enlist this Committee from among the State's top corporate, philanthropic, and community leadership. These individuals will be asked

  - To enlist a Campaign Chair.
  - To review, provide input, and approve Campaign strategies and policies.
  - To represent the Campaign at key Institute and Campaign events.

The Campaign Chair will enlist a Leadership Gifts Team Chair.
1) The Leadership Gifts Team Chair will recruit a Leadership Team to cultivate and solicit the top 10 prospective donors to the Campaign. This Team will be selected by the Chair and will be responsible for a small number of strategic calls on key prospects crucial to the Campaign success. Goal of this team will be set by the Campaign Chair after review of the prospect list and identification of those prospects to be included in the Leadership Prospect List. Team with Campaign Chair set goals of this team.

The Campaign Chair will enlist a Major Gifts Team Chair.
1) The Major Gifts Team Chair will enlist a Major Gifts Team whose responsibility will be to solicit the next 100 prospects.

Major Gifts Team Chair and his/her enlisted team set the goals of this team.

The Campaign Chair will enlist a <u>Public Phase Chair</u>.
1) The Public Phase Chair will enlist five Division Chairs.
2) Each Division Chair will in turn enlist five Team Captains.
3) Each Team Captain will in turn enlist five Team Members.
4) Each Team Member will solicit five businesses, professional groups, or individuals in the Public Phase of the Campaign.
5) Public Campaign Chair and his/her team captains set the goals of this team.
6) The Public Phase Chair will enlist a Public Phase Steering Committee to assist in the goal setting and leadership enlistment process.

The <u>Finance Committee</u> of the Board of Directors will serve as the fiduciary committee of the Campaign. It will review and approve and will serve as the Gift Acceptance Committee of the Campaign, accepting or declining gifts requiring approval beyond the staff level (i.e. gifts other than gifts of cash and securities, such as gifts of property requiring appraisals, etc.) in accordance with the policies adopted.

VII. Campaign Timetable
1) Enlistment of Campaign Steering Committee: November, 2002
2) Enlistment of Leadership Gifts Team: April, 2003
3) Enlistment of Major Gifts Team Chair: April, 2003
4) Enlistment of Major Gifts Team: September, 2003
5) Enlistment of Public Phase Chair: October, 2003
6) Enlistment of Public Phase Division Chairs: November, 2003
7) Enlistment of Public Phase Team Captains: January, 2004 – February, 2004
8) Enlistment of Public Phase Teams: February, 2004 – May, 2004
9) Public Phase Team Training: September, 2004
10) Public Phase Solicitation: October, 2004 – June, 2005
11) Major Prospect Receptions: February – June, September, 2004
12) Executive Briefings: April - June, 2003; September-November, 2003; January-May, 2004
13) Public Kickoff Celebration: October, 2004.
14) Victory Celebration: June, 2005.

Appendix

A. Campaign Volunteer Organization Chart

Appendix A:

Campaign Volunteer Organization Chart

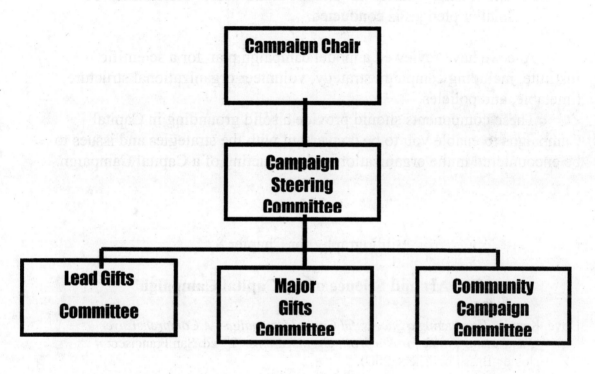

Summary

In this Chapter, we have described a Capital Campaign as distinguished from other forms of fundraising. We have re-capped the evolution of the Capital Campaign from its inception to the present day, including the rise of the Comprehensive Campaign, the prevalence of "Investment Philanthropy" and the increased role of staff solicitation instead of solicitation only by volunteers.

We have examined in detail the requisites for conducting a campaign: The Case for Support, Volunteer Campaign Leadership, a cadre of Prospective Donors, and basic organizational and budgetary Infrastructure.

We have explored the three phases of a Capital Campaign:

1) The Preparatory Phase: in which the constituency relations "Climate" is set for the campaign, the Case for Support is tested in a feasibility study, campaign materials and infrastructure are determined and set in motion, and prospect education and cultivation begins.

2) The Quiet Phase: in which pace-setting commitments and major gifts are cultivated and solicited.

3) The Public Phase: in which broad-based solicitation of smaller pledges is conducted.

And we have reviewed a model campaign plan for a scientific Institute, including campaign strategy, volunteer organizational structure, timetable, and policies.

These components should provide a solid grounding in Capital Campaigns to enable you to be conversant with the strategies and issues to be encountered in the organization and conducting of a Capital Campaign.

***

Bibliography for Chapter 8

"The Art and Science of the Capital Campaign"

Dove, Kent E. *Conducting a Successful Capital Campaign—A Comprehensive Fundraising Guide for Nonprofit Organizations.* 2nd ed. San Francisco: Jossey-Bass Publishers, 2000.

Hopkins, Theodore J., Jr. "Commercializing the Third Sector: Public Benefit and Private Competition," A Paper Delivered at the Fifth International Conference of the International Society for Third Sector Research, July 8, 2002, University of Cape Town, South Africa.

Seymour, Harold J. *Designs for Fund-Raising.* 2nd ed. Rockville, MD: Fund-Raising Institute, 1988.

Spain, William. "Spoils of Aphrodisias: A legendary archaeological site's uncertain future." *Art & Antiques*, June, 1997, pp. 45-46, 48.

***

Chapter 9: "Summary and Final Thoughts"

by William F. Vartorella

> *"We shall not cease from exploration*
> *And the end of all our exploring*
> *Will be to arrive where we started*
> *And know the place for the first time."*
>   *T.S. Eliot, Four Quartets*

Ours has been a voyage of discovery from Marco Polo to Níccolò Machíavellí to Chomolungma (Mt. Everest) and back. Seven hundred years, perhaps, but the more things change, the more they stay the same.

Globally, economies in disarray have turned princes into paupers. Governments are turning their backs on scientists, their once loyal allies in defending the realm and preventing the victors from becoming the vanquished. Like city sieges of old, Governments may starve Science out of its Ivory Tower.[1]

The result: the art of fundraising has become the art of war played on a fluid, target-rich landscape, complete with derelict siege engines (failed donor appeals), Trojan Horse Boards, defeated noble causes, and the spoils of war (endowment). The treasure trove is the elusive Patron, who wears the velvet glove over the iron fist and is Mission-driven.

The ebb and flow of battle rages worldwide, with Asian donors in the lands of the rising sun the new quarry. The sun may have set on the British Empire, but Asia is now the continent of financial exploration and contention.

Platitudes aside, the future of science and discovery depends upon the ability to transform ideas into the *lingua franca* of commerce and to gain *access* to donors.

Noblesse oblige--the view that privilege entails responsibility--is facing its own form of extinction in a New World Order. With

---

[1] See, for example, Susan Gray, "Finding Money to Find E.T.: Cuts in government funds force a group of astronomers to recruit private donors to support their search for extraterrestrial life," *The Chronicle of Philanthropy*, October 3, 1996, pp. 31-33. This cautionary tale covers the gamut from Government to *Fortune* magazine's top moneymakers--such as Microsoft Corporation's co-founder, Paul Allen--to the launch of a "Life in the Universe Trust" which the SETI Institute hopes will attract U.S. $100 million. Prior to 1993, the U.S. Government had spent some U.S. $78 million over 20 years to develop the SETI project. Cf. our earlier comments about the Mars meteorite, which the SETI Institute has used as part of its Case for Support along with the discovery of planets revolving around stars outside our solar system.

primogeniture (feudal rule by which the whole real estate of intestate is inherited by an eldest son) and *entail* (a settlement whereby the succession of a landed estate cannot be bequeathed at whim) artifacts of some tarnished Age of Chivalry, today's scientists are increasingly faced with *nouveau riche* donors.

In the Old World Order, people made money the old-fashioned way: they inherited it or married it. Today's entrepreneur wears her money on her sleeve and is not afraid of the Art of the Deal. When negotiating with these two distinctive types of donors, remember this:

Old Money[2] protects Old Money ("inherited").[3]

---

[2] U.S. Internal Revenue Service (I.R.S.) data are sketchy after 1995, but of the top 1% (some one million U.S. households), roughly *50%* inherited their wealth with an average inheritance of U.S. $782,000. Average wealth of the top 1% was U.S. $7.9 million; average annual income--U.S. $625,000. The *Social Register*, which tracks more than 30,000 individuals (many with inherited fortunes), provides a glimpse into this demographic. See, Judith E. Nichols, "Trend Watch--America's Rich: A Reality Check," *Contributions*, March-April, 2001, p. 18.

[3] During the early 1990s, debate raged in *The Chronicle of Philanthropy* over who was more generous, the poor or the rich. It was fueled by often-cited findings by the Independent Sector, a Washington, D.C.-based coalition of grant makers and charities, which essentially argued that the poor donate a bigger share of their income than the wealthy. Two Boston College researchers, Paul G. Schervish and John J. Harvens, who independently re-evaluated the data, concluded that while poor donors may donate a greater share of their income than wealthy donors, the same could not be assumed when comparing the populations as a whole (e.g., including *non*-donors). "Religious contributions"--gifts or user fees (church maintenance, for instance)--was an important battleground in the accounting. Both these researchers and the Independent Sector agreed on one finding: middle-income individuals give the smallest percentage of income to charity. Seemingly, the bone of contention was two Charts by Independent Sector: one, a percentage of income donated by households that contribute (3.2% by those of U.S. $100,000 or more, compared to higher percentages for selected categories below U.S. $25,000) and the second, a percentage of income donated by all households (2.8% of those earning U.S. $100,000 or more vs. the category, U.S. $10,000-$14,999). For the summary debate, see Kristin A. Goss, "Who's More Generous, the Poor or the Rich? It Depends on How You Count, Scholars Say," *The Chronicle of Philanthropy*, February 9, 1993, pp. 7-8.

Others have weighed in at venues such as *Business Week* and the U.S. Trust Corporation, with participants generally chiding in that the rich could give far more. The U.S. Trust study, which documented increased giving by the wealthy during the U.S. Stock Market surge of the 1990s, also pointed out that *38%* of the respondents indicated the best way to effect a donation was for a friend to ask them *in person*. (Cf., our comment that "people give money to people, not to ideas.") The "environment," for example, resonated as a Top 3 donor cause with 13% of those surveyed. For a summary of "U.S. Trust Survey of Affluent Americans XV," see <www.ustrust.com/affluent.htm>.

But is this the end of the argument? Hardly. A U.S. Treasury Department study released in 1999 indicated that four of five wealthy Americans leave nothing to charity when they die. But, of those who do, the study found that the bequests were a greater share of assets than those less wealthy and the individuals were more likely to have given while alive. Embedded in all of this are discussions of tax breaks associated with the relative cost of charitable giving. See, Thomas J. Billitteri, "Most Wealthy People Bequeath Nothing to Charity, Study Finds," *The Chronicle of Philanthropy*, January 14, 1999, p. 25. Separately, the I.R.S. has indicated that of the wealthy who do provide charitable bequests, about one-third of estate assets (male and female) go to educational, medical, or scientific organizations.

In summary, at the top of the heap, one-half of the wealth in the U.S. is inherited, may or may not be exposed to philanthropy, and clearly is rarely donated at death.

New Money ("entrepreneurial") spends New Money. [4]

Expeditions have traditionally relied on white, male, educated Protestants in the "professional" income brackets (above U.S. $67,000 per year), falling within the 50-64-years-of-age category, whether married or widowed. These "liberal donors" were the revered Patrons of Exploration, cloistered in their walnut-lined clubs and wrapped up in memories of old school ties and dark tales of the Serengeti. They provided at least 80% of the funding for expeditions.

Unfortunately, they, too, are on the verge of extinction and are caught up in passing **trillions** of U.S. dollars in inheritance to their financially over-extended, "Baby-Boomer" children.

The upshot has been a disintegration of traditional streams of income to institutions such as universities and Natural Science museums--the fabled consortial partners of expeditions. As Western society becomes more fragmented and new non-profits continue to emerge at an alarming rate, the competition for money globally will intensify dramatically.

For those seeking a panacea with the Internet as *primary* fundraising tool, think again. Roughly *one-third* of all e-mail addresses change annually.[5] This causes an estimated *53%* "to lose touch with personal and professional contacts, as well as preferred Web sites," according to NFO WorldGroup, which conducted the survey.[6] As these data represent only an on-line panel of U.S. e-mail users above the age of 18, worldwide the annual change of e-mail addresses is anyone's guess. Lost donor contacts = lost

---

[4] Nichols, "Trend Watch--America's Rich," p. 18. As pointed out by Nichols, of the 514 *billionaires* in the world, the U.S. accounted for 170 of them in the late 1990s, compared with just 13 in 1982. Depending upon the quirks of the global economy, that means that one-third of the billionaires are in the U.S. While the names and numbers change in a roller-coaster economy, the growing coterie reflects the New Economy and the advances of the Information Age. According to recent study by U.S. Trust Corporation, wealthy technology executives donated 6% of their after-tax income in 1999 to a host of causes ranging from Human Services (69%) to Health and Medical Research (52%) and the Environment (27%). These data paralleled those of another affluence study conducted by Bankers Trust Private Banking, also in New York. Functionally, it found that a positive relationship existed between the amount and percentage of income contributed to charity and the respondents' level of wealth. For a comparative summary, see Thomas J. Billitteri, "Giving Among Wealthy Detailed in 2 Studies," *The Chronicle of Philanthropy*, August 10, 2000, p. 10. To receive a free copy of the Bankers Trust research, "Wealth with Responsibility Study/2000," call the firm at 800.454.0353.

[5] Anonymous, "Almost one-third of e-mail addresses are changed annually," *Quirk's Marketing Research Review*, December, 2002, p. 72.

[6] *Ibid.* According to the study, e-mail address turnover is driven by "ISP switching, job changes, and consumer efforts to avoid spam." Our question: "At what point are donor solicitations considered 'spam'?"

donor opportunities. But the Internet is an excellent place to prospect and to reap the benefits of "socially responsible investing" (SRI) filters. Websites exist which determine whether companies that want to sell goods and services via their sites meet environmental (or other criteria) of corporate responsibility. In some cases, a percentage of website revenue goes to groups such as Defenders of Wildlife, the Environmental Defense Fund, *et al.*[7]

The list, then, of individual **new donor pools** may be as fragmented as the original expedition donors were homogeneous. But therein lies opportunity. These include,

- **"Baby-Boomers"**: With retirement looming, they worry more about inheriting the good life of their parents than preserving Earth's biodiversity. Best estimates are that this generation will inherit U.S. $4.8 *trillion* through 2015 (although figures in the U.S. $10-*trillion* range have been touted). In 1994, when "the greatest wealth transfer in history" was supposedly underway, *Fortune* cited a First Interstate Bank survey/Chart which laid bare plans of how "Boomers" would spend a U.S. $50,000 legacy. Result: 2% of the money would go to charity.[8] Earlier, *The Chronicle of Philanthropy* raised serious concerns over the "Boomers" intent: early indications they would give "to causes that are very different from those of their parents."[9] In 1999, these dire predictions began coming home to roost, as advocacy groups in the U.S. began articulating the fear that "Boomers" were becoming a "Lost Generation" of donors.[10] Yet, environmental issues continue to resonate as younger donors see evidence in mass media that these organizations are creating institutional and, thereby, global change. Experts indicate this U.S. group --some *77 million "Boomers"*--will demand significant *donor recognition* and a long-term *plan* for giving.
- **Women**: by 2010 this group will control *70%* of the wealth in the U.S. Currently, nearly half of Americans with assets of U.S.

---

[7] Anonymous, "2 New Web Sites Serve Shoppers With a Conscience," *The Chronicle of Philanthropy*, October 7, 1999, p. 40.

[8] Louis S. Richman, "Baby-Boomer Booty," *Fortune*, October 31, 1994, p. 35.

[9] Elizabeth Greene, Stephen G. Greene, and Jennifer Moore, "A Generation Prepares to Transfer Its Trillions," *The Chronicle of Philanthropy*, November 16, 1993, p. 8.

[10] Holly Hall, "The Lost Generation? New study finds a big drop in the percentage of baby boomers who are donors to national advocacy groups," *The Chronicle of Philanthropy*, March 25, 1999, pp. 25-26.

$500,000 or more are women.   In selected niches and locales, such as Palo Alto, California (Women Donors Network),[11] they are moving from "inheritors" to "investor-donors". Best estimates are that "Working Women" is the demographic[12] most apt to give money to innovative, less traditional programs and groups. Tactic here is to tie public education into the fabric of exploration, with attention to interactive projects[13] and displays; classroom exercises. Also worth tracking are women who serve on Boards of Directors of companies. In the U.S., this figure hovers at about 10%. The Principal Investigator (PI) for requests should probably be female.

- **Hispanics**: They are rapidly moving from the recipients of philanthropy to clear stakeholders in the act of giving. More importantly, they understand the nuances of globalization, especially in terms of the wealthy Global North (access to new technologies and global natural resources) further disenfranchising the Global South of their roots, biodiversity, access to new technologies, etc. Surveys indicate that Hispanics overall are strongly attached to the South American nations where they or their ancestors were born--a clear invitation to country-specific research projects, with donors from the Diaspora. The Principal Investigator for expedition activities in which this group is being approached should probably be Latino. (**Asian donors**, especially within the broader corporate context [see below] are clearly a donor force of the future. Yet Hispanic and Asian executives *together* account for only 2% of membership on U.S. corporate Boards of Directors.[14])

- **"Dot-com Survivors"**[15]: when the "boom-went-bust" not everyone in the Internet arena headed for the alms-house. Some

---

[11] The Women Donors Network's membership awards approximately U.S. $250 million annually, which puts it in the grant range of the Rockefeller Foundation.

[12] In two-income families, about one-third of the women earn more annually than their husbands.

[13] "Tele-presence," with remote underwater cameras operated by students and scientists in places such as Monterey Bay, is an excellent example.

[14] Coopers & Lybrand LLP, "Board of Directors' Compensation: 1996," a survey of 301 U.S. companies.

[15] Silicon Valley, long the bastion of the frugal philanthropist, still lags in thinking in terms of "legacy," with *science* rarely a key area of donor interest. A widely reported survey by the Community Foundation Silicon Valley (CFSV) disclosed 45% of the area's top earners gave U.S. $2,000 or less annually to non-profits--with perhaps 6% donating *nothing*. See Thea Singer's interview, "The good-deed doers: Steve Kirsch," *State of Small Business 2000*, p. 140. Kirsch is the founder of four high-tech companies and the co-founder (with his wife) of a U.S. $90-million foundation, which, for example, supports programs to help

had the prescience to cash out early and left for sea breezes and sunny climes. They, now, are the New Philanthropists, committed to hands-on personal involvement.[16] According to Larry Ellison, co-founder and CEO of the Oracle Corporation, the issue is not altruism, but what he has called "enlightened egotism."[17] In our view, these donors will require the most education, the most recognition, and the most patience.[18]

- **Older Donors**--the Last Hurrah: before the Old School Boys disappear, expeditions should make serious efforts toward attracting planned gifts and endowments, including named chairs. Studies continue to find that wealthy people age 65 and older and those "who have possessed their wealth for longer periods" tend to give at higher levels"[19] on an annual basis. Point is the level of giving, not the percentage of overall wealth. The good news is 90% of wealthy donors surveyed over time tend to make gifts directly, rather than using donor-advised funds or community foundations.

In the short-term, with the exception of the last group mentioned, the contributions from these niches will likely be small (U.S. $20,000 or less) until philanthropy becomes institutionalized within their sub-cultures. This is not to say that the above should not be cultivated. They *must* be, as the large NGOs are relentlessly prospecting for donors worldwide. The big

---

reduce air pollution, to develop and implement alternative clean-fuel technologies, and to mitigate the impact of Global Warming.

[16] See *Business Week*'s cover story, "The New Face of Philanthropy," in its December 2, 2002 issue. It notes that the wealthy are doing just fine, despite a declining U.S. Stock Market. See <www.businessweek.com> for the article and list of the top donors, such as real estate developer, Donald Bren, who has given U.S. $400 million to education and environmental groups. For insight into America's top donors under age 45, see the December, 2002 issue of *Worth*, online at <www.worth.com>. The upshot of a spate of articles of late is that today's and tomorrow's donor will act more like Venture Capitalists than check-writers.

[17] Nichols, "Trend Watch--America's Rich," p. 20.

[18] The temptation, during troubled economic times, is to seek out the Third Sector's version of the "Angel Investor"--those philanthropists who have no institutional affiliation with your science or other donors. See Tony Keyes, "The Trouble With Angels," *Upside*, June of 2001, p. 26 for advice to corporations, which also applies to scientists and Institutes. Separately, the problem is, the number of donors interested in gifts of U.S. $10 million or more is relatively small. In a study by Gary A. Tobin, some 502 donors from 1995 to 2000 gave 865 "Megagifts," totaling just under U.S. $30 *billion*. Some 43% went to U.S. private and public education, with only 2.5% targeting the "environment," for example. This, in itself, is contradictory (cf. our earlier remarks, re: wealthy and the environment). Large, prestigious institutions reaped the benefits, according to Elizabeth Schwinn, "Most Big Gifts Benefit a Handful of Large Charities, Study Finds," *The Chronicle of Philanthropy*, April 17, 2003, p. 15.

[19] Michael Anft, "Affluent Americans Feel Compelled to Give to Charity, But Not to Give More Money, New Poll Finds," *The Chronicle of Philanthropy*, November 13, 2003, p. 12.

unknown is the global future of the Middle Class, rising in The People's Republic of China (PRC) but at-risk in the U.S., where there is a widening gap between rich and poor.

Adopting a proactive corporate culture is key to your success.

"Positioning," "niche-specific marketing," and "global branding" are tools that expeditions and Institutes must embrace and develop *now*.

We have discussed the corporate giving model in detail: mentoring, equipment, money. And, while corporate giving as a percentage of profits has dropped by 50% during the past 15 years,[20] the trend of "joint-marketing arrangements" ("cause-related marketing," often in close coordination with sponsorships) with non-profits has been embraced by nine of 10 companies.[21] Their goals: making a difference, enhancing employee loyalty, and the reputation and brand of the corporation. Advice: seek synergy.

Micro-businesses (small, family-owned companies) tend to function similarly and should not be overlooked. The major difference in the U.S., as pointed out by the Better Business Bureau's Wise Giving Alliance, is that small businesses still tend to provide most of their support with cash (82%) and products/services (61%), rather than "cause-related marketing" (roughly 5% or so).[22] While sponsorships may be low on *their* priority list, these businesses offer face-to-face fundraising opportunities and a streamlined decision-making process. Remember: families own 85% of all U.S. companies. For U.S.-based Institutes and expeditions, they present an often-untapped resource.

Then there are the behemoth corporations at your doorstep.

Forbes magazine has charted the most philanthropic companies and the largest corporate donations in 2001, based in part on data supplied by *The Chronicle of Philanthropy*. In spite of financial jitters emanating from September 11, companies still found generosity in their best interest.

---

[20] See Michael E. Porter and Mark R. Kramer's cover article, "The Competitive Advantage of Corporate Philanthropy" in *Harvard Business Review*, December of 2002. For additional information, visit <http://harvard-businessonline.hbsp.harvard.edu>.

[21] Debra E. Blum, "9 of 10 Companies Have Charity Marketing Deals," *The Chronicle of Philanthropy*, June 15, 2000, p. 39. For another view, see PMA/Gable Group Cause Marketing Survey at <www.pmalink.org>.

[22] Don Sadler, "Tax-Wise Strategies for Charitable Giving," *Self-Employed America*, November/December, 2002, p. 12. See, especially, the Chart, "How Small Businesses Support Charities" (Wise Giving Alliance) and his suggestions, re: *pro bono* services first, sponsorships, matching gifts, property/inventory, and— then--cash. Sadler also suggests establishing a "donor-advised account through a community foundation" (p.13), which is beyond our book's treatment, but is something worthy of discussion with your tax specialist and legal counsel.

Ford Motor Company gave the largest dollar amount, U.S. $137.6 million, according to *Forbes*, with **Target**--the discount merchandise chain--heading the list by donating 2.51% of its income.

Asia is heating up, fast. *Export Today's Global Business* shocked the recalcitrant business community with this paean in January of 2001:

> China is hot again, and it is getting hotter by the day. . . . Suddenly, it would seem, all the foreign companies that had been holding off on their plans to invest in China have moved in. The change has come so fast that it hardly shows up yet on the official trade statistics. But any trip to [Shanghai] makes clear that the gold rush mentality of the early to mid-1990s is back.[23]

In December, 2002, *Quirk's Marketing Research Review* featured market research in the PRC--already the world's largest consumer of televisions, refrigerators, and mobile telephones. It detailed the kinds of forces that we believe translate into unprecedented donor opportunities: a communications revolution, urbanization, a burgeoning Middle Class (expanding at 20% per year), pent-up consumer demand, and an "internationalization of style."[24]

Slick publications such as *Action Asia* are running articles focused on exploration and funding in the region.[25] And, lest anyone believe that Japanese companies are not providing significant grants, look to **Fuji Photo Film**, which provided nearly U.S. $8 million to the Smithsonian Institution to bring two giant pandas to its National Zoological Park and to construct a research and habitat facility with a related conservation-education program. It is time to experiment with direct marketing/direct mail, as the Japanese young professionals are receptive, "early-adopters" of Western trends.

A final word on grants from foundations: according to the Foundation Center (2002), more than 90% of grant makers still do not publish *Annual Reports*.[26] While data are sketchy, perhaps 1,500 (?) foundations may have an Internet presence. High-profile grants attract high-profile donors. Do your homework and apply to those where your chance is one-in-five or better, rather than the 7% national average in the U.S. Do not compete needlessly.

---

[23] The Editors, "Shanghai Retakes the Stage," *Export Today's Global Business*, January, 2001, p. 2.

[24] Hy Mariampolski and Pat Sabena, "Qualitative research develops in China," *Quirk's Marketing Research Review*, December, 2002, p. 49.

[25] Anonymous, "Doing it yourself: Thinking of organising your own expedition? Here are a few things you may like to know about funding," *Action Asia*, June/July, 2002, p. 74.

[26] See <www.fdncenter.org/research> for a summary.

"Endowments" continue to be one of the great mysteries for scientists, attributable in part to the lack of global data regarding the number and financial strength for Institutes, expeditions, field stations, etc. and in legal definition (which varies across cultures). Worldwide, probably fewer than two percent (2%) of all non-profits have endowments. This is certainly true in the U.S., where best estimates are about 22,000 of the 1.4 million non-profits (say, 1.6%) have endowments--although they total nearly U.S. $600 *billion*.

Shared solutions to sustainable futures depend upon endowments and, as demonstrated above, the effort can pay *big* dividends.[27]

Lest we depend too heavily on the U.S. model, American non-profits in aggregate tend to rely on

- dues and fees (38%)
- government grants and contracts (30%)
- gifts (25%)
- investment earnings (7%)[28]

for their annual budgets.

The point of our book is that this equation is a formula for disaster.

Endowment earnings, financial (and in-kind gifts) and corporate and foundation support should be order of the day, with government and annual dues much lower on the scale.

Again, the greatest risk to the Future of Exploration is not political intrigue in some exotic locale. It is funding. And the funding--in spite of September 11th, recessions, governmental malaise, skittish donors, and corporate "Robber Barons" under indictment--is *there*, even, we believe, for the most difficult of scientific projects.

This book has been about survival of the fittest--your survival as a scientist.

Our underlying message has focused on the threat of *enigmatic extinctions*, the disappearance of seemingly healthy Institutes and field investigations simply because the money ran out.

---

[27] See also, Donald S. Keel, *"Chapter Three*: Investment Philanthropy & the Psychology of the Invitation," (which includes a variation of the Campaign Model)," in *Into the Field: Strategies for Funding Exploration--Proceedings of the Conference held at Nesbitt Hall, College of Design Arts, Drexel University, Philadelphia, PA on 20-21 April 1996*, edited by P.J. Capelotti, Ph.D. (Philadelphia: The Philadelphia Chapter of The Explorers Club, March, 1997), pp. 41-55.

[28] Kathleen S. Kelly, "Commentary: The Top Five Myths Regarding Nonprofits," <www.prsa.org/_Publications/magazines/Tactics/0800comm1.html>.

The authors believe that expeditions are the sentry, at-risk species of science and discovery. They are like the Black Rhino, once the most numerous of *all* rhino species and now in the crosshairs of intense poaching pressure for its horn, which is valued at U.S. $62,000 per kg on the black market for its ceremonial and reputedly medicinal purposes in the Middle East and Asia. And like the Black Rhino, with a price on its head/horn, for roughly that price an expedition can put a scientist on Mt. Everest, help launch a small scientific payload into low-earth-orbit (LEO) via the Space Shuttle, or absorb part of the cost for the search for the Ice Age Woolly Rhino of the Pleistocene in the wet, boggy crevasses and eroding streambeds of the tundra of the Taimyr Peninsula of Siberia.

Clearly, as poet Antonio Machado has pointed out, "Only a fool thinks price and value are the same thing."

For scientists, knowing the value of their research enables them to price and sell its intrinsic value in the form of an urgent, compelling, and valid Case for Support.

Yet, even the best scientist needs a primer when the unexpected arrives with a vengeance.

"Crisis Management:
a Guidebook of Immutable Laws
for Non-profits in Free-Fall"

When the world seems suddenly "upside-down" and "counter-intuitive," the reality is the Immutable Laws of Fundraising are still in place. "Adversity" often means "opportunity" to re-focus on core values, to explore new donor landscapes, and to think INSIDE the box, rather than to try to re-invent the wheel.

Lest NGOs forget, the reason they exist is to turn utopian visions of how the world should function into works-in-progress of cooperation and renewal.

What follows is perhaps a cautionary tale without a narrative. These 100 tips are intended to underscore the nebulous, but ever-present Immutable Laws of Fundraising and how they apply to Boards, Donors, Corporations, Grants, Capital Campaigns and the host of challenges that give Institute directors and expedition leaders pause.

"Crisis Management" begins with a proven plan. This one is meant to help keep-the-focus, stay-the-course, stop free-fall.

I. The Basics:

1) **People give $ to people, not to ideas.**
2) Never a good time to raise $$$; always competition.
3) Fundraising is a Board function, not a Staff function. (Staff supports Board with documentation for grants, etc.)
4) Best time to raise $ generally is 1 September through 31 December. (Many exceptions.)
5) Nothing is more powerful than an urgent, compelling, valid, and interesting Case for Support.

6) Most powerful fundraising appeal: "Won't you join **me** in giving x $ to y NGO?"

7) Donor Mission is #1, Client Needs are #2, Your Institute/expedition's Mission is #3.

8) Simple plans, simple deals, simple appeals work best.

9) Never beg for $. The issue is creating opportunity for donor participation.

10) If a donor deal seems "too good to be true," it probably is.

II. Boards:

1) Remember the old 4 W's--the Wealthy, the Wise, the Workers, and the Worriers, but *recruit and raise $* from the 3 C's--"Connectedness" with your NGO, expedition, or Institute; "Clout" with potential donors; and "Capacity" for individual giving.

2) Practice "Moves Management," in which you foster relationships with board members and donors over time to achieve shared solutions to a sustainable future for your scientific endeavors.

3) Remove Political, Communications, and Organizational obstacles adroitly with the urgency they deserve.

4) Stagger your Board terms--1, 3, 5 years--in order to counteract the potential for "dysfunctional" members ending up on your Board for "life".

5) Remember: Board members "give," "get," or "get off" the Board--securing $ is their #1 duty (and, yes, they do have fiduciary responsibilities).

6) Create a "Long-range Planning and Development Committee"--which sets in motion the fundraising arm of your Board.

7) If a potential board member says s/he will serve in an "advisory capacity" but will not raise $$$, steer clear and recruit someone else.

8) Require that all board members contribute to the "Annual Fund" and Special Campaigns. (This is known as 100% participation.)

9) A smaller Board tends to be a working Board. No room to hide.

10) Boards must have Strategic Plans and a tactical approach to achieving them.

III. Donors:

1) Old-line, liberal, rich donors are disappearing.

2) New opportunities are women, Hispanics, Asians.

3) Old Money protects Old Money and is difficult to cultivate.

4) New Money is Entrepreneurial.

5) High-tech millionaires traditionally are more difficult to cultivate than Low-tech millionaires.

6) Bank trust officers should always be cultivated. They know where the money is.

7) An individual who volunteers is more apt to help secure in-kind assistance and cash.

8) No one ever insulted a donor by asking for more money, rather than less. But do your research and know what is the appropriate "ask".

9) The person who asks a donor for x $, should also have given x $ or an amount that reflects a "sacrificial gift," e.g., an economic stretch that underscores her commitment.

10) When asking for money, ask directly, then be quiet and listen.

IV. Annual Giving:

1) Have real benefits for each membership category.

2) Constantly work to move members up the category-ladder, re: annual participation.

3) Car decals are moving billboards. Each member gets one.

4) Keep members informed--a conversational monthly sheet is best.

5) Know your constituencies and what they can afford.

6) At least once per year, pitch the benefits of annuities, bequests, etc.

7) If board members don't give annually, why should anyone else?

8) Annual appeals continue even during a Capital Campaign.

9) "Who else is coming to the party and what are they wearing?" People want to know who else supports your Institute, expedition, or NGO and at what level.

10) Don't be the "best-kept secret" in town. Success breeds success.

V. Corporations:

1) Know the company, its products, and market.
2) Learn the company's Supply Chain--these are potential donors as well.
3) Look to Asian conglomerates, their subsidiaries, and joint-venture partners. This is the Asian Century.
4) Requests of less than U.S. $5,000 generally do not go before a full Contributions Committee.
5) Discover which have employee-matching contributions programs.
6) CEOs are key to your donor success, but do not overlook mid-level managers from the community. Rank-and-file tend to be more stable and are key volunteers, mentors, and advocates for your Institute, NGO, or expedition.
7) Create opportunities for your good works to appear *inside* companies--exhibits, etc.
8) Develop mini-events for corporate suppliers as value-added for your sponsors.
9) Corporations prefer simple, educational, non-controversial projects and events.
10) Price projects competitively.

VI. Event Marketing/Sponsorships:

1) Events are forms of membership recognition and long-term sponsor solicitation.
2) Provide opportunities for your sponsors to interact (and thereby, potentially do business together).
3) Sponsors should more than pay for the entire cost of the event. "Profit" is in the public tickets, etc.
4) Your Board should be a sponsor.
5) Every aspect of an event is a sponsor opportunity (e.g., the concession stand might only sell one brand/line of soft drinks--known as "share-of-stomach").
6) Your best sponsors are the ones who have supported you over time. Keep them happy.
7) Identify key sponsor categories and solicit the top prospects in each of these.
8) Think multi-year and offer discounts for those who sign on (but be careful of the economy).
9) After the event, provide sponsors a good sense of total media coverage, attendance, etc.
10) In-kind sponsors (local radio station, for example) can be key to the success of an event.

VII. Direct Mail:

1) "New, improved, and free" are your most powerful pitches.
2) Live stamp.
3) Live signature.
4) "P.S." is often read before the body of the lift letter. Make certain it is a special pitch.
5) One offer per letter. Simple sells.
6) Constantly test a new offer against your best-pulling offer.
7) Don't exchange, sell, or lend lists with anyone, ever.
8) Key times to mail in the U.S.: Sept. 1, Nov. 30, Jan. 30, July 4.
9) A hurricane, recession, Sept. 11th will often kill a direct-mail piece. You need to mail, regardless, to keep your name recognition high.
10) A 2% response rate is excellent. Any mailing that pays for itself is generally considered a success.

VIII. Grants:

1) Never ask for more than the average-grant size that a foundation or corporation gave during the past three years.
2) Position grant proposals as "matching grants." Your match should be "non-cash."
3) Consortial proposals have better chances than single financial requests.
4) Structure grants for three years, rather than one.
5) Budgets: never ask for equipment by brand name.
6) Best way to get equipment is to ask for a long-term "loan," rather than an outright gift.
7) Best time to apply: 4th quarter--less competition traditionally.
8) Worst time to apply: 1st quarter (January). Most competition.
9) Never apply to a foundation where your chances are less than one-in-five, *unless* you have "Clout" (access) with that foundation.
10) Start locally, move regionally, then apply nationally. Best chances are local-regional. International grants are difficult, unless you choose a consortial partner in a developing nation.

IX. Capital Campaigns:

1) Create a valid, urgent, and compelling Case for Support.
2) Feasibility studies (interviews with Board members and key donors) are important, but should be the first step in the actual gift-giving process, rather than merely a report to the Board.
3) Board leadership is crucial. Establish a Goal and get a board member to underwrite the cost of the Campaign (usually 10-15% of the goal) for the first year.
4) Develop a "Gift Range Table" to determine the level of support necessary in different size gift categories in order to meet the Campaign Goal.
5) Adopt a Gift Acceptance Policy to ward off bogus, unethical, or inappropriate gifts and establish clear guidelines regarding who in the Campaign has the authority to solicit/accept various kinds of gifts.
6) Generally, do not announce a Campaign until you have raised 51% of the Goal in the "Quiet Phase."
7) The object is not to get all the prospects solicited; the object is to have each prospect solicited in the best possible way by the best combination of people. Each prospective major prospect, then, constitutes a "mini-campaign."
8) The "Public Phase" is small $$$, but may bring larger, hidden donors to the table.
9) Watch out for the "flash-and-dash" donor. S/he will underwrite a glitzy dinner in order to sidestep a larger gift such as a conservation lab in a museum or your field station or expedition house, for example.
10) People read plaques (and expect them). Donor recognition is crucial. Anonymous wants the most recognition.

X. Power Tips:

1) Register for and use Government Surplus.
2) Recycle equipment to other non-profits (e.g., increase donor recognition opportunities).
3) Keep track of volunteer hours and use them as a non-cash match for grants.
4) Track your Client base and the cost of services, per person, event, etc. Accountability is a big part of attracting long-term funding.
5) HVAC (heating, cooling) is almost impossible to fund alone. Tie exhibit funding to improving infrastructure as well.
6) Affinity Cards (credit cards with your logo) offer passive income generating opportunities for your non-profit.
7) Women hold most of the wealth in the U.S. and need to be cultivated for donations.
8) The more abstract an idea, the more difficult it is to fund. Be concrete and creative.
9) Be proactive rather than reactive. Keep a steady stream of proposals in motion, yet with each specifically tailored to meet Donor, Client, and Your Mission.
10) Finally, a U.S. $1 million grant would be a problem for most NGOs, Institutes, and expeditions because they do not have the infrastructure in place to manage it or sustain the program at the end of the grant period.

To borrow from the words of Marco Polo, we have not told half of what we saw. Embark on your own voyage of discovery, with these--our landmarks.

Finally, remember…

A Funder's Worst Fears:

Projects that are too

- **complex**
- **absolute**
- **controversial**
- **premature**
- **ambitious**

Again, the successful fundraising appeal meets the donor's needs--Mission Statement, Marketing Objectives, $ Comfort Level--on a personal, relationship basis.

We began *Funding Exploration* with a quotation from Aristotle. We shall conclude with Seneca:

> *However, in all our giving, we should seek especially for things that will last, in order that our gift may be as imperishable as possible and bring continuing benefit . . . .*[29]

What greater beneficiary than scientific exploration?

***

---

[29] Waldemar A. Nielsen, "Sound Advice From 2,000 Years Ago," *The Chronicle of Philanthropy*, April 4, 1996, p. 43.

Bibliography for Chapter 9

"Summary and Final Thoughts"

Anonymous. "Almost one-third of e-mail addresses are changed annually." *Quirk's Marketing Research Review*, December, 2002, p. 72.

_____. "Doing it yourself: Thinking of organising your own expedition? Here are a few things you may like to know about funding." *Action Asia*, June/July, 2002, p. 74.

_____. "2 New Web Sites Serve Shoppers With a Conscience." *The Chronicle of Philanthropy*, October 7, 1999, p. 40.

Anft, Michael. "Affluent Americans Feel Compelled to Give to Charity, But Not to Give More Money New Poll Finds." *The Chronicle of Philanthropy*, November 13, 2003, pp. 11-12.

Billitteri, Thomas J. "Giving Among Wealthy Detailed in 2 Studies." *The Chronicle of Philanthropy*, August 10, 2000, p. 10.

_____. "Most Wealthy People Bequeath Nothing to Charity, Study Finds." *The Chronicle of Philanthropy*, January 14, 1999, p. 25.

Blum, Debra E. "9 of 10 Companies Have Charity Marketing Deals." *The Chronicle of Philanthropy*, June 15, 2000, p. 39.

Coopers & Lybrand LLP. "Board of Directors' Compensation: 1996."

Editors, The. "Shanghai Retakes the Stage." *Export Today's Global Business*, January of 2001, p. 2.

Goss, Kristin A. "Who's More Generous, the Poor or the Rich? It Depends on How You Count, Scholars Say." *The Chronicle of Philanthropy*, February 9, 1993, pp. 7-8.

Gray, Susan. "Finding Money to Find E.T.: Cuts in government funds force a group of astronomers to recruit private donors to support their search for extraterrestrial life." *The Chronicle of Philanthropy*, October 3, 1996, pp. 31-33.

Greene, Elizabeth; Greene, Stephen G.; and Moore, Jennifer. "A Generation Prepares to Transfer Its Trillions." *The Chronicle of Philanthropy*, November 16, 1993, pp. 1, 8, 11-12.

Hall, Holly. "The Lost Generation? New study finds a big drop in the percentage of baby boomers who are donors to national advocacy groups." *The Chronicle of Philanthropy*, March 25, 1999, pp. 25-26.

Keel, Donald S. *"Chapter Three*: Investment Philanthropy & the Psychology of the Invitation," pp. 41-55 in *Into the Field: Strategies for Funding Exploration—Proceedings of the Conference held at Nesbitt Hall, College of Design Arts, Drexel University, Philadelphia, PA on 20-21 April 1996*, edited by P.J. Capelotti, Ph.D. Philadelphia: The Philadelphia Chapter of The Explorers Club, March, 1997.

Kelly, Kathleen S. "Commentary: The Top Five Myths Regarding Nonprofits." <www.prsa.org/_Publications/magazines/Tactics/0800comm1.html>.

Keyes, Tony. "The Trouble With Angels." *Upside*, June, 2001, p. 26.

Mariampolski, Hy, and Sabena, Pat. "Qualitative research develops in China." *Quirk's Marketing Research Review*, December of 2002, pp. 44-46, 47-49.

Nichols, Judith E. "Trend Watch--America's Rich: A Reality Check." *Contributions*, March-April, 2001, pp. 18-20.

Nielsen, Waldemar A. "Sound Advice From 2,000 Years Ago." *The Chronicle of Philanthropy*, April 4, 1996, pp. 43-44.

Richman, Louis S. "Baby-Boomer Booty." *Fortune*, October 31, 1994, p. 35.

Sadler, Don. "Tax-Wise Strategies for Charitable Giving." *Self-Employed America*, November/December, 2002, pp. 12-14.

Singer, Thea (interviewer, excerpts). "The good-deed doers: Steve Kirsch." *State of Small Business 2000*, p. 140.

Schwinn, Elizabeth . "Most Big Gifts Benefit a Handful of Large Charities, Study Finds." *The Chronicle of Philanthropy*, April 17, 2003, p. 15.

***

A Selected Bibliography of Funding Information
for
Science and Exploration

with *Abbreviated* Donor Listings

by William F. Vartorella

*Note: what follows is meant as a **supplement** to the scores of potential donor sources detailed within **Funding Exploration**. This is by no means definitive, but merely illustrates the diversity of financial opportunities in a world in which scarcity is the perceived norm. It is a snapshot, frozen in time, based upon experience.*

I. General Reference Works:

From The Foundation Center (NYC, U.S.), see the latest updates:

The Foundation Center Information for Grantseekers. On-line at
<http://fdncenter.org>
1,000 Largest Foundations, by Total Giving
1,000 Largest Foundations, by Grants
America's Wealthy and the Future of Foundations
Grants on Environmental Law, Protection, and Education
Grants for Matching and Challenge Support
Grants for Minorities
Grants for Museums

From The Council on Foundations (Washington, D.C., U.S.):

Annual Report (The Council on Foundations)
Edie, John A. *First Steps in Starting a Foundation*

And, The Expedition Advisory Centre of the Royal Geographical Society (London, U.K.), especially...

Deegan, Paul. *Expedition Supplement: Geographical*. London, U.K.: Royal Geographical Society, October, 1999. 24 pages. Useful primer for the novice explorer, with notes by Sir Ranulph Fiennes, Robin Hanbury-Tenison, OBE, and others. See, especially, "Finances: Mountains of money" and the brief "Directory" with selected references on maps, planning and logistics, solar panels, etc.

Hemming, John; Land, Tony; and Winser, Nigel. *Fund-Raising and Budgeting including Grant-Giving Organizations*. London, U.K.: Expedition Advisory Centre (RGS), January 1991 ff. 31 pages.

Also particularly useful,

Europa Publications. *International Foundation Directory*. London: Europa
Publications, annual.

_____. *World Directory of Awards and Prizes*. London: Europa
Publications, annual.

For "arcane" project funding see,

Searles, Aysel, Jr. *Guide to Financial Aids for Students in Arts & Sciences:
For Graduate and Professional Study*. New York, New York: ARCO
Publishing Company, Inc., 1971 ff. The title understates the wealth of unusual
funding opportunities described therein--Arctic Institute of North America;
Austria Institute; Foreign Area Fellowships for South Asia, Southeast Asia, and
East Asia; French Government Scholarships; Netherland-America Foundation;
American Association of University Women; The Theodore Roosevelt Memorial
Fund; The American Numismatic Society; The Kosciuszko Foundation;
Herbarium Fellowships; The Population Council Fellowships; U.S. Atomic
Energy Commission Special Fellowships in Radiation Protection--and others.
These are Mission-focused and very, very specific.

Another classic with some unusual funding listings is *The College Blue Book*
(see Professional and Reference Books, Macmillan Publishing Company),
which--in addition to scholarships--includes fellowships and grants from
sources such as the American Society of Photogrammetry.

II. Funding Sources for Consortial Projects (Corporate, Foundation & Governmental/NGOs):

Podesta, Aldo C. *Raising Funds from America's 2,000,000 Overlooked
Corporations*. New York, New York: Public Service Materials Center.
Vartorella, William F. "Funding Exploration (and other Exotic
Projects)" on-line Discussion Group: contact <globebiz@camden.net>
* To subscribe, on Subject Line, type
"Subscribe <your name & e-mail address>
In Message text, please list interest area.

Note: The following sources should be researched VERY CAREFULLY, as only selected
Institutes or expeditions (or the universities/museums with whom they may be affiliated) may meet a
listed donor's Mission precisely. The process will take nurturing, education, a creation of volunteer
    activities, and the successful solicitation of equipment loans/free supplies, BEFORE actual
cash grants may occur. Some grants also will probably be regionally focused, through a subsidiary
of a transnational corporation.

Be advised the URLs as well as donor Missions can change.

*Abbreviations: Am.=America, Co.=Company, Corp.=Corporation,
        Fndn.=Foundation, Intern.=International, No.=North*

A. Archaeology, Anthropology, & Early Natural History:

Corporate: Appleton Mills, Carillon Importers, Chesebrough-Ponds USA, Christian Dior NYC, Elco Industries, First Fidelity Bancorporation, First NH Bank, Hanson Industries No. Am., Harris Trust & Savings Bank, Nestle USA, Inc., Omron Systems, Smith Kline Beecham Corp., Subaru of Am., Inc.

Foundation: Wenner-Gren Fndn., Keith Muckelroy Memorial Trust (U.K., young scientists, marine archaeology), Royal Anthropological Institute Ruggles-Gates Fund for Biological Anthropology (U.K., *highly-competitive, open globally*)

B. Arctic and Antarctic:

Foundation: Alaska Conservation Fndn., C.S. Fund, Grand Circle, Tinker Fndn., Gino Watkins Memorial Fund (U.K.), Fuchs Foundation (see, British Antarctic Survey, U.K.), and funding by the Trans-Antarctic Association (via Scott Polar Institute, U.K.; open only to nationals of Australia, New Zealand, South Africa, and U.K.) and the Edward Wilson Fund (polar regions, expeditions; c/o Scott Polar Institute)

C. Biodiversity:

Corporate: Appleton Mills, BHP Minerals Intern., Inc., Clorox Co., Elco Industries, Haseko (Hawaii), Inc., Hoffman-LaRoche, Inc., Holman Corp., Jefferson Smurfit Corp., Ogilvy & Mather Worldwide, Texaco, Oracle Corporation--see <http://www.oracle.com/corporate/giving> (endangered species)

Foundation: for botanical specialty, see Richard Lounsberg Fndn.; Pajeau Wildlife Fndn., Scott Neotropical Fund; Conservation, Food, and Health Society; Ford Fndn., Rockefeller Fndn., Dean Witter Fndn., Giles W. and Elise G. Meade Fndn., Fndn. for Deep Ecology, Fndn. for Agronomic Research, Gordon and Betty Moore Fndn., Pew Charitable Trusts ("Conservation of Living Marine Resources"), Rockefeller Brothers Fund (rainforests, coastal zone management, etc.--East Asia, Central & Eastern Europe, U.S.), Fauna and Flora Preservation Society Fund (U.K.)

Governmental/NGO: World Bank, Biological Council (London, U.K.), International Council for Bird Preservation (U.K., Conservation Awards for European undergraduates in the fields of endangered species, wetlands, tropical forests, marine, and oceanic islands)

D. Environmental Education, Capacity, Justice:

Corporate: Hanson Industries No. Am.

Foundation: Carnegie Corporation of New York, Mitchell Kapor Fndn. (environment & global health), American Honda Fndn., Belvedere Fund, J.C. Downing Fndn.

Governmental/NGO: U.S. National Science Foundation's "Global Learning and Observations to Benefit the Environment (GLOBE)" program (science educators take note, as this provides U.S. groups with funding for hands-on science experience); NASA's "Urban and Rural Community Enrichment Plan for Students" provides training for interdisciplinary aerospace activities in U.S. schools; U.S. National Institute of Environmental Health Sciences, National Human Genome Research Institute--funds projects that addresses social, ethical, and legal implications of environmental health research under its "Environmental Justice: Partnerships to Address Ethical Challenges in Environmental Health" program

E. Ethnic Organizations:

Corporate: AutoAlliance Intern., Inc., Ecolab, Inc., Mercedes-Benz of No. Am., Inc., Mitsubishi Motor Sales of Am., Inc., Motch Corp., Nissan Motors Corp., USA.

Governmental/NGO: see U.S. Office of Postsecondary Education for its "Minority Science and Engineering Improvement Program," which focuses on improvement in science and engineering education at predominantly minority institutions in the U.S.

F. Faculty Development:

Note: this is a little-used strategy and an excellent support of "back-door" support for science and discovery that most universities overlook.

Corporate: Appleton Papers, Ecolab, Inc., Harris Trust & Savings Bank, Long-Term Credit Bank of Japan, Ltd., Melitta USA, Inc., Nissan Motor Corp. USA, Nomura Securities Intern., Norton Co., Shell Oil Co., Subaru of Am., Inc., Toshiba Am., Inc., Toyota Motor Sales USA, Inc.

Foundation: see the Global Fund for Women for unusual opportunities at <http://www.globalfundforwomen.org/3grant/app-guidelines-engl.html> or e-mail <grants@globalfundforwomen.org>. Another excellent source for women in science is the American Association for the Advancement of Science (AAAS), "Directorate for International Programs." (Goal is to increase the participation of women in international scientific research. Special attention is being paid to colleagues in Central and Eastern Europe, the Newly Independent Countries of the former Soviet Union, and other venues. See <http://www.aaas.org/international/wiscnew.shtml>). The James S. McDonnell Foundation has a special "21st Century Science Initiative" that provides awards to encourage researchers to pursue ideas and approaches that are unique and perhaps contrary to the conventional wisdom.

G. International Environmental Issues:

Corporate: BHP Minerals Intern., Hitachi, Ltd., Hoechst Corp., Ogilvy & Mather Worldwide, Samsung Group at <http://www.samsung.com>, British Airways at <http://www.british-airways.com/sitegide/does/a_to_z.shtml>, Tesoro Petroleum at <http://www.tesoropetroleum.com/community.html>.

Foundation: Shell Fndn. has been created to fund sustainable energy and other social investment projects globally. See its "Sustainable Energy Program," which encourages environmentally friendly, sustainable energy use in developing countries. London, England-based, contact <info@shellfoundation.org> or visit its website at <http://www.shellfoundation.org/progs_of_sf.html>.

Governmental/NGO: Also, worldwide, see your government's funding initiatives for programs such as the U.S. Department of Energy's National Energy Technology Laboratory, which seeks cost-shared applications for developing technologies aimed at ensuring affordable energy.

H. Mountaineering:

Emerging funding is in unlikely corporate venues such as Singapore. More traditional sources include the British Mountaineering Council, Mount Everest Foundation (U.K.: British & New Zealand climbers), Nick Estcourt Award (U.K.), Mountaineering Council of Scotland (Scottish-origin expeditions), and high-tech suppliers of exotic and sophisticated equipment.

I. Museums, Natural History & Science:

Corporate: Abbott Laboratories, American Express Co., Amoco Corp., ExxonMobil Corp., IBM, Sara Lee Corp., Shell Oil Co., Slant/Fin Corp., Weyerhaeuser Co.

J. Near Eastern Exploration:

See <http://www.scbell.com/Marketing_&_Fundraising> under "Exploration" for listing (mummy DNA, etc.) and "Funding Egyptology" ARCE paper (available free). E-mail request <globebiz@camden.net>

Foundation: Gerald Avery Wainwright Near Eastern Archaeology Fund (U.K.)

K. Observatories & Planetariums, Physics, Astronomy:

Corporate: Fireman's Fund Insurance Co., Genentech, Inc., Norton Co., Sedgwick, James, Inc.; Toshiba America Fndn., and Phillips Petroleum Fndn., plus a host of aerospace manufacturers/suppliers, including Allied Signal, Arco Chemical, Barnes Aerospace, Beech Aerospace, Boeing, EG&G Aerospace, Grimes Aerospace Fndn., Kaman Aerospace Corp. Giving Program, LTV Aerospace, Lockheed Martin, McDonnell Douglas Fndn., Parker Bertea Aerospace Group, and Sundstrand Corp. Aerospace Fndn.

Foundation: Stewart W. and Willma C. Hoyt Fndn., Fndn. for Deep Ecology

Governmental/NGO: Do not overlook special initiatives for early-career scientists (see, for example, the U.S. Department of Education's individual research programs supporting experimental or theoretical plasma physics).

L. Scientific Organizations:

Corporate: Air France, Benetton Services Corp., BHP Minerals Intern., Inc., Borman's, Inc., Bridgestone/Firestone, Inc., Brown & Williamson Tobacco Corp., CIBA-GEIGY Corp. Pharmaceuticals Div., Eka Nobel, Eastman Kodak, Freightline Corp., Gould Electronics, Industrial Bank of Japan Trust Co., Tomas Lipton Co., Nestle USA, Unilever U.S., Inc., Union Bank, Union Bank of Switzerland (especially, L.A. and NYC Branches).

Foundation: See Edinburgh Trust Number 2 (London, U.K.) for expedition support that requires the participation of a recognized scientific society. Also, worldwide, The Explorers Club Exploration Fund (NYC, U.S.) and for field exploration by youthful scientists, The Explorers Club Youth Activity Fund (NYC, U.S.). For expeditions and "geography," see the National Geographic Society (U.S.) and multiple programs of The Royal Geographical Society (U.K.), the Royal Society (U.K.), and the Royal Scottish Geographical Society (Scotland; must be Scottish-based or Scottish team).

Governmental/NGO: NATO Scientific Affairs Division (Brussels, Belgium) supports consortial projects by NATO members in pure and applied research.

M. Speleological Studies:

Foundation: Ghar Parau Foundation (U.K.), Jeff Jefferson Research Fund (restriction: membership required in British Cave Research Association; U.K.)

N. Underseas Exploration:

Foundation: British Sub-Aqua Club Jubilee Trust (U.K.), PADI Foundation (U.S., "increase understanding of sport diving physics and physiology," underwater science, environmental projects, education)

O. Endowments:

Note: this list is to be used *carefully*, as Missions related to endowments always seem to be in motion. Also, you must be very specific in looking only to those companies with a) Missions central to your Mission, and b) marketing overlays in which these global companies have subsidiaries/interests in regions related to your Institute or expedition. It generally takes considerable effort to receive an endowment grant, so be prepared.

Corporate: Bayer Corp., Boehringer Mannheim Corp., CertainTeed Corp., Clorox Co., CR Industries, First Fidelity Bancorporation, Robertshaw Controls Co., Signet Bank/Maryland, White Consolidated Industries

P. Donated & Endowed Equipment, including Computers:

Note: strategy is to start LOCALLY with a request for an equipment LOAN, not an outright gift. This list is barely representative of what is available.

Corporate: Akzo Chemicals, Inc., Alcon Labs, BP America, Inc., Canadian Pacific, Canon USA, Inc., Epson Am., Inc., Equitable Life Assurance, Eureka Co., Fuji Bank & Trust, Fuji Film Am., Hitachi, Ltd., MCI Communications Corp., Miles, Inc., Sony Corp. of Am.

For *refurbished computers* (depending upon where your Institute or expedition is based; *modest fees may apply*), see Boston Computer Society (has an electronic discussion group specifically for people running computer-donation programs; to subscribe, send an e-mail message to <majordomo@bcs.org>, in the body of the letter, write "subscribe comp-recycle-I"); IBM's "Used Technology Donation Program" may be contacted at <http://www.ibm.com/ ibm/ibmgives/grant/grantapp.shtml>; Non-Profit Computing, Inc. (NYC, U.S.-based, but makes donations *globally*, when shipping can be arranged; contact <npc@igc.org>).

Foundation: see East-West Education Development Fndn. (*recipients* worldwide are selected by the donors of the equipment, *not* by East-West staff; contact <alex@donate.org>); National Cristina Fndn. (links companies and individuals interested in global donations to serve people with disabilities; donors send equipment directly to the beneficiary; disabled scientists--particularly in developing nations--may want to contact the Foundation, which is based in Greenwich, Connecticut U.S.).

Governmental/NGO: also, the U.S. National Science Foundation (NSF) supports a program that encourages the purchase of shared research instrumentation with NSF investigators at other institutions. See, "Research in Undergraduate Institutions" at <http://www.ehr.nsf.gov/crssprgm/rui/start.shtm>. For U.S. Federal Government donations of surplus computer gear, see the "Computers for Learning" website at <http://www.computers.fed.gov>.

Endowment: See The Kresge Foundation Science Initiative for the endowment of scientific instrumentation at research institutions, colleges, universities. NOTE: this is a "challenge grant" program.

Q. Donated Products:

Corporate: Air France, Anchor Glass, Bayer, Benetton, British Airways, Canon USA, Dunlop Tires, Fox, Inc., Ikegami Electronics, KLM Airlines, Marion Merrell Dow, Pearle Visions, Toyota Motor Sales and virtually all the major manufacturers of outdoor gear (tents, clothing, stoves, survival equipment, rods, reels, hunting gear, etc.), which are extremely generous and easy to approach.

R. Executive Volunteers:

The expert's first step in securing gear and then--cash.

Corporate: Aegon USA, Inc., Amdahl Corp., Bates Worldwide, Beretta Corp., BP America, Canadian Pacific, CIBA-GEIGY Corp., Glaxo Wellcome Fndn., Michelin No. Am.

S. By Location (several narrow examples):

Argentina, Brazil, and Chile: See Lampadia Fndn.; Fundacion Antorchas,
      VITAE, and Fundacion Andes
Egypt: Bechtel & Amoco, American Express, IBM
Israel: Intel, Slant/Fin Corp. (one of the *few* companies in the world that
      assists with HVAC for natural history museums)
Italy: Whirlpool, Bristol-Myers Squibb, Hewlett-Packard, IBM, Intel
Mexico: see, for example, consortial U.S.-Canada-Mexico initiatives such as
      the U.S. Department of Education's "Cooperation and Student Mobility
      in Higher Education among the United States, Canada, and Mexico"
      program; excellent opportunity for channeling Institute training in
      the "North Americas."
Panama: Fuller Co.
Russia: Hewlett-Packard Co.; John D. and Catherine T. MacArthur Fndn. (project
      to reinvigorate scientific research by young Russian scholars--see
      <http://www.macfdn.org/announce/russia.htm>)
Scotland: Carnegie Trust for the Universities of Scotland (support for field expeditions by
Scottish university undergraduates)

T. Sponsorships:

See Institute for Civil Society, Inc., "Sports Philanthropy Project," and Robert Wood Johnson Fndn. at <http://www.sportsphilanthropyproject.com>. Also, note individual teams (Toronto Raptors, for example) with borrowed-science images and the biological-sciences emphasis of some athlete-donors.

U. Special Note:

Separately, ABC Workstations, British Airways, British Gas, Gateway, HSBC, Land-Rover, Link 51, RTZ-CRA, and Shell have distinguished themselves as corporate supporters of Natural History and Exploration.

III. *On-Line* Foundations with an Interest in Science and Exploration:

First, see the following:

The Foundation Center's Guide to Grantseeking on the Web. New York, New York: The Foundation Center, 2000.

Reinhard, William. *The Grantseeker's Handbook of Essential Internet Sites.* Gaithersburg, Maryland: Aspen Publishers, Inc., 2000-2001.

Global Links to grants & funding information:

URLs for Grant Seekers: <http://www.sci.csupomona.edu/seis/grants.html>
<http://unicron.unomaha.edu/dept/econ/funding.htm>

Chronicle of Philanthropy Tuesday Download of Grant Opportunities, Nonprofit News, etc. <chronicle-request@nonprofit.com>
In Message, type <subscribe chronicle your name & organization>

Foundation Center Online: <http://www.fdncenter.org>

FundUK & Discussion Group: <http://www.dircon.co.uk>

German Charities Institute: <http://www.dsk.de/dsklinks.htm>

Global Database of Volunteer Opportunities (promotion for your Institute or expedition) at <http://www.contact.org>

GrantSmart: <http://www.grantsmart.org/search/search.html> (searchable database of U.S. tax-related information for more than 60,000 private foundations that file Form 990-PF)

GuideStar: <http://www.guidestar.org/index.html> (searchable by name, keyword, scientific— or other--specialty, location, or revenue: site provides grantseekers information on the programs and finances of more than 660,000 nonprofit organizations and charities)

IdeaList: <http://www.idealist.org> (searchable database of 10,000 nonprofit web sites globally; also, by keyword and location)

Internet Nonprofit Center: <http://www.nonprofits.org> (excellent source for information on nonprofits on the web; includes repository of publications, data about nonprofits and NGOs; links to home pages, related topics)

Nonprofit Web Sites Survey: <scook@ruli.org.uk>

Washington Nonprofit News Wire: <http://www.netlobby.com/marlowe>

Then, see the following:

American Express: http://www.americanexpress.com/corp/philanthropy
Amoco Fndn.: http://www.amoco.com
Autodesk Fndn: http://www.autodesk.com.compinfo/found/found.htm
Dow Chemical Company Fndn.: http://www.dow.com/about/corp/corp.htm
Eddie Bauer, Inc.: http://www.eddiebauer.com/about/eb_philanthropy.asp
ExxonMobil: http://www.exxonmobil.com/contributions/index.html
Hewlett-Packard Co.: http://www.corp.hp.com/Publish/UG/index.html
IBM Corp.: http://www.ibm.com/ibm/imbgives
Intel Corp.: http://www.intel.com/intel/smithso/innov/communit.htm
Japan Fndn.: http://www.nttls.co.jp/infomofa/jfd
S.C. Johnson Wax Fund: http://www.scjohnsonwax.com/community
Henry J. Kaiser Family Fndn.: http://www.open.igc.org/kff
Kresge Fndn.: http://www.kresge.org
Charles A. and Anne Morrow Lindbergh Fndn.: http://www.mtn.org/lindfdtn
MCI Communications Corp.: http://www.mci.com/about/friends
Medtronic: http://www.medtronic.com/public/medtronic/philanthropy
Mitsubishi Electric America Fndn.: http://www.hri.com/MEA/meafhome.html
NEC Fndn. of America: http://www.ias.biglobe.ne.jp/necsocial/e/index.html
David and Lucile Packard Fndn.: http://www.packfound.org
Pew Charitable Trusts: http://www.pewtrusts.com
Rockefeller Brothers Fund: http://www.rbf.org
Scaife Family Fndn.: http://www.scaife.com
United States-Japan Fndn.: http://www.japanese.com/nonprofit/foundation.html
Westinghouse Fndn>: http://www.westinghouse.com/ca/ca.hp.htm

IV. *Selected* Foundation Regional Resources:

Central & Eastern Europe; Balkans; Former Soviet Union:
  See Soros Foundations, especially for special Internet connection initiative
Charities Aid Foundation, *Charities in Russia*
Moscow: International Foundation for Archives Support
  e-mail <culini@culini.msk.su>
Estonian Foundation Centre (26 Estonian foundations)
  Tele.: (2)626-3309; Fax: (2)626-3310
Sabre Foundation, Inc. (book donations in former Soviet Bloc; special Internet
  -Based Technical Assistance Project (TAP) to provide technical
  assistance/training in Internet on-line resources)
  <http://www.sabre.org>, e-mail <sabre@sabre.org>
Mexico: Centro Mexicano para la Filanthropia, A.C. *Directorio de Instituciones
  Filanthropicas*
Venezuela: Fundacion Eugenio Mendoza. *Fundaciones Privadas de Venezuela*
The Hague Club. *Foundation Profiles*
Italy. Fondazione Scientifica Querini Stsampalia (special library/museum focus,
  especially in & around Venice)
  Tele.: (41) 5203433; Fax: (41) 5224954

Japan. Foundation Library Center of Japan
      Tele.: (3) 3350-1857; Fax: (3) 3350-1858
Spain. Centro de Fundaciones (260 member foundations)
      e-mail <centro.fundaciones@mad.servicom.es>
South America and the Caribbean (also, U.S. and Canada): See the Guggenheim
      Foundation's website at <http://www.gf.org> for its Fellows program.
South Pacific. Foundation for the Peoples of the South Pacific (FSP Intern.)
      Address: 25 Thurston St., POB 14447, Sewa. Tele.: 300-392
Ural, Engin (ed.). *Foundations in Turkey*

V. Governmental Grants:

Asia-Pacific Network for Global Change Research (APN): supports regional research on long-term global change in climate, ocean, and terrestrial systems; one goal is to strengthen links between scientists and policy makers. See, <http://www.apn.gr.jp>

European Union (EU): The Fifth Framework Programme (FP5) ends in 2002, but sets the stage for evolving priorities in research, technological development, and demonstration (RTD) projects. See EU for updates.

GEF: funds projects focused upon biodiversity, climate change, international waters, and ozone. Has special programs for land degradation. See small and medium-sized grant programs at <http://www.gefweb.org>.

IAI: goal is to encourage research beyond the scope of the national programs of the 18 nation-members in the Americas and to address scientific issues crucial to the region. Scientific capacity-building and information-exchange on the policy level are key components; <http://www.iai.int>.

Also,

Grants Web: <http://www.srainternational.org/newweb/grantsweb/index.cfm>
      (U.S. government grantmaking areas, with links to federal agencies, funding programs, and application forms; created by Society of Research Administrators)

U.S. Catalog of Federal Domestic Assistance: <http://www.cfda.gov>
      (while our book focuses on *non*-governmental funding, this is an excellent source for U.S.-based Institutes/expeditions which are interested in searching federally-sponsored programs)

U.S. Federal Register: <http://www.access.gpo.gov/su docs/aces/aces140.html>
      (daily publication, announces new U.S. federal grant programs and guidelines; database is searchable from 1995)

UNESCO: <http://www.unesco.org>

VI. *Further Reading:*

A. Books:

Aldred, Cyril. *Akhenaten: King of Egypt.* London: Thames and Hudson Ltd., 1989.

Bakker, Robert T. *Raptor Red.* New York: Bantam Books, 1995.

Christensen, Mark. *Super Car: The Story of the Xeno.* New York:Thomas Dunne Books (St. Martin's Griffin), 2001.

Fastovsky, David E., and Weishampel, David B. *The Evolution and Extinction of the Dinosaurs.* Cambridge, England: Cambridge University Press, 1996.

Harvard, Andrew and Thompson, Todd. *Mountain of Storms: The American Expeditions to Dhaulagiri, 1969 & 1973.* New York: Chelsea House, New York University Press, 1974.

Hawkins, Donald E.; Wood, Megan Epler; and Bittman, Sam. *The Ecolodge Sourcebook for Planners and Developers.* North Bennington, Vermont: The Ecotourism Society, 1995.

Horner, John R., and Lessem, Don. *The Complete T. rex.* New York: Simon and Schuster, 1993.

Hotten, Russell. *Winning: The Business of Formula One.* New York/London: Texere, 2000.
(See especially "Chapter Five: Oiling the Wheels," on sponsorships.)

Karrass, Chester L. *The Negotiating Game: How to get what you want.* New York: Thomas Y. Crowell, 1970.

Kuniholm, Roland. *The Complete Book of Model Fund-Raising Letters.* Englewood Cliffs, New Jersey: Prentice Hall, 1995.

Machíavellí, Níccolò. *The Prince.* Translated and edited by T.G. Bergin. New York: Appleton-Century-Crofts, 1947.

Palmer, Tom G. *Philanthropy in Central and Eastern Europe: A Resource Book for Foundations, Corporations, and Individuals.* Fairfax, Virginia: The Institute for Humane Studies at George Mason University, 1991.

Peat, F. David. *Artificial Intelligence: How Machines Think.* Rev. ed.: New York: Baen Books, Distributed by Simon & Schuster, 1988.

Raeburn, Paul. *Uncovering the Secrets of the Red Planet.* Washington, D.C.: The National Geographic Society, 1998.

Salamon, Lester M. *The International Guide to Nonprofit Law.* New York: John Wiley & Sons, Inc., 1997.

Siegel, Daniel and Yancey, Jenny. *The Rebirth of Civil Society: The Development of the Nonprofit Sector in East Central Europe and the Role of Western Assistance.*   New York, New York: Rockefeller Brothers Fund, 1992.

Sinclair, Michael R. *Hope at Last: A Guide to Grantmaking in South Africa.*   Washington, D.C.: Henry J. Kaiser Family Foundation, 1990.

Stevenson, Jay, and McGhee, George R.. *The Complete Idiot's Guide to Dinosaurs.* New York, N.Y.:
    alpha books, A Division of Macmillan General Reference,   1998.

Sun Tzu. *The Art of War*; translated by Lionel Giles. N.p.: n.n., 1910.

Zubrin, Robert with Wagner, Richard. *The Case for Mars: The Plan to Settle the Red Planet and Why We
    Must.* New York, N.Y.: Simon & Schuster/Touchstone, 1997.

B. Reports and Proceedings:

Capelotti, P.J., editor. "*Chapter Seven*: From Exploration to Discovery--Submissions
    to the Discovery Channel" (notes from remarks made by Angus Yates, *et al.*),
    pp. 81-85 in *Into the Field: Strategies for Funding Exploration--Proceedings
    of the Conference held at Nesbitt Hall, College of Design Arts, Drexel University,
    Philadelphia, PA on 20-21 April 1996*, edited by P.J. Capelotti, Ph.D. Philadelphia:
    The Philadelphia Chapter of The Explorers Club, March, 1997.

Council for Better Corporate Citizenship. *Untitled Press Kit.* Tokyo, Japan:
    Council for Better Corporate Citizenship, 1991.

Exobiology Program Office, NASA HQ. *An Exobiological Strategy for Mars   Exploration.*
    January 1995. 62 pages.

Friends of the *Hunley*, Inc. *Celebrate the History. Solve the Mystery. Raise the Hunley!*
    Charleston, South Carolina: Friends of the *Hunley*, Inc., n.d.

IEG, Inc. "Spanning The Globe." *IEG Sponsorship Report*, December 20, 1999, 4-5.

Independent Sector. "A Survey of Charitable Giving After September 11th, 2001."
    On-line at <http://www.IndependentSector.org>.

Jameson, Stephen C.; McManus, John.W.; and Spalding, Mark D. "International Coral Reef Initiative
    Executive Secretariat Background Paper: State of the Reefs--Regional and Global Perspectives
    (May, 1995)." www.ogp.noaa.gov/misc/coral/sor/sor_asia.html.

Japan External Trade Organization. *Survey of Corporate Philanthropy at Japanese-Affiliated Operations
    in the United States.* New York: JETRO, June, 1995.

Keel, Donald S. "*Chapter Three*: Investment Philanthropy & the Psychology of the Invitation," pp. 41-55
    (includes a variation of the Campaign Model); "*Chapter Four*: Building Your Board--Targeting
    and Creating Constituencies," pp. 56-61 in *Into the Field: Strategies for Funding Exploration--
    Proceedings of the Conference held at Nesbitt Hall, College of Design Arts, Drexel University,
    Philadelphia, PA on 20-21 April 1996*, edited by P.J. Capelotti, Ph.D. Philadelphia: The
    Philadelphia Chapter of The Explorers Club, March, 1997.

The Paleontological Research Institution. "Research. " *Fiscal Year 1996-1997: Annual Report.* Ithaca,
    New York: Paleontological Research Institution, October, 1997.

Trinkley, Michael and Vartorella, William. "Pothunting in the Global Village: A Survey Approach for

Collecting and Standardizing Site Destruction Data" in David G. Anderson and Virginia Horak, eds. *Readings in Archaeological Resource Protection Series. Number 2: Site Destruction in Georgia and the Carolinas*, pp. 87-95. Atlanta, GA: National Park Service, November, 1993.

Vartorella, William F. "*Chapter Two*: The Challenge & Opportunity for Funding Field Expeditions in the 21st Century," pp. 33-40; "*Chapter Five*: Strategies & Tactics for Securing Money (and Equipment) for Exploration," pp. 62-72; "*Chapter Six*: Corporate Support & Expedition Budgets in the New World Order," pp. 73-80; "*Chapter Eight*: Planning for the Future of Exploration: The 21st Century Donor for Field Expeditions--A Profile," pp. 86-96; "*Chapter Nine*: A Selected Bibliography for `Funding Exploration' with Abbreviated Donor Listings," pp. 97-104 in *Into the Field: Strategies for Funding Exploration--Proceedings of the Conference held at Nesbitt Hall, College of Design Arts, Drexel University,Philadelphia, PA on 20-21 April 1996*, edited by P.J. Capelotti, Ph.D. Philadelphia: The Philadelphia Chapter of The Explorers Club, March, 1997.

U.S. Congress. House. Committee on Energy and Commerce. *Financial Responsibility at Universities. Hearings* before the Subcommittee on Oversight and Investigations of the Committee on Energy and Commerce, House of Representatives, on Indirect Cost Recovery Practices at U.S. Universities for   Federal Research Grants and Contracts, 102d Cong., lst sess., March 13 and May 9, 1991.

World Resources Institute. "Status of the world's coral reefs: East Asia." www.wri.org/reefsatrisk/reefasia.html.

C. Articles--Journals and Professional Publications:

Alexeeva, Olga. "The Taste of Pineapple." *Foundation News and Commentary*, January/February 1996, 14.

Alpert, Mark. "Making Money in Space." *Scientific American Presents the Future of Space Exploration Quarterly*, Volume 10, Number 1 (Spring, 1999), 92-95.

Anonymous. "Catalog Sales in Japan." *South Carolina World Trader*, Volume 4, Number 8 (October, 1996), 9.

_____. "Charities Urged to Focus on Management Strategies." *The Chronicle of Philanthropy*, September 6, 2001, 42.

_____. "Companies Forecast First Significant Increases in Giving in 5 Years." *The Chronicle of Philanthropy*, September 21, 1995, 12.

_____. "Matters of Fact." UNDP *Choices*, Volume 12, Number 2 (June, 2002), 28.

_____. "Patagonia in Japan: U.S. Outdoor Gear Catches On." *Focus Japan*, April, 1998, 11.

_____. "Technology: New Approach to Linking Corporations, Charities." *The Chronicle of Philanthropy,* May 30, 2002, 31.

Baatz, E.B. "Business Strategy: The Big Picture." *CIO*, August 1996, 24.

Bapna, Deepak; Maimone, Mark; Murphy, John; Rollins, Eric; Whittaker, William; and Wettergreen,

David. "Nomad's Land: Robotic Rehearsal for the New Frontier." *GPS World* (June, 1998), 22-28, 30-32.

Blum, Debra E. "After the Attacks: Consumers Choose Products Based on Corporate Philanthropy, Studies Find. " *The Chronicle of Philanthropy*, November 29, 2001, 24.

_____. "American Foundations Increase Giving to Support International Projects." *The Chronicle of Philanthropy*, January 11, 2001, 23. See also, Chart, "International Giving by American Foundations," whose source is Foundation Center.

_____. "Companies' Charitable Gifts Follow Their Revenue and Go Overseas." *The Chronicle of Philanthropy*, July 15, 1999, 12.

Boorstein, Jonathan. "P.S.--Think Again: Survey shows postscripts, first-class stamps and free offers aren't necessarily what the people want." *Direct*, March 1, 1998, 38-39.

Chart--"Global Warming" in *"CIO* 100 World Leaders." *CIO*, August, 1996, 38.

Chart. *CIO*, September 15, 1995, 18.

Corbley, Kevin P. "Identifying Villages at Risk of Malaria Spread." *Geo Info Systems*, January 1999, 34-37.

Currie, P.J., Dong Z.-M., and D.A. Russell. "1993. Results from the Sino-Canadian Dinosaur Project." *Canadian Journal of Earth Sciences* 30: 1997-2272.

Egol, Len. "Endnote on Book Club India." *Direct*, January, 1996, 67.

Farkas, E.J. "Preliminary Report of the Human Remains from the Theban Tomb No. 32 (Season 1991)." *Acta Archaeologica Academi*ae *Scientiarum Hungaricae*, 45 (1993), 15-31.

Feeback, Ronald W., and Vartorella, William F. "A `Back to Basics' Studio for $10,000." *Educational & Industrial Television,* Volume 13, Number 10 (October, 1981), 52-54.

Flanagan, Joseph. "Raising the *Hunley*." *Common Ground: Archaeology and Ethnography in the Public Interest*, Summer/Fall, 2001, 12-23.

Gose, Ben. "Terrorist Attacks Did Not Cause Major Shift in Focus of Most Grant Makers." *The Chronicle of Philanthropy*, September 5, 2002, 15-16, 18.

Gray, Susan. "Charities' Income From Sponsorships Up 10%--Chart: How Corporate Spending to Sponsor Events Has Grown." *The Chronicle of Philanthropy*, March 26, 1998, 20.

Greene, Stephen G. "A World of Difference: Spending by non-profit groups in 22 nations exceeds $1-trillion--and is growing, says a global team of researchers." *The Chronicle of Philanthropy*, November 19, 1998, 31-33..

_____. "Belt-Tightening at Two Foundations Puts the Squeeze on Charities." *The Chronicle of Philanthropy*, October 17, 2002, 11.

_____. "Fund Raiser Aims to Cultivate Support for Living Laboratory." *The Chronicle of Philanthropy*, April 18, 2002, 58.

_____. "Grappling With Social Needs." *The Chronicle of Philanthropy*, February 21, 2002, 15-16.

Hall, Holly. "Joint Ventures With Business: A Sour Deal?" *The Chronicle of Philanthropy*, April 6, 1993, 21-22.

Haller, Vera (with Amicone, Hay). "Scribes in Cyberspace." *Beyond Computing*, October, 1995, 18-21.

Hess, Peter E. "Deep Shipwreck in High Courts." *Delaware Lawyer*, Volume 17, Number 1 (Spring, 1999), 16-19.

Hildebrand, Carol. "Branding the Globe." *CIO Enterprise*, Section 2 (March 15, 1998),   34-35, 38-40, 42.

Holstein, William J. "We're Naïve About Japanese Philanthropy." *The Chronicle of Philanthropy*, January 14, 1992,   38-39.

International Organization for Chemical Sciences in Development (IOCD). "International Symposium: Chemistry and Pharmacology of Plants Used in African Traditional Medicine." *IOCD Update*, Fall, 2002, 4.

_____. "Meeting in Western Africa: Purchasing, Servicing and Maintenance of Scientific Equipment." *IOCD Update*, Fall, 2002, 1.

Jurdak, Roy. "Do's & Don'ts of Translation." *The Source Blue Book--1997 Edition* (*Atlanta International Magazine*), n.d., 31, 37.

Lee, Pascal. "From the Earth to Mars--Part One: A Crater, Ice, and Life." *The Planetary Report*, Volume XXII, Number 1 (January/February, 2002), 12-17.

Lewis, Nicole. "Charitable Giving Slides." *The Chronicle of Philanthropy*, June 27, 2002, 27, 30, 33.

_____. "Social-Service and International Groups Were Winners in 2001, Report Says." *The Chronicle of Philanthropy*, June 27, 2002, 28.

Lipman, Harvy, and Schwinn, Elizabeth. "The Business of Charity: Nonprofit groups reap billions in tax-free income annually." *The Chronicle of Philanthropy*, October 18, 2001, 25-26 ff.

M.L. "Newswatch--Global Confidence Survey: Legends of the Fall." *CFO*, September, 2001, 26.

Orosz, Joel J. "Opinion: Big Funds Need a `Skunk Works' to Stir Ideas." *The Chronicle of Philanthropy*, June 27, 2002, 47.

Pachtman, Arnold. "Getting to `Hao!' *International Business*, July/August 1998, 24-26.

Pascoe, Jason; Ryan, Nick; and Brown, Peter. "Context Aware: the Dawn of Sentient Computing?" *GPS World*, September 1998, 22-29.

Piske, Klaus. "The 10 Most-Common Mistakes Americans Make When Direct Marketing to Europe." *Target Marketing*, March 2002, pp. 61, 64-65.

Quirk's Marketing Research Review and its website at <www.quirks.com>.

Satava, Richard and Blackadar, Thomas. "The Physiologic Cipher: Telemedicine on Everest." *GPS World*, October, 2001, 20.

Schutt, John. "Searching for Meteorites." *GPS World*, August, 1996, 13.

Stehle, Vince. "European Philanthropy Experts Disagree on Rules for Giving in Era of Euro." *The*

Chronicle of Philanthropy, May 21, 1998, 37.

Vartorella, William F. "A Catalyst for Change: The New Philanthropy in the Global Village." *NonProfit Strategist*, Volume 7, Issue 1 (February, 2001), 4-5.

_____. "A Simple Guide to a Fundable Field Season." *The Glyph*, Volume 1, Number 12 (March, 1998), 13-14.

_____. "An Insider's Guide to Getting Equipment Grants." *Nonprofit Management Strategies*, October, 1992, 1,7,11.

_____. "Avoiding Budget Traps: Ten Simple (and inviolable) Rules for Constructing a Competitive Budget." *FRI Monthly Portfolio,* January, 1994, 1-2.

_____. "Cooperation, Not Competition: Beating the Odds in the Grants Game through Consortial Projects." *FRI Monthly Portfolio,* May, 1993, 1-2.

_____. "Corporate Fund Raising in Transition: Posers, Players, and Power Proposals." *Fund Raising Institute (FRI) Monthly Portfolio*, Volume 33, Number 7 (July, 1994), 1-2.

_____. "Creating Sustainable Funding for Natural History Collections in the New World Order— Foundations and Corporations: Old Allies, New Opportunities." *Museum Management and Curatorship* (England), Volume 15, No. 3 (September, 1996), 328-333.

_____. "'Digging for Dollars' or the Quest for a Sustainable Archaeology." *The Glyph* (AIA, San Diego). *The Glyph*, Volume 1, Number 11 (December, 1997), 13-15.

_____. "Doing the bright thing with your company logo." *Advertising Age*, February 26, 1990, 31.

_____. "Evolution, Predator Traps, and Money Pits: Re-thinking Collection Extinction." *SPNHC Newsletter*, Volume 13, Number 2 (August, 1999), 1, 9, 13.

_____. "Exploring Inner Space: the Mind of the Donor." *Human Performance in Extreme Environments*, Volume 3, Number 1 (September, 1998), 113-116.

_____. "Funding in the Extreme: Pushing the Envelope, Managing the Risk." *Human Performance in Extreme Environments,* Volume 2, Number 1 (June, 1997), 27-29.

_____. "Preparing for the 'Asian Century': Donor Prospecting in Japan through Direct Mail." *Taft Monthly Portfolio,* Volume 38, Number 4 (April, 1999), 1-2, 7.

_____. "Seven Deadly Sins of Expedition Fundraising." *Expedition News*, Volume Four, Number Two (February, 1997), 3-4.

_____. "Simple Application of Convergent/Divergent Funding Theory to (Micro-) Extreme Environments." *Human Performance in Extreme Environments*, Volume 5, Number 2 (June, 2001), 128-130.

_____. "Simple Tools for Navigating a Budgetary 'Lunar Landscape.'" *Human Performance in Extreme Environments*, Volume 4, Number 1 (April, 1999), 27-29.

_____. "Some Common Errors and Misconceptions about Direct Mail." *Fund Raising Management,* April, 1991, 24-25.

_____. "The 'Archaeology' of Finding Equipment." *The Glyph,* Volume I, Number 13 (June, 1998), 11, 13-14.

Whelan, David. "Corporate Giving Rose in 2000, Survey Finds." *The Chronicle of Philanthropy*, January 24, 2002, 11.

Wilhelm, Ian. "Foundations Gave $ 29-Billion Last Year, a 5.1% Increase, Report Says." *The Chronicle of Philanthropy*, April 18, 2002, 16.

World Bank. *Private Infrastructure Project Database, 1996.* "Private Investment Projects, 1984-1995" in "Let's Make A Deal." *International Business*, December 1996/January 1997, 6.

Zelade, Richard. "Leading the Pack." *International Business*, December 1996/January 1997, 6.

D. Articles--Magazines, Newspapers:

Adler, T. "Providing the data to protect biodiversity." *Science News*, Volume 148, November 18, 1995, 326.

Africano, Lillian. "Eight War Zones, 20 Visas, 17 Countries, and 33,000 Miles: Two Friends Retrace Marco Polo's Treacherous Route." *Biography*, February, 1999, 78-88, 108.

Agle, D.C. "Rover Boys: Three crews of Apollo astronauts experienced an out-of-this-world driving adventure." *AutoWeek,* July 30, 2001, 16-17.

Anonymous. "A Guide to Social Investing. " *My Generation*, November-December, 2001, 30.

_____. "Competition--A Japanese View: Why America has Fallen Behind." *Fortune*, September 25, 1989, 52.

_____."Hold On--There's More." *Entrepreneur*, September, 1998, 128-129.

_____. "Outlook: Database--Jurassic Juggernaut." *U.S. News & World Report*, Sept. 25, 1995, 16.

_____. "Where the U.S. R&D Is" (Chart). *Fortune*, March 25, 1991, 85.

_____. "Where to Donate (and find) Surplus Goods." *Successful Meetings*, June, 1996, 42.

Evans, Bob. "Personal Finance: Socially Responsible Investing: You Don't Have to Sacrifice Profits for Principles." *Self-Employed America*, March/April, 1997, 14-15.

Farnham, Alan. "Managing: Ideas & Solutions--Brushing Up Your Vision Thing." *Fortune*, May 1, 1995, 129.

Frazer, Lance. "Threatened pharmacopoeia: The world's coral reefs." *The Rotarian*, October 2002, 12-13.

The Futures Group. "Number of Middle-Class Workers" (*Fortune* Chart). *Fortune*, May 30, 1994, 76.

Knight-Ridder Tribune. "Chart: Average life expectancy," June 28, 1992, n.p.

Kuhn, Susan E. "How Business Helps Schools." *Fortune/Special Issue*, Spring, 1990, pp. 91-94, 96, 98, 100, 102, 104, 106.

Martin, Justin. "Good Citizenship is Good Business." *Fortune*, March 21, 1994, 15-16.

Monastersky, Richard. "For the Sake of Sue--What will happen to the world's best *T. Rex*?" *Science News*, Volume 148 (November 11, 1995), 316-317.

Monk, John. "*Hunley* price tag rising for S.C. taxpayers." *The State* (a newspaper, Columbia, South Carolina U.S.A.), October 27, 2002, 1, A 16-A 17.

O'Donnell, Francis, and Belliveau, Denis. "Marco Polo's Guide to Afghanistan." *Smithsonian*, Volume 32, Number 10 (January, 2002), 44-47, 49-51.

Orlean, Susan. "Where's Willy? Everybody's favorite whale tries to make it on his own." *The New Yorker*, September 23, 2002, 56-63.

Pollack, Kenan. "Outlook: Species--It's a Tough World Out There." *U.S. News & World Report*, November 17, 1995, 23.

Ramsey, Nancy. "How Business Can Help the Schools." *Fortune*, September 16, 1992, 147-148, 150, 154, 156, 160, 162, 166, 168, 172, 174.

Various Authors. "The New Automotive Universe 2000." *Automobile Magazine*, July, 2000, 76-80, 82, 84-85. Richard Feast, "As the dust settles, our stellar experts analyze the new order," 76-77. Georg Kacher, "The view from Europe," 78-79. Peter Nunn, "The view from Asia," 80, 82. Paul Lienert, "The view from America," 82, 84-85.

Vartorella, William F. "Pod zltou vlajkou: Sponzorovanie timu F1 a boj o Strednu Europu" ("Under the Yellow Flag: F1 Team Sponsorships and the Battle for Central Europe"). Trans. by Peter Fritz, Editor. *F1 Sport International/Slovenske Vydanie*, July, 2002, 24-25.

Vartorella, William F. "F1 Racing at the Ragged Edge: Team Sponsorships and the Slovakia Connection." *Grand Prix Business*, February, 2004, 30-33. English abstract, page 88.

E. Unpublished Papers:

Hopkins, Theodore J., Jr. "Commercializing the Third Sector: Public Benefit and Private Competition." Paper Delivered at the Fifth International Conference of the International Society for Third Sector Research, July 8, 2002, University of Cape Town, South Africa.

Przychodzen, Agnieszka, and Smith, P.H. "Challenger Flies to Mars." A paper delivered at the Third International Mars Society Convention, August 10-13, 2000, Ryerson Polytechnic University, Toronto, Ontario, Canada.

Vartorella, William F. "Exploring the Corporate Jungle: the Role of Global Philanthropy in Preserving the Rainforest and Matching Eco-Vision with Company Missions." Paper presented at a two-day international symposium, "Building on Our Potential," Shanklands Rainforest Resort, Cooperative Republic of Guyana, 3 December 2001.

_____. "From `Denizens to Dinosaurs': Entrepreneurship and Collections Management--A Workshop." Paper presented at the 14th Annual Meeting of the Society for the Preservation of

Natural History Collections, "Finance and Funding Workshop," Ripley Center, The Smithsonian Institution, Washington, D.C., 28 June 1999.

_____. "Global Funding for Egyptology in the 21st Century: An Appraisal and Recommendations for Change." Paper presented at the 43rd Annual Symposium of the American Research Center in Egypt (ARCE), Seattle, Washington: Spring, 1992.

_____. "Patrons, Petroglyphs, and Sustainable Futures: Strategies and Tactics for Philanthropy in Global Markets--A Workshop." Paper presented at the Congresso Internacional de Arte Rupestre, "Atravessando Fronteiras," Universidade de Tras-os-Montes e Alto Douro (UTAD), Vila Real, Portugal, 10 September 1998. *Transmitted live via the Internet from UTAD.*

***

Biographies:

I. William F. Vartorella, Ph.D., C.B.C.:

During the past 25 years, Bill Vartorella has worked on exotic projects in Egypt, Venezuela, Romania, Brazil, Morocco, Guyana, Canada, and the U.S., etc. including archaeology, endangered species, GIS applications to historic corridors, biodiversity, eco-tourism, marine sciences, satellite communications, health care, bio-anthropology, utopian societies, the arts, museum conservation labs, education, publishing, manufacturing, rural communities, women's issues, motorsports, and saving threatened antiquities. Since 1971, he has secured U.S. $$$ millions from a host of governmental, foundation, and corporate sources, including the U.S. Agency for International Development (USAID), Arcadia Foundation, Cannon, Carnegie, the David Koch Foundation, Fox Family Foundation, Freedoms Foundation, National Trust for Historic Preservation, Park Foundation, the U.S. Army, *Reader's Digest* Travel and Research Fund, National Historical Publications and Records Commission (NHPRC), National Endowment for the Humanities (NEH), etc. and Fortune 500 companies in Japan, Canada, Holland, and the U.S. The author of nearly 100 articles, papers, and book chapters in disciplines ranging from archaeology to utopian studies, Vartorella's work has appeared in *Advertising Age*, *American Writers Before 1800*, *Communal Societies*, *Educational and Industrial Television*, *F1 Sport/Slovakia*, *Grand Prix Business*, *Journal of Human Performance in Extreme Environments*, *Museum Management and Curatorship*, *National Preservation Report*, and *Readings in Archaeological Resource Protection Series*, as well as *Expedition News* and *The Explorers Newsletter*. His articles on global philanthropy and corporate culture appear regularly in publications distributed in more than 30 countries, including *Fund Raising Management*, *Nonprofit Board Report*, *Nonprofit Management Strategies*, *Non-Profit Strategist*, *Nonprofit World*, *Taft Monthly Portfolio*, and *What's Working in Nonprofit Fundraising*. In 1992, he delivered a paper before the 43rd Annual Symposium of the American Research Center in Egypt (ARCE/Seattle) entitled, "Global Funding for Egyptology in the 21st Century: An Appraisal and Recommendations for Change." In August of 1996, Vartorella gave a sponsored paper and funding workshop at the Second World Congress on the Preservation and Conservation of Natural History Collections, which was co-hosted by and held at Cambridge University. In 1997, his work was featured prominently in the *Proceedings* of a Symposium held at Drexel University entitled, "Into the Field: Strategies for Funding Exploration." In 1998, he presented a sponsored workshop at the International Rock Art Congress held at UTAD in Vila Real, Portugal, which was simulcast live on the Internet. In 1999, Vartorella co-chaired a fundraising workshop at the annual meeting of the Society for the Preservation of Natural History Collections held at The Smithsonian Institution in Washington, DC. In 2001, he was a sponsored speaker on corporate support for sustainable rainforests at an international seminar in Guyana. Trained in part as an archaeologist, Vartorella has worked on excavations in Great Britain and the U.S. and, in 1993, proffered draft text and recommendations for the UNIDROIT draft convention on stolen or illegally exported cultural objects. His expedition experience also includes logistics for marine science in Venezuela and Brazil. Exotic scientific projects have included ancient Egyptian mummies, cardiovascular disease prevention in Romania, and high-technology motorsports (electric and other open-wheel formulae). He has served on the boards of three U.S.-based foundations for Egyptology and marine sciences. Vartorella earned his Ph.D. in Mass Communications from Ohio University (Athens, Ohio) and a C.B.C. credential in business and professional advertising from B/PAA (NYC). He is a registered consultant with numerous transnational NGOs, especially in developing regions. He has trained more than 7,000 nonprofit executives worldwide, both in seminars (grants, board development, strategic planning, etc.) and at special retreats. For 18 years, he has served as Executive Vice-President of Craig and Vartorella, Inc., which works with clients worldwide on shared solutions for just, sustainable futures, particularly in developing countries. He is a Fellow of both The Explorers Club and the Royal Geographical Society.

II. Donald S. Keel:

Don Keel has nearly 40 years' experience organizing multi-million-dollar fundraising campaigns, directing institutional advancement programs, and producing promotional video presentations that have won national awards in the U.S. He has been vice-president of two U.S. colleges and associate vice-chancellor of a public university, campaign director for a national consulting firm, and president of his own award-winning consulting company. His successful campaign strategies have enabled a broad range of not-for-profit organizations including colleges, universities, museums, YMCAs, ethnic minority organizations, and cultural institutions to raise hundreds of millions of U.S. dollars (two of these campaigns surpassed their goals by more than U.S. $10 million each). Through his promotional video presentations, Keel has developed a unique way to present the primary values of an organization in a manner that resonates with the target audience. The result has been the creation of persuasive presentations that have won regional and national awards from the Council for Advancement and Support of Education (CASE), including the highest national award made by that organization. Keel is co-originator of Obstacle-Based Thinking (OBT), an innovative real-world strategy for preventing the most common obstacles encountered in development from hindering organizational progress. This strategy enables objective analysis of serious obstacles commonly encountered in the development of advancement programs and a *modus operandi* for removing them from the path of progress. He has been a presenter at the 2001 and 2002 International Conferences of the Association of Fundraising Professionals in St. Louis, Missouri and Toronto, Canada. Keel has also presented OBT to U.S. state and regional conferences in Rhode Island and Massachusetts. He presented the Association of Fundraising Professionals (AFP) First Course Module, "Managing Development Office Operations," in 2001. He has also been a presenter, along with *National Geographic* and The Discovery Channel professionals, at two Explorers Club, two-day symposia on funding field exploration (Philadelphia, Pennsylvania and New York City, New York USA). Keel's projects have included major stints in New York City, Washington, DC, the southeastern and southwestern U.S., and the Caribbean, where he worked closely with global philanthropists, opinion leaders, and policy makers. In addition to his international seminars on OBT, Keel's workshops include board issues (recruitment, training, retention), "Investment Philanthropy" (donor return on social investment), and applications of his unique capital campaign model, which is based on the psychology of invitation. Keel is a graduate of The Pingry School and the University of North Carolina at Chapel Hill, where he majored in philosophy.

III. Kathryn Anne Monk, Ph.D., D.I.C., B.Sc. (Hons.), F.R.E.S., F.R.G.S.:

Recently, the Director General - Iwokrama International Centre for Rain Forest Conservation and Development, Guyana, South America, Dr. Kathryn Monk has 21 years post-doctoral experience in institutional, environmental, and natural resource management worldwide.

As a scientist, her research and field expeditions have led her to South America (Guyana), Southeast Asia (mainly Indonesia and Malaysia), the Middle East (mainly Kuwait and Bahrain), and Africa (mainly Kenya). Dr. Monk's work on team-based biodiversity and ecosystem conservation has been recognized through the award of two honorary research positions with Canadian and British universities, supported by the production of more than 50 publications and conference presentations.

Her scholarly work has appeared in such journals as the *Biological Journal of the Linnaean Society*, *Science*, and *Oryx*, on projects varying from the biogeography of insects, to the decline in orangutan in northern Sumatra and seabird colonies in eastern Indonesia, to the development of GIS databases using remote sensing for tropical forestland inventories. Work papers have also been similarly diverse, including alternative methods of forest conservation and development, the need for protocols on benefit sharing and intellectual property rights, and biodiversity monitoring in tropical ecosystems. Dr. Monk is the author or contributor to several books and monographs, including the regionally seminal *The Ecology of Nusa Tenggara and Maluku* (Singapore: Periplus Editions Ltd.; Oxford: Oxford University Press).

Her experience in the funding arena has included many research grants from such groups as the Royal Society and private foundations, the organization of and participation in many international field expeditions, plus consultancies for such institutions as the

Zoological Society of London (the Leuser Development Programme, Sumatra, Indonesia) and the World Bank, Indonesia. The Leuser Development Programme, for example, was a 53 million euro project funded by the European Union and Government of Indonesia for an Integrated Conservation and Development Programme to develop a novel participatory managerial system and regional support for a new 2.5-million hectare conservation area (the Leuser Ecosystem) in northern Sumatra.

Earlier, Dr. Monk assisted Dalhousie University, Canada, in a five- year, C$36 million, CIDA-funded initiative to upgrade environmental management skills, through institutional capacity building for the Environmental Management Development in Indonesia (EMDI) project.

Most recently, she directed The Iwokrama Centre - an autonomous international research and development institution established in 1996 to develop and demonstrate methods for conservation and just, sustainable use of tropical forests. Dr. Monk was brought in to guide the Centre through a transition stage from being a fully donor-funded development project towards some financial self-reliance within the context of an experimental business center. The Centre is located in the capital, Georgetown, and operates a field station some 200 kilometers inland in the 360,000-hectare Iwokrama Forest for which it has direct management responsibility. The Centre has received support from government and non-governmental organizations, including DFID, CIDA, EU, ITTO, Commonwealth Secretariat, and UNDP.

Dr. Monk holds earned degrees from the University of London (Imperial College at Silwood Park), U.K. (Ph.D., Ecological Entomology and D.I.C. Entomology) and the University of Durham, U.K. (B.Sc. [Hons.] Biology, Ecology Option). She is a Fellow of both the Royal Geographical Society and the Royal Entomological Society of London, and is a Member of the Malaysian Nature Society and of the British Ecological Society.

***

BOOK REVIEWS

"Bill Vartorella and Don Keel's *Funding Exploration* is an indispensable guide for making one's dreams and aspirations of field research and exploration a reality. Having organized and/or participated in diving expeditions for over 20 years from the Caribbean to Maine, the Great Lakes, Guam and Alaska, the one thing that these expeditions have in common is the inevitable quest for....funding. Using the advice and recommendations in this book, any exploratory endeavor can put together the resources and money necessary to carry out their mission."

Peter E. Hess, Esq.
1993 USS MONITOR Deep Diving Expedition Leader

"Bill Vartorella and Don Keel understand very well the several connecting issues relating to the exploration of Mars analogues on Earth. The authors make a number of suggestions for fundable projects of great utility to those scientist-explorers in the here and now who are preparing for sophisticated robotic and human explorations of the Red Planet in the near future."

Dr. Marilyn Dudley-Rowley, Advisor, NASA Mars Reference Mission

"This book is pure gold for expedition leaders & field scientists!"

Marie Levine
Executive Director, Shark Research Institute

Shangri-La Publications, 3 Coburn Hill Rd, Warren Ctr., PA 18851 USA   866-966-6288

SHANGRILAPUBLICATIONS.ORG